D1420479

St. Martin
and
His Hagiographer

History and Miracle
in Sulpicius Severus

by
Clare Stancliffe

CLARENDON PRESS · OXFORD
1983

Oxford University Press, Walton Street, Oxford OX2 6DP

London Glasgow New York Toronto
Delhi Bombay Calcutta Madras Karachi
Kuala Lumpur Singapore Hong Kong Tokyo
Nairobi Dar es Salaam Cape Town
Melbourne Auckland
and associated companies in
Beirut Berlin Ibadan Mexico City Nicosia

Oxford is a trade mark of Oxford University Press

Published in the United States
by Oxford University Press, New York

British Library Cataloguing in Publication Data
Stancliffe, Clare
St. Martin and his hagiographer.
1. Martin, Saint, Bishop of Tours
2. Severus, Sulpicius — Criticism and interpretation
3. Christian Saints — France — Tours
— Biography
I. Title
270.2'092'4   BR1720.M3
ISBN 0-19-821895-8

Typeset by Hope Services (Abingdon)
Printed in Great Britain
at the University Press, Oxford
by Eric Buckley
Printer to the University

MATRI
QUAE STUDIO VERITATIS FOVENDO
SEMINA SCIENTIAE CURAVIT

Preface

My first debt is to Sulpicius Severus, who has left us with such a brilliantly written *Life of Martin*—and with so many puzzles. I have been pondering his account of Martin, off and on, for some twelve years, and still it holds my interest. I hope that this book may enable others to share that interest.

My second debt is to Professor J. M. Wallace-Hadrill, who acted as my supervisor for the Oxford thesis on which this book is based. He has always made himself available for listening to my ideas or reading my work; but chiefly I value the freedom he gave me to pursue my own choice of subject in my own way. The corollary, of course, is that I alone bear responsibility for the book which follows: its defects must not be laid at his door.

There are many others who have helped in various ways. I would like to thank Professor Owen Chadwick for most generously giving me his own copy of Halm's *Sulpicii Severi opera*; and Professor Henry Chadwick for reading the original thesis and offering encouragement at a time when it was much appreciated. I also benefited from the general interest in late antiquity shared by many in Oxford around 1970; and if Peter Brown's 'Rise of the Holy Man' lectures imparted the spirit of late antiquity, I am no less grateful to J. F. Matthews's lectures which provided flesh and sinews, and so helped an early medievalist to make herself at home in the late Roman Empire. Amongst my fellow postgraduates who contributed to a lively seminar on the later Roman Empire, I would particularly single out for thanks Philip Rousseau, who shared his own ideas with me at a time when I had little to give in return.

At Cambridge, I would like to thank the Principal and Fellows of Newnham College for making my two years there so happy and so productive. Although much rewritten since, the study which follows is recognizably the same as that first penned at Newnham. Nor should I forget the valiant typing of Mrs Josephine Morris, in Hertfordshire, and Mrs Margaret Gilley, in Durham. My thanks also go to the Bodleian and Ashmolean libraries, Oxford; to the Cambridge University Library; to the University Library of Newcastle upon Tyne; and to the Dean and Chapter Library and the University Library, Durham—especially for use of the Levison Collection.

Further afield, I am most grateful to M. Charles Lelong for answering my queries about his recent archaeological discoveries at Marmoutier; also to the nun who showed us round the excavations there, and to Père Vincent Desprez for expertly guiding us round the archaeological discoveries made at Ligugé.

The process of revising and rewriting over an extended period of time is always complex. I have tried to take into account all recent work of importance in the final revision, but inevitably a halt has to be called somewhere. I particularly regret that the proceedings of a French conference on hagiography, *Hagiographie, cultures et sociétés IVe-XIIe siècles* (Paris 1981), reached me too late to be of use.

In connection with the final revision I would like to thank Mr Alexander Murray for reading the thesis and making suggestions for revision; Professor R. A. Markus for reading two chapters of the final version; and Dr E. D. Hunt, for reading through the completed whole, and picking up various small points which needed attention.

Last, there is a debt to my immediate family. That to my parents reaches back to the days when my mother fought to persuade my school to teach me Greek in lieu of needlework, and herself backed up the able efforts of my Latin teacher. More recently she has read most of the book which follows, and has made various helpful suggestions; while from my father I suspect that I have learnt more of the art of composition than from any teacher. The final debt is to my husband, Ben de la Mare, who has read the whole book with great attention, and who has shared with me the task of translating its many Latin quotations, enhancing both their fluency and their accuracy. More than this, he has sustained me through many months of toil; and his confidence never flagged, however rough the going.

C.E.S.

Contents

Abbreviations

AA	*Auctores Antiquissimi*
AB	*Analecta Bollandiana*
BLE	*Bulletin de littérature ecclésiastique*
CCSL	*Corpus Christianorum, Series Latina* (Turnhout)
CIL	*Corpus Inscriptionum Latinarum* (16 vols., Berlin 1862 ff.)
CSEL	*Corpus Scriptorum Ecclesiasticorum Latinorum* (Vienna)
C.Th.	Theodosian Code, edd. T. Mommsen & P. M. Meyer, *Theodosiani libri xvi . . .* (2 vols., Berlin 1905), vol. I.
DACL	*Dictionnaire d'archéologie chrétienne et de liturgie*, by F. Cabrol & H. Leclercq (15 vols., Paris 1903-53)
Dict. Sp.	*Dictionnaire de spiritualité ascetique et mystique*, ed. M. Viller (Paris 1937 ff.)
ET	English translation
Fontaine, *Vie*	J. Fontaine: Sulpice Sévère, *Vie de Saint Martin*, vol. I, introduction, text, and French translation; vols. II & III, commentary (*SC* 133-5; 1967, 1968, & 1969).
Fontaine, 'L'Ascétisme chrétien'	J. Fontaine, 'L'Ascétisme chrétien dans la littérature gallo-romaine d'Hilaire à Cassien', *La Gallia romana* (Rome 1973), pp. 87-115.
GCS	Die griechischen christlichen Schriftsteller der ersten drei Jahrhunderte

JRS	*Journal of Roman Studies*
JTS	*Journal of Theological Studies*
MGH	*Monumenta Germaniae Historica*
pb. edn.	paperback edition
PG	*Patrologia Graeca*, ed. J.-P. Migne
PL	*Patrologia Latina*, ed. J.-P. Migne
REA	*Revue des Études Anciennes*
RH	*Revue historique*
SC	*Sources Chrétiennes* (Paris)
SRM	*Scriptores Rerum Merovingicarum*
van Andel	G. K. van Andel, *The Christian Concept of History in the Chronicle of Sulpicius Severus* (Amsterdam 1976).
Vite dei Santi	*Vite dei Santi dal III al VI secolo*, general editor C. Mohrmann (Fondazione Lorenzo Valla, 1974 ff.)

Note on Texts of Sulpicius Severus

Pending the promised *CCSL* edition, I have used the following:
    Vita Martini and *Epistulae*: text in J. Fontaine, *Vie de Saint Martin*, I (*SC* 133; 1967).
    Dialogi and *Chronica*, text in C. Halm's edition, *Sulpicii Severi opera* (*CSEL* 1; 1866).
In the notes, I abbreviate these works of Sulpicius as *VM*, *ep.*, *D*, and *Chron*.

The *Dialogues* present something of a problem, because the original fifth-century division (represented by the Italian family of MSS and the Book of Armagh) was into two books, whereas Halm followed the French 'Martinellus' family of MSS, dividing them into three books. Because I have used Halm's text, I have perforce followed his division into three books, and given references accordingly. I regret that G. Augello, *Sulpici Severi Dialogi*, Palermo 1969 (apparently a Latin text with Italian translation: see F. Murru in *Latomus* 38, 1979, p. 960, n. 2 and addendum pp. 980–1), came to my notice too late for me to make use of it.

Introduction

St. Martin of Tours was one of the first confessors: one of the first Christians to be honoured as a saint because of his way of life rather than the manner of his dying. Today he is remembered largely for one particular deed which is familiar from medieval carvings and stained-glass windows. In these, Martin the soldier is portrayed in the act of cutting his cloak in half so as to share it with a shivering beggar; and, as we might expect from artists working in a feudal society, Martin may there be depicted as an armoured knight, mounted on horseback.[1]

In historical reality, however, Martin belonged to the later Roman Empire; and, unlike his later admirers in feudal Europe, Martin's Gallo-Roman biographer, Sulpicius Severus, regarded his years in the army as an embarrassment. They were barely redeemed by his acts of charity, and by his fearless resolution to quit soldiering with the words, 'I am a soldier of Christ. I may not fight.' For Sulpicius, it was primarily Martin's post-army life that marked him out as a man of God; and it is with his interpretation of St. Martin, not with the later cult, that this study will be concerned.

Martin left the Roman army in 356, and, according to Sulpicius, journeyed to Poitiers to join its bishop, Hilary, the protagonist of the Nicene faith. After further travels and adventures, Martin returned there and founded a monastery not far from the city. Here he is shown resuscitating a disciple who had just died; and his growing reputation as a man of God, whose prayers were answered, led to his being popularly

---

[1] Cf. B. H. Rosenwein, 'St. Odo's St. Martin: the uses of a model', *Journal of Medieval History* 4 (1978), pp. 317–31.

elected as bishop of Tours *c*.371. However, Martin did not let his new responsibilities as bishop deflect him from the monastic life, and he soon established a monastery at Marmoutier, just across the river Loire from his episcopal city. It was thus in the dual role of bishop of Tours and abbot of Marmoutier that Martin spent the rest of his life. He died in 397.

It is tempting to view Martin's years at Tours as falling in the Indian summer of Roman Gaul: a period of recovery and sunny optimism which was brought to an abrupt end only after his death. But that is to take too superficial a view. In many areas the devastation wrought in the third century had bitten deep, and recovery was uneven. Between 250 and 276 Germanic freebooters had crossed the weakly-guarded Rhine frontier and rampaged across Gaul, leaving behind them a trail of destruction and a tell-tale rash of coin hoards. The Touraine was among the areas stricken. A historical fragment tells us that Tours itself was besieged; and eloquent testimony can be found in the erection there of massive city walls, some thirteen feet thick, built out of former monuments and enclosing only a quarter of the original urban area.[2] The surrounding countryside also suffered: for instance, archaeology has revealed pottery kilns abandoned in mid-production at Mougon, while nearby at Cravant the remains of a villa have been found, its well filled with human bones. The evidence of coins points to its destruction in the 270s.[3]

For the survivors, of course, life carried on; and towards the end of the century Diocletian succeeded in bringing Gaul once more within the *pax romana*. None the less, internal insecurity and barbarian pressure on the Rhine frontier persisted. Renewed invasions in the middle of the fourth century were repulsed first by the Caesar Julian, and then again by Valentinian I, an effective military emperor. In 367 Valentinian, following earlier precedents, established his

---

[2] T. Reinach, 'Le Premier siège entrepris par les Francs, *RH* 43 (1890), pp. 34-46; J. Boussard, 'Étude sur la ville de Tours du Ier au IVe siècle', *REA* 50 (1948), pp. 315-16; *idem, Carte archéologique de la Gaule romaine*, 13: *Carte et Texte du Département d'Indre-et-Loire* (Paris 1960), pp. 11-12.

[3] J. Boussard, 'Essai sur le peuplement de la Touraine du Ier au VIIIe siècle', *Le Moyen Age* 60 (1954) pp. 273-6; *idem, Carte*, nos. 60, 63.

court at Trier, thus placing himself with in easy reach of the threatened frontier; and the government headquarters for the prefecture of the Gauls remained there till around the turn of the century, when they were transferred to Arles.[4] The wisdom of this move was demonstrated in the winter of 406-7, when the Rhine frontier once more gave way under Germanic pressure: this time, for good.

These tumultuous events form at least one backcloth for the life of Martin. They account for the insecurity which is reflected in false rumours of a barbarian attack on Trier; and, at a deeper level, they throw light upon Martin's conviction that the end of the world was imminent. In this context we might ponder the words of a French archaeologist and historian, who has drawn attention to the lasting effects of the third-century invasions upon the Touraine: 'We may suppose that [Martin's] mission had for its setting a waste land, and that it was directed to a people living in fear, barely beginning to rebuild the ruins.'[5]

However, we must not let ourselves be misled into assuming that this grim picture was typical of all Gaul in the fourth century. Southern Gaul, which was more heavily romanized to start with, had also been less seriously affected by the third-century invasions. In Aquitaine, the leisured life of the senatorial aristocracy was able to continue, almost as if nothing had happened;[6] and it was here, on his estate of Primuliacum, that Sulpicius Severus spent his life. Southern Gaul's greater degree of romanization, culture, and economic prosperity must be borne in mind amongst other factors when we consider the contrast between Martin and Sulpicius, between Marmoutier and Primuliacum.

Another area which shows signs of prosperity in the fourth century is the Rhineland. Paradoxically, the necessity for maintaining a large army there, which had to be fed, clothed, and armed, stimulated economic activity. An additional

---

[4] I incline to follow Palanque's dating of this move to *c*.395, rather than Chastagnol's 407: J.-R. Palanque, 'La Date du transfert de la Préfecture des Gaules', *REA* 36 (1934), pp. 359-65; and 'Du nouveau sur la date du transfert de la Préfecture des Gaules?', *Provence Historique* 23 (1973), pp. 29-38, replying to A. Chastagnol, 'Le Repli sur Arles', *RH* 249 (1973) pp. 23-40.

[5] Boussard, 'Le Peuplement', p. 276.

[6] See, for instance, M. Labrousse, *Toulouse antique* (Paris, 1968), pp. 567-72.

factor which furthered the revival of this area was the presence of an emperor at Trier for most of the time from 367 to 392. As an imperial capital, Trier provided a focus for political, social, and cultural life within Gaul for a generation. Valentinian's son and successor, Gratian, was educated by the foremost Gallic rhetorician; and, against a murky background of sporadic barbarian invasions, Gratian's reign stands out for the patronage afforded to men of letters, in place of his father's military parvenus.[7]

Gratian's reign was also marked by a renewed concern to throw the weight of imperial recognition and favour behind the Christian church. After Constantine's death, the development of close church-state relations in the western part of the empire had been hindered by the heretical Arian tendencies of Constantius, followed by Julian's return to paganism (360-3). Although Valentinian I was an orthodox Christian himself, he chose not to concern himself too nicely with religious affairs; and, in any case, his second wife was a pronounced Arian. It was thus not until Gratian's reign that the old state religion of Roman paganism was disestablished, while church and emperor drew closer together.

This development was sustained after Gratian's death in 383. His supplanter in Gaul, Magnus Maximus, sought to make amends for his usurpation by posing as an ultra-catholic emperor, in contrast to the Arianizing tendencies of the legitimate court at Milan. This led him to take a hard line with the suspected heretic, Priscillian, and his followers: a point on which he clashed with the bishop of Tours. Meanwhile, in Milan, Ambrose succeeded in stiffening the young Valentinian II against the pagan senators' request for the restoration of the Altar of Victory to the senate house; and two years later, he was able to outmanœuvre Valentinian's aggressively Arian mother, thus laying the Arian bogy. The final outlawry of paganism followed not long after: in 391 the Emperor Theodosius issued a law which conclusively banned all pagan sacrifices, and even forbade access to the

---

[7] A. R. Lewis, *The Northern Seas* (repr. New York 1978), pp. 20-4. E. M. Wightman, *Roman Trier and the Treveri* (London 1970), pp. 58-67. John F. Matthews, *Western Aristocracies and Imperial Court, A.D. 364-425* (Oxford 1975), chs. 2-3.

temples. A pagan revival a couple of years later under the usurping emperor, Eugenius, proved short-lived, ending with the latter's overthrow in 394. Christianity as the sole official religion of the Roman Empire had come to stay. Martin's episcopate thus fell at a critical period for the church in western Europe. In Gaul, Christianity was already on its way to dominance in the towns by 360; but it was only in the following decades that it became the religion of the senatorial aristocracy, and that it began to make some headway with the peasants in the countryside. Martin was involved in the conversion of both these classes, and his activities illustrate the process whereby people were led to abandon their pagan beliefs in favour of Christianity. The increasing connection between church and state is also reflected in Martin's life: positively, in his visits to the imperial court at Trier in order to intercede for prisoners; and negatively, in his horror at the trial and execution of Priscillian; and, more generally, in his distaste at the way in which ambitious church leaders clustered round the imperial court, concerning themselves more with worldly power and position than with the things of the spirit.

This development jarred upon Martin's conception of the proper role of a Christian bishop. As a disciple of Hilary of Poitiers, Martin viewed with misgiving the growing worldliness of the church. His own understanding of the Christian calling can be seen in his decision to become a monk. Formal monasticism was then a new, eastern, phenomenon, and Martin was one of the first Christians in the Latin-speaking half of the empire to embrace this way of life. His new-fangled asceticism antagonized the easy-going Gallo-Roman bishops of his day, but it won him the respect of many lay people, both peasants and aristocrats. These looked to Martin as to a true man of God, and turned to him for help and healing. As bishop and monk, healer and evangelist, Martin of Tours was an important figure in his own right; and his career provides a fascinating insight into that period of church history which saw Christianity's triumph over paganism, its increasing involvement with politics, and the first beginnings of western monasticism.

But this study is not a biography of Martin; nor could such a work be written in any straightforward sense. This is because nearly everything that we can hope to know of Martin comes from the pen of his younger contemporary and disciple, Sulpicius Severus; and Sulpicius wrote not a biographical, but a hagiographical account. This poses special problems of interpretation, but it also provides additional interest; for the *Vita Martini* was written at a time when the genre of hagiography was still in the process of formation, and this life was itself destined to become one of the most influential models for that genre.

During the fourth century, with the era of Christian persecutions now over, the monks began to replace the martyrs as the contemporary Christian heroes whose lives might be held up for imitation. Athanasius paved the way with his *Life of Antony*, written in 357 or shortly thereafter. This was twice translated into Latin in a matter of years. Next came Jerome's three saints' lives; and then, Sulpicius' *Life of Martin*, completed in 396. Sulpicius followed this *Life* with three open letters, also about Martin; and finally with the *Dialogues* (*c*.404-6), in which Martin was favourably compared with the ascetics of Egypt. Taken together with a few others, these works by Athanasius, Jerome, and Sulpicius were to establish the new literary genre of hagiography, which was to enjoy such popularity in the middle ages.

The author of this influential life of Martin, Sulpicius Severus, knew his subject at first hand. Although he was never a member of Martin's monastery at Marmoutier, Sulpicius visited Martin there to gather information for his book, and in his own way he tried to model his household in Aquitaine after its example. As a well-educated Gallo-Roman who was personally acquainted with his subject, we would expect his account to be accurate and well informed.

For all this, Sulpicius' portrayal of Martin as a saint, whose *virtus* was attested by numerous miracles, failed to win universal acceptance within Gaul. Shortly after the publication of the *Vita* an anonymous critic was heard to enquire how it was that a man who enjoyed the sort of powers over nature, with which this book credited Martin, could himself recently have suffered burns. That was in

396-7. By the time the last book of the *Dialogues* came to be written nearly ten years later, the sceptics had forced Sulpicius on to the defensive in his account of Martin's deeds. What is more, certain monks from Martin's own monastery appear to have been of their number, for some of them refused to believe that their abbot had really been visited by saints, angels, and demons, as Sulpicius' writings claimed. We thus have the strange paradox of parts of the Martinian writings, which were written by a contemporary who knew Martin personally, being rejected by other contemporaries who were equally well acquainted with him: amongst them, monks from Martin's own monastery. This is certainly odd.[8]

The first scholar to approach this conundrum with the tools of modern historical scholarship was E.-C. Babut, whose *Saint Martin de Tours* was published in 1912. Babut's explanation for the scepticism of Sulpicius' contemporaries was a logical one: they refused to believe many stories told about Martin because they were well aware that these stories were not true. Sulpicius had twisted the chronology of Martin's life and borrowed miracle stories from elsewhere in order to glorify his hero. His primary motive was to portray Martin as a 'saint', in the same tradition as Athanasius' hero, Antony. This, however, was not because Sulpicius knew Martin well and was convinced that he was a saint. Instead, his adoption of Martin as his hero was dictated by the fact that Martin was the only bishop who was in sympathy with Sulpicius' sectarian stance; for Babut thought that Sulpicius belonged to an extreme, rigorist minority, which was out of communion with the rest of the church from 385 to 417.

Babut's book pioneered the modern critical approach to Sulpicius' Martinian writings. True, in exposing the weaknesses of Sulpicius' account, he sometimes pushed his scepticism beyond the bounds of credibility; and no one today would accept every jot of his thesis. None the less,

---

[8] It is not, however, unparalleled. In the 12th century Walter Daniel's *Life of Ailred* met with comparable scepticism from two contemporary prelates; and Daniel, in his *Letter to Maurice*, reacted much as Sulpicius did in his *ep.* 1 and *D* III. See *The Life of Ailred of Rievaulx* by Walter Daniel, ed. F. M. Powicke (London etc. 1950), pp. 66 ff.

in modified form it can claim followers, chiefly in Germany. In France, which honours Martin as a patron saint, his book has tended to be unpopular; but for all that, it has proved fruitful in indirect ways, compelling scholars to reconsider Sulpicius' account, and stimulating various ripostes. Outstanding amongst these is the detailed study published by Père Delehaye in 1920, and this in itself comprises an important contribution to Martinian studies.[9] More recently, Sulpicius' *Vita Martini* and *Letters* have been re-edited by J. Fontaine, with full introduction and notes; and the same scholar has devoted several articles to aspects of the subject, which are particularly helpful from a literary angle.

However, there is still a certain amount of confusion and disagreement. Babut's study has made it impossible to hold to the old, uncritical acceptance of every detail of Sulpicius' Martinian writings; but his own rival thesis is itself untenable *in toto*, and no one since then has attempted a synthesis of the whole subject. The primary source of the confusion is that, since Babut wrote, we have had only studies which undermined particular aspects of his thesis, or which enlarged our understanding of certain areas of Sulpicius' works. These have greatly enriched our knowledge and our understanding in some spheres, but they have not resolved the overriding puzzle which Babut sought to solve: namely, the sceptical reception given to Sulpicius' portrayal of Martin *c*.400 AD, with all its implications for the (un)reliability of the Martinian writings. I attempt to grapple with this question, although along rather different lines from Babut.

My underlying objectives are fourfold. First, I seek to gain insight into what Sulpicius set out to do in his Martinian writings: and so I start in Part I with Sulpicius and his writing of the Martinian works. Then, after looking at Sulpicius' portrayal of Martin and the problems this raises (Part II), I go on to explore the way in which our reading of the Martinian works—specifically of the miracle stories—relates to Sulpicius' and to his own contemporaries' understanding of them (Part III): and that is my second major concern. Next, I suggest an alternative explanation for fourth-century hostility to Sulpicius' presentation of Martin. Finally, in Part V, I consider how Sulpicius' portrayal of Martin is likely to relate to the monk-bishop of flesh and blood whom Sulpicius had himself known, and thus to throw light upon Martin himself. This study is cast in the form of a quest because it is a reaching out after understanding. It follows the time-honoured historical principle of starting from a definite body of material, in this case Sulpicius' Martinian writings, and of stretching out towards what is further from our grasp, in this case Martin and the impact which he made upon his contemporaries.

Perhaps a further word of explanation about Part III, 'The Thought-World', might be in place. Any historian who is concerned with the intellectual history of a society as far removed from our own as that of late antiquity encounters some problems in this sphere. However, the Martinian writings of Sulpicius Severus raise them in an acute form. First, because miracle stories do not just crop up incidentally in the course of his main narrative; rather, they *are* his main narrative. Secondly because, as we have seen, some of Sulpicius' own contemporaries refused to believe in the *virtutes* which he ascribed to Martin. And here, already, I flounder because of the gulf between a twentieth-century and a fourth-century understanding of such matters. *Virtus*, and its plural *virtutes*, is a key word in the Martinian writings; but whereas for Sulpicius and his contemporaries the one word carries meanings of excellence, moral perfection, spiritual power, and miracles, our own lack of any single word to convey all this is symptomatic of our different patterns of thought. In other words, *virtus* and *virtutes* are at the heart of Sulpicius' presentation of Martin, and of the controversy that arose from this; and we are ill-equipped to understand them.

My sketch of 'the thought-world' in Part III is an attempt to remedy this. It makes no pretence at being a full exposition of the subject: that would lie outside the scope of this book. It merely aims to pin-point those areas where fourth-century assumptions differed radically from our own, and which are crucial for a true understanding of how Sulpicius and his contemporaries would have perceived Martin's *virtutes*.

Of course, if all this were common knowledge, I could have contented myself with showing how Sulpicius' Martinian works fit into their late antique background, and leave it at that. But my impression is that such understanding is not very widespread, at least in this country; nor am I aware of any adequate synthesis in English to which I could refer readers. Indeed, a German historian recently began a study of another late antique saint's life with the comment that saints' lives are still *terra incognita* for historians;[10] and if that is true of Germany, then it applies with even greater force in this country—hence the need to set the scene in a general way before entering upon more detailed discussion.

In the course of this work I have necessarily found myself wrestling with two unfavourable critiques of Sulpicius' portrayal of Martin, which are by no means identical.[11] One is that of Babut, whose wayward, but often perceptive, views still require consideration. Although I do not concur with his conclusions, I hope that I have at least faced his criticisms of Sulpicius' writings squarely. The second adverse critique, to which I have given more space, is that of Sulpicius' own contemporaries. I have tried to show that this had a different origin from the charges levelled by Babut, and that the underlying explanation for it lies in the varying ideals and the dissensions of the fourth-century church.

In this way I have sought to solve the riddle posed by Sulpicius' portrayal of Martin, and its rejection by some of Sulpicius' contemporaries; and I hope that one result will be to enable the reader to form an estimate not only of Sulpicius and his writings, but also of Martin of Tours and his work. I also hope that, in the process, an oblique shaft of light may

---

[10] F. Lotter, *Severinus von Noricum, Legende und historische Wirklichkeit* (Stuttgart 1976), p. 1; he includes a helpful discussion about ways of approaching hagiography and the interpretation of miracle stories (cf. my review in *JTS* n.s. 29, 1978, pp. 576-7). A useful historiographical survey of various approaches to hagiography and miracle stories is given by F. Graus, *Volk, Herrscher und Heiliger im Reich der Merowinger* (Prague 1965), ch. 1. Unfortunately, little has been published on this field in English; it is works in German and French which form the major contribution.

[11] Sometimes, particularly in Part II, I may appear guilty of confusing the two. But this is only because I am there probing along Babut's lines—and Babut did assume that the two were identical—in order the better to distinguish between the fourth-century and the twentieth-century criticisms in Part III.

have been thrown on to the history of the Gallic church and the beginnings of western monasticism in the fourth century; on to the genesis of western hagiography and questions relating to the use of miracle stories; and on to the way in which men in late antiquity viewed the workings of the cosmos: their 'world picture'.

PART I
SULPICIUS SEVERUS

2

Sulpicius' Conversion[1]

Sulpicius Severus came from a noble, though not senatorial, family of Aquitaine.[2] The date of his birth is unknown, but he was a younger contemporary of Paulinus of Nola who was born *c*.355.[3] Our knowledge of his private life is scanty as his own correspondence is lost, and neither his *Chronicle* nor his Martinian writings afford us much in the way of personal details. For the years 395-404 we can glean a fair amount of information from Paulinus' letters to him, and this roughly covers the period of his conversion and literary output. Apart from a passing reference in Jerome's commentary on Ezekiel (410/12),[4] which at least suggests that he survived the immediate impact of the 407 Germanic invasions, our only other source of information is chapter nineteen of Gennadius' *De viris inlustribus*, written at the end of the fifth century. This adds to our knowledge by telling us that

[1] By 'conversion' I mean primarily 'conversion to asceticism'. For Paulinus, and so probably for Sulpicius himself, serious commitment to Christianity led naturally to embracing the ascetic life: see J. T. Lienhard, *Paulinus of Nola and Early Western Monasticism* (Theophaneia 28; Cologne & Bonn 1977), ch. 2.

[2] Gennadius, *De viris inlustribus* 19; ed. E. C. Richardson, *Texte und Untersuchungen* 14, i (1896), p. 69. A. B. E. Hood, 'Sulpicius Severus and his Background' (unpubl. Oxford B.Phil. thesis, 1968), pp. 12-13. A useful dossier of what earlier writers (from Paulinus of Nola to Erasmus and beyond) have said of Sulpicius is given by H. de Prato, *Sulpicii Severi opera ad MSS. codices emendata* (2 vols., Verona 1741 & 1754), I, xxxiii-liv. It is interesting, though perhaps irrelevant, that an inscription at Bordeaux was set up by one Sul(picia) Severa: *CIL* XIII, i, no. 858. Cf. also *CIL* XIII, i, no. 586, and R. Dezeimeris in *Société archéologique de Bordeaux* 6 (1879), at pp. 116-18, 123: a reference I owe to Hood, p. 13.

[3] Paulinus, *ep.* 5, 4-5 (*CSEL* 29, pp. 27-8). For the date of Paulinus' birth, see P. Fabre, *Saint Paulin de Nole et l'amitié chrétienne* (Paris 1949), 13-16.

[4] *Comm. in Hiezechielem* XI, xxxvi, 1/15: 'et nuper Severus noster in dialogo cui "Gallo" nomen imposuit' (*CCSL* 75, p. 500).

Sulpicius was a priest, and that in his old age he was temporarily deceived by the Pelagian heretics. Later he recognized his error, and resolved to atone for sin contracted through loquacity by holding his peace.[5] This implies that he was still alive in the 420s when the semi-Pelagian controversy broke out in southern Gaul. We do not know the date of his death.

To judge from his apparent success as a lawyer and from the quality of his writings, Sulpicius must have received a good education. Presumably this was in Gaul, perhaps at Bordeaux, as his friendship with Paulinus implies. The main stress in late classical education lay on rhetoric, an art for which Aquitaine was then famous. The object was to learn how to express the emotions of an imaginary character realistically, and the general attitude towards this form of education may be summed up in Augustine's words: 'This is where men gain mastery of words. This is where they come by that fluency, so necessary to persuade in business affairs, and to expound ideas.'[6] It was therefore a natural step for a man in Sulpicius' position to become an advocate when he had finished his training in rhetoric: here was a field in which eloquence was all-important, and it provided an excellent ladder for an ambitious young man whose class was not in itself sufficient to procure him a government post.[7] The other step in the same direction was a profitable marriage, which Sulpicius duly made: we hear of the wealth brought by his marriage into a senatorial family, and of stenographers afforded him by his mother-in-law.[8] We do not know whether Sulpicius was a pagan or a Christian. The latter is more likely, but it does not make much odds: he had the background, education, and ambitions which formed common ground

---

[5] Cf. Proverbs 10:19; Gennadius, loc. cit. No contemporary addressed Sulpicius as 'presbyter', but this does not necessarily mean that Gennadius' information is wrong. Hood, p. 77, points out that the Verona MS of the Martinian works, written in 517, calls Sulpicius 'a monk of Marseilles' (*CSEL* 1, p. 137). But although in many respects this is plausible, there is one overwhelming objection: that Gennadius would surely have mentioned this, for he was himself a priest at Marseilles.

[6] Augustine, *Confessiones* I, xvi (26) (*CSEL* 33, p. 23); cf. also I, xvii (27).

[7] A. H. M. Jones, *The Later Roman Empire* (3 vols., Oxford 1964), I, 511–12; III, 147 n. 97. Hood, pp. 14 ff.

[8] Paulinus, *ep.* 5, 5; Sulpicius, *ep.* 3, 2. Cf. Augustine *Confess.* VI, xi (19).

amongst educated men of the world in the later fourth century. At the moment of his conversion to the ascetic life, his friend Paulinus compared Sulpicius' fortunes favourably with his own: '(You were) nearer the prime of life, more richly praised, less burdened with ancestral wealth, but no poorer in intellectual resources; and, enjoying an outstanding name for eloquence, you were still immersed in the bustle of the law courts—that theatre of the world.'[9]

Outwardly, Sulpicius was prospering, and the path ahead of him appeared smooth and straightforward. But, meanwhile, he could scarcely avoid being touched by the destiny of those closest to him; and this in time led him to question the direction of his present life, with its pursuit of worldly success. The greatest shock may well have come from the death of his wife, for all that we know nothing of its circumstances.[10] In the event, Sulpicius appears to have remained or drawn closer to his mother-in-law, a pious lady named Bassula, than to his own father, who had little sympathy for the otherworldliness of a radical Christianity.[11]

The effect of his wife's death on Sulpicius must remain a matter for conjecture, but we are on surer ground when we postulate the influence of his intimate friend, Paulinus. This rich nobleman had gradually been moving towards a total dedication of his life to God over a number of years.[12] He had served as governor of Campania in Italy in 381, and from then onwards he entertained a special devotion towards its local saint, Felix of Nola. From Italy he retired back to his extensive family estates in Aquitaine, and married a devout Spaniard, Therasia. She probably stimulated Paulinus' growing piety, and contributed to his decision to seek baptism in Bordeaux. A further influence may have been exercised

---

[9] Paulinus, *ep.* 5, 5.

[10] It is implied by Paulinus' reference to Sulpicius' conversion as having occurred despite his 'post coniugium peccandi licentia et caelebs iuventas' (*ep.* 5, 5). Fontaine, surely rightly, takes the 'freedom to sin' as being that of a young man whose marriage has now come to an end, thus restoring him to the single state (*Vie* I, 22 and cf. p. 26). Sulpicius' continuing close relationship with his mother-in-law precludes the possibility that his marriage ended in quarrelling and divorce, rather than in the death of his wife.

[11] Paulinus, *ep.* 5, 6; Fontaine, *Vie* I, 26-8.

[12] Fabre, *Saint Paulin*, 25-38; Lienhard, pp. 24-51.

by Martin of Tours, who healed Paulinus from an eye complaint.[13] Then, around 389, tragedy struck. Paulinus' brother
met with violent death, and he himself was threatened with
loss of life and property, and moved from Aquitaine to Spain.
On top of this, when his wife gave birth to a son, the baby
died after only eight days. These calamities helped to spur
Paulinus and Therasia to their final decision, in 393, to
renounce the world and to embrace the monastic life. They
began to sell off their extensive family estates, and in 395
they journeyed to Nola, where they were to spend the rest
of their lives by the shrine of St. Felix.

This radical reorientation of his friend's life was not
without its effect on Sulpicius. Indeed, looking back from
397, Paulinus could imply that they had moved together
along the path leading to conversion; though more strictly
contemporary evidence shows that Paulinus was the first to
make the decision, and that he had then urged his friend to
follow suit.[14] It was probably through Paulinus that Sulpicius
acquired his interest in Martin of Tours. Paulinus, having met
Martin and experienced his healing powers, would have
been in a position to tell Sulpicius of 'his faith, his way of
life, and his spiritual power', those qualities that inspired
Sulpicius to visit Martin and write about him. So it was that
Sulpicius made his first pilgrimage to Tours, in 393 or 4:
partly to see the holy man for himself, and partly to gather
material for the projected biography.[15] The fact that Sulpicius
was then intending to write the life of a monk-bishop implies
that he had begun to think about what the monastic life
entailed. It also suggests that he had already read the *Life of
Antony*, and perhaps Jerome's saints' lives and other ascetic

[13] *VM* 19, 3. Paulinus was once in Martin's company at Vienne: Paulinus,
ep. 18, 9.

[14] Cf. *ep.* 11, 5-6 (of 397) with *ep.* 1, 1 (of early 395): Sulpicius has announced
his decision to dispose of his property to Paulinus, 'sollicito et optanti'. Doubtless
Sulpicius had been the recipient of letters comparable to those which Paulinus
sent to other potential recruits to asceticism: e.g. *eps.* 25 and 25* addressed to
Crispinianus.

[15] *VM* 25, 1. This visit must post-date Paulinus' sale of his estates which started
in 393 (Fabre, *Saint Paulin*, 35), and antedate Paulinus' *ep.* 1 to Sulpicius, written
early in 395 (Lienhard, 178).

literature.[16] As yet, however, Sulpicius had made no decision to adopt the monastic life himself; for Martin spent the time pressing him to free himself from the burdens of secular life in order to follow Jesus unimpeded, and urging on him the example of Paulinus, who had achieved the impossible by fulfilling the gospel command to sell all and give to the poor.[17]

Sulpicius was impressed by Martin and his monastery of Marmoutier, and urgency would have been added to his appeal if Martin voiced his conviction that the end of the world was imminent.[18] In all events, the pleas of Martin and Paulinus soon bore fruit. In 394 or early 395, Sulpicius took the plunge. He resolved to strip himself of his possessions and throw up his legal career in order to devote his whole life to following Christ, as Martin and Paulinus were doing. He thus became, if not a 'monk' as we would understand that term, at least a 'servant of God'.

In making this decision, Sulpicius was acting in accordance with the views of a small, but significant, minority among his Christian contemporaries. In order to gain perspective on his conversion, we must turn aside to glance briefly at the beginnings of the monastic movement in the west.

[16] Sulpicius knew the *Vita Antonii* and other ascetic literature by 396: below, ch. 6, ii.
[17] *VM* 25, 4-5.
[18] *VM* 25, 2-3. *D* II, 14.

3

Monastic Beginnings

From early times the Christian church included a small minority who had renounced career, possessions, and marriage in order to live a wholly God-oriented life. These ascetics were in many ways the forerunners of the monks. Monasticism proper, however, arose only in the late third and fourth centuries when such ascetics began to cut themselves off from society, secluding themselves from all day to day contact with non-monks, and often grouping themselves into communities.

Traditionally, this new development began with St. Antony. About 270 AD this future saint, then an unlettered Egyptian lad of about twenty, heard in his local church the gospel passage, 'If you wish to be perfect, go, sell all that you have and give to the poor; and come, follow me, and you will have treasure in heaven.' (Matt. 19:21.) Antony sold all his goods and took up a life of asceticism, retreating further and further into the deserts of Egypt in pursuit of peace for the contemplation of God; but there were times when he made himself accessible to the crowds flocking to him, and guided those disciples who sought to imitate his way of renunciation. By Antony's death in 356 the monks of Egypt could be numbered in their thousands; and Athanasius' *Life of Antony* soon made known the ideal of the monastic life, even to those who lived far beyond the boundaries of Egypt.[1]

Antony was not the sole inspiration behind Egyptian monasticism, for Pachomius was simultaneously guiding the

---

[1] On early Egyptian monasticism see D. J. Chitty, *The Desert a City* (pb. edn, London & Oxford, 1977).

development of cenobitic communities. However, the story of Antony can be taken as typical in its portrayal of a radical break with civilization. In Egypt, there was generally a sharp cleavage between the traditional Greek culture of the Egyptian cities on the one hand, and, on the other, the raw beginnings of a new Christ-centred life in the desert.

When monasticism reached the west in the second half of the fourth century, it changed somewhat. This was partly because it did not remain an alien introduction in the Latin west, but became naturalized, often being grafted on to earlier ascetic—and Roman—traditions which were indigenous there. Also, it tended to appeal to a more cultured class than in Egypt.[2] As a result, western monasticism developed characteristics which set it somewhat apart from its Egyptian progenitor. A general point is that, in the west, the split between monastery and secular society was not as absolute. One example lies in the greater readiness of western monks to accept incorporation within the church's pastoral and priestly ministries: whereas an Egyptian might cut off his thumb in order to render himself ineligible for ordination, westerners like Eusebius of Vercelli or Martin of Tours combined the monastic life with episcopal office. Another difference lies in the west's less hostile attitude to traditional Roman culture. An impressionistic view is that the typical monastic convert in Egypt was a peasant farmer, but in the west a well-born aristocrat, an ambitious intellectual, or an educated official. Inevitably, such men could not undo their literary education when they rid themselves of their material possessions and became monks. Instead, they used the rhetorical devices of the schools to preach the gospel of

---

[2] For early western monasticism in general see R. Lorenz, 'Die Anfänge des abendländischen Mönchtums im 4. Jahrhundert', *Zeitschrift für Kirchengeschichte* 77 (1966), pp. 1–61. On Christian antecedents of monasticism in Africa, see G. Folliet, 'Aux origines de l'ascétisme et du cénobitisme africain', *Saint Martin et son temps* (Rome 1961), pp. 25–44; for Gaul, Fontaine, 'L'Ascétisme chrétien', pp. 90–105. For the influence of aristocratic Roman traditions, see J. Fontaine, 'Valeurs antiques et valeurs chrétiennes', in *Epektasis*, edd. J. Fontaine and C. Kannengiesser (Paris 1972), pp. 571–95; and particularly Fontaine, 'L'Aristocratie occidentale devant le monachisme', *Rivista di storia e letteratura religiosa* 15 (1979), esp. pp. 35–53. Cf. also M. Heinzelmann, *Bischofsherrschaft in Gallien* (Munich 1976), pp. 185–211, although H glosses over the very real gulf between pagan and monastic values in the fourth century: cf. below ch. 20, n. 68.

Christ, and transferred to the Bible the attention they had hitherto lavished on the pagan classics of Rome.

Martin of Tours, however, does not conform to this pattern. His father was a soldier from Pannonia who had risen through the ranks; and Martin, though able to read, lacked the literary education which enabled intelligent men from modest backgrounds to rise to dizzy heights in the late empire.[3] Instead, Martin, as the son of a soldier, was drafted willy nilly into the Roman army at the age of fifteen, despite boyhood dreams of the church or the desert. Although he was baptized three years later, he remained a soldier until 356, and it was only after this that he began to explore the possibilities of the monastic life. Sulpicius represents him going first to Hilary at Poitiers, and it may be that Hilary's clergy then lived some kind of communal, premonastic life.[4] However, his first recorded ascetic experiences took place in Italy *c.*357-60, years in which Arianism was in the ascendant. As for the sources of his inspiration: Martin may well have encountered monasticism in his boyhood in Italy, as Sulpicius indicates; also, his adoption of the solitary life may have been stimulated by the Arian persecution, much as one root of Egyptian monasticism may lie in the stimulus given to anachoresis (withdrawal) by earlier pagan persecutions.[5]

Martin is said to have first established a hermitage for himself at Milan. Then, having been expelled by the Arian bishop, he and a priest withdrew to the Mediterranean island of Gallinara, where they lived off roots, like Egyptian solitaries. This, however, was only a temporary expedient, occasioned by the Arian persecution. In 360 this was relaxed, and Hilary, the exiled bishop of Poitiers and Martin's spiritual mentor, returned home. Martin speedily rejoined him, and

---

[3] Martin could read: *VM* 26, 3; but 'inlitteratus' (i.e. uneducated): *VM* 25, 8. For what follows, see *VM* 2 ff. For the chronological and other problems involved, see below chs. 9 and 10.

[4] Fontaine, 'L'Ascétisme chrétien', pp. 94-8.

[5] On *VM* 2, 4, see below, ch. 9, iii, and cf. notes 46-7. Fontaine, *Vie* II, 591-601. For persecution possibly stimulating Egyptian monasticism, see Chitty, pp. 6-7.

established another hermitage at Ligugé, an estate only five miles out from Poitiers.[6]

Excavations carried out at Ligugé during the 1950s and '60s have brought to light much of interest concerning this phase of Martin's life.[7] The site had formerly been occupied by a modest Roman villa, but this had fallen into ruins before Martin's arrival. The southern wing of the villa contained a very long room, partially sunk below ground level: presumably a cellar or store room, probably for grain. It was at the western end of this that Martin built his church: a simple rectangular building with a semicircular apse at the east end, the whole measuring approximately 47 feet by 16 feet (14.35m × 4.80m). The side walls were placed right up against those of the store room, and it was built directly on the store room's concreted floor. The church looks as though it was rather hastily put together: it was not a polished work, designed for posterity. At the north-west and south-west corners stairs led up on to the ground level, where there were two rooms of the former villa leading off each other, carrying on along the east–west axis.

Around the end of the fourth century, the westernmost of these rooms was to emerge as the focus of another religious building of cruciform plan. It has been suggested that this was a martyrium, commemorating the place where Martin resuscitated the dead catechumen. The connection between these archaeological remains and Martin is fortunately made explicit by a sarcophagus carrying the inscription: ARIOMERES SERUOS DOMNI MARTINI ORA PRO ME. This inscription is definitely pre *c*.550, and probably dates from *c*.430–60.

Approximately 33 yards to the north of the church, in the centre of the former villa's courtyard, a little building

---

[6] *VM* 7,1 records the foundation of this monastery; its name is supplied by Gregory of Tours, *De virtutibus S. Martini* IV, 30 (*MGH, SRM* I, ii, repr. 1969, p. 207). The reliability of this identification is attested by recent excavations, for which see following note.

[7] A general overview, complete with plans, is provided by J. Coquet, *L'Intérêt des fouilles de Ligugé* (revised edn. Ligugé 1968). More readily accessible are the summaries given by F. Eygun in *Gallia* 12 (1954), 21 (1963), and 25 (1967). A more detailed discussion is provided by Coquet's articles in *Revue Mabillon* 44 (1954), 45 (1955), and 51 (1961): see my Select Bibliography, below.

consisting of three rooms was erected, probably in the fourth century: it must date from after the villa's desertion, as it reuses some of its stone, while it itself was embraced within a far more grandiose semicircular building that was destroyed in the fifth century. One of the rooms of the small building had a hypocaust. The whole was of crude construction, and it has been plausibly suggested that this was where Martin lived. The large, semicircular building might then be an *exedra*, built about 400 AD to enshrine Martin's dwelling-place when this had perhaps become a focus for pilgrimage.[8]

The fact that Martin founded his hermitage within striking distance of Poitiers is significant, for it shows that Martin, despite his earlier experiments, did not imitate Antony in settling in total isolation from society. It further implies that the bishop of Poitiers played an important role in Ligugé's foundation, and in the spiritual formation of Martin.[9] Disciples were attracted to Martin at Ligugé, and traditionally this foundation marks the starting point of Gallic monasticism —although we should remember that Ligugé itself probably resembled a *lavra*[10] rather than a fully-fledged monastery. It is interesting to note that, right at the beginning, we see an ascetic community being founded within striking distance of an episcopal city, and with the guidance of the bishop himself.

In these respects the foundation of Ligugé foreshadows Martin's later monastery of Marmoutier, where the links between city and solitude, episcopal life and monastic life, become even closer. Martin was elected bishop of Tours *c*.371, but continued to live as a monk, at first using a little

---

[8] Cf. the way in which Marmoutier became a pilgrimage site before *c*.460: below, ch. 24, n. 65. In that chapter I discuss further the fifth-sixth century developments at Ligugé.

[9] It has been suggested that Hilary came into contact with eastern monasticism during his exile in Asia Minor, and that he may have transmitted some of its ideas to Martin: Fontaine, *Vie* I, 155–9; P. Rousseau, *Ascetics, Authority, and the Church in the Age of Jerome and Cassian* (Oxford 1978), pp. 85–6, 149–50. Hilary, in his patronage of monasticism, was not typical of fourth-century Gallic bishops: cf. below, ch. 20, ii–iii.

[10] I.e. a settlement of hermits living in their own huts, but under the direction of an abbot.

cell next to the cathedral. Then, overwhelmed by throngs of visitors, he built a wooden cell for himself on the other side of the Loire, about two miles out from the city. Disciples joined him there, building their own cells or hollowing out caves in the soft stone cliff, and in this way there arose the monastery of Marmoutier. Despite its unplanned beginnings, Sulpicius' description of the monastery—probably reflecting the community of the early 390s—shows that by that date it was something more than a gathering of hermits.

There were about eighty disciples, who were formed after the example of their blessed master. No one possessed anything of his own there: they made over everything to common ownership. No buying or selling was allowed, as is customary with most monks. No craft was practised there, with the exception of the scribe's, and even this was entrusted to the younger men, while the older ones remained free for prayer. Seldom did anyone leave his cell, except when they came together at the place of prayer. When the time of fasting had passed, they all took food together. No one touched wine, unless sickness compelled him. Many were clad in camel's hair: softer clothing was regarded as an object of reproach. What is all the more remarkable is that many of them were said to be nobles, who, having been brought up quite differently, schooled themselves to bear with this humbling and demanding life.[11]

The Marmoutier way of life may not have been as precisely regulated or closely supervised as that of a Pachomian monastery, but it still smacks of cenobitism. Each monk had his own cell, but there was also a feeling that all these cells belonged together and comprised one foundation.[12] The monks met daily for corporate worship, followed by a communal meal. There was also a pooling of economic resources: one monk acted as steward, and not only food, but also clothing was dispensed centrally.[13] Furthermore, the prohibition on trade, coupled with a story of Martin reprimanding a monk for buying horses and slaves, implies that Martin possessed not merely the moral authority of a soul-friend, but the actual authority of an abbot. Proficient

---

[11] *VM* 10, 5-8. See Fontaine's notes ad loc., esp. pp. 687-90 on Sulpicius' stylization of Marmoutier.

[12] See *D* III, 14, 8-9, and cf. *VM* 23, 6, where Anatolius' 'cellula' obviously forms part of 'omne monasterium' of Clarus.

[13] *D* III, 10, 2; III, 14, 6.

monks, like Clarus, were able to graduate from this moderately regulated existence to pursue a more eremetical life
nearby.[14]

As has been pointed out, many of these features recall the
primitive cenobitic monasticism of Egypt, such as Jerome
described.[15] There is, however, one major difference: the
Marmoutier monks did no manual work to support themselves. For their subsistence, they presumably derived something from the assets of those joining the community. Beyond
this, they looked to the church for support.[16] As bishop of
Tours, Martin would have been nominally responsible for
apportioning that church's income, which derived from any
property it had been given, plus the offerings of the faithful.
Presumably the proceeds were shared between the establishment and running costs of the cathedral and other churches
throughout the diocese, works of charity, salaries to non-
monastic clergy in the diocese, and the upkeep of Marmoutier
and other monastic foundations.[17] References to the
Marmoutier monks running short of food and clothing
suggest a fairly spartan existence; but we must set alongside
these a story which reveals that the monastery was able to
hire the services of a peasant with his ox cart to haul timber.[18]
Thus some, at least, of the rough work was performed by
hired labour; and when we add that the only work undertaken
by the monks was the copying of manuscripts, and that
Marmoutier on the outskirts of Tours was very much in
touch with civilization, then we may see in its way of life
a modification of eastern monasticism in a direction that
other, more cultured converts would take very much further.

Martin's development of monasticism in Gaul provides
one important background to Sulpicius' conversion. There

---

[14] *VM* 23, 1-2; Fontaine, *Vie* III, 993-4. For Martin scolding a monk for his
purchases, see *D* III, 15, 2.

[15] Fontaine, *Vie* II, 679-80, citing Jerome *ep.* 22, 35, q.v. (*CSEL* 54, pp. 197-
200).

[16] *D* III, 14, 6.

[17] Cf. Possidius, *Vita Augustini* 23-25, 1 (*Vite dei Santi* III, pp. 188-94);
J. Gaudemet, *L'Église dans l'Empire romain* (Paris 1958), pp. 288-311.

[18] *VM* 21, 2-4. For shortage of food and clothing, see *D* III, 14, 6, and cf. III,
10, 1-2.

is, however, a second context for this which also deserves recognition: that is, the phenomenon of 'conversion' amongst educated westerners in the later fourth century. I refer here not to the widespread adhesion to Christianity at that time, in the sense that people began to fall in with the emperor's religion, substituting church-going on Sundays for sacrifices to the pagan gods; rather, I allude to the fact that some of the most intelligent and sensitive people were then becoming converted to the ascetic life, opting out of a career and family life in order to devote themselves wholly to the service of Christ.[19] Such converts were often inspired by stories of the eastern monks; but, whereas Martin's rigorous monasticism followed such models in an easily recognizable way, the more educated converts tended to embrace a somewhat modified asceticism that cannot easily be defined —particularly as it was very variously understood.

The sheer incongruity of such cultured converts attempting to follow Antony literally into the desert is illustrated by Jerome's experiences in the desert near Antioch, *c*.374–6. Even there, the well-educated Jerome was accompanied by his library, and by copyists.[20] Within three years he was back in civilization. Thereafter he acted as spiritual adviser to noble ladies in Rome, counselling them to adopt a rigorous ascetic regime *in their own homes*; and when he was forced to leave Rome in 385 he did not return to the desert, but established his own monastery at Bethlehem. This enabled him to write extensively, and to maintain contact with western Christians by means of frequent letters and visitors.

Another example of the response made by educated westerners to the call of the desert is provided by the story of the two imperial officials who stumbled upon a little ascetic household just outside Trier. There, they read the *Life of Antony*, and its appeal was immediate. In place of a protracted and laborious struggle to gain promotion, with its highest peak being the risky achievement of imperial favour, Antony's example proferred a new goal. If they renounced the world, they could straightway become not

[19] Cf. A. D. Nock, *Conversion* (Oxford 1933), p. 7; Lienhard, pp. 33–5.
[20] J. N. D. Kelly, *Jerome* (pb. edn. London 1975), ch. 6, esp. pp. 48–9; Rousseau, op. cit. pp. 100 ff.

'friends of the emperor', but 'friends of God'. Abandoning their careers and fiancées forthwith, they resolved to remain with the ascetic community they had found.[21]

Yet another response to eastern monasticism can be seen in the double conversion of Augustine, then a successful rhetoric teacher at Milan, and of his friend Alypius, a lawyer.[22] In Augustine's case the ground had been prepared by a fruitful encounter with neoplatonism; but their actual conversion in 386 was precipitated by hearing first of Antony, and then this story of conversion at Trier. However, Augustine and Alypius did not follow Antony to the desert, nor the two officials into an existing monastery. Instead, Augustine set up his own Christian household where he and his companions lived their own version of a life dedicated to Christianity. Their ascetic retreat near Milan had much in common with the cultured Roman tradition of withdrawal from public affairs to enjoy a life of *otium*, or leisure for higher pursuits.[23] Then, after baptism, Augustine and his friends returned to Africa, and the emphasis shifted. In 388 they settled on Augustine's family estates at Thagaste, which Augustine made over for the communal use of the group that clustered around him. Here 'he lived for God, in fasting, prayer, and good works, *meditating day and night upon the law of the Lord*', and communicating his faith in sermons and books.[24]

The community at Thagaste appears as a halfway house between the philosophical retreat near Milan, and the full monastery which Augustine founded at Hippo in 391. It consisted of men who had all become *servi Dei* and renounced the world; but all were friends, and their way of life allowed a certain freedom in coming and going, and a freedom to pursue their intellectual interests, which makes scholars chary of calling their community a 'monastery'.

---

[21] Augustine, *Confessiones* VIII, vi, 15 (*CSEL* 33, pp. 182-3).

[22] Augustine tells his own story in his *Confessions*, VI-IX, esp. VIII, vi-viii, & xi-xii. For interpretation and references to other works see Peter Brown, *Augustine of Hippo* (London 1967), pp. 79-137.

[23] Brown, pp. 113, 115 ff. In Latin, *otium*, 'leisure', is positively conceived, while business and public affairs are seen as *negotium*, the deprivation of such leisure. These words correspond to the Greek σχολή and ἀσχολία: E. Benveniste, *Indo-European Language and Society* (ET London 1973), pp. 115-17.

[24] Possidius, *Vita Augustini* 3,2 (*Vite dei Santi* III, p. 138). Folliet, pp. 35-9.

However, we must beware of being too restrictive in our use of this term; for, about this time, the African *Passio Typasii* could anachronistically describe as a 'monasterium' the hermitage that its hero had set up *c.*300 on his family estates, after he had been discharged from the army.[25] This reveals the western, pre-Antonian background to the sort of life which Augustine established at Thagaste; and, at the same time, the way in which this was being influenced and reinterpreted in the light of the new monasticism from Egypt. Thus, the inspiration behind Thagaste must be sought in three sources: in indigenous African asceticism, in Egyptian monasticism, and in the Roman philosophical ideal of a life of leisure dedicated to cultural and philosophical pursuits.

It is against this manifold background that we must set the conversion of Sulpicius Severus. The story of Antony (probably) and the example of Martin (certainly) played their part in this by influencing Sulpicius directly. But the significance of the other examples lies elsewhere, in showing something of the different ways in which a cultured westerner of the later fourth century might respond to the call of monasticism. They reveal that the conversion of the two friends, Sulpicius and Paulinus, is no isolated phenomenon, no 'special case'. On the contrary, they would join a diverse but recognizable body of *conversi*: men who had been converted from an ordinary life in the world to become 'servants of God', but who refashioned the rigorous monasticism of Egypt in a manner appropriate to their own cultural background.

---

[25] *Passio S. Typasii veterani* 4 (*AB* 9 (1890), p. 119). Cf. Fontaine, *AB* 81 (1963), p. 44. On the date of the *Passio Typasii* see below, ch. 10.

4

Sulpicius, *servus Dei*

(i) Primuliacum

Sulpicius' decision to exchange a secular career for the service of God was made in the teeth of opposition from his father, albeit with the approval of his mother-in-law. Sulpicius renounced his claim to his father's lands and sold the property which his marriage had brought him, using the proceeds to help the poor.[1] He kept only one estate for his own use; and, even with this, he transferred its legal ownership to the local church, retaining nothing but the usufruct for himself.[2] This estate, Primuliacum, was his equivalent of Augustine's Thagaste. Its exact whereabouts are unknown, but it appears to have been within striking distance of Toulouse and Narbonne, probably lying to their west.[3]

---

[1] Paulinus, *ep.* 1, 1; *ep.* 5, 5-7 (*CSEL* 29, pp. 2, 28-9).

[2] Paulinus, *ep.* 24, 1-4. The significance of Sulpicius' conversion tends to be played down because he did not make as clean a break with his past life as did Paulinus (Fontaine, *Vie* I, 42 ff; cf. Lienhard, p. 98). As far as the retention of Primuliacum is concerned, A. Rousselle-Estève has pointed out that whereas Paulinus, a priest, would be supported by the church, Sulpicius as a layman needed to retain some land to secure his own livelihood: 'Deux exemples d'évangélisation en Gaule à la fin du IVe siècle: Paulin de Nole et Sulpice Sévère', *Fédération historique du Languedoc méditerranéen et du Roussillon*, 43e Congrès (Montpellier 1971), pp. 93-4. Compare Augustine at Thagaste.

[3] For the general area, see Fontaine, *Vie* I, 32-40, and also Leclercq, *DACL* XIV, 2, cols. 781-98. However, Fontaine's discussion requires modification in four particulars. (i) We should not build too much on the Eluso of Paulinus, *ep.* 1, 11, because at this early date (394-5) Sulpicius was not necessarily settled at Primuliacum. (ii) We cannot deduce from Sulpicius' references to Aquitaine in *D* I, 27, 2 and *Chron.* II, 41, 3 anything more than that Sulpicius came from Gaul south of the Loire, i.e. the civil diocese of Aquitaine; see A. Chastagnol, 'Le Diocèse civil d'Aquitaine au Bas-Empire', *Bulletin de la Société nationale des Antiquaires de France* (Paris 1970), pp. 272-90, esp. 282-7. (iii) Primuliacum cannot have been actually within the *civitas*/diocese of Toulouse, as Fontaine

It was at Primuliacum that Sulpicius settled to live his version of the monastic life, possibly in association with his mother-in-law, Bassula.[4] Although Sulpicius did not join Martin's monastery of Marmoutier (any more than Augustine joined an existing monastery in Italy), his inspiration for the Primuliacum community was clearly drawn from Martin and his disciples. Paulinus reported that Sulpicius' messengers had described him as 'a servant of God, no slave to mammon. Martin breathes right through you, and in you Clarus lives, and the gospel is brought to fullness.'[5] The Clarus mentioned here epitomizes the link between Primuliacum and Marmoutier as surely as Sulpicius' continued pilgrimages to Tours.[6] Clarus was one of Martin's well-born disciples who had settled near Marmoutier, where his outstanding faith attracted disciples. He died shortly before Martin and was revered as a saint by Sulpicius and Paulinus, being buried beneath the altar at Primuliacum.[7]

Paulinus praised Sulpicius for living as a *peregrinus* in the world. Instead of crowding his house with furniture and wealth, 'you fill (it) with pilgrims and needy people, marking

suggests, because Sulpicius' bishop was called Gavidius (*Chron.* II, 41, 4), whereas the bishop of Toulouse in 405 was Exsuperius, his predecessor Silvius (L. Duchesne, *Fastes épiscopaux* I (2nd edn. 1907), p. 307). (iv) I would deduce from Paulinus *ep.* 28, 3: (a) that the province of Narbonensis lay between Primuliacum and Nola as the roads ran (Victor travelled on foot—NB 'ne inputes pedibus eius'); and (b) that Primuliacum probably did not lie actually within the province of Narbonensis; for Victor returned 'de Narbonensi . . . ad te' (i.e. Sulpicius), before setting off anew for Nola.

When we add to all this the other evidence discussed by Fontaine, particularly the reference to Toulouse in Sulpicius *ep.* 3, 3, and the fact that a Bordeaux messenger could drop off a letter at Primuliacum en route between Nola and Bordeaux, then the area west of the Toulouse *civitas* becomes by far the most likely neighbourhood for Primuliacum. See map 2, and cf. below ch. 20, iii.

[4] See Paulinus, *ep.* 5, 6 & 19; *ep.* 31, 1. P. G. Walsh, *Letters of St. Paulinus of Nola* (2 vols., Westminster Maryland, & London, 1966/7, 1967), I, 220 n. 18, suggests that Bassula 'played the same role in the foundation of the monastery at Primuliacum as Therasia played at Nola.' This is possible; but if so, it is odd that she does not figure in the *Dialogues*, which are set at Primuliacum, and name their participants and audience (*D* III, 1).

[5] Paulinus, *ep.* 27, 3. On Martin as a model to be followed, see also Sulpicius, *ep.* 2, 17.

[6] Paulinus, *ep.* 17, 4.

[7] *VM* 23, 1–2; Paulinus, *ep.* 32, 6. Is the Sabatius who was Clarus' disciple at Marmoutier (*VM* 23, 7) identical with the Sabbatius who appears at Primuliacum in *D* III, 1, 4?

out one corner for yourself. [You act] as a fellow servant alongside the slaves of your household. You do not, like a paterfamilias, appropriate the temporary shelter of your home, but, rather, you lodge there like a hired servant or a tenant.'[8] Presumably the 'pilgrims and needy people' are the 'fratres spiritales', whom Paulinus hoped would accompany Sulpicius to swell the devotees of St. Felix at Nola, as well as the 'pueri' who appear to be Sulpicius' servants, now associated with him in the ascetic life. These were normally tonsured, and dressed in monastic garb.[9] In addition, boys were entrusted to Sulpicius to be raised in the monastic life and prepared for the priesthood.[10] These must be Sulpicius' spiritual sons, to whom Paulinus refers elsewhere.[11]

There may also have been other monks living near Primuliacum, but not belonging to Sulpicius' community. For, in the literary setting of the *Dialogues*, while the first day's discussion is just between Sulpicius and two friends, the following morning a crowd of neighbouring monks and clerics appear. These lived close enough to have got wind of the story-telling session, and had come to join in.[12]

Beyond the immediate vicinity of Primuliacum Sulpicius was closely linked with his friend, Paulinus, in his pursuit of the ascetic life. At first, Paulinus pressed Sulpicius to visit him at Nola, and Sulpicius' failure to do so strained their relationship considerably.[13] By 400, however, Paulinus had accepted that their friendship would have to rely on the medium of regular letters, exchanged annually by couriers,

---

[8] *Ep.* 24, 3.

[9] Dress and tonsure: cf. Paulinus' request, *ep.* 22, 2, which was met by Sulpicius, *ep.* 23, 2. 'Fratres spiritales', Paulinus, *ep.* 5, 15. 'Pueri', Paulinus, *ep.* 11, 1; Sulpicius, *ep.* 2, 5; *D* II, 14, 5 and III, 3, 5. There was probably a considerable overlap between the 'fratres spiritales' and the 'pueri'. A parallel to the latter is found in Basil's monasticism in Asia Minor, where 'a slave woman could even accompany her mistress to the ascetic life and continue her service', W. K. L. Clarke, *St. Basil the Great* (Cambridge 1913), p. 95.

[10] See Paulinus, *carmen* 24, lines 669–768 (*CSEL* 30, pp. 228–31); Babut, *Saint Martin*, p. 41.

[11] *Ep.* 27, 3-4. Paulinus' sorrow at having no such sons himself excludes the possibility that these *pueri* are simply monks under another guise, as there was a brotherhood of monks at Nola (*ep.* 23, 8). See Walsh, II, 320, n. 13.

[12] *D* I, 1, 1; III, 1, 3-5. Similarly Clarus had his own monastery close to Marmoutier, *VM* 23, 2.

[13] Paulinus, *ep.* 5; *ep.* 11, 12-14; *ep.* 17.

preferably monk-couriers. The most popular of these was Victor, who by common agreement acted as messenger between Primuliacum and Nola, dividing his time equally between the two.[14] Paulinus would send Sulpicius a 'eulogy' of Campanian bread as he did to the African monk Alypius. Some years later Sulpicius sent his friend garments of camel's hair, which Paulinus welcomed: they pricked him into recollection of his sins and remembrance of the biblical heroes Elijah, David, and John the Baptist.[15] Each friend bewailed his own sinfulness and praised the examples of other holy men. Sulpicius sent Paulinus his *Life of Martin* and, presumably, his other Martinian works.[16] Paulinus proudly read them out to his relative, Melania the Elder, to Nicetas bishop of Remesiana (Dacia), and to many other holy men. Saints' lives ranked alongside the Bible as important reading matter for ascetics, and it is reported that Melania was particularly partial to them.[17] Paulinus also delighted in imitating such minor actions of Martin as the washing of another's hands, although he admitted that he had only once gone so far as to wash another's feet, a Christ-like service which Martin had performed for Sulpicius.[18]

This small detail is perhaps significant. It suggests that the ascetic life as practised by Paulinus and Sulpicius was rather more easy-going and gentlemanly than it was at Marmoutier under Martin. Whereas the latter resolutely refused to let great men of the world dine with him, Sulpicius felt uneasy at the prospect of turning such men away, and himself insisted on admitting the ex-vicar Eucherius and the *consularis* Celsus to listen to Gallus' stories about Martin.[19] Another important difference is that at Marmoutier only the younger monks were given texts to copy; the older ones were entirely

---

[14] See, e.g., Paulinus, *ep.* 28, 1. Lienhard, pp. 182–7.

[15] Paulinus, *ep.* 5, 21 (cf. *ep.* 3, 6). *Ep.* 29, 1.

[16] Paulinus, *ep*, 11, 11. *Ep.* 32, 7 (at end) implies that Paulinus has received at least Sulpicius' second letter; *D* III, 17, 3–5, that he would soon receive the *Dialogues*. Similarly, Paulinus sent Sulpicius his literary compositions: *ep.* 28, 6.

[17] Paulinus, *ep.* 29, 14. Her grand-daughter, Melania the Younger, appears to have shared this penchant: *Vie de Sainte Mélanie*, chs. 23 and 26 (ed. D. Gorce, *SC* 90, pp. 174, 178–80).

[18] *Ep.* 23, 4–5; cf. *VM* 25, 3.

[19] Cf. *D* I, 25, 6 (Martin) with *D* III, 1, 6–7 (Sulpicius).

free for prayer. Sulpicius, on the other hand, remained a very literary figure. He followed up his *Vita Martini* with three Martinian letters and the *Dialogues*, and also composed a historical work, his *Chronicle*. He had stenographers at his disposal, and paid attention to style: particularly in the Martinian writings, where the *clausulae* at the end of sentences are meticulously worked out.[20] He pressed Paulinus for literary compositions and for historical information for his *Chronicle*. He built a church and baptistery at Primuliacum, and adorned the latter with representations of Martin and Paulinus, writing some dedicatory verses. Not satisfied with these, he asked Paulinus to compose some more.[21]

It is certainly some way from here to the holy man whom Sulpicius himself described as 'inlitteratus' (*VM* 25, 8). Yet we should beware of making too much of the consequences of this difference. Paulinus' and Sulpicius' whole-hearted admiration for Martin appears to have been matched by Martin's regard for them;[22] and Sulpicius' presentation of Martin as an unsophisticated holy man may well be literary exaggeration, designed to highlight the *vera sapientia* in contrast to the vanities of *inanis philosophia*, which often passed as *sapientia* among the worldly.[23] In fact, there is nothing surprising—or reprehensible—about Sulpicius' monasticism if we relate it not simply to the idealized picture of Marmoutier which Sulpicius has given us, but also to the life and ideals of educated western converts, such as Augustine at Thagaste, or Paulinus of Nola and his correspondents.

Paulinus certainly regarded himself as a monk, and his community at Nola as a monastery; and his claim is given substance by his renunciation of all property, and by his continence, his dress, his taking of only one meal a day, and his participation in regular worship at Nola.[24] However, it is a far cry from Nola to the deserts of Egypt. Paulinus lived in chastity alongside his wife, rather as Sulpicius may have done

[20] Sulpicius, *ep.* 3, 2. P. Hyltén, *Studien zu Sulpicius Severus* (Lund 1940), ch. 3.

[21] Paulinus, *ep.* 28, 5-6; *ep.* 32, esp. § 2-5.

[22] *VM* 25, 2-5; Sulpicius, *ep.* 2, 14. For a possible parallel to this mutual regard see *Verba seniorum* X, 76 (*PL* 73, cols. 925-7).

[23] Cf. *VM* 1.

[24] For Paulinus' monasticism, see Lienhard, esp. pp. 30-1, 58-81, 101-6.

with his mother-in-law; but strict monasticism required the segregation of women into separate communities.[25] Nor, for all his move to Nola, did Paulinus sever connections with the world outside his monastery. Certainly, he cut free from the non-Christian world; but he maintained, or even initiated, contact with Christians from many places, both through regular correspondence, and also through entertaining guests at Nola. He went to Rome once a year for the celebration of St. Peter's day, while Nola itself was a pilgrimage centre, attracting crowds of visitors. Paulinus played an active part in fostering the cult of St. Felix there. Although there were already four basilicas, Paulinus added a fifth, embellishing it with mosaics and verse inscriptions. He also kept alive his literary talents, composing a panegyric on the Emperor Theodosius, and yearly devotional poems in honour of St. Felix. Thus, although the Bible had now replaced the pagan classics, Paulinus continued to give much of his time to literary and cultural pursuits. There is no suggestion that he ever undertook any manual work.

In these ways, Paulinus' way of life after his conversion parallels Sulpicius'. Both were involved in building churches, writing edifying compositions, and fostering a saint's cult; both remained in close contact with the world outside their monastery, travelling a certain amount; and both continued to be looked after by others as far as their material needs were concerned, although the men performing these menial tasks were now members of their monastic brotherhoods. The differences between this way of life and that of Egyptian monasticism are obvious; but before we decry it, we should recall two things.

The first is that some of the differences had already been foreshadowed in Martin's monastery of Marmoutier. As we have seen, the Marmoutier monks did not support themselves by manual work, and they appear to have hired peasant labour to perform at least the heavier tasks. Further, the one craft allowed at Marmoutier was that of copying manuscripts. Thus, Martin's monasticism already contained the seeds of that literary monastic culture which was to be so typical of

---

[25] E.g. Sulpicius, *D* II, 11.

western monasticism; and Sulpicius and Paulinus, in writing
hagiographical literature, were writing in a specifically
edifying genre which was to enjoy a long future there.[26]
In addition, Martin as bishop had been responsible for
building churches in his diocese; and, when travelling, he
was normally accompanied by monks, thus revealing that
Marmoutier monks were not sharply segregated from the
outside world.[27] In these respects Martin's way of life has
more in common with that of Sulpicius and Paulinus than is
commonly recognized.

A second point is that our picture of life at Primuliacum
may well be distorted by its literary presentation in the
Dialogues. We have little evidence of how daily life was lived
there, and the classical ethos evoked by the *Dialogues* may be
a literary creation rather than a mirror of reality. To take one
example: we know that Sulpicius added a larger basilica next
door to the one that already existed at Primuliacum, and that
he built a baptistery between them. This implies communal
worship, which is what we would expect by analogy with
Nola and elsewhere; and this assumption is confirmed by
Paulinus' lighthearted request that Sulpicius would 'prepare
(his) whole band of dedicated young men, with which you
charm God by day and night, to direct the force of their
prayers against my sins . . .'[28] However, if we had nothing
but the evidence of Sulpicius' *Dialogues*, we might well fall
into the error of assuming that regular worship had no place
at Primuliacum. For the *Dialogues* represent Gallus as being
woken in the morning, telling stories of Martin all day, and
of his audience dispersing in the evening, with no mention
whatever of services.[29]

As with worship, so perhaps with other aspects of the
ascetic life. While in the *Dialogues* there is some chaffing
Gallus about the appetites of Gallic monks and their inability
to content themselves with the scanty fare of their African

[26] J. Leclercq, *The Love of Learning and the Desire for God* (ET, 2nd edn. pb.,
London 1978), *passim*, and esp. pp. 199 ff.

[27] Building churches, *VM* 13, 9; Gregory of Tours, *Historiae* X, 31, 3 (below,
ch. 23, n. 16). Accompanied by monks, *VM* 13, 7; *ep*. 3, 6–7; *D* II, 3, 1.

[28] *Ep*. 27, 4; a reference which I owe to Babut's attentive eye: *Saint Martin*,
p. 41.

[29] *D* II, 14, 7; III, 1; III, 17, 1. For Nola, see Lienhard, pp. 78–80.

brethren, we might also note that it was a monk from Primuliacum, Victor, who was responsible for instituting more meagre eating standards at Nola, cooking gruel not of wheat, but of millet with beans pounded in it. Something of the qualms which this dish aroused in Paulinus can be discerned behind the playfulness with which he expresses his relief that Victor had spared him the other ingredients of Ezechiel's hotch-potch.[30]

Thus, as far as outward ascetic practices are concerned, life at Primuliacum was probably very similar to life at Nola. Paulinus regarded the Primuliacum brothers as 'monks', just like the brothers at Nola; though we, perhaps, would prefer to restrict that term more narrowly, and to class Sulpicius and Paulinus as *conversi*, or *servi Dei*.[31]

More significant than the name or the external trappings of monasticism is the question, did Sulpicius seriously try to grapple with a life dedicated to God, particularly a life of prayer? For that was the *raison d'être* of Sulpicius' model, Marmoutier, as of other monastic communities down the ages. Unfortunately, it is a question that is easier to ask than to answer, for our sources are woefully deficient. But we must at least remember that our ignorance about Sulpicius' spiritual life could as easily be due to its non-representation in the type of sources we have, as to the lack of such an inner life. One indication is the fact that, according to Gennadius, Sulpicius wrote letters on the love of God and contempt for the world. If these had survived, we might have a very different picture of Martin's biographer from that commonly propounded today. We must also remember that our sources for Sulpicius' life break off in about 404, whereas he probably lived on into the 420s, and matured spiritually with age. The letters mentioned by Gennadius (and Sulpicius' ordination?) may belong to this later period.[32] A further

---

[30] *D* I, 4, 5-5, 2; I, 8, 5. Paulinus, *ep.* 23, 6-8. Cf. Babut, p. 41.

[31] Primuliacum brothers as monks: Paulinus, *ep.* 22. Sulpicius is called a *servus Dei* by Paulinus of Milan, *Vita Ambrosii* 1, 1 (cit. below, p. 99). On this group, see E. Griffe, 'La Pratique religieuse en Gaule au Ve siècle: *saeculares et sancti*', *BLE* 63 (1962), esp. pp. 253-4. Also Brown, *Augustine* p. 132.

[32] Gennadius, *De viris inlustribus*, 19; above, pp. 15-16. These letters are lost, or unidentified. The letters attributed to Sulpicius, which Halm published as an appendix (*CSEL* 1, pp. 219-56), can be shown on stylistic grounds to be falsely so attributed: Hyltén, pp. 156-7.

point to ponder is the probable parallel with Paulinus. Both Sulpicius and Paulinus give the impression that their attention was focused on the externals of monasticism;[33] but for Paulinus there exists other evidence which reveals that he did have a deeper understanding of the monk's calling.[34] The same may well be true of Sulpicius. We do once catch a glimpse of him sitting alone in his cell, preoccupied, as often, with 'hope for things to come and weariness with the present, fear of Judgement, dread of its punishments. This led on to the thing that prompted my whole train of thought: recollection of my sins. All this saddened and overwhelmed me.'[35] Is this aimless, involuntary brooding, or a spiritual exercise?[36] We cannot be certain. But one pointer is that Sulpicius, like Martin, believed that the end of the world was imminent;[37] and this would surely have given an immediacy to his fears of Judgement and punishment, raising them to something more than mere day-dreaming.

(ii) Sulpicius and the Bible

Further clues as to Sulpicius' Christian life at Primuliacum may be sought in his use of, and attitude towards, the Bible. The reading of scripture and the offering of prayer were closely associated in the monastic life. Martin, for instance, devoted every moment to one of these, and even when reading, 'he never slackened his spirit from prayer'.[38] The reason was that the monastic tradition of *lectio divina* regarded the Bible as the source and the springing-off point for contemplation: the first step up the *scala paradisi*, which led on, through prayer and meditation, to the divine vision.[39]

[33] Cf. Fontaine, *Vie* I, 45; Lienhard, pp. 81, 144.

[34] E.g. *ep.* 24, 5 to end.

[35] Sulpicius, *ep.* 2, 1; cf. *D* II, 6, 3.

[36] Fontaine asks the question, and opts for the former (*Vie* III, 1185 ff.).

[37] Below ch. 7, n. 32. Paulinus probably thought similarly: Lienhard, pp. 139–40. See also van Andel, pp. 117–30.

[38] *VM* 26, 3; cf. Cyprian, *Ad Donatum* 15, 'Sit tibi vel oratio assidua vel lectio; nunc cum Deo loquere, nunc Deus tecum.' Cit. D. Gorce, *La Lectio Divina*, I (Wépion-s-Meuse & Paris, 1925), p. 183 n. 1. See Gorce, pp. xi-xix, 64–70, 182–6.

[39] Gorce, pp. 360–1.

One consequence is that monastic writings tend to be deeply impregnated with the Bible, particularly the Psalms. Sulpicius' works, however, scarcely fit into this pattern: for Halm's index lists only five scriptural citations in the Martinian works, and seven in all. This presents a striking contrast with the letters of Sulpicius' friend, Paulinus, who was for ever pouring his own thoughts into the words of scripture. However, we should not jump too hastily to the conclusion that the Bible meant little to Sulpicius. To start with, Halm grossly underestimated the number of biblical allusions in Sulpicius' writings. Recent scholarship has shown that there are some ten in the *Vita Martini*, rather than the two which Halm noted; and similar adjustments must be made for all Sulpicius' works. What is more, Sulpicius' presentation of Martin often seems to carry biblical overtones, even when we hesitate to point to one specific source, thus suggesting that Sulpicius had a deep familiarity with the Bible.[40]

None the less, the fact remains that Sulpicius' writings are not permeated by the Bible in the way that Paulinus' are. A revealing example of the difference occurs when Sulpicius incorporates information from one of Paulinus' letters into his *Chronicle*. Sulpicius reproduces the information, and echoes some of Paulinus' words; but he transposes it all into his own style, and omits Paulinus' quotations from the Psalms.[41] This procedure of deliberately eschewing the words of the Bible occurs all the way through the *Chronicle*, for again and again we see Sulpicius taking his facts from the Old Testament, but re-presenting them in a classical idiom.[42] This shows that the relative paucity of scriptual allusions in Sulpicius' writings arises from his deliberate

---

[40] Fontaine, *Vie, passim*, for *VM* and epistles. For *VM*, see also the useful index in Smit *et al. Vita di Martino*, in *Vite dei Santi* IV, p. 373. (I have given the figure of ten, not twelve, because I am not convinced by Smit's suggested parallels with Ep. Ti. 1:7; and Ep. Hebr. 13:6.) For Sulpicius' *Chronicle*, see van Andel, pp. 10–22. For Sulpicius' familiarity with the NT in general, see Fontaine *Vie* I, p. 116, and cf. pp. 100–1.

[41] Van Andel p. 49.

[42] For his use of the OT as a source, see van Andel pp. 10–26, who also shows (pp. 10–12) that he used a Latin translation of the *Vetus Latina* type, and possibly the Septuagint as well. For its transposition into a classical idiom, below ch. 13.

policy as an author: he chose not to lard his work with biblical phrases.

It is worth asking why Sulpicius' writings appear to be so little influenced by the Bible.[43] There are two separate answers. The first lies in the simple fact that Sulpicius is a product of the late Roman Empire, and was therefore educated in secular schools, and encouraged to model his style on the great classical authors of pagan Rome.[44] He was a mature man, probably in his thirties, when he first decided to embrace Christian asceticism; and it would be most remarkable if he had fundamentally changed his literary style at that time of life. His case bears no comparison to that of a medieval monk, who would have been trained from boyhood in a monastery, and so received his grounding in Christian, not classical, Latin.

The second answer must be sought by pondering the sort of works of Sulpicius which we still possess, and the purpose and readership of those works. For although all Sulpicius' letters to Paulinus are lost, from Paulinus' replies we might deduce that the Bible played a more prominent part in them than in his surviving books.[45] The reason, I would suggest, is that when Sulpicius wrote to Paulinus, he was addressing a fellow *conversus*. As regards the Martinian works and *Chronicle*, however, the evidence is that Sulpicius was there attempting to reach beyond the little circle of dedicated Christians to attract cultured readers, educated, like himself, in the well-loved Roman classics.[46] The language of the *Vetus Latina* Bible would have jarred horribly on them—as, very probably, on Sulpicius himself. Sulpicius spoke their language partly because that was the natural thing for him to do, and partly to try and wean them from the pagan classics on to Christianity. In this, he had a different aim from Paulinus, who regarded attempts to win over the pagans as mistaken. Thus, whereas the prominent role of scripture in

---

[43] Hyltén claims (p. 4) that Sulpicius' style was influenced by the Bible. This is not much in evidence; but note Fontaine *Vie* I, 100-1 and 114-16.

[44] See ch. 6 below. On Sulpicius' style see Fontaine's sensitive appreciation: *Vie* I, ch. 3, esp. pp. 100-10.

[45] Cf. below, p. 43.

[46] Below, ch. 7.

Paulinus' writings can rightly be taken as indicative of the importance of the Bible for him, we should not infer the opposite from the relative paucity of biblical allusions in Sulpicius' extant writings. Given the cultured, not overtly Christian, component of his audience, we should no more expect frequent biblical reminiscences in Sulpicius' literary works than in Augustine's *City of God*.

Now that we have disposed of the negative evidence bearing upon Sulpicius' attitude to the Bible, we are free to look anew for positive indications of how he regarded it. The best place to start is his *Chronicle*. This tells the story of the people of God from the creation of the world up to Sulpicius' own day, and for three-quarters of the work the Old Testament forms the principle source. Sulpicius explains that he has set out to compress the whole course of sacred history into two books, leaving out virtually no facts. At the same time, he makes it clear that he has deliberately excluded 'universa divinarum rerum mysteria' from his compass, as he felt that these could be sought only within the text of the Bible itself.[47] This shows that Sulpicius regarded the Bible as something that could be read on two levels: on the surface there was the straightforward narration of events, the *simplex historia*; veiled beneath this lay the *mysteria*, prefigurations of the future which were discernible only to the wise.[48] In his *Chronicle* he deliberately concentrates on the *simplex historia*, which probably explains why he passes so rapidly over the prophetical books, whose narrative content was slight.[49] Thus, for instance, on Ezekiel he writes: 'The mystery of things to come and of the resurrection were revealed to him. His book is one of great weight, and should be read with care.'—and that is all.[50] The only mystery which

---

[47] *Chron.* I, 1; cf. also II, 14, 7.

[48] E.g. *D* II, 6, 6-7; *Chron.* I, 2, 4. Cf. van Andel, pp. 60-8.

[49] S. Prete, *I Chronica di Sulpicio Severo* (Vatican 1955), pp. 31-2. However, given Sulpicius' avowed aims, his silence over the Prophets in his *Chron.* does not necessarily show that they meant little to him, as Prete suggests. Rather, his awareness of approaching doom and his critical attitude to the avarice and luxury of contemporary society would surely have made him sympathetic to such prophets as Jeremiah and Ezekiel: *D* I, 21, 4 may be a reminiscence of Jeremiah 22:14. See also van Andel, esp. pp. 69, 107-9, 130.

[50] *Chron.* II, 3, 9.

Sulpicius felt he ought to expound is that of Nebuchadnezzar's dream of the statue with feet of iron and clay, which he interpreted as signifying the internal dissensions and the admixture of barbarians within the Roman Empire of his own day: and this meant that the end of the world was at hand.[51]

It was perhaps Sulpicius' feeling of imminent catastrophe that led him to expound this *mysterium*. More characteristic is his comment on the lengthening of Abraham and Sarah's names, 'cuius quidem rei non inane mysterium non est huius operis exponere.'[52] Such reticence makes it difficult to say much about how Sulpicius felt the Bible should be interpreted at a non-literal level; but it is likely that he was referring to a typological form of exegesis such as had been widespread in the church from the second century, and formed part of the basic catechetical instruction given to all Christians.[53]

In this sphere, Sulpicius was probably influenced by the ideas of Hilary of Poitiers. Like Sulpicius, Hilary had a great respect for the chronological narration of facts, and adopted a historian's style for his account of the 'facta' and 'dicta' of the Gospels; and he also saw these external events as forming a veil through which their spiritual meaning might be discerned.[54] This means that theoretically his approach was similar to that of Sulpicius, although in practice their writings are dissimilar, owing to Sulpicius' exclusive concentration on straight chronological narrative. Now Sulpicius had read Hilary's *Tractatus Mysteriorum*, and this could well have been responsible for transmitting to him Hilary's approach to the Bible.[55] Indeed, we should probably see an

[51] *Chron.* II, 2-3, 7. Sulpicius' interpretation of the dream was commonplace by his day: S. Mazzarino, *The End of the Ancient World* (ET London, 1966), pp. 36, 40, 48.

[52] *Chron.* I, 6, 2; cf. van Andel, p. 64.

[53] Sulpicius includes a few examples of this type, e.g. *Chron.* I, 24, 5, on Deborah: 'haec in typum ecclesiae [forma] praemissa sit'. On typology see J. Daniélou, *Gospel Message and Hellenistic Culture* (ET London 1973), pp. 198, 201 ff., 226 ff. etc.; and J.-P. Brisson (ed.), Hilaire de Poitiers—*Traité des mystères* (*SC* 19), pp. 41-55.

[54] See J. Doignon, *Hilaire de Poitiers avant l'exil* (Paris 1971), pp. 230-9, esp. p. 238.

[55] van Andel, pp. 62-7. Cf. J. Daniélou in *Hilaire de Poitiers, évêque et docteur* (Paris 1968), pp. 11-13.

echo of Hilary's wording in Sulpicius' 'non inane mysterium', and a respectful acknowledgment of him in Sulpicius' reference to the 'prudentes', who discern a future mystery in the Old Testament account of Lamech.[56] Certainly these phrases, taken in conjunction with his friendship with Paulinus, whose letters are full of spiritual interpretations of the Bible, show that Sulpicius was no stranger to such an approach.

However, the evidence suggests that Sulpicius himself felt more in tune with the straightforward historical sense of the Bible, and did not class himself as one of the *prudentes* who were equipped to draw out its inner significance.[57] This impression is borne out by what may be the only surviving evidence of Sulpicius' own interpretation of a biblical passage which is preserved—in a corrupt form—in one of Paulinus' letters to him. Paulinus is commenting on the first verse of the Song of Songs, 'bona ubera eius super vinum', which he takes as signifying that the milk of New Testament grace is better than the wine of Old Testament justice. He then continues to give us Sulpicius' preferred interpretation: 'Sed hoc, ut tu mavis intellegi, serum indicetur, quo prima nascentium multra coalescit'.[58] Although this reading is anything but certain since the manuscript tradition is corrupt for this passage, all the constructions which can be put on this sentence agree on the fact that Sulpicius' interpretation was a literal one, in contrast to Paulinus' never-ending flow of spiritual meanings.

I think we should therefore conclude with reference to Sulpicius' *lectio divina* that he did indeed read the Bible with care, and may have spent more time trying to penetrate its mysterious depths than he is usually credited with: he seems to have discussed biblical questions with Martin, as well as with Paulinus.[59] None the less, his own bent was a literary-historical one, and he therefore tended to view the Bible in these terms. In place of the manual work which Jerome

---

[56] *Chron.* I, 2, 4. Cf. van Andel, pp. 63–4.

[57] Cf. Paulinus, *ep.* 43, 3: 'Nam me fateor tantorum nominum et mysteriorum pondera nec digito ausum tangere.' (*CSEL* 29, p. 365.)

[58] Paulinus, *ep.* 23, 27. I have given Walsh's suggested emendation (*Letters* II, 307–8) as, like him, I cannot make adequate sense of Hartel's edition which gives 'semini detur' in lieu of 'serum indicetur (*CSEL* 29, p. 184).

[59] *VM* 25, 6. Fontaine, *Vie* I, 114–16; III, 1069–70.

recommended to his virgins, Sulpicius, like Jerome himself, probably spent his time in literary study. We should perhaps view this not as an opting out of the monastic *labor et studium*, but rather as his own means of pursuing the Christian ideal.[60]

(iii) Sulpicius' Temperament and Personality

Before concluding this study of Sulpicius' post-conversion life, we must give some consideration to the various interpretations of his personality that have recently been propounded; for these influence the way in which his life and writings are viewed.

According to Fontaine, Sulpicius was unstable in character, touchy and pessimistic, and a prey to inner conflicts and to a feeling of his own inadequacy. This led to resentment, aggressiveness, and biting censure on the one hand, and to an equally uninhibited set of affections on the other.[61] Sulpicius is thus presented at a psychological level as a complex man of violent temperament, always ready to dart from one extreme to the other. Meanwhile, the way in which these characteristics were manifested was partly determined by his literary education, which meant that he never let slip a chance of displaying his literary brilliance, albeit at the expense of someone else or to the detriment of elementary delicacy. Such appears to be the gist of what Fontaine is saying, but it is perhaps worth quoting a few lines to illustrate his rhetorical approach. Talking of the affinity between Sulpicius and Sallust and Tacitus, he says: 'Chez Sulpice, ces penchants vont jusqu'à des attitudes d'agressivité et de ressentiment, sinon, parfois, jusqu'à une susceptibilité amère, exacerbée, qui confine au délire de la persécution. . . . Ses vrais rapports avec autrui ont toujours été plus ou moins inhibés par une profonde défiance de soi. D'où une égale surenchère dans la louange et le blâme . . .'[62] Fontaine is surely right in sensing that Sulpicius

---

[60] Whereas Martin was always praying or reading (*VM* 26, 3), Jerome was always reading or writing (*D* I, 9, 5). For Sulpicius, see *VM* I, 6; below ch. 7, i; and Paulinus, *ep.* 11, 4.

[61] *Vie* I, 54–8. Cf. also Fabre, *Saint Paulin*, p. 281.

[62] *Vie* I, 56.

and Sallust were in many respects kindred spirits;[63] but I would question whether we have enough material to enable us to go further than this, and to analyse Sulpicius' psychology in this way.

Lack of direct evidence from Sulpicius himself compels Fontaine to rely largely upon the letters which his friend Paulinus wrote to him. Judging from the way in which Paulinus poured out his feelings about the unique bond which united him to Sulpicius,[64] we should expect something of the same gamut of feeling in Sulpicius' own letters, and therefore should not take any expression of his emotions as a sign of emotional instability. If Sulpicius admired his friend's spiritual gifts and bewailed the incompleteness of his own attempt to break away from his former life,[65] so, equally, did Paulinus;[66] and in both cases we should take the extravagant praise of the other and denigration of self with a pinch of salt. If, from Paulinus' response, it appears that Sulpicius had complained because his friend had deprived him of his letter bearers,[67] then one must also add that this was not the only occasion when Paulinus seized with delight upon Christian couriers, and detained them at Nola.[68] Indeed, Paulinus' lamentation at having no spiritual sons like Sulpicius', coupled with his grave disappointment at his friend's failure to bring his lads to Nola, suggests that the boot was on the other foot.[69] As for Paulinus' letter which begins, 'Why do you demand more love from me?':[70] its extravagant language 'reflects the reconciliation effected between Sulpicius and Paulinus after the period of strained relations' caused by Sulpicius' failure to come to Nola;[71] it is Paulinus, not Sulpicius, who complains that his 'appetite

---

[63] Cf. van Andel, pp. 69-74. J. Fontaine, 'L'Affaire Priscillien ou l'ère des nouveaux Catilina; observations sur le "Sallustianisme" de Sulpice Sévère', in *Classica et Iberica* (= Festschrift in hon. of J. M.-F. Marique), ed. P. T. Brannan (Worcester Mass. 1975), pp. 355-92.

[64] *Ep.* 11, 1-6.

[65] Fontaine, *Vie* I, 57. Paulinus, *ep.* 24, 1.

[66] *Ep.* 5, 4; *ep*, 11, 11-12; *ep.* 24, 20-2.

[67] Fontaine, loc. cit.

[68] See Paulinus, *ep.* 18, 1; *ep.* 28, 3.

[69] *Ep.* 27, 3; *ep.* 5, 15; *ep.* 17.

[70] *Ep.* 23, 1; Fontaine loc. cit. and n. 2.

[71] Walsh, *Letters* II, p. 301.

for love' is heightened, rather than satisfied, by Sulpicius' attentions; it is not at all clear from the wording that Sulpicius has 'complained of not being loved';[72] and even if he has, then this must be seen in the context of Paulinus' chilliness in epistles 17 and 22.

Finally, while it seems clear that Sulpicius had broken his promises to visit Nola, I am not wholly convinced that Sulpicius' reason was an unwillingness to forgo the remaining comforts of Primuliacum. Sulpicius himself pleaded ill-health, though this excuse wore too thin to satisfy Paulinus.[73] Sulpicius also appears to have expressed a belief that Paulinus would soon be too poor to invite him, and that he was afraid of going hungry;[74] but, judging from the culinary régime of Victor at Nola, it seems doubtful whether Sulpicius' material standard of living would have been much lower there than at Primuliacum; instead, it looks like a jocular excuse. Why, however, was he so reluctant to exchange Primuliacum for Nola? In part, perhaps, because of a natural preference for his own land and contentment with his own ascetic household; in part, perhaps, because his mother-in-law's stenographers facilitated his literary activities; in part, perhaps, because from the first he showed a desire to explain and defend the ascetic life within Gaul, and did not simply shut his ears to all criticisms as Paulinus recommended; and this desire was maybe heightened by his great regard for Martin, and by the need to defend Martin's reputation within Gaul.[75]

In conclusion, I think we must admit that the evidence for Sulpicius being a man with a 'personnalité singulière' is slight, and rests upon a subjective impression rather than upon a plausible body of evidence. It is worth pointing out that some scholars have thought very differently. After close examination of Sulpicius' account of Priscillianism in his *Chronicle*, Prete has pointed to his 'senso di moderazione e di equilibrio' in seeing the rights and wrongs of both parties, while on the basis of a passage in the *Dialogues* Babut himself

[72] Fontaine, *Vie* I, 57.

[73] Cf. Paulinus *ep*. 5, 8 and *ep*. 17, 4.

[74] Paulinus, *ep*. 11, 12-13; cf. Fontaine loc. cit.

[75] Cf. below, ch. 7. The last suggestion was originally made to me by J. M. Wallace-Hadrill.

has pointed to the contrast between the virulent Jerome, and Sulpicius' restraint.[76] For my own part, I would add that I discern no signs of a deeprooted lack of self-confidence in Sulpicius. As for his 'pessimism': this does not brood over and distort everything, but only breaks through occasionally —and, we might add, understandably, when we recall that the Roman Empire was then visibly disintegrating, as Sulpicius clearly perceived; and when we realize that all was far from well with the Gallic church.[77] Thus, while I would concur in seeing Sulpicius as a man given to 'great enthusiasms and also violent antipathies',[78] I do not think he was fundamentally unbalanced in temperament.

In fact, the more we know of the background to Sulpicius' life, the more he fits into place as a cultured *conversus*. In the mean time, I have discussed these theories about Sulpicius' personality because they underlie many interpretations of his life, and of his Martinian works. Ever since Babut wrote in 1912, there has been a tendency for scholars to compare the ascetic life of Primuliacum with that of Martin's Marmoutier, to the depreciation of the former. The assumption has been that because Sulpicius did not renounce his cultural and literary concerns, and live in stark austerity, we need not take his ascetic conversion very seriously; and that when he decries the behaviour of the Gallic clergy and their hostility towards strict ascetics, we should see this only as evidence of his embittered personality, not as testimony to the real state of the Gallic church. I shall return to this second point in chapter 20, and here do no more than question the first one; for much of the confusion has arisen from comparing Sulpicius' ascetic life with that of Martin, whereas a fairer comparison would be with that lived by other contemporaries who combined literary culture and asceticism, as did Jerome and Paulinus. Like them, Sulpicius belonged to that diverse, but recognizable, body of Christians, the *servi Dei*.

---

[76] Prete, p. 95. E.-C. Babut, 'Sur trois lignes inédites de Sulpice Sévère', *Le Moyen Age* 19 (1906), p. 213.

[77] Empire disintegrating: above, n. 51. Typical outbursts of Sulpicius occur in *D* I, 21; *Chron.* II, 51, 9-10, on which see below, ch. 20, iii.

[78] Fabre, *Saint Paulin*, p. 281.

5

The Ascetic Brotherhood, East and West

'I ask, what loss of family love or of friendship do I suffer from an inhuman father or indifferent brother or forgetful friend, when you alone amply make up for all these bonds . . . of love?'[1] So Paulinus wrote to Sulpicius when smarting at the hostile reaction to his own conversion; and his words are worth pondering, for they reveal something of the traumatic dislocation and subsequent restructuring of relationships which occurred when a *conversus* turned his back on the normal ways of the world, seeking after Christ along the path of asceticism. A pagan would regard the adoption of such a 'living death' as 'madness'; but more devastating still was the similar reaction of shocked disapproval on the part of ordinary, conventional Christians.[2]

One effect of this was to encourage ascetic converts to band together against the hostile world: former ties of class and kinship were replaced by a new network of friendships between fellow *conversi*. This led to the formation of a far-flung brotherhood of ascetics, which spanned the Roman Empire. In his own province, a convert might well find himself an odd man out, viewed with suspicion. But when he opted out of the conventional society around him, the convert at the same time opted into an ascetic culture whose ideal was epitomized by Antony and the monks of Egypt, and which drew disciples from all over the empire.

---

[1] Paulinus, *ep.* 11, 4.

[2] For pagans, see Rutilius Namatianus, *De reddito suo*, lines 515-26 (ed. P. van de Woestijne, Ghent 1936, pp. 57-8); for Christians, cf. Ausonius' hurt incomprehension at Paulinus' conversion, *eps.* 27-31 (ed. H. G. E. White, 2 vols., 1919-21, London & New York, vol. II, esp. pp. 108, 124 ff., 134); Lienhard, pp. 36-9, and cf. p. 122.

The community of interest between such ascetic converts was strong enough for one to initiate correspondence with another whom he had never met, though often a common friend or a reading of the other's books supplied a link. Thus Alypius seems to have taken advantage of the presence of Paulinus' courier in Carthage to introduce himself to his fellow *conversus*, enclosing some of Augustine's works. On the strength of these, Paulinus wrote back not only to Alypius, but to Augustine as well.[3] All were one in Christ, and thus all limbs of the same body. Augustine, in turn, although he had never set eyes on him, felt that he already knew Jerome: partly through reading his works, but more especially through Alypius' visit to him. For 'when he saw you, I too saw you, but through his eyes', as Alypius and he were one in spirit.[4]

This letter of Augustine's was written to introduce one of his monks, Profuturus, to Jerome. Through such letters of recommendation, a normal practice in a world hinged on patronage, the network of ascetic relationships was frequently extended. Thus, for instance, Paulinus could recommend the monks Postumianus and Theridius to Sulpicius, whom they had never met before.[5] If we were to identify this Postumianus with the interlocutor in Sulpicius' *Dialogues*, we would have another example of the ramifications of ascetic relationships; for the latter brought back to Sulpicius news of Jerome and the Egyptian ascetics. Such links with the east are clearly implied in the *Vita Martini* as well as the *Dialogues*,[6] and we may take a few more instances to give us some insight into those particularly affecting Sulpicius.

First there is Silvia, the sister-in-law of that Rufinus who came from Eauze in southern Gaul and rose under Theodosius I to precarious heights at the court of Constantinople, only to perish gruesomely in 395.[7] Given the provenance and career of her brother-in-law, Silvia herself is likely to have

---

[3] Paulinus, *ep.* 3 to Alypius; *ep.* 4 to Augustine.

[4] Augustine, *ep.* 28, 1 (*CSEL* 34, i, pp. 103–4).

[5] Paulinus, *ep.* 27, 2 (and cf. 27, 1), which must refer to these two monks as Sulpicius was long since acquainted with Sorianus (see *ep.* 22, 1).

[6] *D* I, 1, 1–3; III, 17, 2–18, 1. *VM* 24, 3.

[7] J. F. Matthews, 'Gallic Supporters of Theodosius', *Latomus* 30 (1971), p. 1078; Alan Cameron, *Claudian* (Oxford 1970), ch. 4.

originated from Aquitaine or thereabouts, and to have travelled to the east in connection with her family c.388.[8] The *Lausiac History* records that she journeyed from Jerusalem to Egypt in the company of Melania the Elder, Palladius, and the deacon Jovinus, a visit which probably took place in the 390s. This Silvia is surely identical with the lady of that name who promised to bring back relics from the east for Sulpicius' monk-courier, Victor: relics which were probably destined for Sulpicius' new church at Primuliacum.[9] In common is the name, the link with Aquitaine, the ascetic ideal which was associated both with pilgrimage to the east and with the collection of relics, and the fact that both Sulpicius and the Silvia of the *Lausiac History* gravitated towards the circle of Rufinus and Melania, rather than the rival camp of Jerome.[10] In the face of this evidence it seems reasonable to affirm the identity of the two Silvias.

Another such link figure who appears to be a friend of Sulpicius in Gaul, Paulinus in Italy, and Jerome in the Holy Land, is Desiderius. Sulpicius dedicated his *Vita Martini* to 'Desiderio fratri carissimo', and I think we can accept as virtually certain the identity of this Desiderius with the friend and fellow monk of Sulpicius to whom Paulinus sent a letter by the hand of Victor, Sulpicius' courier.[11] Is this Desiderius to be identified with the priest of that name from southern Gaul who visited Jerome in 398, received the dedication of Jerome's translation of the Pentateuch c.400, and took part in enlisting Jerome's sharp pen against the ideas of Vigilantius in 405?[12] We cannot 'prove' the identity of the two Desiderii, but it is very likely: both were ascetic

---

[8] E. D. Hunt, 'St. Silvia of Aquitaine', *JTS* n.s. 23 (1972), esp. pp. 354–62.

[9] Paulinus, *ep.* 31, 1.

[10] Cf. Peter Brown, *Religion and Society in the Age of Saint Augustine* (London 1972), p. 210. For Sulpicius' position, see below, ch. 21.

[11] *VM*, preface; Paulinus, *ep.* 43.

[12] Below ch. 20, iii. On Desiderius see A. Feder, *Studien zum Schriftsteller-katalog des heiligen Hieronymus* (Freiburg im Breisgau 1927), pp. 144–8: although Feder goes too far in concluding (p. 146) that the Desiderius addressed by Paulinus as his 'sancto et merito venerabili fratri' must therefore have been a priest. Paulinus uses an identical formula when writing to ascetics who were definitely not priests, including women! E.g. *eps.* 38 and 39.

converts, and both came from the same geographical area. Further, Paulinus and Sulpicius already had connections with Jerome in the Holy Land; and nearer home Paulinus, Jerome, and Jerome's Desiderius all had a further link in the person of Exsuperius, bishop of Toulouse. In addition, both namesakes were educated men with an interest in biblical exegesis, a subject which also bulks large in Jerome's writings and Paulinus' correspondence with Sulpicius.

Such east/west links provide us with the physical background for the literary parallels which occur in our texts. Thus, for instance, we find the story of the Egyptian monk whose obedience was tested by his being given the task of watering a dried-up stick till it should take root and flourish in Sulpicius' *Dialogues*, Cassian's *Institutes*, and the *Apophthegmata patrum*.[13] While their accounts are not identical, both Sulpicius and the *Apophthegmata* give this tale a similar miraculous twist: in three years the stick had rooted and grown into a flourishing tree. But in Cassian's account, the abba came to the brother, John, at the end of one year's toil, and pulled up the rootless stick, telling John that he need water it no longer.[14] Owen Chadwick, who discusses these three versions, came to the conclusion that Cassian's must be based upon an earlier version of the story since he could 'hardly have changed a story with a miraculous point to a story without the miracle.' I am not convinced by this, as Cassian had no love for thaumaturgy, and tended to give stories a moral or theological slant;[15] but it is at least certain that Cassian did not derive this story from the account in the *Dialogues*, for he names the monk as John of Lycopolis, whereas Sulpicius does not mention his name.[16] Further, Sulpicius cannot have derived his account from

[13] I omit the *Vitae patrum* version, as this depends directly on the Greek *Apophthegmata*: Rousseau, *Ascetics*, p. 254.

[14] Sulpicius, *D* I, 19; *Apoph.* John Colobus § 1 (*PG* 65, col. 204); Cassian, *Institutes* IV, 24 (*CSEL* 17, pp. 63-4). See O. Chadwick, *John Cassian* (Cambridge, 2nd edn. 1968), p. 21.

[15] As Chadwick himself recognizes in the following paragraph: ibid. pp. 21-2, and cf. p. 51.

[16] Sulpicius and Cassian tell the same stories on other occasions: e.g. *D* I, 12, 1 and *Institutes* V, 27. C. Butler again thinks that Cassian is not dependent on Sulpicius' account, *The Lausiac History of Palladius* (2 vols., Cambridge 1898 & 1904) I, 212-13.

Cassian, since he wrote some twenty years earlier;[17] and the Greek story in the *Apophthegmata* would probably not have been influenced by either of the other versions, written as they were in Latin in the west.[18] In other words, we appear to have three versions of the same story, which at a written level are all independent of each other; and both the Latin accounts derive orally from separate pilgrimages made to Egypt at the end of the fourth century.[19]

Similar circumstances may account for the parallels which are discernible between Sulpicius' *Vita Martini*, and the *Historia monachorum in Aegypto*. The similarities between these two works have puzzled scholars, as Rufinus only translated the *Historia monachorum* into Latin some time after 400 AD, by which time the *Vita Martini* was already written; and it is most unlikely that there was any direct literary relationship between the Greek original on the one hand, and the virtually contemporaneous *Vita Martini* on the other. None the less, the number of similar stories which are told in both works is striking. In both we find instances of holy men being healed by an angel, of their calling up the shade of a dead man to question him, of their transfixing pagan processions to the spot, and of the devil visiting them in their cells in an attempt to deceive them. While we cannot reach certainty, my own feeling is that there was some link between these works, and that this was probably due to the oral transmission of stories about holy men.[20]

We can even suggest a possible channel for such trans-

[17] Sulpicius' *Dialogues* cannot date from as late as 430, as Chadwick states (op. cit. pp. 8 and 21): see below, ch. 7, ii. For the date of the *Institutes*, see Chadwick, pp. 37-9.

[18] It is true that Postumianus proclaimed that *VM* was known throughout Egypt (*D* I, 23, 6), and that Sulpicius planned the same distribution for *D* (*D* III, 17, 7); but this needs to be taken with a pinch of salt. In any case, the *Apophthegmata* account names the monk, which Sulpicius does not, and this rules out straight derivation from him. Nor is derivation from Cassian likely: (a) Cassian gathered his material in Egypt in the first place; (b) by the 420s, when Cassian was writing, links between east and west were far more precarious, and they were dealt a crippling blow by Vandal control of the Mediterranean in the years following 429.

[19] On Postumianus' visit, see below ch. 7, ii; on Cassian's, Chadwick, pp. 12-18. Rousseau has been led independently to posit oral sources for some of Cassian's information: *Ascetics*, pp. 221, 254-5.

[20] See below, appendix. For further details, see my unpublished Oxford D.Phil. thesis, 'Sulpicius' Saint Martin' (1978), appendix.

mission in the person of an Aquitanian priest called Vigilantius.[21] Vigilantius originated from Saint-Martory, in the foothills of the Pyrenees. In 395 he visited the Holy Land as a protegé of Paulinus of Nola. This means that he could have heard the pilgrims' account which was later written down as the *Historia monachorum in Aegypto* at first hand, fresh from the pilgrims' own lips: for they had returned early in 395 from their tour of Egyptian ascetics, and they were associated with—or even belonged to—Rufinus' community on Olivet, which Vigilantius is likely to have visited.[22] Later in 395 Vigilantius returned to the west. Indeed, if the arguments given below in chapter 21 are accepted, Vigilantius was at this time a member of Sulpicius' brotherhood at Primuliacum, and went back there. Although Vigilantius later turned against asceticism and against the dubious practices then becoming associated with the cult of the martyrs, at this date he was still in sympathy with the ideals of Paulinus and Sulpicius. He was therefore well placed for retailing to them stories about the Egyptian monks which he had heard while he was in the Holy Land. These stories, in their turn, could have influenced Sulpicius in his choice and his presentation of incidents to include in the *Vita Martini*.

There was certainly scope for the recurrence of the same stories in different literary works. For one thing, all ascetics looked back to the Bible, and many of the stories they tell have an obvious affinity with biblical stories. Thus, for instance, stories about the devil masquerading as Christ may well derive ultimately from II Corinthians 11:14: 'Satan himself masquerades as an angel of light', coupled with expectation of the parousia. Such stories occur in the *Historia monachorum*, *Historia lausiaca*, and the *Life of St. Pachomius*, as well as in the *Vita Martini*.[23]

---

[21] For further discussion and references, see below, ch. 21.

[22] *Historia monachorum in Aegypto*, ed. A.-J. Festugière (Brussels 1961); ET, *The Lives of the Desert Fathers*, by B. Ward and N. Russell (pb. edn. Oxford & Kalamazoo, 1981). For a clue to their date of return, see epilogue §10. On their link with Olivet, prologue §2, and cf. I, 19. On Vigilantius and Olivet see below ch. 21, n. 26.

[23] B. Studer, 'Zu einer Teufelserscheinung in der Vita Martini des Sulpicius Severus', *Oikoumene: studi paleocristiani pubblicati in onore del Concilio Ecumenico Vaticano II* (Centro di Studi sull' Antico Cristianesimo, Università di Catania, 1964), p. 357.

Side by side with this common biblical culture there was also a shared ascetic culture which operated chiefly at an oral level. Stories about the achievements of holy men had become a popular medium for instruction by the end of the fourth century, and indeed were one of the chief means whereby asceticism spread. As we have seen, the story of Antony was in itself sufficient to inspire some hearers to follow suit. Such circumstances led to the setting down on paper of the lives of holy men. Thus Athanasius wrote his famous *Vita Antonii* for monks overseas, who had wanted to know the details of his life 'so that you may train yourselves in eager rivalry of him'; and Jerome had a similar objective in many of his writings: most explicitly in the *Vita Malchi*, which he described as 'a story of chastity for the chaste'.[24]

In this way the links which bound together the ascetics of east and west were not merely the physical ones of visits and pilgrimages, but also cultural ones, comprising a common way of looking to the Bible and to stories of holy men to provide them with models for their own way of life. So it was that Jerome could write to Paulinus, recommending as a pattern for monks the lives of Paul, Antony, Julian, Hilarion, and Macarius, and beyond them, Elijah and Elisha.[25] It is partly against this background of ascetic *vitae* and *exempla* that we should place Sulpicius' own compositions about Martin, although, as we shall see, there were also many other factors at work in their genesis.

---

[24] *Vita Antonii*, preface (*PG* 26, col. 837). *Vita Malchi* 10 (*PL* 23, col. 62). Cf. Rousseau, *Ascetics, passim*, and esp. pp. 70, 94.

[25] *Ep.* 58. 5.

6

Sulpicius' Literary Background

Long before his conversion to asceticism immersed him in Christian ascetic culture, Sulpicius was at home in the classical culture of the ancient world. From a social angle, his conversion involved exchanging the one world for the other: he opted out of traditional Roman society when he opted into the ascetic life. But from a cultural angle, no such radical exchange took place.[1] Rather, his reading of Christian authors was grafted onto his previous classical culture, and the latter remained the root stock, through the fruit it bore was Christian.

If we wish fully to understand the Martinian writings, then Sulpicius' literary and cultural formation are important. For they will have fashioned his outlook; and, in particular, they will have influenced the way in which Sulpicius saw and presented Martin through the medium of the written word. The specific question of how far classical and Christian norms determined the literary forms of the Martinian writings can best be left to a later chapter; but, first, it would be helpful to know something of Sulpicius' education and intellectual development.

Unfortunately, direct evidence is lacking. We can but say in general terms that, as Sulpicius grew up at a time when the public educational system of the Roman Empire was still flourishing, his education would have followed the time-honoured Greco-Roman model.[2] The primary stage consisted

[1] Sulpicius (esp. *VM* 1, 3) is misunderstood by T. J. Haarhoff, *Schools of Gaul* (Johannesburg 1958²), p. 169, and by P. Courcelle, *Late Latin Writers and their Greek Sources* (ET Cambridge Mass. 1969), pp. 235–6. Cf. below, ch. 7, pp. 73–5.

[2] For what follows, see H. I. Marrou, *A History of Education in Antiquity* (ET pb. edn. London 1977), part III, esp. chs. 4–6, and 8; Haarhoff, pp. 52–118.

of learning to read and write and do sums. The secondary stage, at the grammarian's school, was largely devoted to the reading, the memorizing, and the study of traditional classical authors. Amongst Latin writers, Virgil occupied the foremost place; but Terence, Sallust, and Cicero, together with Horace, Plautus, and many others, were also included. The teacher would first read a passage aloud, and then give a detailed explanation. This included both a minute grammatical and stylistic analysis, and also a more general exposition, which ranged over mythology, history, geography, and anything else pertinent to the text. However, grammar apart, these other subjects were not taught separately, in their own right, but only as background for the appreciation of literature. As for science, it was almost wholly neglected.

The final stage of education was devoted to rhetoric, to learning the art of expressing oneself fluently and convincingly. This began in the higher stages of the grammarian's school, and was continued under specialized rhetoric professors. The student practised by being set imaginary speeches, *declamationes*. These comprised *suasiones*, speeches of advice to some historical or mythological personage at a certain juncture (e.g. 'Should Cato commit suicide after Utica?'); and *controversiae*, imaginary legal cases which had to be pleaded for, or against. Rhetoric tended to overshadow or oust other subjects of study. For instance, history tended to be reduced to a gallery of good or bad examples to be paraded in one's speeches, and the intellectual discipline of philosophy was frequently neglected: Augustine was set to read Cicero's *Hortensius* not for its philosophical content, but because of its stylistic excellence.[3]

Would Sulpicius have learnt Greek? That he would have been *taught* Greek is fairly certain; for the fourth century still retained the traditional practice of studying Greek and Roman authors *pari passu*, taking boys through Homer and Menander at the same time, or even before, they were introduced to Virgil and Terence.[4] However, the crux is: did Sulpicius learn Greek sufficiently well to enable him to read

[3] *Confessiones* III, iv, 7. For the teaching of history see Haarhoff, pp. 210–17.
[4] Marrou, pp. 258–64; Haarhoff, pp. 220–31.

Greek books later in life? It was certainly possible to acquire such a facility in Greek in south-west Gaul in the late fourth century: witness the hellenism of Pacatus, or of Rutilius Namatianus.[5] However, the actual experiences of Paulinus of Nola at Bordeaux and Augustine in Africa—and, if Rufinus is to be believed, of himself and Jerome in Rome—suggest that, all too often, school Greek was insufficient to enable Latin speakers to get to grips with Greek authors on their own.[6] None the less, we must not dismiss their school Greek as worthless. After all, later in his life Augustine succeeded in building upon it sufficiently to enable him to make considerable use of Greek texts;[7] and even Paulinus' case was not as hopeless as it first appears: for, in the same breath as calling Greek 'an unknown language', he lets slip that, however, imperfectly, he *has* translated a work of Clement from the Greek.[8]

What, then, of Sulpicius' knowledge of Greek? The evidence of his *Chronicle* implies that he was able to make some use of it, for in his account of the Arian controversy he makes 'a creditable attempt' to explain the differences between the terms ὁμοούσιος, ὁμοιούσιος, and ἀνομοιουσία; and, earlier on, he was able to draw upon Julius Africanus' *Chronographiae*, a synchronization of religious and secular history written in Greek.[9] It has also been suggested that Sulpicius obtained information about Persian affairs from Greek writers such as Plutarch and Strabo; but this appears doubtful.[10]

All in all, the education which Sulpicius received was much as it would have been three centuries earlier. It was firmly based upon the Greco-Roman classics, and virtually unaffected by the rise of Christianity. The teaching of Christian beliefs and morals was the affair of the family, and of the church;

[5] Courcelle, pp. 210-12; NB also Paulinus' correspondent, Jovinus: G. Bardy, *La Question des langues dans l'église ancienne* (Paris 1948), pp. 219-20.

[6] Marrou, pp. 259-62; Courcelle, pp. 131-3, 139-45; p. 38, n. 1.

[7] Courcelle, pp. 145-53.

[8] *Ep.* 46, 2; Bardy, pp. 218-19.

[9] Sulpicius, *Chron.* II, 40, 1-3; van Andel, p. 93. Julius Africanus: van Andel, pp. 26-8; Prete, *I Chronica*, pp. 48-9. For the possibility that Sulpicius used the Septuagint, see above ch. 4, n. 42.

[10] It is suggested by Prete, pp. 49-50, and van Andel, p. 36; but Pompeius Trogus was probably Sulpicius' source: see below, esp. n. 17.

it in no way replaced the standard classical education. Thus
Sulpicius' formal education would have been entirely classical
in content, which explains the persistence of Greco-Roman
influence after his conversion. His grounding in Christianity
would have been acquired separately, probably through a
thorough pre-baptismal catechetical course, supplemented
by his own reading, by sermons, and by intercourse with
others—not least, with Martin.[11]

Happily, we can get some way beyond these generalities
by making use of the indirect evidence afforded by Sulpicius'
writings. His prose style has been carefully analysed by
Hyltén, who has revealed its sophistication. In the *Chronicle*,
a historical work, Sulpicius adopts the style of earlier Roman
historians like Sallust and Livy, who wrote unrhythmical
prose; but in his Martinian works, the *clausulae* at the end
of his sentences display his mastery of the metrical and
rhythmical prose that was then fashionable.[12]

More pertinent to our present concerns is the fact that
Sulpicius' writings also give us a fair idea of the books he had
read. This goes some way towards providing him with a literary
context, and so will be detailed here. The subject-matter falls
naturally into two categories: classical, and Christian.

(i) Classical Authors known to Sulpicius[13]

Of all the classical authors known to Sulpicius, pride of place
must needs go to Sallust. Not only was Sulpicius familiar
with the *Catiline Conspiracy* and *Jugurthine War*; not only
did their style influence that of his *Chronicle* so heavily
that Sulpicius has been dubbed 'the Christian Sallust'. Even
more significant is the fact that Sulpicius' perception of past
and present events was coloured by his reading of that
trenchant historian.[14] Sulpicius accepted Sallust's view that

---

[11] Marrou, op. cit. pp. 314–29; *VM* 25, 4–7; cf. *D* II, 12, 1; II, 13.

[12] Hyltén, esp. pp. 31–4, 53–7; cf. H. Hagendahl, *La Prose métrique d'Arnobe*
(Göteborg 1937), pp. 18–26, esp. p. 21, n. 1.

[13] I give references only to works not mentioned in Halm's index (*CSEL* 1,
p. 258). Hyltén, pp. 4–6, and van Andel, esp. ch. 1, are helpful.

[14] For what follows see van Andel, pp. 69–74.

peace gives rise to moral decline, epitomized by a desire for wealth and for power, whence arise factions. It was in this spirit that Sulpicius regarded the divisions of the post-Constantinian church in Gaul, the bishops' avarice and concern with power-grabbing, and their hostility towards the pure, simple Christianity represented by Martin. Half the long list of vices which he attributes to the contemporary church at the end of his *Chronicle* are typically Sallustian vices: *invidia*, *factio*, *libido*, *avaritia*, and *desidia*. Nor is it only in his *Chronicle* that we discern Sallust's influence; for, as we shall see, the opening of the *Vita Martini* appears to have been written as a kind of conscious dialogue with Sallust.[15]

Besides Sallust, Sulpicius was well acquainted with Tacitus' *Annals* and *Histories*; also with Livy's *History*, and probably with the *Roman Histories* of Velleius Paterculus, and the *Breviarium* of his own contemporary, Eutropius.[16] He further shows himself unusually well-informed about Persian affairs for a Latin historian. His source here was almost certainly the *Philippic Histories* of Pompeius Trogus, an Augustan historian who wrote in Latin about Greek (includ-ing Persian) history. This is all the more likely as Trogus came from Gallia Narbonensis, close to Primuliacum. Unfortunately, apart from the prologues summarizing the contents of each book, Trogus' original work is nearly all lost, though an epitome made by Justin survives. Such evidence as we have, however, points to Sulpicius' use of Trogus himself, rather than the epitome.[17]

---

[15] Below, ch. 7, i.

[16] Tacitus: Halm, pp. 82–3; van Andel, pp. 24, 40–8. Livy: Fontaine, *Vie* II, 414 n. 2. Velleius: E. Klebs, 'Entlehnungen aus Velleius *Philologus* 49, n.s. 3 (1890), pp. 288–98. Eutropius: below, p. 179.

[17] Cf. van Andel, pp. 36–9. But whereas van Andel argues for Sulpicius' use of Justin's epitome of Trogus, plus some other source(s) (Plutarch and Strabo, p. 36; Trogus, p. 39), the evidence he cites points strongly to Sulpicius' use of Trogus himself, not Justin; and this obviates our postulating additional sources. Sulpicius, *Chron.* II, 9, 5 is closer to Trogus fragment 30a than to Justin 1, 9, 1; and *Chron.* II, 23, 3 is closer to Trogus prologue 34 than to Justin 34, 3, 6. Also, Sulpicius could have known of Ochus' Egyptian campaign and of the succession of Arses (*Chron.* II, 14, 4 and 16, 8) only from Trogus (see prologue 10); they are not mentioned in Justin's epitome (see *M. Iuniani Iustini epitoma historiarum philippicarum Pompei Trogi*, ed. O. Seel, Stuttgart 1972, pp. 90–1, and cf. p. 309). The same very probably goes for the other details mentioned by Sulpicius but lacking in Justin, which van Andel notes (p. 37).

After history, we may pass on to biography. Of this genre, Sulpicius seems to have known at least Suetonius' *De vita Caesarum*; for Suetonius' pattern of biography influenced the formal structure of the *Vita Martini*; and a verbal echo of the *Augustus* indicates that Sulpicius knew this work at first hand.[18]

History and biography apart, Sulpicius also reveals a thorough acquaintance with the classics of Latin literature. Amongst epic poems, he quotes from Virgil's *Aeneid* and Statius' *Thebaid*, while satire is represented by Juvenal.[19] In addition, there are convincing verbal reminiscences of Ovid's *Metamorphoses* and Horace's *Epistles*, together with a close parallel which suggests that he knew Phaedrus' *Fables*.[20] Of playwrights, there are quotations from Terence's *Andria*, and indirectly we also know of one from Plautus' *Aulularia*.[21] As for Cicero, Sulpicius almost certainly knew the *In Catilinam* and *Cato maior de senectute*, and there are many echoes of other works of his which Sulpicius may well have read: the *Pro Sestio*, *De oratore*, *De legibus*, *Tusculan Disputations*, and very probably the *Academica posteriora*.[22] Finally, convincing verbal reminiscences imply that Sulpicius knew Apuleius' *Golden Ass*.[23]

In addition to these works whose parallels with Sulpicius' have, in the main, already been investigated, we should also consider Valerius Maximus' *Facta et dicta memorabilia*. There are interesting similarities between such stories as that of Servius Tullius, who was seen asleep and 'circa caput flammam emicuisse', and the 'globum ignis de capite illius [i.e. Martini] vidimus emicare'; or between the story of how a daemon came repeatedly to wake Mark Antony during the night at Actium, and how an angel kept rousing Count

---

[18] Below, ch. 8, i, esp. n. 18.

[19] van Andel, pp. 23–4.

[20] Ovid: van Andel, p. 25. Horace: Fontaine, *Vie* II, 378 and n. 3. Phaedrus: ibid. III, 960, n. 2.

[21] Terence: *D* I, 9, 3; Fontaine, *Vie* II, 387, n. 1. Plautus: Paulinus, *ep.* 22, 3.

[22] *Catil.*: Fontaine, *Vie* II, 368 n. 2. *Cato*: ibid. III, 1080, n. 1. *Sest.*: ibid. II, 646, n. 2. *Orat.*: ibid. III, 1034, n. 1. *Leg.*: ibid. II, 579, n. 1. *Tusc.*: ibid. II, 381, n. 1. *Acad. post.*: B. R. Voss, *Der Dialog in der frühchristlichen Literatur* (Munich 1970), pp. 311–12, esp. n. 23.

[23] C. Morelli, 'Apuleiana', *Studi italiani di filologia classica* 20 (1913) p. 186.

Avitianus.[24] It is true that in both cases similar stories are also told of other men by other authors;[25] but the number of possible parallels is striking,[26] as are the similar ways in which anecdotes are linked by the two authors,[27] although no single parallel is close enough to prove direct borrowing.

In any case, Sulpicius' acquaintance with the classical literature of Rome was clearly extensive; and it is interesting to find our impression that Sulpicius continued to draw widely on this culture after his conversion confirmed by Paulinus of Nola's playful allusion to his continued citation of Virgil and Plautus.[28]

(ii) Christian Authors known to Sulpicius

As regards Sulpicius' Christian literary culture, the various canonical books of the old and new testaments obviously formed the groundwork. This has already been discussed.[29] But his religious reading also included much else.

To start with, his familiarity with the canonical books of the Bible did not preclude his reading at least one apocryphal book: he used the *Passio sanctorum apostolorum Petri et Pauli* for his *Chronicle* account of Simon Magus being borne aloft over Rome by demonic minions, and crashing to his destruction when the latter were driven off by the apostles' prayers.[30] It is also possible that he derived from the

---

[24] Valerius 1, 6, 1 (ed. C. Kempf, Berlin 1854, pp. 136-7); cf. Sulpicius *D* II, 2, 1. Valerius 1, 7, 7, and *D* III, 4.

[25] See P. Antin, 'Autour du songe de S. Jérôme', in his *Recueil sur saint Jérôme* (Collection Latomus 95, Brussels 1968), pp. 76-7.

[26] E.g. triumph, not funeral: Valerius 2, 10, 3 and Sulpicius *ep.* 3, 21. Attack with drawn sword fails: Valerius 2, 10, 6 and *VM* 15. Cf. also Valerius 2, 10, 6 and *D* II, 4.

[27] E.g. Valerius, 3, 2, introduction (p. 244), 'Nec me praeterit . . .' and *VM* 24, 4, 'Non praetereundum . . .'; Valerius 7, 3, 8, 'Veniam nunc ad eos, quibus . . .' and *D* III, 11, 1, 'Veniam ad illud, quod . . .'; Valerius 1, 8, *ext.* 2, 'Et quoniam ad externa transgressi sumus . . .' and *D* II, 6, 1, 'Et quia palatium semel ingressi sumus . . .'

[28] Paulinus, *ep.* 22, 3.

[29] Above, ch. 4, ii.

[30] *Chron.* II, 28, 5; cf. *Passio SS. apost. Petri et Pauli* chs. 50-6, ed. Tischendorf, Lipsius, and Bonnet, *Acta Apostolorum Apocrypha* (2 vols. in 3, repr. Hildesheim 1959), I, pp. 163-7.

apocryphal *Ascension of Isaiah* the detail in his second epistle about the prophet's limbs being cut off with saws and metal plates; for that work includes a chapter on Isaiah's martyrdom, according to which he was sawn apart with a tree saw. However, Sulpicius might have derived this detail from an intermediary; and in any case, the story of Isaiah's martyrdom was well known in the late fourth century.[31]

Babut suggested that Sulpicius was deeply influenced by such apocrypha.[32] These latter do, it is true, have some parallels with the Martinian works in their stories of mass conversions,[33] and their general stress on thaumaturgy.[34] However, such elements were common enough elsewhere, and there is nothing to indicate that Sulpicius had definitely read any apocryphal work apart from the *Passio . . . Petri et Pauli*. On the other hand, he may well have done so, or have known stories out of them through hearsay; for the Priscillianists were not the only readers of such apocrypha in the fourth century.[35]

A very different group of Sulpician sources consists of those chronographical and historical Christian books which supplied Sulpicius with material for his *Chronicle*: viz. Julius Africanus' *Chronographiae*, Hippolytus' *Chronicle* (available

---

[31] *Ascension of Isaiah*, ch. 5; ET in E. Hennecke, *New Testament Apocrypha* (2 vols., ET London 1963-5), II, 650-1; cf. C. C. Torrey, *The Apocryphal Literature* (New Haven, 1945), pp. 133-5. This work was well known in late fourth-century Spain, probably thanks to the Priscillianists: Jerome, *Comm. in Esaiam* XVII, 64 (*CCSL* 73A, p. 735). Sulpicius ref.: *ep.* 2, 10; cf. Fontaine, *Vie* III, 1223-4. On the widespread knowledge of this story see R. Bernheimer, 'The Martyrdom of Isaiah', *Art Bulletin* 34 (1952), esp. pp. 21-2, 32-3. Or might Sulpicius have been simply embroidering upon Hilary, *Contra Constantium*, 4 (cf. *Vie* III, 1218, n. 1)?

[32] *St. Martin*, pp. 227-8, 234-6, and cf. p. 317.

[33] Babut, pp. 228-9, compares the *Acts of John* account of the destruction of the temple at Ephesus and the resulting conversions with the Levroux episode (*VM* 14, 3-7). But cf. Delehaye's well-founded criticisms: 'S. Martin', pp. 51-6.

[34] See Babut, pp. 234-6, singling out resurrections. Another possible example is the saint's power to command creatures, and the comparison made between their obedience, and men's indifference: cf. *Acts of John* 61 and Sulpicius, *D* III, 9, 4 and cf. *D* I, 14, 8. But the idea was commonplace: e.g. Ambrose, *De virginibus* II, 20 (ch. 3).

[35] See H. Chadwick, *Priscillian of Avila* (Oxford 1976), pp. 24-5, 78. The circulation of apocrypha in southern Aquitaine was doubtless assisted by the existence of Priscillianist sympathisers in the neighbourhood: cf. below ch. 20.

in a Latin translation), and Jerome's translation and continuation of Eusebius' *Chronicle*.[36]

For more theological works, the Latin Christian tradition right up to the later fourth century was dominated by the work of African writers, particularly Tertullian and Cyprian. Their importance for Hilary has been clearly demonstrated.[37] With Sulpicius, their influence is harder to detect, but his writings contain likely reminiscences of Tertullian's *De resurrectione carnis* and *De idololatria* and of two of Cyprian's letters, while further echoes of other works by Tertullian remain a possibility.[38] Sulpicius also knew Minucius Felix's dialogue, *Octavius*.[39]

There can be no doubt as regards Sulpicius' acquaintance with martyr literature, for he explicitly states that he had read the passions of various martyrs who suffered under Diocletian.[40] He does not give further details, but his account of Martin's encounter with Julian at Worms is clearly influenced by the confrontation of future martyr and Roman emperor or official as portrayed in various martyrs' *acta*, especially those of African soldier-martyrs. The parallels with the *Passio Typasii* are particularly striking; but as chronological considerations make it unlikely that Sulpicius could have known this work by 396, it is better just to signalize the general correspondence with works of this genre, and to forgo the temptation to reach greater precision.[41]

Sulpicius' interest in martyr literature, his particular veneration for Cyprian, and the Cyprian—Hilary—Sulpicius link, all these have led Fontaine to speculate upon the possibility that Sulpicius knew Pontius' *Vita Cypriani*, the life of the great martyr-bishop of Carthage.[42] This hypothesis

[36] Prete, pp. 47-9; van Andel, pp. 26-36, 89-90.

[37] Doignon, pp. 210-25.

[38] Tertullian: Fontaine, *Vie* III, 1335 and n. 2, II, 698 n. 2; cf. also III, 1057 n. 1, 1100 n. 1, 1199 n. 1, and 1287, n. 1. Cyprian: ibid. II, 584 n. 1, III, 1219 n. 1. NB also the respectful mentions of Cyprian in *D* I, 3, 2, and III, 17, 5. Cf. Fontaine, *Vie* I, 118.

[39] Y.-M. Duval, 'La Lecture de l'*Octavius* de Minucius Felix à la fin du IVᵉ siècle', *Revue des Études Augustiniennes* 19 (1973), pp. 57-8, n. 8. Cf. also Voss, *Der Dialog*, pp. 312-3 and n. 24.

[40] *Chron.* II, 32, 6.

[41] See below, ch. 10, pp. 141-2, 144-8, and n. 45.

[42] *Vie* I, 69-70, and cf. 118.

can now, I think, be confirmed; for close study reveals two verbal similarities, which, taken with other parallels of content, make it highly likely that Sulpicius did indeed know this work. With Pontius' 'non quo . . . lateat tanti viri vita', we may compare Sulpicius' 'nefas putarem tanti viri latere virtutes',[43] while the phrase 'longum est ire per singula' appears in identical form in both works.[44] In addition, both authors mention the kindness with which their heroes met the hostility shown them; in both we find the idea that the martyr's honour can be achieved even by those who have not suffered physical martyrdom; and in both this idea is followed by the lament of the disciple, who feels torn between rejoicing in his hero's triumphal death, and bewailing his own fate in being left behind.[45] In view of all these similarities, we may surely accept that Sulpicius knew Pontius' *Vita Cypriani*; especially as by that date awareness of this work was not restricted to Africa and to that omnivorous reader, Jerome. It was also used by Prudentius in Spain, not far from Sulpicius' Aquitaine.[46]

While Sulpicius' familiarity with the *Vita Cypriani* has not hitherto been recognized, his acquaintance with Athanasius' *Vita Antonii* has been widely accepted since Babut wrote in 1912. Babut rightly saw that Athanasius' work pioneered the genre of hagiography, and that Sulpicius' *Vita Martini* followed in its wake.[47] However, Babut seriously over-estimated Sulpicius' debt to the *Vita Antonii*—particularly when he claimed that Sulpicius borrowed whole episodes from Antony's life and wantonly attributed them to

---

[43] *Ponzio, Vita e martirio di San Cipriano*, ed. M. Pellegrino (Alba, 1955), 1, 1; cf. *VM* ded. letter, 5.

[44] *V. Cyp.* 5, 1; *VM* 19, 5. This is striking; but NB that similar phrases occur elsewhere: e.g. 'singillatim crudeliter factu eius exequi longum est' (Suetonius, *Tib.* 42, 1); 'et quia longum est per diversa tempora carptim ascensum eius edicere . . .' (Jerome, *V. Hil.* 10).

[45] *V. Cyp.* 5, 6; *VM* 26, 5 and 27, 2-3. *V. Cyp.* 1, 2 and 19, 2; Sulpicius, *ep.* 2, 9-12. *V. Cyp.* 19, 3; Sulpicius, *ep.* 2, 7 and *ep.* 3, 19-21, with the *dolere - gaudere* antithesis.

[46] See Y.-M. Duval in *Epektasis*, ed. Fontaine and Kannengiesser, p. 558 and n. 65; cf. p. 562, n. 103. On the link between Spain and Aquitaine see Fontaine, ibid., pp. 587 ff., and Fontaine, 'Société et culture chrétiennes sur l'aire circum-pyrénéenne au siècle de Théodose', *BLE* 1974, pp. 241-82.

[47] Cf. *St. Martin*, pp. 75-83, esp. 82-3; pp. 89-90.

Martin.[48] Some parallels with the *Vita Antonii* are discernible in the early chapters of the *Vita Martini*, and Athanasius' work exerted some influence upon Sulpicius' treatment of Martin and the devil.[49] But its real importance lies, along with Jerome's saints' lives, in inspiring Sulpicius with the general idea of writing about Martin; not in providing him with source material or with a model which he could adopt wholesale. We shall return to these matters later; here, we may simply note that Sulpicius knew the work, and knew it in Evagrius' Latin translation.[50]

Of perhaps more fundamental importance for his influence upon Sulpicius is another fourth-century author, Hilary of Poitiers: in particular, the outspoken Hilary of the *Contra Constantium* with its denunciation of church leaders who could be bought with gold to fawn upon a heretical emperor, 'an enemy full of blandishments . . . , Constantius the Antichrist'.[51] The pervading influence of this work of Hilary's is apparent in Sulpicius' writings, as in his account of how Martin alone of all the bishops retained his apostolic authority, refusing to be subservient to the Emperor Maximus.[52] There are also two passages where Sulpicius was consciously echoing Hilary: in his second epistle, when he was recounting the martyrs' trials which Martin would have undergone had he lived in an age of outright persecution, and in the *Dialogues*, where he was describing the habitual effects of Martin's prayers on demoniacs.[53] In addition, Sulpicius used Hilary's *Adversus Valentem et Ursacium* in his *Chronicle*, and probably also the *De synodis*, a letter sent to the Gallic bishops while Hilary was still in exile.[54] As regards Hilary's exegetical

[48] See the criticisms of Delehaye, 'S. Martin', pp. 41-7.

[49] Below, ch. 8, i; and cf. ch. 17, ii.

[50] This is above all apparent from *VM* 2, 1, which obviously echoes Evagrius' translation of *V. Ant.* 1: not the older Latin version (ed. G. J. M. Bartelink, *Vita di Antonio, Vite dei Santi* I, p. 6), nor the Greek original. See B. R. Voss, 'Berührungen von Hagiographie und Historiographie in der Spätantike', *Frühmittelalterliche Studien* 4 (1970), pp. 57-8.

[51] Ch. 5 (*PL* 10, col. 581).

[52] *VM* 20, esp. §1; cf. *Contra Const.* 5 and 6.

[53] Cf. Sulpicius, *ep.* 2, 9-10 and Hilary, *Contra Const.* 4 (noted by Fontaine, *Vie* III, 1218 n. 1); Sulpicius *D* III, 6, 3-4 and *Contra Const.* 8 (noted by Delehaye, 'S. Martin', p. 49).

[54] van Andel, pp. 86-9.

works, we have already seen that Sulpicius knew his *Tractatus mysteriorum*, and it is highly likely that he was also acquainted with his *Commentary on Matthew*.[55]

Another fourth-century Latin churchman whom we might expect Sulpicius to have read is Ambrose: like Hilary, a pro-monastic, anti-Arian bishop, who refused to kowtow to emperors, and who sided with Martin as regards the impropriety of Priscillian's trial. Even if Ambrose did not encounter Martin in Trier at the time of this trial, friendly communication between the two bishops is implied by the fact that Martin received relics of the Milanese martyrs Gervasius and Protasius, whose bodies were triumphantly discovered by Ambrose around that time.[56] However, there is no conclusive evidence that Sulpicius had read any of Ambrose's works, though there are some points in common which may imply it. There is one indication that Sulpicius may have known Ambrose's *De viduis*;[57] and it could be that the association of saints Agnes, Thecla, and Mary in a vision of Martin's owes something to the occurrence of all three in Ambrose's *De virginibus*.[58] In addition, there are certainly some similarities between Sulpicius' second letter, and Ambrose's *De excessu fratris sui Satyri*; but this may be simply because both belong to the tradition of consolation literature.[59] Overall, then, we may leave the question of Sulpicius' knowledge of Ambrose's works with the verdict of likely, but not proven.

There is, however, one contemporary churchman whose writings definitely influenced Sulpicius: Jerome. It is most

---

[55] Above, ch. 4, ii; van Andel, p. 89.

[56] Gregory of Tours, *Hist.* X, 31, v; *In gloria martyrum* 46 (*MGH, SRM* I, ii, p. 69). See also Chadwick, *Priscillian*, pp. 129, 133 ff., 138; Sulpicius, *D* III, 11–13.

[57] Sulpicius' reference to Deborah as a type of the church (*Chron.* I, 24, 5, on which see van Andel pp. 64–5) may come from Ambrose's *De viduis*, VIII, 47 and 50 (*PL* 16, cols. 262, 263). But it might simply derive from oral catechetical instruction.

[58] *D* II, 13, 5–6; see Fontaine, *Vie* III 1216, n. 1. This, however, would presumably indicate that Ambrose's work was known to Martin, rather than Sulpicius. Note also that Mary and Thecla are named (along with other holy women) in Jerome's famous *ep.* 22, 41, which was apparently known in Martinian circles around 398: see *D* I, 8, 4–9, 2.

[59] Cf. *De excessu* I, 20–1 (*PL* 16, col. 1353), and *ep.* 2, §§8, 15 and 16. Fontaine, *Vie* III, 1243–4, notes.

instructive to see how many similarities there are between the
teaching of Sulpicius' Martin, and of Jerome. Both, for
instance, have a rather negative attitude towards marriage,
whereas Ambrose openly accepted it as a good.[60] Both
taught that bishops should honour a strict ascetic; both
used the metaphor that no soldier is accompanied by his
wife on the battlefield; both were against the practice of the
clergy entertaining important men of the world, although
here again they differed from Ambrose.[61] Both Sulpicius
and Jerome praised their heroes for treading underfoot the
glory of the world;[62] both agreed that gifts should be
distributed instantly to the poor, and that monks should
possess nothing of their own;[63] and both writers castigated
those monks and clerics who did not maintain such strict
standards.[64]

While some of these similarities may be due simply to
common biblical and ascetic precepts,[65] such traits as regarding marriage as a falling away from goodness, or refusing
entertainment to men of the world, are more idiosyncratic.
Further, Sulpicius explicitly expresses his admiration for
Jerome, whose castigations he regards as particularly apposite
for church life in Gaul. In this context he cites verbally
from Jerome's famous letter *De virginitate*, addressed to
Eustochium.[66] This means that Sulpicius knew this letter at
the very least, and it is likely that he knew others, also.
Jerome's epistle 117, addressed to a mother and daughter
in Gaul, was apparently known to Vigilantius;[67] and Jerome

---

[60] Martin regarded marriage as 'pardonable' (*D* II, 10, 6), which is reminiscent
of Jerome, *Adversus Jovinianum* I, 7-9 (*PL* 23, cols. 228-33). For Ambrose's
more balanced teaching, see his *De virginitate* VI, 31-4 (*PL* 16, cols. 287-8).

[61] Cf. *D* II, 12, 5-6 and Jerome, *ep.* 24, 5, 2; *D* II, 11, 4 & 6-7 and Jerome,
ep. 22, 21, 8; *D* I, 25, 6 and Jerome, *ep.* 52, 11, 1.

[62] *D* II, 4, 2, 'mundi gloriam calcans'; Jerome, *Vita Hilarionis* 30, 'stupeo quam
gloriam illum et honorem calcare potuisse.' (*PL* 23, col. 44.)

[63] *D* III, 14, 6; Jerome, *ep.* 52, 16, and cf. *V. Hil.* chs. 18 and 27.

[64] Below, ch. 19.

[65] E.g. on the saint's refusal of gifts, see II Kings 5:15-27, specifically recalled
by Jerome, *V. Hil.* 18.

[66] See *D* I, 8, 2-9, 5, where two verbal reminiscences of Jerome's *ep.* 22 occur.
The shorter, not given by Halm, is 'nos usque ad vomitum solere satiari' (*D* I, 8,
5), echoing Jerome's 'saturantur ad vomitum' (*ep.* 22, 34, 3). Cf. also *VM* 16,
2-3 and *ep.* 22, 30, 3.

[67] See Jerome, *Contra Vigilantium*, 3 (*PL* 23, col. 341).

expected such letters to circulate amongst his sympathizers, and wrote with an eye to a future audience.[68]

In addition to some of Jerome's letters, verbal parallels show that Sulpicius definitely knew his *Vita Pauli*.[69] He probably also knew Jerome's *Vita Hilarionis*, where a popular explanation for drought is 'Antonii mortem etiam elementa lugere', which is very similar to Sulpicius' ascription of changed weather to Martin's death: 'eiusdem mortem lugeret'.[70] We may also see a discreet allusion to this work of Jerome's towards the end of the *Vita Martini*, where Sulpicius is expatiating upon Martin's ceaseless fasts, vigils, and prayers: 'Vere fatebor, non si ipse, ut aiunt, ab inferis Homerus emergeret, posset exponere'. The reference here to the 'as they say' looks like a deliberate allusion to Jerome, who had claimed apropos of his attempt to describe Hilarion's life: 'Homerus quoque si adesset, vel invideret materiae, vel succumberet.'[71] Note further that in both works we find the same idea of 'national saints';[72] and also that there are points in common between some of the stories told of Martin and of Hilarion, such as their fearlessness when confronted with brigands.[73]

We may conclude, then, that Sulpicius knew Jerome's life of Hilarion, as well as that of Paul; also, the letter on virginity to Eustochium, and, as we saw earlier, Jerome's translation and continuation of Eusebius' *Chronicle*. In addition, Sulpicius may well have known other works of Jerome's, such as his *Life of Malchus*, and further letters. What is significant, though, is that it is not just a matter of Sulpicius having read these works by Jerome: he took them

---

[68] Jerome, *ep.* 123, 17, 3; *ep.* 117, 12. See Feder, ch. III esp. pp. 112-13, 139-54.

[69] Delehaye, 'S. Martin', p. 48; below, ch. 22, n. 48; Stancliffe, 'Sulpicius' Saint Martin', pp. 79-80.

[70] *V. Hil.* 32; *D* III, 7, 3 (discussed below, p. 221). For another probable verbal reminiscence see above, n. 62.

[71] *VM* 26, 3; *V. Hil.* ch. 1. NB also Sulpicius' use of *succumbimus*, *VM* 26, 1. See Fontaine, *Vie* III, 1089-90, and cf. Babut, p. 105, n. 1. Note also that Jerome alludes to Sallust in his opening chapter of *V. Hil.* (cf. *V. Hil.* 1 and Sallust *Cat.* 3, 2 and 8, 4), as does Sulpicius in *VM* 1 (below, ch. 7, i).

[72] *D* III, 17, 5-6; *V. Hil.* 14, and cf. ch. 24. Below, ch. 21, at end.

[73] Cf. *VM* 5, 5, and *V. Hil.* 12. Fontaine compares their treatment of demoniacs: *Vie* II, 846, 848.

to heart. This is suggested by the number of possible parallels between Jerome's works and the Martinian writings, coupled with Sulpicius' explicit tributes to Jerome. A further pointer in the same direction is the likelihood that Jerome's saints' lives and letters provided Sulpicius with two monastic technical terms which he could not have derived from the Latin translations of the *Vita Antonii*: viz. *anachoreta*, and *cellula*.[74] We may add that the traffic between Jerome and Sulpicius was not entirely one way. By 412 at the latest Jerome knew of Sulpicius' *Dialogues*, and it is likely that he also knew the *Vita Martini*, though he never mentions it explicitly.[75]

Through his friend, Paulinus, Sulpicius was also indirectly in touch with the party clustered around Jerome's once-loved *bête noire*, Rufinus. After receiving the *Vita Martini*, Paulinus read it aloud to Rufinus' protector, Melania, and in 403 or 404 he forwarded Sulpicius' request for historical information to Rufinus.[76] Such contacts may have something to do with the similarities discernible between the Martinian writings and Rufinus' translation of the *Historia monachorum*; and it has also been suggested that Rufinus may have used Sulpicius' *Chronicle* for his continuation of Eusebius' *Ecclesiastical History*.[77] On Sulpicius' side, it is almost certain that he had read Rufinus' *De adulteratione librorum Originis* before writing the *Dialogues*.[78]

In conclusion, we may say that Sulpicius was well read in classical literature, particularly in history, where he was deeply influenced by Sallust. Similarly with Christian writings, he was probably attracted not by theological works, but rather by history, and by martyr and ascetic literature: i.e *passiones* and *vitae*; and particularly by Jerome's ascetical writings and Hilary's polemical ones. History, biography,

---

[74] J. Gribomont, 'L'Influence du monachisme oriental sur Sulpice Sévère', *Saint Martin et son temps*, pp. 140-1, 144-5.

[75] Above ch. 2, n. 4; below, ch. 21.

[76] Paulinus, *ep.* 29, 14; *ep.* 28, 5. See P. Brown, 'The Patrons of Pelagius', in Brown's *Religion and Society*, pp. 210-11; and C. P. Hammond, 'The Last Ten Years of Rufinus' Life', *JTS* n.s. 28 (1977), esp. pp. 380-2.

[77] Doignon, p. 431; van Andel, pp. 91, 155-6. On the complex relationship between the Martinian writings and Rufinus' translation of the *Historia monachorum*, see Stancliffe, appendix.

[78] Below, ch. 21, n. 43.

and polemic, classical and Christian: this is what we know Sulpicius to have read. Let us now look at how this diverse cultural background combined with historical circumstances to play its part in the genesis of the Martinian writings.

7

The Genesis of Sulpicius' Writings

(i) The *Vita Martini* and *Epistles*

Sulpicius' first work was his life of Martin of Tours, for which he had been collecting material when first he visited the holy man in 393 or 4. Over the next three years he came to know Martin quite well, and two monks were sent from Tours to tell him of Martin's death in November, 397.[1] By that time the *Vita Martini* was already completed. This is shown by a vision which Sulpicius saw just before the news reached him. In this vision, Martin smilingly 'held out to me in his right hand the little book which I had written about his life.'[2] Indeed, the *Vita* must by then have been finished for a while, as it was already in general circulation: it had reached Paulinus in Italy,[3] and also some other readers who felt less favourably disposed. Amongst the 'many' who had read it was a sceptic, who had been heard asking how it was that the man whom Sulpicius had depicted as having power over death and fire should in fact have got himself burnt recently. Martin must have been still alive at the time this doubter read the *Vita*; and, it would appear, had recently been hale enough to be visiting Trier.[4]

---

[1] *D* II, 13, 3-4; *ep.* 2, 14 & 6.

[2] *Ep.* 2, 3; cf. *VM* pref. 1.

[3] Paulinus, *ep.* 11, 14. Hood, appendix, argues that Paulinus had not yet seen the book, but only got word of its existence from Sulpicius; and that Sulpicius did not put the *VM* into general circulation until after Martin's death. However, he fails to notice that Paulinus, with his juxtaposition of 'divina gloria' and 'humana memoria', and with his allusion to Sulpicius' work as 'clothing' for Christ, is echoing *VM* 1 and 3: see below, p. 76.

[4] *Ep.* 1, 2; *D* II, 9, 5.

Further precision about the date of the *Vita*'s publication is possible, with the evidence pointing to 396. As we have seen, Sulpicius was in regular correspondence with Paulinus, and Paulinus does not mention the work in his epistle 5 to Sulpicius, written in the summer of 396, but only in epistle 11, which he wrote in the spring of 397.[5] From this we may deduce that Sulpicius sent a copy to Paulinus with the couriers, who, according to the normal routine, would have journeyed to Nola in the autumn of 396; and we may further surmise that the book was completed some time between then and the autumn of 395, when the previous letter-bearers would have set out for Nola.

We have one additional piece of information to help us date the *Vita*. Sulpicius represents Martin as dying soon after Clarus; and, as the latter was already dead when the book was written, it cannot have been finished very long before Martin's own death.[6] The most likely date for its completion is thus some time during the summer of 396.

Sulpicius' purpose in writing a life of the bishop he revered is in part bound up with the question of the audience he wrote for. The *Vita* is dedicated to Desiderius, a fellow Aquitanian who belonged to the same ascetic circles as Sulpicius and Paulinus of Nola. Alongside this dedication we may place Sulpicius' closing words, where he expresses the hope that his little book will give pleasure to 'omnibus sanctis'.[7] This shows that Sulpicius thought of his immediate audience as comprising the circle of ascetic converts in Gaul, and probably beyond, which I have already described.

However, as we have seen, such ascetic converts were often regarded with hostility, even by their fellow Christians. Indeed, the majority of the Gallo-Roman episcopate would appear to have opposed the asceticism of Martin and his followers. Sulpicius shows himself fully aware of this,[8] and must have written his laudatory account of Martin in this

---

[5] Lienhard, pp. 178-82. The recurrence of the phrase 'evangelii non surdus auditor' in *VM* 2, 8 and Paulinus, *ep.* 5, 6, is puzzling. Was Sulpicius so attracted by Paulinus' phrase that he incorporated it into *VM* when revising this later in the summer of 396? Cf. Fontaine, *Vie* II, 471-2.

[6] *Ep.* 2, 5; *VM* 23, 1.

[7] *VM* 27, 6.

[8] *VM* 27, 3-4.

awareness. One objective may have been to defend Martin against his opponents' smears; another, to idealize the ascetic life that Martin had lived as a bishop. This means that the *vita* is tantamount to ascetic propaganda. As such, it amounts to an indirect indictment of worldly bishops, for it idealizes the virtues which they so conspicuously lacked. Sulpicius was not exactly writing the *Vita Martini* for the Gallo-Roman episcopate; but he was, in a sense, writing against them.[9]

A third category of audience is implied by the elaborate dedicatory letter and preface to the *Vita Martini*. It has been suggested that these represent a conscious dialogue with the cultural traditions of antiquity.[10] In the opening words of his preface, Sulpicius deliberately evokes Sallust's *Catilinae Conjuratio*. There, Sallust had stressed mortal man's transience in the world, a fate which could be partially overcome through attaining a glory founded upon *virtus*, by deeds or words. Thus Sallust saw the highest goal of man's life as the attainment of everlasting fame, and he himself, disillusioned with political life, had set out to achieve this by writing history. Sulpicius stands this idea on its head, much as Augustine was to do some twenty years later.[11] Having brought Sallust's *credo* alive in his readers' minds by his evocative opening, Sulpicius then pricks the bubble: 'For what has the glory of their writings profited them, seeing that it is a glory which will perish with this world?' he asks. These pagans 'spes suas fabulis, animas sepulcris dederint'. This mortal fame is to be contrasted with the life which is eternal, and which is entered into by all those who have lived religiously in this world—not by those who have sought glory the pagan way through writing, fighting, or philosophy. There is thus a double contrast: between what will perish with this world, and what is eternal; and between the death of a man's soul, where only his memory lingers on, and, on the other hand, the life of a man. It is as though

[9] Loc. cit., and cf. Fontaine, *Vie* I, 80-4. This concern is even clearer in the *Dialogues*: see I, 12, 1-2; II, 8, 1-2.

[10] Fontaine, *Vie* I, 72-5; II, 359 f., 393-422, q.v. for references to what follows.

[11] *De civitate Dei* V, 13-17. Cf. Brown, *Augustine* pp. 311-12: 'Augustine drains the glory from the Roman past in order to project it far beyond the reach of men, into the "Most glorious City of God".'

the Christian is able to rise above the traditional Roman world-view, and to see the world from the perspective of God's infinity. Viewed like this, the *saeculum* shrinks from filling the whole to becoming but a part of God's universe, and its time-span dwindles from being the only measure to becoming a thing which itself will pass, in contrast to the eternity of God.

And yet, Sulpicius does not wholly turn his back upon the views of pagan Roman historiography. Sallust's disillusionment with public life and subsequent withdrawal is in some ways comparable to the recent action of Paulinus of Nola and Sulpicius himself.[12] Further, Sulpicius, like Sallust, proposes to earn merit not so much by his way of life, as by his writing; and like other ancient historians he had the moral purpose of eternalizing one man's life as a model for future generations to imitate. Thus the prefatory chapter to the *Vita Martini* reads like a dialogue with the great historians of pagan Rome, above all, with Sallust. Sulpicius does not reject their views so much as correct them: he replaces their aim of writing about pagan heroes to win earthly fame with his own aim of writing about a Christian hero to win eternal life. Martin will incite men to *true* wisdom, *heavenly* 'militia', and *divine* 'virtus'.[13] And it is precisely at this point, just as he appears to be brushing aside the great cultural traditions of the Greco-Roman world, that he reclaims the Roman historiographical tradition as his own: by continuing with a phrase from Livy.[14]

What is the purpose of this brilliantly executed preface, and of its dialogue with traditional Roman culture? It can only be that Sulpicius wished, amongst other things, 'et litteratos convincerem', just as he would do some eight years later when writing his *Chronicle*.[15] We must not be so blinded by the eventual success of Christianity as to forget that in 394, precisely when Sulpicius was planning the *Vita*

---

[12] Cf. Fontaine, 'Valeurs antiques', pp. 571–95.

[13] *VM* 1, 6, picking up (in a different order) the 'pugnando vel philosophando' of *VM* 1, 4, and substituting 'divinam virtutem' for 'stultae illius virtutis' which Sallust had sought by writing. Cf. also I Cor. 1:18–25.

[14] Fontaine, *Vie* II, 414.

[15] *Chron.* I, 1, 4. So also Fontaine, loc. cit. and *Vie* I, 72–5, q.v.

Martini, the pagan Nicomachus Flavianus held the office of consul, and was busy reviving pagan rites in Rome.[16] A recent study has drawn attention to how the Roman aristocracy, in the aftermath of Julian's reign, 'identified itself with a classical past in which Christians were to have no share.' The effect was to transform 'the confrontation of religions into a confrontation of cultures.'[17] Against this background, we can perceive the significance of Sulpicius' evocation of the literary brilliance of the great Roman writers, and his re-channelling of their traditions to the service of Christianity. While other Christians were content to exult in the speedy overthrow of the regime of the ex-rhetor, Eugenius, and the pagan, Nicomachus Flavianus, Sulpicius set out to woo the *literati*.

Thus the general historical circumstances from which the *Vita Martini* took its existence were complex. It was not simply the life of a monk retold for ascetic circles.[18] It was also intended for a far wider audience: for contemporary churchmen in Gaul, and for those compatriots whose loyalties to Christianity were still torn by their love for the classical culture in which they had been nurtured.

These circumstances might in themselves appear sufficient to explain the genesis of the *Vita Martini*, but I would suggest that there were in addition more personal factors at work. It is as well to recall that the composition of the *Vita* spans the crucial period of Sulpicius' conversion and its immediate aftermath, from 393/4 when first he went to visit Martin and his future was undecided, to 396, by which time he had made his choice and refashioned his life after the pattern of Martin. Like Sallust, Sulpicius had abandoned his worldly career, and

[16] Matthews, *Western Aristocracies*, pp. 241-3. I am virtually persuaded by Matthews' arguments to date the setting of the *Carmen contra paganos* to 394 (*Historia* 19, 1970, pp. 464-79, esp. 470-1). Even without it, the remaining literary evidence (esp. Rufinus, *HE* II, 33) suffices to show that there *was* a pagan reaction in 394, and that it did scare contemporary churchmen: J. J. O'Donnell's discussion (*Phoenix*, 32, 1978, pp. 129-43) does not justify his concluding paragraph.

[17] R. A. Markus, 'Paganism, Christianity and the Latin Classics in the Fourth Century', *Latin Literature of the Fourth Century*, ed. J. W. Binns (London 1974), pp. 1-21, esp. p. 8.

[18] Cf. Fontaine, *Vie* II, 423: 'Paradoxalement, au moment de s'engager dans son œuvre, Sulpice semble penser ... plus à la *Conjuration* qu'à la *Vie d'Antoine*.'

turned his hand to writing; but Sulpicius was far more intimately bound up with the subject he proposed to write about than Sallust had been. Like Livy, Sulpicius looked for a reward for his work; but it was a Christian reward that he looked for, and one that his whole way of life was oriented towards. We might compare his hopes with those of his contemporary Pionius, who concluded his transcription of *The Martyrdom of St. Polycarp* with the words:

Finally, I, Pionius, made my transcription from Isocrates' copy, after I had made diligent search for it in accordance with the revelation of the saintly Polycarp, collecting the pages after they were all but worn out with age, that the Lord Jesus Christ might also gather me together with his elect into his heavenly kingdom . . .[19]

Like Pionius, Sulpicius hopes that his literary endeavours will bring him a heavenly prize; and Paulinus rather delightfully regards the *Vita* as Sulpicius' 'fleece', his equivalent of Martin's gift of half his cloak to a beggar. In return, he suggests, Christ the Lamb will clothe Sulpicius with some of his own wool at Doomsday.[20]

We might also notice the active role assigned to Polycarp by Pionius: the same idea can be seen with Sulpicius and Martin. In a sense the *Vita Martini* is intended both for God and for Martin, the latter standing as Sulpicius' patron *vis-à-vis* the former. On the one hand Martin's own life is testimony of God's continuing action in fourth-century Gaul, for Christ is present in—and acting through—his saints.[21] It is because of this that Sulpicius can express the hope that whoever *believes*, rather than reads, his life of Martin will be rewarded by God.[22] On the other hand, the *Vita Martini* can also be seen as the offering of a disciple and client to his master and

---

[19] *Martyrdom of St. Polycarp* 22, 5; ed. and tr. H. Musurillo, *The Acts of the Christian Martyrs* (Oxford 1972), pp. 20-1. On Pionius see H. Delehaye, *Les Passions des martyrs et les genres littéraires* (2nd edn. Brussels 1966), ch. 1, §1, esp. pp. 33-43. Was the copying of MSS at Marmoutier (*VM* 10, 6) conceived of as a task beneficial in itself?

[20] *VM* 1, 6; Paulinus, *ep.* 11, 11, and cf. *VM* 3, 3-4.

[21] *D* III, 10, 5. Cf. *D* I, 14, 8 and I, 22, 5. NB also Paulinus, *carmen* 15, 257-8: 'Nonne unus in omni / Christus adest sancto?' (*CSEL* 30, p. 62).

[22] *VM* 27, 7.

patron.[23] In his own lifetime, Martin had shown himself a powerful intercessor in the court of heaven: most notably, when his prayers that an unbaptized disciple should be restored to life were answered.[24] This role of heavenly patron for his followers received even clearer expression after Martin's death. When breaking news of this to Aurelius, Sulpicius described the vision in which he had seen Martin smiling and holding out to him the *Vita Martini*; he had then begged and obtained his usual blessing from Martin, and struggled to follow him and Clarus when they ascended into heaven. His vain efforts woke him, and it was at this moment that one of his lads came to tell him of Martin's death. Sulpicius broke down at this news, but then tried to console Aurelius and himself with the realization that Martin would still be present when men were talking of him or praying, and would protect them with his blessing as the vision he had just seen testified; for Clarus' ascent in the wake of his master proved that heaven was open to Martin's followers. Sulpicius himself had grave doubts of his ability to follow the holy man, but rested all his hopes upon the intercession of Martin: 'that what I am unable to obtain on my own, I may at least gain thanks to Martin's prayers for me.'[25]

Thus I would suggest that the motif of writing to gain an eternal reward had a far deeper and more personal meaning for Sulpicius than for the pagan historians, and the feelings it engendered were consequently all the more intense. Sulpicius' very being and future were intimately bound up with the person of Martin, who 'loved me . . . above all others.'[26] He had thrown up his career in the world as Martin had advised, thus drawing upon himself the hostility and incomprehension of his contemporaries. Yet he was aware of the differences between his own way of life and that of Martin, and therefore attributed all the more

---

[23] Cf. Fontaine, *Vie* I, 65. Sulpicius' vision of Martin holding the *Vita* and blessing him (*ep.* 2, 3-4) shows that Sulpicius felt that he had obtained Martin's blessing for his *VM*.

[24] *VM* 7.

[25] *Ep.* 2, 16-18. Cf. *ep.* 2, 8, 'Praemisi quidem patronum . . .' Cf. also *ep.* 3, 21. Cf. P. Brown, *The Cult of the Saints* (Chicago, London, 1981), pp. 54-68.

[26] *Ep.* 2, 14. Cf. *D* II, 13, 3-4.

importance to his literary work and to Martin's intercessory powers.[27]

There is one other way in which the *Vita Martini* may be more intimately bound up with Sulpicius' inner feelings than one might at first suppose. The conversions of both Paulinus and Sulpicius had aroused hostile comment; but whereas the former made a clean break with his old way of life by moving to Nola, Sulpicius remained in his native Aquitaine and refused all Paulinus' invitations to join him. Instead, he resolved to explain the course they had taken to the hostile world.[28] Paulinus disapproved of this aim and sought to dissuade him by quoting from the psalms which recalled a situation when the chosen people of God cut themselves off altogether from the heathen nations surrounding them:

'My brother, . . . let us pay no heed to the taunts and hatred of the unfaithful. . . . *The poison of asps is under their lips* . . . *Their heart is vain, their throat is an open sepulchre.* Let us beware their leaven, lest it corrupt the whole. For it is written, . . . *With the holy thou shalt be holy, and with the wicked thou shalt be perverted'.*[29]

Only those who came in humility and admitted their ignorance were to be helped. Those who were happy with their worldly life, their pleasures, careers, and wealth, should be left to their own devices.[30]

This letter was written early in 395 when Sulpicius was already working on his life of Martin; and, although the latter does not immediately strike us as Sulpicius' *apologia pro vita sua*, we should bear in mind that it was the first work produced by a man newly converted to the Christian asceticism which Martin exemplified; that it was written at a time when Sulpicius felt very sensitive to the hostility or incomprehension of the people around him, including, probably, his own father;[31] that the conversion of a well-born

---

[27] He claimed to have undertaken the writing of the *VM* partly to make up for the deficiencies in his own way of life: *VM* 1, 6.

[28] Paulinus, *ep.* 1, 4: 'Tu igitur qui laboras, ut scribis, rationem pro meo ac tuo facto reddere . . .'

[29] *Ep.* 1, 2, citing psalms 13, 3; 5, 10–11; and 17, 26 (*CSEL* 29, p. 3).

[30] *Ep.* 1, 4 & 7.

[31] 'Respuens patrimoniorum onera ceu stercorum . . . caelestem patrem anteverteras terreno parenti, exemplo apostolorum relicto patre in navicula

and well-educated man in the prime of his life to ascetic Christianity was still unusual enough to make it likely that the convert would wish to boost his own morale and to justify his decision in the eyes of the men amongst whom he lived; and that we know from Paulinus that Sulpicius was planning to explain their conversions at the very period when he was engaged upon the *Vita Martini*.

This means that the *Vita* is anything but the work of a *désengagé* author. While Martin was still alive a particularly close friendship had sprung up between the two men, and Sulpicius sought to model his whole way of life upon Martin's. Thus, in lovingly depicting his hero's life and ideals, Sulpicius was also setting out his own aspirations of which Martin was the living embodiment. Something of the depth of their relationship can be gauged by noting that not only Sulpicius' way of life, but also his theological and ecclesiastical ideas appear to derive from Martin. Striking concerns of Sulpicius are his preoccupation with the imminent end of the world, his condemnation of secular interference in ecclesiastical concerns, and his harsh criticism of the wealth, ambition, and avarice of the established church. In all three cases Sulpicius gives us evidence to show that Martin himself held these views;[32] and his depiction of Martin is in one sense a blueprint for his ideal of a Gallic bishop.

If we add to all this Sulpicius' dependence upon Martin as his advocate with God, it becomes perfectly understandable that criticisms of the *Vita Martini* should have cut him to the quick. Within a year came the sceptical query about the thaumaturge's inability to prevent himself from getting burnt, and in his first epistle Sulpicius immediately leapt to his hero's defence. He assimilated the critic to the perfidious Jews or accused him of the folly he had earlier

---

fluctuante, scilicet in huius vitae incerto cum retibus rerum suarum et inplicatione patrimonii derelicto Christum secutus', wrote Paulinus to Sulpicius in 396: *ep.* 5, 6. On father-complexes and holy men, see P. Brown, *JRS* 61 (1971), p. 99.

[32] Martin's teaching on the imminence of Antichrist, *D* II, 14, 1–4; Sulpicius' beliefs, *VM* 24, 3; cf. also *Chron.* II, 28, 1; 29, 5–6; 33, 3. Martin's opposition to government interference in an ecclesiastical case, *Chron.* II, 50, 5; Sulpicius', *D* I, 7, 2. Martin's views on the relative worth of bishops and ascetics are illustrated by *D* II, 12, 6, though I doubt whether his abhorrence of the ways of conventional bishops was as extreme as Sulpicius' (e.g. *D* I, 21, 3–4; *Chron.* I, 23, 5–6).

attributed to the pagans, while drawing a close parallel between Martin and the apostles Peter and Paul: like them, Martin had achieved greatness not the easy way, but through enduring hardships triumphantly; and he retold the offending story to illustrate his point. Shortly afterwards Martin must have died, for Sulpicius' next works were the two letters describing his vision at Martin's death, and the latter's godly end and triumphant funeral.[33] Here is the first fully-developed portrayal of Martin as a martyr *voto atque virtute*, albeit *sine cruore*: white martyrdom. Here also is the insistence on Martin's place in heaven, and his role as guardian for his faithful followers on earth.

(ii) The *Chronicle* and the *Dialogues*

Sulpicius' other two works, the *Chronicle* and the *Dialogues*, appear to be roughly contemporaneous with each other. The chronological axis of the former was the year of Stilicho's consulship, which fell in AD 400.[34] This suggests composition in that year and those immediately following. A further clue lies in the fact that the *Chronicle* uses material taken from a letter of Paulinus to Sulpicius, which was only written in 403.[35] J. Bernays argued that the extracts from this letter were added in to the *Chronicle* after the relevant part of the text (near the end) was already written.[36] His view has recently been challenged, though not disproved; in my eyes it remains likely, though certainty either way is impossible. In all events, this means that publication cannot have taken place till the latter half of 403 at the earliest. A *terminus ad quem* is suggested by the absence of any mention of the barbarian invasions which devastated Gaul from 406-7. This implies publication before the end of 406.

The *Dialogues* likewise have no mention of the barbarian invasions, and a definite *terminus ad quem* is given by Jerome's

---

[33] *Eps.* 2 and 3.

[34] *Chron.* II, 9, 7; II, 27, 5.

[35] *Ep.* 31, brought to Sulpicius in spring, 403: Lienhard, pp. 182-7.

[36] *Ueber die Chronik des Sulpicius Severus* (Berlin 1861), p. 3, n. 4. His view has been challenged by van Andel, pp. 51-2.

mention of them c.410/12.[37] A *terminus a quo* is provided
by Sulpicius' account of the Origenist controversy. Postumianus is represented as having just returned from a pilgrimage
to the east.[38] On his outward voyage three years previously,
his first port of call had been North Africa. Soon afterwards
he visited Alexandria at a time when the Origenist controversy had brought the patriarch and the monks into
confrontation, and the works of Origen had been banned
by episcopal synods.[39] This dates Postumianus' visit to
c.400, which gives a dramatic date for the *Dialogues* of
c.403; consonant with this is the mention by one of the
interlocutors of the *Dialogues* that it was then the eighth
year since Martin had voiced his views on Antichrist.[40]
The interest shown in the Origenist controversy suggests
that this passage was written while the latter was still a live
issue, and the natural assumption is therefore that the
Dialogues were written c.404-6: a dating which finds added
confirmation if my suggestion about the link between
Sulpicius' *Dialogues* and the Jerome-Vigilantius controversy
is accepted.[41]

There is some evidence to suggest that the *Dialogues* were
originally published in two instalments, as the last dialogue
shows a far greater concern for naming witnesses of Martinian
miracles, and explicitly states that this is due to the reputed
disbelief of many people, who are said to be dubious about
'some of the things which were recounted yesterday', i.e. the
contents of *Dialogues* I and II.[42] A further point is that,
originally, the *Dialogues* consisted of two parts, not the three
into which the work is divided in modern editions. These two
parts comprised (i) *Dialogues* I and II in Halm's edition; and
(ii) *Dialogue* III. Proof of this comes both from the earliest
manuscript tradition, and from the references of Gallic

---

[37] Above, ch. 2, n. 3.

[38] *D* I, 1, 1.

[39] *D* I, 6, 1. Theophilus' *volte-face* against Origen occurred in 399, and in 400
he convoked a synod condemning him. See A. Guillaumont, *Les 'Képhalaia
Gnostica' d'Évagre le Pontique et l'histoire de l'Origénisme* (Paris 1962), pp. 62-4.

[40] *D* II, 14, 4. As Martin died in November 397, this sets a *terminus ad quem*
of 405.

[41] Below, ch. 21.

[42] *D* III, 5, 2-3. This was noted by de Prato, I, 266.

writers of the fifth and sixth centuries who described the work, most notably Gennadius.[43] This division into two parts thus corresponds with what were probably two chronological instalments.

As for the scope, purpose, and public of these later works: the *Chronicle* gives a short history of the people of God, from the creation of the world to the time of writing. The first one and a half books deal with Old Testament events. Then, after a bare mention of Christ's birth and crucifixion and a rapid run-through of church history up to Constantine's accession, Sulpicius devotes the remaining nineteen chapters to the fourth-century church, especially the Arian and Priscillianist heresies. Martin is mentioned only for his role in the Priscillianist controversy. This sets the *Chronicle* somewhat apart from Sulpicius' other writings, which centre on Martin.

However, it is not wholly unrelated. Sulpicius' avowed aim in his *Chronicle* was 'to instruct the ignorant and to refute the learned', and this, coupled with his desire to retell the biblical story in classical style, shows that he was attempting to win over the educated to Christianity, just as in the *Vita Martini*.[44] Further, he selected his material from the Old Testament and from recent history in order to put across his own convictions about the church: particularly the incongruity of wealthy bishops, and the need for religious leaders to stand up to secular rulers and reject their interference in religious matters.[45] Both these convictions are strongly voiced in his Martinian works, where Martin is portrayed as the model bishop. Finally, in his *Chronicle* Sulpicius presented the bishops' fear of Priscillianism as their reason for regarding asceticism so unfavourably.

---

[43] de Prato, I, 266–8. In addition to the Verona and Brescia MSS used by de Prato, the 'D' text from the Book of Armagh (*c.*807) also illustrates the primitive division into two dialogues: *Liber Ardmachanus: the Book of Armagh* (ed. J. Gwynn, Dublin & London 1913), fol. 201v, and cf. fols. 210r and 215r.

[44] *Chron.* I, 1, 4. Van Andel further argues that Sulpicius' *Chron.* seeks to convert the educated before they are overtaken by the imminent end of the world (see esp. pp. 139–42). Given Sulpicius' expectations of the impending end, this may well be true, and van Andel's thesis is of great interest. However, he makes more of the subject than the reticence of Sulpicius' *Chron.* justifies.

[45] van Andel pp. 12, 14, 80–3, 94–5, 107–8, 115. Cf. *VM* 20 and n. 32 above.

Although he was careful to reject Priscillian's teaching, he indicated how the dissensions which had arisen over his trial and execution had so embittered church life that the true people of God (presumably Martin and his followers) found themselves insulted and scorned.[46] Here again we see a relationship between the *Chronicle* and the Martinian writings.

It is the latter, however, which are our primary concern: viz. the *Vita*, epistles, and *Dialogues*. As we have seen, the epistles grew out of the *Vita*, completing and defending its portrayal of Martin. In particular, the first epistle was explicitly written in reaction to a sceptical response to the earlier work. A similar background underlies the *Dialogues*,[47] where an apologetic purpose is far more in evidence than in the *Vita*. The scene is set by Postumianus' return from his travels in Africa, Egypt, and the Holy Land. Sulpicius asks him about the fortunes of asceticism in the east in comparison with its position in Gaul; for at home, practice of the ascetic life was thwarted by the bishops.[48] Thus, from the beginning of the *Dialogues* the contrast between the asceticism of Martin and his followers and the behaviour of the rest of the Gallic clergy is brought out into the open, and set against the background of the wider church: in particular, the customs and achievements of the monks of Egypt. Indeed, one of the main themes of the *Dialogues* is the comparison (syncrisis) between the *virtutes* of Martin and those of the Egyptians, with Sulpicius insisting that Martin had himself done everything that had been accomplished by all the Egyptian monks put together, and more, and that he had achieved this under far more trying circumstances.[49]

The *Dialogues* thus constitute an apologetic on two fronts simultaneously. On the one hand, they were written to bolster up the *Vita*'s portrayal of Martin in the face of scepticism and hostility from the Gallic clergy; on the other hand, they sought to portray Martin's asceticism as the same in kind as that practised by the Egyptian heroes of the desert, and to prove that Martin was second to none of them.

---

[46] *Chron.* II, 50-1.   [47] Cf. *ep.* 1, 2-4 and *D* I, 26, 4-6.
[48] *D* I, 2, 2-5.   [49] *D* I, 24-5; cf. II, 5, 1-2.

Greece may have had the apostle Paul, and Egypt any number of holy men; however, Martin alone was enough to ensure that Europe would not have to take second place to Asia.[50] In this connection, we may note a strong desire on Sulpicius' part to defend Gallic monasticism against the strictures of Jerome—or at least, while he readily admitted that Jerome's harsh comments on ascetic abuses had much bearing on the Gallic situation, Sulpicius took care to underline the strictness of Martin's own practices, which left nothing to be desired.[51]

In conclusion, we might say that the background to the writing of the *Vita* and *Dialogues* was similar, but not identical. Like the *Vita*, the *Dialogues* were written for ascetic circles in Gaul and beyond; but apologetic—and didactic[52]—concerns are more in evidence, and the interests of non-Gallic readers have been more obviously borne in mind. Like the *Vita*, the *Dialogues* were written with an eye to the contemporary Gallic church; but in the later work there is more direct criticism, where earlier this had just been implied by the contrasting virtues of Martin's life;[53] and, conversely, the concern to defend Martin is far clearer in the *Dialogues* than in the earlier work. As for the third category of readers postulated for the *Vita*, those cultured Gallo-Romans who were unwilling to exchange Virgil and Sallust for the Bible: they again were anticipated. Gallus feels it is appropriate to introduce a quotation from Statius, 'because we are talking amongst educated men', and there are also literary allusions to Terence, Sallust, and Virgil.[54] We may thus conclude that, in general, the audience and purpose of both *Vita* and *Dialogues* were similar; and the chief difference between them is that in the *Dialogues* the controversial nature of Martin's ideal is brought out into the open, whereas for most of the *Vita* it is simply implied. This difference was probably due partly to the reception

---

[50] *D* III, 17, 6–7.

[51] *D* II, 8, 2; cf. *D* I, 8, 4–9, 3.

[52] E.g. *D* I, 12, 1–2; II, 7, 1–8, 1; II, 12, 7–8.

[53] *D* I, 21; I, 26, 3–6; II, 12, 9–10, etc. *VM* has only ch. 27, 3–4.

[54] *D* III, 10, 4; I, 9, 3; I, 3, 3; II, 4, 5. Cf. also the literary affectation of apologizing for uncouth style: *D* I, 27, 1–5.

given to the *Vita*; partly, perhaps, to an increasing polarization of the differences between ascetics and bishops in Gaul between 396 and 406; and partly to a difference in genre. More will be said of these matters later on.

8

The Literary Forms of the Martinian Writings

As we seek to understand the literary form of Sulpicius' Martinian works, we need to bear in mind their many-sided background. This consists not just of Sulpicius' library, but also of the oral traditions which would have reached him, and the historical circumstances which surrounded the writing of each individual work. For instance, one idiosyncracy is that Sulpicius' portrayal of Martin consists not just of a *Vita*, but also of letters and dialogues. If we assumed that this was how Sulpicius had planned his work from the beginning, and then searched for literary precedents, we would get nowhere. Instead we should recall that the *Vita* was published before its hero's death, and so the two letters describing Martin's end and funeral were needed to round off its account; also, that the *Vita* idealized a controversial figure and was launched amid ecclesiastical dissension within Gaul, whence the need for its defence immediately, in epistle 1, and some years later, in the *Dialogues*. With this proviso regarding the importance of non-literary influences, let us now consider the literary form of the Martinian writings, and their relationship to the literary traditions of antiquity.

(i) The *Vita Martini*

The *Vita Martini* can be subdivided into four unequal parts:[1] (i) a dedicatory letter and preface setting out the aims and

---

[1] Cf. F. Kemper, *De vitarum Cypriani, Martini Turonensis, Ambrosii, Augustini rationibus* (Münster diss. 1904), p. 21; and, for a more complex schematization, Fontaine, *Vie* I, 88-96.

scope of the work (letter to Desiderius and *VM* 1); (ii) a chronological narration of Martin's life from birth to his election as bishop and establishment of the monastery of Marmoutier (2-10); (iii) an account of the miraculous deeds which Martin performed while bishop of Tours (11-24); and (iv) an account of Sulpicius' visit to Martin, which leads on naturally to a description of the latter's interior life and asceticism (25-7). Within this general framework section (iii) on Martin's miracles can be further subdivided, viz: (a) Martin combating false religion (11-15); (b) Martin's cures and exorcisms (16-19); (c) Martin and the Emperor Maximus (20); and (d) stories illustrating Martin's gift of *discretio spirituum* (21-4). The whole life shows traces of careful planning, and we have every reason to believe Sulpicius when he says he has been selective in his choice of material.[2]

Since the literary construction of the *Vita* was so clearly thought out, it is legitimate to ask what genre Sulpicius was following, and how he would have seen his work in relation to the literary traditions of antiquity. Fortunately, his dedicatory letter and preface provide a clear starting-point. Their meaning has been richly drawn out by Fontaine, who points to two main areas of concern on Sulpicius' part: first, his close attention to literary style; and secondly, his attitude to Roman historiography.[3] The opening sentences of Sulpicius' preface, as we have seen, pick up Sallust's aim of achieving *virtus* by writing, and proceed to redirect it to a specifically Christian goal. In the second part of the preface (*VM* 1, 6-9), the traditions of Roman historiography are even more in evidence. Sulpicius describes the task he has chosen and says something of the content of his work, and of its beneficial functions; and he also talks of his selectivity, and of his concern for truth. All this is typical enough of Roman historiography, as a glance through *Die Topoi in den Proömien der römischen Geschichtswerke*[4] reveals. In view of this, it is perhaps not surprising to find Paulinus of Nola describing the *Vita Martini* as a *historia*.[5]

---

[2] *VM* 1, 8; Fontaine, *Vie* I, 85, n. 1.
[3] *Vie* II, 359 ff.; also Voss, 'Berührungen', pp. 58 ff.
[4] By E. Herkommer (Tübingen diss. 1968), q.v.   [5] *Ep.* 11, 11.

I use the word 'perhaps' because in antiquity biography was generally regarded as belonging to a different genre from straight historiography. 'Whereas history describes in detail what its personages *do*, biography is more concerned with revealing what sort of person they *are*', and selects its material to that end.[6] We might add that the biographer, even more than the historian, aimed at readability rather than at historical precision. However, although this distinction between history and biography was widespread, it was not absolute: as the republic had given way to the principate, so individuals had come to dominate Roman historiography;[7] and where should we draw the line between Livy's history, Sallust's monographs, Tacitus' *Agricola*, and Suetonius' biographies? Seen against this background, it becomes less surprising to find Sulpicius unaware of any incongruity in placing his *vita* in the tradition of Sallust. Apart from this, the only other feature in his preface which smacks more of historiography than biography is his concern for truth.[8] His assertion, 'alioquin tacere quam falsa dicere maluissem' is reminiscent of Cicero's dictum that no historian 'quid falsi dicere audeat'.[9] However, Fontaine has pointed to a legal background for Sulpicius' plea that his readers should 'fidem dictis adhibeant'; and it may well be that we should regard Sulpicius' asseverations of truthfulness in the light of similar protestations in the *Dialogues*, and take it as a sign of genuine concern, not just a *topos*.[10]

In other respects, Sulpicius behaves like a typical biographer. Thus his concern not to overburden his readers is more a feature of biography than of historiography, and can be

---

[6] E. I. McQueen, in *Latin Biography*, ed. T. A Dorey (London 1967), p. 18; cf. E. Jenkinson on Nepos, ibid. p. 5. For late antiquity see A. Momigliano, 'L'età del trapasso fra storiografia antica e storiografia medievale (320–550 D.C.)', *Settimane di Studio* . . . 17 (Spoleto 1970), pp. 92-3.

[7] A. J. Woodman, *Velleius Paterculus* (Cambridge 1977), pp. 30-45; cf. McQueen, pp. 17-21; Momigliano, 'L'età', pp. 104-5.

[8] *VM* 1, 9 gives far more emphasis to this than does Athanasius' 'utrobique curam veritatis habens' (*PL* 73 cols. 127-8).

[9] *VM* 1, 9; Cicero *De orat.* II, (15,) 62: a work which Sulpicius had probably read (above, ch. 6, n. 22). According to Fontaine, the 'conpertum et probatum' of Sulpicius' preceding sentence is also Ciceronian (*Vie* II, 427).

[10] Fontaine, *Vie* II, 426-7; below, ch. 22.

paralleled from Nepos.[11] Biographical norms also help to account for his selection of material for the *Vita Martini*.[12] Sulpicius regarded Martin as 'sanctissimus', and, like many of his contemporaries, he assumed a direct correlation between holiness and the ability to work miracles. It was therefore natural for him to devote a large part of his account of Martin to miracle stories, which in his view 'reveal[ed] what sort of person' Martin was.

However, the most decisive evidence that Sulpicius was writing within the traditions of antique biography lies in the formal structure of the *Vita Martini*. As far back as 1904, Kemper sought to trace the Suetonian pattern of biography in the *Vita Martini*.[13] Since he wrote, the uniqueness and the characteristics of the Suetonian type of biography have been whittled down; but it still remains true that Suetonius was influential, and that he did on the whole write his lives according to a certain pattern, even if the latter often betrays variation. Typically, this pattern consists of a chronological account of the subject as far as the peak of his career, followed by a description *per species* of his achievements, and then of his personality.

Kemper regarded the *Vita Martini* as fitting into this schema, with chapters 2-9 giving a chronological account of Martin's life up to his attainment of office; chapters 10-24 describing his public life as a bishop; and chapters 24-7 describing his private life. Although Sulpicius never rigidly follows any model, and although he faced difficulties in accomodating the life of a monk-bishop to such a scheme,[14] used by Suetonius for emperors, I still think there is truth in Kemper's thesis, notwithstanding more recent arguments to

[11] XVI, 1, 1, cit. Jenkinson, in *Latin Biography*, loc. cit.
[12] Cf. Voss, 'Berührungen', p. 61 (although NB that the *VM* did have an apologetic aim, which also affected Sulpicius' choice of material).
[13] Kemper, pp. 41 ff.; cf. F. Leo, *Die griechisch-römische Biographie nach ihrer litterarischen Form* (Leipzig 1901), pp. 2 ff., esp. 8.
[14] E.g. W. Schatz, 'Studien zur Geschichte und Vorstellungswelt des frühen abendländischen Mönchtums' (Freiburg im Br. dissertation, 1957), p. 65, points out that all Martin's miracles wrought as a bishop depend on his asceticism, not his episcopal office. This is true, but it does not necessarily undermine Kemper's case. The inconsistency arises from the paradox of a monk-bishop; cf. below, pp. 94-5.

the contrary.[15] Sulpicius' own words in his preface, 'Igitur sancti Martini vitam scribere exordiar, ut se vel ante episcopatum vel in episcopatu gesserit', accurately describe his procedure, and are themselves an example of the rhetorical device of *divisio*, much loved by Suetonius.[16] Further, chapters 2–10 do contain a chronological account of Martin's career up to his election as bishop and foundation of Marmoutier; the following fourteen chapters devoted to his miraculous deeds as bishop are strictly arranged according to subject-matter;[17] and the final three chapters are about Martin's personality and way of life, with a possibly Suetonian echo in the phrase 'interiorem vitam illius et conversationem cotidianum'.[18]

The *Vita Martini* thus belongs to the tradition of antique biography. However, it is not just a biography, but a Christian biography. This much is a statement of the obvious. Yet, as soon as we reach after greater precision, we run up against conflicting opinions about how it should be categorized. Some scholars put it in a series of Latin episcopal lives, whose subjects are, respectively, Cyprian, Martin, Ambrose, and Augustine.[19] Others would differentiate sharply between a bishop's *vita* and a monk's *vita*, and would class the *Vita Martini* amongst the latter. The series then runs from Athanasius' *Vita Antonii* to Sulpicius' *Vita Martini*, and continues with Eugippius' *Commemoratorium* on Severinus,

[15] By Schatz, pp. 63–6; and G. Luck, 'Die Form der suetonischen Biographie und die frühen Heiligenviten', *Mullus*; Festschr. T. Klauser (= *Jb. f. Antike u. Christentum*, Ergänzungband I, 1964), p. 238. Although in *Vie* I, 65–6, Fontaine appears to be negative about the possibility of direct Suetonian influence on the *VM*, in *Vie* II, 423, he appears to go almost as far as I would go. I would agree with his remarks on p. 60 and n. 1.

[16] G. B. Townend, 'Suetonius and his Influence', in *Latin Biography*, ed. Dorey, pp. 84–6.

[17] Luck appears blind to this; and he is mistaken when he asserts that proper names often provide the cue for a new story (p. 238). Sulpicius' careful composition in the *Vita* is thrown into relief by the absence of any such attempt to bind his material together thematically (or chronologically) in the *Dialogues*. Cf. Fontaine *Vie*, I, 85, n. 1.

[18] *VM* 26, 2; cf. Suetonius, *Augustus* 61, 1, 'referam nunc interiorem ac familiarem eius vitam...' ed. H. Ailloud (Budé series, 3rd edn. Paris 1961) p. 113, noted by Luck loc. cit. The possibility that Sulpicius was here echoing Suetonius is increased by the fact that the phrase, 'interior vita', was apparently not yet in use in Christian spirituality; cf. Fontaine, *Vie* III, 1081 and n. 1.

[19] Kemper, and cf. Pellegrino (as above, ch. 6, n. 43), pp. 34 ff., esp. 37.

and Gregory the Great's *Dialogues*.[20] A third proposal, which leads to a somewhat similar classification, is to categorize lives on the basis of their attitude towards the miraculous. This entails a distinction between such works as the *Historia monachorum*, the *Lausiac History*, and the lives by Athanasius, Jerome, Sulpicius, and Eugippius on the one hand; and, on the other, the encomium-style lives such as those composed by Hilary of Arles and Ennodius of Pavia, with which Possidius' *Vita Augustini* and Ferrandus' *Vita Fulgentii* are also grouped on the grounds that they, like the encomia, betray little interest in miracles.[21]

With so many conflicting suggestions, it is as well to be clear precisely what Christian biographies were available in Latin at the time when Sulpicius was writing.[22] The oldest was the *Life of Cyprian*, written by Cyprian's deacon, Pontius, soon after the bishop's martyrdom in 258. Next, there was Evagrius' translation of Athanasius' *Life of Antony*. Finally, there were the three ascetic lives composed by Jerome: the *Vita Pauli*, written at Antioch between 374 and 382, and the *Vita Malchi* and *Vita Hilarionis*, both written at Bethlehem between 386 and 392. Sulpicius, as we have seen, knew all these lives with the probable exception of the *Vita Malchi*. However, of these five so-called 'lives', those about Cyprian, Paul, and Malchus are very different from the *Vita Martini*, and in some ways are not classifiable as lives at all.[23] Our concern therefore lies only with Athanasius' *Vita Antonii* and Jerome's *Vita Hilarionis*.

The *Vita Antonii* does not fit into any straightforward schema.[24] One can say that Athanasius' introductory letter forms a prologue; that chapters 1–4 tell in brief the story of Antony from his birth to his establishment as an ascetic; and that chapters 5–14 narrate his progress in the ascetic life

---

[20] Schatz, part I, esp. pp. 66–7; Mohrmann in *Vite dei Santi* III, pp. xxx ff.

[21] F. Lotter, *Severinus*, pp. 17, 50 ff., esp. 58.

[22] In general, see Pellegrino, pp. 7–30.

[23] On *V. Cypr.* see Pellegrino, pp. 75–83; Delehaye, *Les Passions*, pp. 69–77; and Mohrmann, *Vite dei Santi* III, pp. xii–xxvi. On Jerome's *vitae* see D. Hoster, *Die Form der frühesten lateinischen Heiligenviten* (Cologne Diss., 1963), pp. 50–69.

[24] The diverse suggestions of Holl and Reitzenstein are outlined by Schatz, pp. 27–40. The chapter nos. given refer to Athanasius' text, not Evagrius' tr.

and warfare against the demons, culminating in his glorious emergence after twenty years. Starting from the other end, chapters 89–94 tell of Antony's death and then summarize his achievements, concluding with an envoi. The middle section, however, comprising chapters 15–88, cannot be categorized so neatly. Its subject-matter illustrates two main themes. The first is Antony's charisma, which derives from God. His powers of wisdom, of discerning spirits, of knowing the future and having visions, and of healing, are all instances of this charisma. Secondly, these chapters show Antony encouraging, teaching, and helping the martyrs, the monks, and people still living in the world—including even emperors; but yet withdrawing periodically for further *askesis* and wrestling with the demons. There is much that is didactic here, but it also illustrates Antony's fame and popularity, and how he coped with it. Within this long section there are, of course, some groupings that can be made: e.g. Antony's sermon, which consists of an exhortation to monks, largely on demons (chs. 16–43); the fruits of Antony's spiritual gifts, including miracles (chs. 56–66); his dispute with the philosophers (chs. 72–80). Yet basically this material is not arranged schematically,[25] and there are some chapters which relate rather to a chronological ordering, such as those concerned with his visits to Alexandria (chs. 46, 69–71). An approximate chronology is also implied by Antony's periodical public appearances, which are interspersed with solitary retreats, first near his native village, then in the tombs, next in a fort in the desert, and finally in his inner mountain. One might say, then, that the life follows a rough chronological pattern, from Antony's birth to his death; but that within this basic pattern Athanasius has grouped together some chapters devoted to similar themes.

Jerome's *Life of Hilarion* is far easier to break down into a regular schema, consisting of seven sections: (i) a preface (ch. 1); (ii) a brief narrative covering Hilarion's life from birth to conversion (chs. 2–3); (iii) Hilarion's ascetic life and warfare against the demons (chs. 4–12); (iv) Hilarion's miracles (chs. 13–23); (v) his guidance of Palestinian monasticism

---

[25] E.g. instances of Antony's wonderful deeds occur in chs. 15, 48, 56–66, 70–1, 82–4.

(chs. 24-29); (vi) his wanderings to escape fame (chs. 30-43); (vii) his death and translation (chs. 44-47).[26] Jerome sees Hilarion's life as falling into distinct phases, and this has enabled him to tell the story both chronologically and, to some extent, *per species.*

If we compare the *Vita Martini* to these two works, certain differences are immediately apparent. First, there is no conversion to asceticism on the part of Martin. He may have wanted to become a monk when he was only twelve;[27] but in fact he remained with his parents, and then entered the army. He may, like Antony, have heard the Christian message that he should take no thought for the morrow;[28] but whereas this prompted Antony to give away his remaining property and adopt the ascetic life, Martin remained a soldier, fulfilling the precept by giving away half his cloak. The break with his past life came rather when he confronted the Caesar Julian with the words, 'Christi ego miles sum: pugnare mihi non licet.'[29] But here the similarities are with the accounts of martyrs, not of monks; and Martin does not immediately adopt an ascetic life, but simply goes to seek out the bishop of Poitiers. When at last we do hear of Martin establishing himself in a monastery, Sulpicius gives us no hint that he sees this as in any way marking a new phase in Martin's life.[30] In fact, the way in which Sulpicius tells the story of Martin's life presents his election as bishop and foundation of Marmoutier as the turning-point. Up to chapter 9, we have a straightforward chronological account, as we have seen, while from chapter 11 onwards the material is arranged under topics. This arrangement necessarily differentiates the *Vita Martini* from the lives of Antony and Hilarion: while the latter each have but a single chapter covering their hero's life from birth to conversion, Sulpicius has seven such chapters, which in effect makes the first two-fifths of his *Vita* a chronological account.

---

[26] A similar breakdown is given by Hoster, pp. 70 ff., esp. p. 79.

[27] *VM* 2, 4. Cf. below, ch. 11.

[28] *V. Ant.* 3; *VM* 2, 8.

[29] *VM* 4, 3; cf. below, ch. 10.

[30] *VM* 6, 4. The same might be said of Martin's foundation of Ligugé, *VM* 7, 1.

This difference in formal arrangement is mirrored by a rather different subject-matter in these lives. We do not see Martin making progress in the ascetic life, as had Antony and Hilarion; the emphasis goes rather on Martin's *constantia*, and the continuities of his life from childhood to old age.[31] Also, although the devil does figure in the *Vita Martini*, his opposition is not so closely linked to Martin's pursuit of the ascetic life as it is for Antony, Hilarion, and other eastern monks. There are indeed two parts of the *Vita Martini* where eastern parallels do spring to mind, both concerned with the devil's appearances to Martin. The first comes in the chronological part of the *vita*, telling how Martin left Hilary to go and convert his parents. *En route* he encountered the devil in human guise, who promised him permanent opposition in his life of service to God. Martin put him to flight with the same verse of scripture as Antony had used against the demon of fornication, who had appeared to him as a black boy. Apart from the scriptural citations, however, there is little in common between the two accounts.[32] The second consists of chapters 21-4, illustrating Martin's charisma of *discretio spirituum*, the discernment of spirits. As we shall see, eastern ascetic modes of thought are indeed relevant, although they are not the only influences discernible in these chapters.[33]

Apart from these relatively few cases, however, we cannot fasten upon the miracle stories of the *Vita Martini* as being specifically those proper to a monk *as opposed to* a bishop.[34] The point is, that Sulpicius was concerned to present Martin as a true monk *and* a true bishop. He makes no secret of the fact that he feels that all bishops in Gaul should live as Martin lived, even to the extent of owning no property—a fact which suggests that he thought monk-bishops should be the norm. Martin, alone of all the Gallic bishops, possessed *apostolica auctoritas*: an episcopal authority which was

[31] *V. Ant.* 3-14; *V. Hil.* 4-11, and 32. For Martin, see *VM* 10, 1-2; Fontaine, *Vie* I, 63-4; II, 661-2, III, 1321; and below, ch. 11. I cannot agree with Schatz, p. 67.

[32] *VM* 6, 1-2; *V. Ant.* tr. Evagrius, ch. 4; see Delehaye, 'S. Martin', p. 45.

[33] Below, ch. 17, ii.

[34] In this the *VM* resembles, rather than differs from, the *V. Ambrosii*, despite Mohrmann, *Vite dei Santi* III, pp. xxx ff. esp. xxxiv.

founded precisely upon his ascetic virtues of humility and *constantia* in the face of the court's attempts to cultivate him.[35] What is more, it is precisely this quality of apostolicity which reappears apropos of one of his healing miracles.[36] Martin may indeed use the weapons of asceticism in order to influence God and thus 'miraculously' achieve his aims; but these aims are those of a bishop, a pastor of his people. Thus we see Martin healing the sick and the possessed as Jesus had done, and overthrowing pagan temples so that he could found churches or monasteries in their place, as other bishops were to do. Martin's asceticism is indeed an asceticism harnessed to the service of the church, and this to a far greater extent than we find in the lives of Antony or Hilarion.[37] Thus as far as the content of the *Vita Martini* is concerned, it is but a half-truth to describe it as a monk's *vita*: it is that of a monk-bishop.

To return now to the question of structure, we must surely conclude that Sulpicius' arrangement of material in the *Vita Martini* owes nothing to the *Vita Antonii*: the former's chronological first part, followed by its account of Martin's miracles as a bishop arranged *per species*, has no parallel in Athanasius' work.[38] The correspondence with the *Vita Hilarionis* is slightly stronger, in that Jerome does at least group together Hilarion's miracles wrought in Palestine. However, these are not arranged *per species*, so much as to illustrate the growth of Hilarion's fame;[39] and there is no equivalent to Sulpicius' final chapters on Martin's interior life. Parallels in the arrangement of subject-matter are therefore very limited. Thus, in terms of formal structure, the *Vita Martini* is closer to Suetonius' *De vita Caesarum* than to any of the Christian biographies that Sulpicius would have known.[40]

[35] Cf. *VM* 20, 1-7 and 10, 1-2.

[36] *VM* 7, 7 and note by J. W. Smit ad loc., *Vite dei Santi* IV, p. 269.

[37] Cf. P. Rousseau, 'The Spiritual Authority of the "Monk-Bishop"', *JTS* n.s. 22 (1971), pp. 406-19; Pellegrino, pp. 42-4.

[38] So also Fontaine, *Vie* I, 70-1.

[39] Cf. Hoster, p. 74.

[40] As for the question of why Sulpicius should have preferred the Suetonian model to that of *V. Ant.* or *V. Hil.*: I would suggest that it was partly because Suetonius was the biographical norm for Latin speakers; partly because Sulpicius

The real parallels between the three saints' lives we have been discussing lie not in the sphere of literary form, but, to a certain extent, in the content and the intention of these lives. We should be thinking in terms of the very idea of writing the life of a holy man, of propagating the ascetic ideal in this way, and of 'proving' one's hero's holiness through the sort of stories one told about him. Thus Jerome wrote his *Vita Pauli* and *Vita Hilarionis* largely in response to Athanasius' *Vita Antonii*. The *Vita Martini* has a far more complex background than this, and, as far as its content is concerned, it is the life not just of a monk, but of a monk-bishop. However, the fact remains that Sulpicius was also very aware of the ascetic *vitae* of Athanasius and Jerome, as his *Dialogues* show. There, he demonstrates that Martin has outdone the ascetics of Egypt in his miracles, and therefore that he is able to rank alongside the most perfect of the eastern monks. This means, of course, that the lives of eastern monks probably influenced Sulpicius' choice of stories about Martin, and the general way in which he presented his hero.[41] But does this have anything to do with literary genres? Or, to put it more precisely: should the early saints' lives which contain many miracle stories (such as those about Antony, Hilarion, and Martin) *ipso facto* be differentiated from those (such as the *Vita Augustini*) which do not?

In order to understand such a question we must make a detour from fourth-century saints' lives, in order to glance briefly at the ultimate forerunners that have been suggested for them. This involves going back to the Hellenistic period, when some pagan cult sites had a professional class of functionaries called οἱ ἀρεταλόγοι, whose task was ἀρετὰς λέγειν, i.e. to publicize the miracles wrought there by the gods. Collections of such miracles were kept in book form, and modern scholars have coined the term 'aretalogies' to

---

may have been unsure of the chronology of many of M's miracles; and partly, because if he had told the story chronologically, it might have been difficult not to end on a decrescendo (see *D* III, 13 3–6; cf. Babut *St. Martin*, chs. 3 and 4; below, ch. 24). I do not think it implies that Sulpicius saw M's episcopate as turning him into an official: see below, ch. 11.

[41] Cf. above, ch. 7, ii; ch. 5; and below, ch. 17, ii.

describe such collections.[42] This much is now generally accepted. In 1906, however, Reitzenstein attempted to give a far broader currency to the term aretalogy by designating as such those miraculous accounts of prophets and philosophers which were legendary in character, and lacked both a coherent formal structure and historical accuracy.[43] In such works, miracle story was piled on miracle story, and although the authors might seek to present their accounts as historical, this meant nothing. Their sincerity was confined to their pious intentions, for they told the stories primarily for the purpose of religious edification, and to arouse wonder at the miracles recounted. Such aretalogies could be found in both the pagan and the Jewish-Christian traditions. As regards the former, Reitzenstein pointed to the *Life of Apollonius of Tyana*, and the presumed models which Lucian was parodying in his *Alexander, Death of Peregrinus*, and *Philopseudes*. For the latter, after pin-pointing the odd parallel to these works in the canonical and especially the apocryphal acts of the apostles, he concentrated primarily on early monastic literature: i.e. the lives by Athanasius and Jerome, and such compendious works as the *Historia monachorum* and *Lausiac History*.

A fundamental weakness of this 'aretalogical' approach lies in its confusion between literary genre on the one hand, and content on the other. Even the proponents of 'aretalogy' admit that antiquity did not recognize any precise literary genre of this name.[44] This being so, the extended use of this word by modern scholars serves only to confuse the issue by implying the existence of a coherent body of material, which, on examination, turns out not to exist.[45] Properly, we should adopt only those distinctions between literary genres which were recognized in the period with which we are dealing; and

[42] Nock, *Conversion*, pp. 83-93, esp. p. 89; Morton Smith, 'Prolegomena to a discussion of Aretalogies, Divine Men, the Gospels and Jesus', *Journal of Biblical Literature* 90 (1971), pp. 174 ff. H. C. Kee, 'Aretalogy and Gospel', ibid. 92 (1973) pp. 403-4.

[43] *Hellenistische Wundererzählungen* (Leipzig), pp. 1-99. Babut followed Reitzenstein's lead: *St. Martin*, pp. 89-108.

[44] Reitzenstein, p. 98, 'das Wort Aretalogie . . . das im Altertum vielleicht nicht einmal ganz in diesem Umfange verwendet worden ist'; Smith, pp. 175-6, 195-6.

[45] See Kee, esp. pp. 404-9.

this means that we should reserve the word 'aretalogy' strictly for a collection of miracle stories such as was kept at Hellenistic cult sites.

Despite this, some modern scholars are prepared to follow Reitzenstein's lead. Thus Lotter sees a parallel with Hellenistic aretalogy in Jerome's decision 'proprias narrare virtutes' of Hilarion, in contrast to Epiphanius' brief letter which simply praised him 'locis communibus'.[46] From here he goes on to Sulpicius' *Dialogues*, where it is said that Gallus 'Martini narrasse virtutes'; and he sees this idea, that the hagiographer's task was the narration of miracle stories, as dominating many other early saints' lives. Over against this thaumaturgical tradition of hagiography, Lotter also distinguishes a different, non-miraculous tradition, which is represented by the encomia on Honoratus and Hilary of Arles. In these, virtue was shown not in thaumaturgy, but in a readiness 'signa fugere et occultare virtutes'. In the same non-thaumaturgical tradition Lotter would place the lives of Epiphanius of Pavia, Augustine of Hippo, and Fulgentius of Ruspe. He recognizes that in terms of literary form, the latter two lives belong to a different tradition from the others, which are encomia. However, the distinction which he makes rests not on literary form, but on the way in which the subject's personality is conceived, and the justification for honouring him as a saint.

But did men of the fourth and fifth centuries themselves distinguish between lives that gave a pre-eminent place to miracles, and those that did not? Or are we simply projecting our own categories on to the consciousness of those living a millenium and a half ago? Certainly, Jerome's preface to the *Vita Hilarionis* will not bear the meaning which Lotter invests it with. The natural interpretation is that whereas Epiphanius has praised Hilarion with all the commonplaces which literary convention demanded, Jerome intends to say something of Hilarion's own specific *virtutes*.[47]

To illuminate the question of how men of that period regarded the various types of Christian *vitae* then being written, let us turn to Paulinus of Milan's preface to his *Vita Ambrosii*:

[46] *Vita Hilarionis* 1, (*PL* 23, col. 29); Lotter, pp. 50–9.
[47] So, also, *Vite dei Santi* IV, pp. 73–5, and cf. p. xli.

'You urge, revered father Augustine, that just as the blessed men Athanasius the bishop and Jerome the priest set down the lives of holy men living in the wilderness, Paul and Antony, as also the life of Martin, the revered bishop of Tours, was composed in fine prose by Severus, servant of God, so I too should set down the life of the blessed Ambrose, bishop of the church at Milan.'[48]

Apparently Paulinus—and Augustine—saw no incongruity in adding the life of a great bishop to this series of monks' and monk-bishops' lives. The next stage in the development of Latin monk-bishops' lives comes with Possidius of Calama's *Vita Augustini*, written a decade or so later, in the 430s. Although Possidius does not explicitly name his predecessors, he refers to how a similar task of writing *vitae* about similar Christian figures has previously been carried out 'a religiosissimis sanctae matris ecclesiae catholicae viris'; and this must refer to the *Life of Ambrose*, which Augustine had commissioned, and beyond that to the *Vita Martini*, and, in all likelihood, the *Vita Cypriani*.[49]

With the lives of Martin, Ambrose, and Augustine, we thus have a nascent tradition of *vitae* devoted to western bishops, two of whom were also monks. Precisely because the authors of the two later lives were conscious of belonging to this tradition, and because the situation of all three subjects was so similar, it is instructive to compare them. When we do so, we can discern some similarities in their arrangement: preface; chronological account from birth to consecration/ordination; deeds as bishop; personal life; death.[50] However, the *content* of the main part of these lives, i.e. the deeds performed as bishop, is very dissimilar. In the *Vita Martini* we hear largely of Martin's campaigns against paganism, his healings and exorcisms, and his encounters with the devil; and the stories are chosen in such a way as to throw Martin's *virtutes*, his thaumaturgical powers, into strong relief. The *Vita Ambrosii* certainly contains plenty of miracles; but the primary emphasis goes on upholding the power and dignity of the catholic church against the state, and against heretics. There are thus many stories illustrating Ambrose's firm stand against

---

[48] 1, 1 (*Vite dei Santi* III, p. 54).
[49] *V. Aug.* praef. 2 (*Vite dei Santi* III, p. 130). Cf. Kemper, p. 38.
[50] Kemper, p. 41.

emperors, and many illustrating the discomfiture of his adversaries. The *Vita Augustini* focuses even more on one major theme: that of how Augustine's ceaseless work of expounding the word of God was responsible for the building up of the catholic church, and the weakening of heretical groups. Of course, the emphases given by our three biographers would have arisen in part out of the character of their subjects' lives: Martin did do much to destroy paganism around Tours; Ambrose, as bishop of the imperial capital, certainly played an important role *vis-à-vis* the imperial court; and the centrality to Augustine's episcopate of his expounding the word of God and combating heresies is evident from other sources. None the less, there are large areas of these bishops' lives of which their biographers say nothing, such as Martin's daily round as a bishop, or Ambrose's patronage of asceticism, or the repercussions of the sack of Rome on Augustine, which led to his writing the *De civitate Dei*.

The conclusion I would draw is that all three of these lives were selective; and that the authors made their selection on the basis of what seemed important to them, and what fitted in with their own intentions in writing. Of the three biographers, only Paulinus of Milan gives the impression of being scarcely the master of his material, and he is also the only one to write at the behest of another. As a result, his *Vita Ambrosii* is more a straightforward setting down of what he remembers about his former bishop than a deliberately contrived interpretation of Ambrose's achievements and significance.[51] With Sulpicius and Possidius, however, things were different. Each constructed his work carefully, selecting his material to fit in with his aims. Sulpicius, as we see elsewhere, was writing his Martinian works against a complex background of hostility towards much that Martin stood for; and, as he wished to demonstrate his hero's perfection as a monk and bishop, he had a particular reason for concentrating on the latter's miracles, which 'proved' his holiness.

However, the background to Possidius' *Vita Augustini* was quite different. Here, it was not so much Augustine, as the

---

[51] Cf. J.-R. Palanque, 'La *Vita Ambrosii* de Paulin', *Revue des sciences religieuses* 4 (1924), esp. pp. 40–41, 409–16.

church, which needed to be upheld. For Possidius wrote at a time when the Vandals were sweeping across North Africa, burning churches as they went, and these calamitous years may well have seen a recrudescence of Donatism.[52] It is therefore small wonder that Possidius laid such emphasis on Augustine's strengthening of the catholic church. It was this, Augustine's channelling of his talents to the building up of the corporate church, that concerned Possidius: not so much the holiness of Augustine as an isolated individual. Also, it would seem likely that Possidius had imbibed his master's outlook on miracles; and that, while not disbelieving in them, he regarded them as of lesser importance than the possession of moral qualities. Thus, like Sulpicius, he selected his material to suit his objectives; but, unlike Sulpicius, miracle stories as such did not directly contribute to his objectives, and therefore he did not focus attention on them.

My conclusions from a comparison of these three lives are that we cannot profitably distinguish between them in such a way as to subdivide early Christian biography into distinct categories along Lotter's lines. The prefaces to the lives of Ambrose and Augustine show that contemporaries themselves made no such distinctions, whether between monks' lives and bishops' lives, or between more hagiographical lives and more historical lives. There seems to be no good reason for treating miracle stories as a 'special case', and classifying lives that contain them as different in kind from other lives. In late antiquity, all Christians accepted the reality of God's intervention in the course of human events, and 'miracle stories' were therefore regarded as no less 'historical' than other stories. The old classical conventions of historiography, which designated such material as 'superstitio' and excluded it from history proper, were of little relevance to Christians; for these would look back to the Gospels for the prototype of a life under God, showing forth many signs of God's power.[53]

[52] W. H. C. Frend, *The Donatist Church* (Oxford 1952), p. 229 and n. 1, pp. 301 ff.; cf. R. A. Markus, 'Donatism: the Last Phase', *Studies in Church History* 1, ed. Dugmore and Duggan (London 1964), pp. 118–26.

[53] A. Momigliano, 'Popular Religious Beliefs and the Late Roman Historians', in his *Essays in Ancient and Modern Historiography* (Oxford 1977), pp. 141–59; W. den Boer, in *Studia Patristica* IV, ed. F. L. Cross (= *Texte u. Untersuchungen* 79), 1961, p. 354. Cf. below, chs. 15 & 16.

In the fourth century, the genre of hagiography was still a new one, which had arisen under new circumstances. The age of persecutions was now over, and other Christian ideals were being put forward to take the place of the martyr ideal. However, at this period, the traits and the type of life that characterized the 'holy man' were still a matter of debate. Was he a martyr? A bishop? A hermit who lived entirely on his own, having no contact with other men? Or a monk who was ready to teach and help those who sought him out, and to spend some time guiding other people? The simultaneous existence of many different holy-man ideals led to the constant adaptation of *vita* forms, with each author making his own selection and presentation of material in accordance with his own ideas.[54] Soon, the genre of hagiography would settle down to its long and successful reign in a culture where people knew what its norms were, and what sort of birth and achievements a man must be credited with if he were to be acclaimed as a saint. But around 400 AD we are still in the formative period of hagiography; and the vitality and diversity of the new genre is richly illustrated by the fact that it could include works as unlike as Jerome's *Vita Pauli* on the one hand, and on the other, Possidius' *Vita Augustini*.

(ii) The *Epistles* and *Dialogues*

It is not necessary to say much about the literary form of Sulpicius' epistles, other than that they complement the *Vita*, and should be read in conjunction with it. The letter form had been used by Christians since the days of St. Paul, and our earliest accounts of martyrs' passions occur in letters from the churches of Lyons and Vienne, and of Smyrna. This is perhaps relevant for the context of epistles 2 and 3. Even more apposite for the literary background of epistle 2 is the classical genre of consolation literature, which was taken over by Christian writers and blossomed in the later fourth century. Of the Latin writers of that period, Ambrose, Jerome, and Paulinus of Nola all made use of it, often in letters; and it is

<hr />

[54] Hoster, pp. 145, 159-61, 83.

to this tradition that Sulpicius' letter to Aurelius belongs.[55]
Rather different is Sulpicius' first letter, which seeks to
answer the scepticism of an unnamed man over Martin's
thaumaturgical powers. This is an open letter dealing with
one specific incident in Martin's life. Here, we see the
flexibility of the letter form, which could be used to answer
specific criticisms as well as to supplement the *Vita*.

More important than the literary form of the epistles is
that of the *Dialogues*. Sulpicius himself says that he has
adopted this form only for literary reasons: 'But although
I adopted the dialogue form, whereby the reading might
gain in variety, and in order to relieve tedium, I declare
that I conscientiously secure the historical truth (nos pie
praestruere profitemur historiae veritatem).'[56] The setting
is the return of Sulpicius' friend, Postumianus, after three
years of pilgrimage in the east. Postumianus then retails the
story of his journey, and discusses the Origenist controversy
and St. Jerome.[57] There follow some twelve chapters recounting miracles which Postumianus had seen or heard of
while in Egypt, interspersed with one pointing the contrast
to Gaul, where churchmen were dogged by vanity.[58] These
miraculous achievements of the ascetics of Egypt are then
contrasted with those of Martin, who is shown to be superior
to the Egyptians in that he alone performed all the different
kinds of miracles which individual ascetics had worked in
Egypt; that he did this despite the most unfavourable conditions, surrounded as he was by obstreperous churchmen;
and that he alone raised the dead to life.[59] Then, at the
insistence of Postumianus and Sulpicius, a disciple of Martin
called Gallus launches into an account of those *virtutes* of
Martin which Sulpicius has omitted from his earlier writings,
and which Gallus claims to have witnessed with his own
eyes.[60] There follow fourteen chapters about Martin's deeds,
including quite a long section illustrating Martin's ideals

---

[55] See C. Favez, *La Consolation latine chrétienne* (Paris 1937).
[56] *D* III, 5, 6.
[57] *D* I, chs. 3-9.
[58] Egypt: *D* I, chs. 10-20 & 22. Gaul: *D* I, 21.
[59] *D* I, 24-5.
[60] *D* I, 26, 7-27, 8.

about women and marriage;[61] this story-telling only ended with evening, when the arrival of a visitor was announced. The following day the stream of stories about Martin was continued, this time before a larger audience; again the story-telling ran on until the setting of the sun concluded the session.[62]

Within this framework, there are two outstanding features of the *Dialogues*: one is the number of asides explicitly attacking the Gallic church of the day, or referring to its hostility;[63] the second is the open avowal that the aim is to prove Martin's superiority in *virtus* to that of the Egyptian ascetics.[64] Apart from these two features, the content of those parts devoted to Martin is very similar to that of the *Vita*: in both works we have tales of Martin destroying pagan temples, healing the sick, raising the dead, exorcizing the possessed, and being visited by saints, angels, and demons. Both works contain stories which are equally miraculous, and we should therefore reject the view which, while regarding the *Vita* as belonging to the Roman biographical tradition, which was an offshoot from historiography, none the less classifies the *Dialogues* as a *Wundertatenbericht*.[65]

Elsewhere, in fact, this same scholar discusses the *Dialogues* at greater length, and there portrays them as the outcome of a synthesis between two different genres:[66] on the one hand, the *hochliterarisch* dialogue, whose proper subject-matter had originally been philosophy; on the other hand, the popular *Reise-Erzählung*, which also went to the making of the *Historia monachorum* and *Historia lausiaca*. Traces of the influence of Ciceronian dialogues are certainly discernible. However, rather than the *Reise-Erzählung*, I would invoke the general tradition of Christian literature, particularly the Bible and the nascent tradition of hagiography which we have already discussed; and as well as the philosophical dialogue of Ciceronian type, I would raise the question of classical

---

[61] *D* II, 6, 1-8, 5; II, 10, 4-12, 11.

[62] *D* II, 14, 5 - III, 1, 8. *D* III, 17, 1.

[63] *D* I, 2, 2-5; I, 8, 4-9, 3; I, 12, 2; I, 21; I, 24, 3; I, 26, 3-6 etc.

[64] *D* III, 2, 2; I, 24-6; II, 5, 1-2; III, 17, 7.

[65] Voss, 'Berührungen', pp. 60-1, 68-9. See appendix below for a table allowing easy comparison of miracle stories in *VM* and in *D*.

[66] Voss, *Dialog*, p. 312.

biography in dialogue form.[67] One Greek life in dialogue form, dating from the third century BC, has been found; and it may be that this type of biography was not as unknown as the chances of survival imply. Shortly after Sulpicius' *Dialogues* on Martin, a Greek author, Palladius, wrote a *Dialogus de vita S. Joannis Chrysostomi*. Thus, on the question of literary form, I would suggest that Sulpicius' casting of his material as a dialogue owes something to the Roman dialogue tradition of Cicero and Minucius Felix; and something, probably, to a surviving classical tradition of biography in dialogue form.

Thus, on the basis of the content of the main body of Sulpicius' *Dialogues*, (which is much the same as the content of chapters 11-24 of the *Vita Martini*); and on the basis of other lives written in dialogue form in antiquity, I would suggest that we see the *Dialogues* as belonging, at least in large part, to the genre of biography.[68] However, there is more to Sulpicius' choice of this particular form of biography than a simple desire for variety, or even the fact that such variety was forced on him by the impractibility of writing two *vitae* of the same man. One point, made by Père Delehaye,[69] is that the dialogue form was less hidebound by literary conventions than straight biography, and this made it easier for Sulpicius to give historical details: he was free to quote Martin's own words and to specify people by name in a way which would have been considered bad taste in biography.[70] This was particularly important as the veracity of Sulpicius' portrayal of Martin had come under fire, and it was therefore crucial for him to be able to name eyewitnesses for the deeds he recorded.[71] Further, not only was Sulpicius trying to buttress his account against the

[67] See P. R. Coleman-Norton, 'The Use of Dialogue in the *Vitae Sanctorum*', *JTS* 27 (1926), pp. 388-95. Cf. Momigliano, 'L'età del trapasso', p. 94; *The Development of Greek Biography* (Cambridge, Mass. 1971) pp. 47 and 80.

[68] See now P. L. Schmidt, 'Zur Typologie und Literarisierung des frühchristlichen lateinischen Dialogs', in *Christianisme et formes littéraires de l'antiquité tardive en occident*, Fondation Hardt *entretiens*, vol. 23 (Geneva 1977), esp. pp. 121-4, who groups together the dialogues of Sulpicius and Gregory the Great as 'hagiographical dialogues'.

[69] 'S. Martin', pp. 82-3.

[70] Delehaye, loc. cit. Quoting Martin's words: *D* II, 11, 3-7.

[71] *D* III, 5, 2-3; cf. I, 27, 8. Below, ch. 22.

scepticism of readers; he was also trying to argue a case that Martin was superior to the Egyptian ascetics, and to bring home to Gallic churchmen that there were many things wrong with the Gallic church of his own day, and that they could do worse than learn from the example of Martin. Biography was no stranger to apologetics in the ancient world, and it had already been used by Nepos as a vehicle for comparing Greek and Roman men and achievements.[72] Indeed, syncrisis (comparison) was a literary commonplace of the biographical encomium. Even more pertinent is Jerome's use of biography to challenge the undisputed primacy of Antony as the first monk, and to insist that a Syrian saint, Hilarion, was in every way as good as the Egyptian 'father of monasticism'. This provides a forerunner for Sulpicius' use of biographical material to make a (favourable) comparison between the Egyptian ascetics and Martin.[73]

For this purpose, the dialogue form was even more apposite than straight biography: it is admirably suited for discussion and controversy, as Palladius' dialogue about John Chrysostom illustrates. I would suggest that its adoption by Sulpicius was partially due to this attribute. By giving the bulk of the narrative to Postumianus and Gallus, Sulpicius was able to avoid direct responsibility for the views put forward.[74] It is interesting to note that Gennadius describes Sulpicius' *Dialogues* as a '*Conlationem Postumiani et Galli* se mediante et iudice de conversatione monachorum Orientalium et ipsius Martini'. Minucius Felix's dialogue *Octavius*, which may well have influenced Sulpicius, likewise consists of a disputation.[75]

The *Dialogues* thus comprise a subtle combination of additional biographical material about Martin, coupled with arguments and defence of an apologetic nature. The latter feature is more marked than in the *Vita*, but, ultimately, the two works both bear witness to the same complex

---

[72] Momigliano, *Development*, p. 98; NB that Nepos' biographies were still being read in late antiquity (ibid. p. 99).

[73] See above, ch. 6, n. 72, and below, ch. 21, n. 53.

[74] See *D* I, 9, 3; II, 8, 3–4.

[75] Gennadius, *De vir. inl.* 19 (ed. Richardson, p. 69). *Octavius*: above, ch. 6, n. 39.

background. Like the *Vita*, the *Dialogues* owe their existence in their present form both to the cultural traditions of antiquity, and to the particular historical circumstances out of which Sulpicius wrote.

PART II

SULPICIUS' MARTIN: SOME PROBLEMS

9

The Chronology of Martin's Life

When we turn from Sulpicius to look at his presentation of Martin, we encounter certain difficulties. The most basic of these concerns the chronology of Martin's life, and this will be tackled first of all.

It may be asked why so much space needs to be given to so humdrum a subject. The need stems in the first place from the chronological confusion of our sources. Of course, if it were just a matter of a year here or a few months there, it could probably be left to the footnotes. But, alas, Sulpicius' Martinian writings harbour a chronological discrepancy of some twenty years; and it is clearly important to our understanding of Martin to know, for instance, whether he was a soldier for five, or twenty-five, years.

There is also a further, more intriguing reason for our concern. In 1912 Babut suggested that the inconsistencies of Sulpicius' chronology for Martin arose from the fact that Sulpicius was seeking to foreshorten Martin's years as a soldier, for apologetic reasons. In other words, he argued that Sulpicius deliberately falsified the chronology of Martin's life. Whereas other suggestions made by Babut have received short shrift, this one was taken up and cogently re-presented by Fontaine in 1961. This makes an examination of Sulpicius' chronology essential not just for establishing the major dates of Martin's life, but also for tackling the wider question: can Sulpicius' Martinian writings be regarded as in any sense trustworthy, from a historical point of view?

An examination of the chronology is, therefore, essential to our main task, and I shall begin by setting out that given by Sulpicius. This can then serve as the basis for subsequent discussion.

(i) Chronological résumé of Martin's life, according to Sulpicius Severus[1]

Martin was born at Sabaria in Pannonia, now Szombathely (Hungary), near the Austro-Hungarian frontier; he was brought up at Pavia, in Italy. His father was a soldier, who rose to the rank of tribune. Although both his parents were pagans, Martin showed an interest in Christianity from an early age. When he was ten, he sought refuge in a church and asked to be made a catechumen—despite parental opposition. At the age of twelve, he conceived a desire for a hermitage.

However, Martin's father was hostile to his son's religious yearnings. He therefore saw to it that, in accordance with a law compelling sons to adopt their fathers' professions, Martin was drafted into the army at the young age of fifteen. Martin fought in the select corps of the imperial guard, the *scholae*, first under the Emperor Constantius [337-61], and then under the Caesar Julian [caesar, 355-60]. After three years as a soldier his experiences at Amiens impelled him to seek baptism, at the age of eighteen. However, he did not immediately leave the army, for his tribune hoped to join him in renouncing the world as soon as his tribunate was over. Buoyed up by this promise, Martin carried on in the army for approximately two more years. He was then able to utilize a personal encounter with the Caesar Julian to obtain his release from the army, at a time when Julian was distributing a donative to his troops. This took place when the Roman army had gathered in the territory of the Vangiones to drive back Germanic invaders beyond the Rhine frontier [356].

After leaving the army Martin sought out Hilary, bishop of Poitiers, and remained some time with him. Hilary tried to ordain Martin deacon, but on the latter's persistent refusal he ordained him exorcist instead. Not long afterwards Martin

---

[1] This compressed account follows Sulpicius' chronological survey in *VM* 2-9, unless indication is made to the contrary. I have supplied dates in square brackets for those reigns or events which can be securely dated from other sources. Sulpicius himself never dates any event in Martin's life by reference to consuls or the regnal years of emperors: that would have been out of place in a biography; cf. Delehaye, 'S. Martin', pp. 81-2.

crossed the Alps into Italy and so returned home (probably to Pannonia[2]), in the hopes of converting his parents. He then strove to stem the tide of Arianism in Illyricum, but earned a beating for his pains and was forcibly expelled. Once back in Italy he learnt that the Gallic church was convulsed now that Hilary had been driven into exile by the Arians; he therefore established a hermitage for himself at Milan. Hounded out from there also by the Arian bishop, Auxentius, he settled on the island of Gallinara, where he lived as a hermit with one companion until Hilary returned from exile [360]. Having missed Hilary at Rome, Martin followed him to Poitiers and established himself in a monastery nearby [i.e. Ligugé]. Here he was joined by disciples, and he acquired fame by resuscitating one of these who had just died, and shortly afterwards performing a similar miracle elsewhere.

At about the time of the second of these miracles, the see of Tours fell vacant. The citizens were determined to have Martin as their new bishop, and one of them pretended that his wife was ill in order to inveigle Martin into leaving his monastery to go and heal her. Once in Tours, Martin was acclaimed bishop by the people and duly consecrated, despite the reluctance of some of the bishops assembled for the purpose. This occurred during Valentinian I's reign [364-75].[3]

In addition to pastoral work, Martin's position as bishop brought him into direct contact with the imperial court at Trier. At one stage he was on friendly terms with the Emperor Maximus [383-8], and he was invited to a banquet along with the prefect and consul Evodius [consul, 386], and other high-ranking men. On another occasion he dined privately with Maximus and his wife, this taking place when Martin was a septuagenarian (*Martino . . . septuagenario*).[4]

Martin returned to Trier on a later occasion soon after Priscillian's death [c.385]. After impassioned altercations he reluctantly agreed to join with the anti-Priscillianist bishops in consecrating Felix to the see of Trier; and he

---

[2] See Fontaine, *Vie* II, 572 n. 1.
[3] *D* II, 5, 5.
[4] *VM* 20; *D* II, 6-7, esp. 7, §4.

lived for sixteen years after this.[5] He was still alive at the time when the synod of Nîmes met [394 or 396], and while Sulpicius was writing his life [*c*.394-6].[6] He had been dead for no more than seven to eight years by the time the *Dialogues* were written [probably *c*.404-6].[7]

Such is the chronological outline given by Sulpicius. One difficulty is immediately apparent: if Martin was aged twenty when Julian dismissed him in 356, as the *Vita* implies, how could he have reached his seventies by *c*.385? The other problem arises over the date of Martin's death. If Martin lived for sixteen years after Felix's consecration *c*.385, then he must have died *c*.401. However, we have evidence that Brice was bishop of Tours at the time of the synod of Turin in 398;[8] a letter of Paulinus of Nola's, which was written in 398, implies that Martin, like Felix, is a *dead* saint;[9] and Sulpicius himself informs us that Martin died soon after Clarus, and Clarus was already dead when the *Vita Martini* was finished in 396.[10] On top of all this Gregory of Tours, who was well informed about his predecessors, explicitly dates Martin's death to 397. As Gregory's date fits perfectly with the implications of these other sources, I shall set Sulpicius' chronology on one side for the time being, and first consider that given by Gregory.

---

[5] *D* III, 11-13, esp. 13, §6.

[6] *Ep.* 2, 3 & 6; and, for the synod of Nîmes, *D* II, 13, 8. This took place on 1 Oct. in the consulship of Arcadius and Honorius, which could denote either 394 or 396. However, the latter date is more likely, as in 394 Theodosius would have only just (6 Sept.) reconquered the west from Eugenius, and bishops are unlikely to have foregathered for a synod at such a critical time. See L. Duchesne, *Fastes épiscopaux de l'ancienne Gaule* (3 vols. 2nd edn. Paris, 1907, 1910, and 1915), vol. I, p. 366.

[7] *D* II, 14, 4; above ch. 7, ii.

[8] This is apparent from two of Pope Zosimus' letters; see É. Griffe, *La Gaule chrétienne à l'époque romaine* (3 vols., 2nd edn. Paris 1964-5) I, 347. See also (especially for the dating of the synod of Turin) J.-R. Palanque, 'Les Dissensions des églises des Gaules à la fin du IVe siècle et la date du concile de Turin', *Revue d'histoire de l'église de France* 21 (1935), pp. 481-501.

[9] *Ep.* 17, 4: 'Qua fide speras Christi gratiam in honore Martini, eadem Christi offensam time in offensione Felicis.' (*CSEL* 29, p. 127.) Dated to 398, after July, by Lienhard, pp. 178-82; to 398 or 399 by P. Fabre, *Essai sur la chronologie de l'œuvre de saint Paulin de Nole* (Paris 1948), pp. 23-7.

[10] *VM* 23, 1; *ep.* 2, 4-6. Babut, p. 57.

(ii) The Evidence of Gregory of Tours

Gregory, bishop of Tours *c.*573-94, was writing nearly two centuries after Martin's death. None the less, the precision of his information about his predecessors is explicable only on the assumption that he was able to draw upon earlier episcopal records, which had begun at least with Martin's predecessor, and been continued ever since.[11] The final chapter of his *History* amounts to an independent booklet 'On the bishops of Tours'. The question we have to ask is, what chronological details did Gregory's source(s) for this chapter provide him with? Close perusal suggests that up to and including Martin's successor, the year (and possibly the actual day) of the consecration of each new bishop was recorded at Tours, and dated either by consular years, or by the regnal years of the emperors.[12] From the mid-fifth century, this external dating seems to have been dropped, and instead the length of each episcopate was recorded, with increasing precision: from the seventh bishop onwards this is given not just in years, but in months, and often days. In this way, Gregory is able to provide a chronological sequence of the bishops of Tours from the first one right up to his own day. Certainly, there are some chronological problems;[13] and when Gregory attempted to synchronize events dated according to different systems, or to make his own calculations, he could easily get a year or so out. But this does not negate the fact that Gregory's basic chronological structure appears well founded. It has withstood the searching scrutiny of L. Duchesne remarkably well; and it is also worth pointing out that Gregory's chronology for the episcopates of Martin and the following three bishops fits with the evidence of the synodal

[11] The fact that Gregory was related to all but five of the previous bishops of Tours (*Hist.* V, 49) suggests that family traditions provided one source. But his chronological details presuppose some documentary records, also, and epitaphs are another possibility.

[12] *Hist.* X, 31. Gregory cannot have been working from the length of the episcopates for the early bishops of Tours, for in that case he would not have given us two slightly different calculations for the length of Martin's episcopate (below, n. 25).

[13] On which see L. Duchesne, *Fastes épiscopaux* II, 282-3; *Les Anciens Catalogues épiscopaux de la province de Tours* (Paris, 1890), pp. 22-7.

decrees of a council held at Tours in 461, when Perpetuus signs as bishop of Tours.[14] Thus, when we find Gregory giving us dates for Martin's consecration and death which he cannot have deduced from Sulpicius, we should take them seriously; for all the indications are that he derived them from a written source kept at Tours.

The first firm Martinian date which Gregory gives is that of Martin's consecration as bishop. Gregory sets this in the eighth year of the reign of Valens and Valentinian (371-2), and elsewhere notes that it occurred on 4 July.[15] The only difficulty is that 4 July did not fall on a Sunday in 371 or 372, although Sunday was the normal day for an episcopal consecration. This prompted Delehaye to opt for Sunday 4 July 370, and to suggest that Gregory made a mistake of one year when attempting to collate the episcopal records of Tours, dated by consular years, with the regnal years of emperors. This is possible; but, equally, Martin's consecration might not have occurred on a Sunday.[16] We may, however, conclude with some assurance that Martin was consecrated bishop of Tours either in 370, or 371, or 372.

The other primary date which Gregory gives, and which he does not derive from Sulpicius, is that of Martin's death.[17] Gregory dates this to the consulship of Caesarius and Atticus (397), which he equates with the second year of Arcadius' and Honorius' reign.[18] Now, it so happens that the date of

---

[14] *Hist.* X, 31, iv-vi; cf. *De virt. S. Martini* I, 6. Delehaye, 'S. Martin', p. 30.

[15] *Hist.* X, 31, iii; II, 14.

[16] Cf. Delehaye, 'S. Martin', p. 28; and Duchesne, *Les Anciens Catalogues* p. 24 n. 1. For the ruling on Sunday consecrations, see Griffe, *La Gaule chrét.* II, 231-2.

[17] Though note that Gregory's reckoning of two sixth-century events after Martin's death (*De virt. S. Mart.* I, 32; II, 1) would date the latter to 400 or 401. However, Delehaye ('S. Martin', p. 30) has shown that both computations are made of the same elements and so cannot be taken as confirming each other. As he suggests, Gregory was probably misled by Sulpicius' reference to Martin living 'sedecim annos' after Felix's consecration.

[18] *De virt. S. Mart.* I, 3; *Hist.* I, 48, and cf. also X, 31, iii-iv. Arcadius and Honorius succeeded jointly on Theodosius' death in January 395, which would most naturally give 396 as their second year. But it is possible that some chronographers assigned all 395 to Theodosius (see E. J. Bickerman, *Chronology of the Ancient World*, London 1968, pp. 64-7); or that Gregory made an error of one year when collating the years of the consuls with the regnal years of the emperors (Delehaye, p. 28).

397 fits perfectly with the circumstantial evidence mentioned above for placing Martin's death before the end of 398: with Paulinus' hint that Martin was dead by 398-9, with papal evidence that Brice had already succeeded Martin as bishop of Tours by 398, and with Sulpicius' indications that Martin died soon after 396. On the other hand, all three are *implying* Martin's death between 396 and 398, not stating it; and this means that they can scarcely be seen as the sources for Gregory's statement. Gregory must have been drawing upon local records kept at Tours, for he knows not only the exact date of Martin's *depositio*, but also that there was a twenty-day interregnum before the consecration of Martin's successor, Brice. And, unless he had detailed local evidence available, why should he have placed Martin's death in 397, when Sulpicius, whom he quarried for other chronological information on Martin, implied that it occurred some four years later? Further, while Sulpicius' solitary reference to 'sedecim postea vixit annos' can be harmonized with Gregory's date if we postulate simple scribal error,[19] the number and the precision of Gregory's statements about Martin's death preclude our explaining away his date of 397 in a similar fashion. I think we should therefore accept the present scholarly consensus which follows Gregory and attributes Martin's death to 397.

As for the actual date of his death: Gregory twice tells us that it occurred in the middle of a Sunday night;[20] twice, that Martin's episcopate lasted for a number of years and four and a bit months;[21] and once, that the feast of Martin's *depositio* (i.e. funeral) was celebrated at Tours on 11 November.[22] In 397, 8 November was a Sunday, and this might be the actual date of Martin's death; but Delehaye has argued convincingly that no weight can be attached to the Sunday tradition.[23] The *depositio* on 11 November, however, would have come from reliable tradition; and this is further confirmed

---

[19] *D* III, 13, 6; see below, §iii.

[20] *De virt. S. Mart.* I, 3; *Hist.* I, 48.

[21] Below, n. 25. As Martin's consecration took place on 4 July, these calculations give us a date in November.

[22] *Hist.* II, 14.

[23] 'S. Martin', pp. 29-30.

by the preamble to the acts of the council of Tours, which met either on 14 or 18 November, 461, after its episcopal participants had foregathered in Tours to celebrate the festival of Martin's *receptio* (funeral).[24]

The remaining figures given by Gregory are calculations of the length of Martin's episcopate,[25] and of his age when he died. To discover the latter, Gregory seems to have utilized Sulpicius' *Martino . . . septuagenario* statement, and reckoned seventy years back from Evodius' consulate, 386, thus placing Martin's birth in the eleventh year of Constantine's reign, i.e. 316.[26] So Gregory's dating of Martin's birth to 316 cannot be taken as independent evidence confirming Sulpicius' *Martino . . . septuagenario*. On the contrary, note that Gregory utilizes Sulpicius' words when describing Martin's birth, once even mentioning that his source is an 'earlier history'—a reference which must indicate Sulpicius' Martinian works;[27] note also that Gregory (virtually) never mentions the age or date of birth of any other bishop of Tours.[28] Taken together, these facts compel us to recognize that Sulpicius was Gregory's sole source of information on this subject.

Let us, therefore, take from Gregory the date of *c*.371 for Martin's consecration, and 397 for his death; and let us leave

---

[24] *Concilia Galliae a. 314–506*, ed. C. Munier (*CCSL* 148, pp. 142–3). On the meaning of *depositio* and *receptio* see Delehaye, 'S. Martin', pp. 127–8.

[25] Estimated variously as 25 years, 4 months, and 10 days (*De virt. S. Mart.* I, 3); 26 years, 4 months, and 17 days (*Hist.* X, 31, iii); or, he died during the twenty-sixth year of his episcopate (*Hist.* I, 48). See Delehaye, pp. 28–9.

[26] *Hist.* I, 36; Babut, p. 167, n. 1; Delehaye, p. 29. J. Fontaine cites no evidence to support his belief that Gregory's date is independent of Sulpicius' chronological indications: 'Vérité et fiction dans la chronologie de la *Vita Martini*', *Saint Martin et son temps*, p. 194.

[27] Gregory, *De virt. S. Mart.* I, 3: 'Gloriosus domnus Martinus, . . . sol novus exoriens, sicut anterior narrat historia, apud Sabariam Pannoniae ortus, ad salvationem Galliarum opitulante Deo diregitur.' (As well as comparing *VM* 2, 1, quoted below, NB *D* III, 17, 6: 'sed nequaquam a Christo Gallias derelictas, quibus donaverit habere Martinum.') Gregory, *Hist.* I, 36: 'Huius [i.e. Constantini] imperii anno undecimo . . . beatissimus praesul Martinus apud Sabariam Pannoniae civitatem nascitur parentibus gentilibus, non tamen infimis.' Cf. Sulpicius, *VM* 2, 1: 'Igitur Martinus Sabaria Pannoniarum oppido oriundus fuit, . . . parentibus secundum saeculi dignitatem non infimis, gentilibus tamen.' Note also Gregory, *Hist.* X, 31, iii: 'De cuius [i.e. Martini] vita tres a Severo Sulpicio libros conscriptos legimus.'

[28] Gregory lists nineteen earlier bishops, but gives the ages only of Martin and of his own immediate predecessor, whom he would have known: *Hist.* X, 31.

the date of Martin's birth until we have examined Sulpicius' writings more closely.

(iii) Unravelling Sulpicius' Chronology

We have seen that Gregory of Tours, apparently drawing on local written records, dated Martin's death to 397. Sulpicius, however, put it sixteen years after the consecration of Felix to the see of Trier, which itself followed shortly after the execution of the Spanish heresiarch, Priscillian, *c.*385.[29] Even if we dated Priscillian's execution and Felix's consecration to 384, the earliest conceivable date, counting inclusively that would still yield 399 as Sulpicius' date for Martin's death. And this, as we have seen, is too late not just for Gregory of Tours, but also (by implication) for other sources contemporary with Sulpicius.

Why should Sulpicius have implied that Martin's death occurred *c.*401, when in fact it seems to have taken place in 397? Sulpicius certainly knew the date of Martin's death;[30] so, there being no reason for him to falsify it, the answer is probably that 'sedecim' (sixteen) is not what he originally wrote, but a scribal corruption. This explanation is widely accepted amongst modern scholars, although there are three different theories as to how the corruption came about. The original text might have read 'sed decem', which could readily have given rise to 'sedecim';[31] or it might have read either 'xiii' or 'xiu';[32] either of these could easily have been corrupted to 'xui'. As, on independent grounds, I regard 385 as the most likely date for Priscillian's execution, I would opt for an original reading of 'xiii'. Counting inclusively (as

---

[29] Priscillian's death occurred some time between late 384 and early 387, probably either in 385 or 386. Chadwick, *Priscillian*, pp. 132–8, gives a magisterial survey, coming down in favour of 386. I myself prefer the date 385, as this is the one given by our three earliest sources (the chronicles of Sulpicius and of Prosper, and the anonymous Gallic chronicle of 452); and Sulpicius at least was writing within twenty years of the event, and evinces a strong concern for correct chronology in his *Chronicle*.

[30] Above, p. 71.

[31] Fontaine, 'Vérité et fiction', p. 196 and n. 19.

[32] 'xiii' is suggested by Duchesne, *Les Anciens Catalogues*, p. 24, n. 1; 'xiu' by B. Vollmann, *Studien zum Priscillianismus* (St. Ottilien 1965), pp. 4–5, n. 6.

Sulpicius does in his *Chronicle*[33]), this would yield the date of 397 for Martin's death; and it would then harmonize with Gregory of Tours' dating. I should perhaps emphasize that we are here in the realm of 'hypothesis', not 'fact'; but this is the only plausible explanation of our conundrum, and I shall therefore adopt 397 as the date of Martin's death as a working hypothesis.

Next, let us tackle the date of Martin's birth. Here, as we have seen, Sulpicius is our only primary source of information, and the problem arises from the fact that he gives us two quite different indications. In the *Vita*, he seems to show us Martin leaving the army in 356 at the age of twenty, implying that Martin was born in 336.[34] In the *Dialogues*, however, he refers to Martin as *septuagenarius* (a septuagenarian) at the time when he dined alone with the Emperor Maximus and his wife, i.e. *c*.385.[35] There is thus a discrepancy of some twenty years between the chronology implied by the *Vita*, and that implied by the *Dialogues*.

Once we recognize, regretfully, that Gregory's dating of Martin's birth to 316 is deduced from Sulpicius' writings, not from Tours records, we find ourselves adrift from *terra firma*, tossing on the high seas of uncertainty. Have we any means of deciding which passage of Sulpicius is more reliable? Is there any *a priori* reason for thinking that one chronology is more likely than the other?

Those in favour of the 'long chronology', envisaging Martin being born *c*.316, have put forward two general arguments to support their contention.[36] First, that it

[33] E.g. *Chron.* II, 27, 5: AD 29–400 is reckoned as 372 years.

[34] *VM* 3, 5-5, 1; see in particular C. Jullian, 'La Jeunesse de Saint Martin', *REA* 12 (1910), at pp. 261-7.

[35] *D* II, 7, 4. Maximus overthrew Gratian and established his court at Trier in August, 383; but it was some time before he could persuade Martin to regard him as anything other than a usurper (*VM* 20, 2-3), so 384 is the earliest likely date. The *terminus ad quem* must be Priscillian's execution, for the bitterness and mistrust it engendered (*D* III, 12) would have shattered the relaxed friendship of Martin and Maximus. The year of Evodius' consulate cannot be used to date even the banquet mentioned in *VM* 20 precisely: Delehaye, 'S. Martin', p. 22; Fontaine, *Vie* III, 933.

[36] The comradeship between Martin and his tribune, advanced as an argument by Fontaine (*VM* 3, 5; 'Vérité et fiction' p. 207), scarcely tells against the 'short chronology', as Martin at the time of his baptism was eighteen by either reckoning. See also Fontaine, *Vie* II, 503-4.

accords better with Hilary's attempt to ordain the newly-released Martin to the diaconate in 356, as the minimum age for a deacon was then theoretically twenty-five or thirty years.[37] Secondly, that Sulpicius' description of Martin's last hours, especially Martin's own reference to his decrepit old age, would fit better with a man dying at the age of eighty-two, rather than sixty-one.[38]

Neither argument can carry much weight. On the first point, Ambrose's rapid elevation to the episcopate at the uncanonical age of twenty-four shows that rulings about proper ages for ordination could easily be disregarded; and it is likely that the Christian community at Poitiers in 356 was still small, and so would have welcomed a forthright recruit like Martin, even if he were only twenty.[39]

On the second point, we must recognize that expectations of life were so much lower in the fourth century than they are today that there would be nothing odd in Martin calling himself an 'old man', and dying, at the age of sixty-two. A grim picture emerges from detailed research on life expectations in the Roman Empire. Let us take the prospects of soldiers serving in the Danube provinces, where conditions were probably similar to those encountered by Martin in north-east Gaul and the Rhineland. Of those joining up at the age of seventeen, about half would be dead by the time they were forty; only 13.7% would survive to the age of sixty-two; and a mere 2.5% to the age of eighty-two. Nor are these short life spans primarily due to the dangers of soldiering. Taking civilians in the same area, only 21.7% would survive to be sixty-two, and 4.2% to be eighty-two.[40]

These figures show that, in the Roman period, men aged prematurely according to our modern expectations. This invites us to stand on its head the argument about the likely age of Martin on his death-bed. Not only does the idea of

---

[37] *VM* 5, 2. Fontaine, 'Vérité et fiction' p. 207.

[38] Sulpicius, *ep.* 3, 13: 'fatiscentem aetatem', 'senectus'. Babut, *St. Martin*, p. 167; Griffe, *La Gaule chrét.* I (1st edn., 1947), 201.

[39] Gaudemet pp. 124–7. On Christianity in Poitiers, see J.-R. Palanque in *Hilaire et son temps* (Paris 1969), pp. 12–13; Doignon, pp. 30–47.

[40] A. R. Burn, 'Hic Breve Vivitur: a Study of the Expectation of Life in the Roman Empire', *Past and Present* 4 (1953), pp. 2–31, esp. p. 23.

Martin dying worn out and old at the age of sixty-one become plausible; we must then go on to ask: how probable is the scenario presupposed by the 'long chronology'? Is is likely that Martin would have retired at the age of forty, after a gruelling twenty-five years in the army, and then straightway embarked on an equally demanding new way of life, with the vitality to carry on for another forty years or more? Of course, it is possible: witness Theodore of Tarsus, a Greek monk who was consecrated Archbishop of Canterbury at the age of sixty-six, ·and finally died after a fruitful episcopate at the age of eighty-eight; or the even more remarkable Ossius, bishop of Cordova, who lived to be over a hundred.[41] These cases must caution us against too negative a view. None the less, a Martin born in 336 seems more likely.

It is also suggested by a number of small points. For instance, Martin's flamboyant gesture in confronting Julian with an open refusal to fight, and in offering to go into battle unarmed rather than be thought a coward, together with his near fatal experiment in pursuing the ascetic life on a tiny Mediterranean island, living off wild roots: all this smacks of a young man, not a forty-year-old.[42] Further, it would make sense for a twenty-year-old Martin, baptized just two years previously, to have gone almost straight off to convert his parents once he had extricated himself from the army. But it would have been odd if he had acted like this at the age of forty, twenty-two years after his own baptism.[43]

In fact, if we postulate 336 as the year of Martin's birth, then many details of his childhood and army days fall naturally into place, whereas on the 'long chronology' hypothesis they require special explanation. The most obvious case is Sulpicius' remark that Martin 'desired the desert' when he was twelve years old.[44] This would certainly be anachronistic for the year 328; and so, if we envisage Martin being born *c*.316, we

---

[41] Bede, *Ecclesiastical History of the English People* IV, 1 and V, 8; ed. B. Colgrave and R. A. B. Mynors (Oxford 1969), pp. 330, 472. V. C. de Clercq, *Ossius of Cordova* (Washington 1954), pp. 49-52.

[42] *VM* 4, 2-5; 6, 5-6. I owe this point to my husband, Ben de la Mare.

[43] Jullian, 'La Jeunesse', p. 265.

[44] *VM* 2, 4.

must explain it away as 'hagiographer's licence': the retro-spective projection on to Martin's boyhood of the ascetic ideal he was later to make his own.[45] The 'short chronology', however, dispenses with the need for this. By 348 it is likely that news of the desert monks had indeed reached Pavia, where Martin grew up. Athanasius spent most of his second exile (339-46) in Italy, visiting Milan and Aquileia as well as Rome. He was accompanied by Egyptian monks, and accord-ing to Jerome they spread news of St. Antony and of the monasteries founded by Pachomius.[46] In Vercelli, near Pavia, Eusebius adopted the monastic life at some unknown date before being exiled in 355.[47] Milan, Vercelli, and Pavia form a triangle of neighbouring cities; and if word of the desert fathers had reached the first two, then it had probably reached the last one, also.

The short chronology also makes better sense of Martin's military career. First, there is the sentence, 'Ipse armatam militiam in adulescentia secutus inter scolares alas sub rege Constantio, deinde sub Juliano Caesare militavit'.[48] This implies that Martin did not join the army till Constantius became emperor after Constantine's death in 337; and indeed, since Martin was serving in Gaul only three years after joining the army (*Vita* 3, 1), the implication is that he joined no more than three years before Constantius won control of Gaul (battle of Mons Seleucus, 353): i.e. not till 350 at the earliest.[49] However, Fontaine has pointed out

---

[45] Fontaine, 'Vérité et fiction', pp. 225-6. Fontaine sees *VM* 2, 2-4 as a hagiographical commonplace, the 'holy childhood' of a future saint (*Vie* II, 441-52). But the text affords no support: no miracles mark Martin's birth and childhood (cf. *Vie* II, 442). Instead it is narrated in the same straightforward way as Martin's incorporation into the army. Note that Sulpicius uses exactly the same expression, 'cum esset annorum—' for the ages of 10, 12, 15, and 18. Why should we take the first two figures symbolically, the last two literally? (Cf. 'Vérité et fiction', pp. 222-31.) But *cave* the Roman preference for round numbers (Burn, pp. 4, 18-19).

[46] Jerome, *ep*. 127, 5 (*CSEL* 56, p. 149); Lorenz, p. 4; Rousseau, *Ascetics*, p. 81.

[47] Lorenz, p. 9.

[48] *VM* 2, 2, giving Halm's punctuation (*CSEL* 1, p. 111).

[49] Cf. Babut, *St. Martin*, p. 169, n. 3. What, then, was Martin, one of Constantius' *scholares*, doing at Amiens in the winter of 353-4 or 354-5 (*VM* 3, 1)? For Constantius spent the former winter in Arles, the latter in Milan (Ammianus Marcellinus XIV, 5, 1; XIV, 10, 16). A possible explanation lies in the fact that

that, if one puts a comma after *secutus,* one can take this sentence to mean that Martin in his youth fought in the army (as an ordinary soldier), and was then promoted to the *scholae,* picked cavalry regiments closely associated with the person of the emperor, under Constantius.[50] This is possible.

Another point is that Sulpicius represents Martin as being baptized at the age of eighteen, carrying on as a nominal soldier for another two years or so, and then, when fighting became imminent, seeking his release from Julian.[51] Now, if Martin had been baptized after the winter of 353-4 (perhaps at Easter 354), and remained with the *scholares* attached to Constantius until Julian's appointment as caesar (November 355), then it would have been quite possible for him to have come through the next two years without fighting in any major engagement until Julian's campaign of 356.[52] But that he 'solo licet nomine militavit' for twenty-two years after his baptism is highly unlikely.

Equally, the donative incident makes much better sense on the short chronology hypothesis. For, given the church's ambivalent attitude to the shedding of blood (even by soldiers in the course of duty), we can see that a youthful Martin, who had so far escaped fighting since his baptism two years previously, could well have been brought to a moment of decision by, probably, his first taste of war, coupled with the distribution of a donative immediately before another battle.[53] Acceptance of the donative would have engaged his loyalties to the army for the duration of that season's campaign[54] —a campaign directed by a general

the winter of 353-4 saw a mopping-up operation of Magnentius' supporters (ibid. XIV, 5), and Amiens had links with Magnentius (J. Bidez, 'Amiens, ville natale de l'empereur Magnence', *REA* 27, 1925, esp. pp. 314-16). *Scholares* were regularly used on such missions: see R. I. Frank, *Scholae Palatinae* (Rome 1969), ch. 6, esp. pp. 102-4.

[50] 'Vérité et fiction', pp. 204-5.

[51] *VM* 3, 5-4, 3.

[52] In 354 Constantius marched against the Alamanni, but concluded peace without fighting. In 355 there was a major battle in which at least some of the *scholares* (the *scutarii*) took part, but Constantius with another part of the army was not involved: Ammianus XIV, 10 and XV, 4 (esp. §1). On the *scholares'* duties see Frank, ch. 6.

[53] See below, ch. 10.

[54] Fontaine, *Vie* II, 520-1.

who meant far more serious business with the Germans than Constantius had. Conversely, the idea of a soldier who had seen twenty-five years of service in the army choosing that moment to request his release is most implausible.

In this discussion of the pros and cons of the two chronologies, one final question must be raised: in view of the empire's parlous military plight, its need for more soldiers, and its harsh legislation compelling the sons of veterans to enrol in the army, would it have been *possible* for Martin to obtain his release after a mere five years of soldiering? The answer appears to be, yes, though with difficulty. An interesting parallel is provided by Victricius, bishop of Rouen *c*.380–407, and a former soldier. As with Martin, Victricius' request to be freed from the army for Christ's service was at first strongly opposed. But his determination, coupled with a miracle, eventually secured his release.[55] Further examples are provided by Victor, Sulpicius' monk-courier, and by his companion-in-arms, Crispinianus. Victor had formerly been in the army, but we do not know the circumstances of his release. His friend, Crispinianus, carried on as a soldier although he was a Christian. Paulinus had no qualms about urging him to transfer from the service of Caesar to the service of Christ. Although Crispinianus was a young man, and as such could not have been eligible for retirement for many years, Paulinus never entertained the idea that Crispinianus would have to remain in the army because he was constrained to do so by law. Instead, he talked as though the decision to leave the army and become a monk was purely one for Crispinianus' will, with the chief deterrent being Crispinianus' desire to marry and have children: not his fear of torture and execution.[56] All in all, the evidence suggests that a determined young man might well be successful in obtaining his premature release from the army, though, if he struck unlucky, he might have to suffer for his audacity.[57]

[55] Paulinus of Nola, *ep.* 18, 7; discussed below, pp. 143–4.

[56] Paulinus, *ep.* 25 (esp. §5) and 25*.

[57] See also P. Siniscalco, *Massimiliano: un obiettore di cosciènza del tardo impero* (Turin 1974), p. 129; and cf. *C. Th.* VII, 20, 12 (2). Also A. Rousselle, 'Aspects sociaux du recrutement ecclésiastique au IVe siècle', *Mélanges de l'école française de Rome: Antiquité* 89 (1977), p. 359, n. 132. Nepotian appears to be another example: Jerome, *ep.* 60, 9 (cit. below, ch. 21).

So far our discussion about the general likelihood of one or the other chronology, while not conclusive, has pointed us more in the direction of the 'short chronology'. Let us now turn to the two key texts, scrutinizing them in detail and setting them in context, to see which direction they indicate.

The passage in the *Vita* occurs in the chronological section which traces Martin's life up to his consecration as bishop.[58] Whereas the subsequent section is arranged by topics, with almost no chronological indications, this earlier part is full of precise chronological detail: 'when [Martin] was aged ten ... twelve ... fifteen ... eighteen ...', we read. In these chapters the chronology provides the connecting thread, and such Martinian stories as do occur are firmly subordinated to this.

The immediate context of the passage under discussion is set by the famous story of Martin, still an unbaptized soldier, giving away half his cloak to a beggar. That night Martin saw a vision of Christ dressed in his half-cloak, and this fired him to seek baptism immediately:

(*VM* 3, 5) Quo viso, vir beatissimus ... bonitatem Dei in suo opere cognoscens, cum esset annorum duodeviginti, ad baptismum convolavit. Nec tamen statim militiae renuntiavit, tribuni sui precibus evictus, cui contubernium familiare praestabat: etenim transacto tribunatus sui tempore renuntiaturum se saeculo pollicebatur. (6) Qua Martinus expectatione suspensus per biennium fere posteaquam est baptismum consecutus solo licet nomine militavit.

(4, 1) Interea inruentibus intra Gallias barbaris, Julianus Caesar, coacto in unum exercitu apud Vangionum civitatem, donativum coepit erogare militibus ...

The story continues with Martin coming before Julian to receive his donative, and instead insisting on his immediate discharge. The obvious interpretation is that Martin was baptized at the age of eighteen; but that he remained in the army for another two years before gaining his discharge from Julian in a campaign which can only be that of 356.[59]

---

[58] Chs. 2–10. See above, ch. 8, i.

[59] No .earlier campaign (as suggested, e.g., by Delehaye 'S. Martin', p. 26) is possible. 356 was Julian's first campaigning season, and it was definitely under Julian that Martin served (Jullian, 'La Jeunesse', pp. 263–5). In any case, Sulpicius represents Martin as going straight from the army to join Hilary, already

This interpretation must remain the normal one. However, ingenious alternatives have been suggested in an attempt to harmonize this passage with the Martinian chronology implied by the *Dialogues*: i.e. with a Martin born *c*.315, and serving in the army *c*.330-56.

First, there is the suggestion originally made by Babut in 1912, which was further developed by Fontaine in 1961.[60] They assume that chapters three and four of the *Vita* do indeed depict Martin being released from the army in 356 at the age of twenty, and explain it by saying that Sulpicius was here guilty of deliberate misrepresentation. They point to the revulsion, widely felt in the fourth century, against ordaining anyone who had served in the *militia* (which included the civil service and army)—especially if he had continued to serve after baptism. This is particularly pertinent for Martin's case, as Brice explicitly accused Martin of being defiled by his army career. Sulpicius would therefore have had every reason for trying to conceal the fact that Martin had remained a soldier for over twenty years after he had been baptized. However, Martin's former military career was too well known to be wholly suppressed, so Sulpicius compromised by assigning him an army stint of five years, that being the absolute minimum. At the same time he insisted that Martin had been a soldier only in name; in his behaviour, he was already more of a monk than a soldier.

A second approach is to explore the various ways in which the last sentence of chapter three can be interpreted. Need the phrase 'per biennium fere' necessarily refer to the verb 'militavit'? Thus Griffe offers the translation: 'After being held in suspense by this expectation for about two years after he had been baptized, Martin did his military service,

---

bishop of Poitiers and famous for his catholic faith (*VM* 5, 1), but not yet exiled. Since Hilary came to the fore of the Arian—catholic controversy only after the synod of Milan in 355, and had in any case only fairly recently been consecrated bishop, neither Constans' campaign of *c*.341 nor Constantius' of 354 will do. 356 is therefore the earliest possible date. At the same time it is the latest possible, as Hilary went into exile some time during that year.

[60] Babut, *St. Martin*, pp. 71-2, 167-70, 121-2; Fontaine, 'Vérité et fiction', esp. pp. 205-22.

but only as a nominal soldier.'[61] In other words, the two
years refers only to the length of time that Martin was kept
waiting by his tribune, when Martin was perhaps a *tiro*;
Sulpicius gives no indication of how long Martin actually
remained in the army.

A slight variation has been suggested—without much
conviction—by Fontaine: viz. to punctuate the sentence,
'Qua Martinus expectatione suspensus per biennium fere,
posteaquam . . .'[62] This would have the meaning: 'Martin,
having been kept in suspense for about two years by this
expectation, fought only in a nominal way after he had
received baptism.' This is preferable, but still not very
satisfactory; for, as Fontaine points out, the rhythm naturally
suggests a slight pause after *suspensus*, rather than that we
should run the following three words in with the participial
clause; and the word order is certainly odd. If that was how
Sulpicius meant us to take his sentence, why did he not write,
'Qua Martinus expectatione per biennium fere suspensus',
and thus make his meaning clear?[63] Did he deliberately wish
to make this passage ambiguous so as to encourage readers
to think that Martin had spent only another two years in
the army?—In which case, we are half-way back to Babut's
suggestion. Besides, the 'nec statim' of *Vita* 3, 5 implies a
relatively short period in the army after baptism. Two years
would do, but not twenty-two.

This last objection can also be levelled against the third
suggestion, an earlier one of Griffe's, that we should read
'vicennium', twenty years, in place of 'biennium', two
years, in the last sentence of chapter three.[64] Initially, this
may still appear an attractive hypothesis.[65] However, the
manuscripts give no grounds for suspecting the reading

---

[61] É. Griffe, 'La Chronologie des années de jeunesse de saint Martin', *Bulletin
de littérature ecclésiastique* 62 (1961), pp. 116–17.

[62] *Vie* II, 507 & n. 2.

[63] Ibid. pp. 507–8.

[64] É. Griffe, *La Gaule chrétienne* I (1st edn. 1947), pp. 203–4.

[65] While substitution of 'b' for initial Latin 'v' was not typical of late Roman
Gaul as a whole, it did occur in Béarn and Bigorre (cf. Latin *verruca* > French
verrue, but > Béarnais *burugo*); and Primuliacum could have lain in or near this
area: cf. below, ch. 20, iii, and map 2.

'biennium'. Indeed, it was already there in the text used by Paulinus of Périgueux in the 460s.[66]

As we consider these hypotheses, we have to admit that all three have serious drawbacks. In the first case we are required to make a major assumption about Sulpicius' character and reliability as a historian;[67] in the second, we have to wrench a Latin sentence in a most unnatural manner in an attempt to make it fit with our own preconceived ideas; while in the third case, we are forced to assume that the manuscript reading of the *Vita* had become corrupt within seventy years of publication. None of these suggested solutions is impossible; but, equally, none is very plausible.

Let us now turn to our second text, *Dialogues* II, 7. The context here is of Gallus telling stories about Martin and the emperors; and, in particular, the story of how Maximus' wife insisted on her husband entertaining Martin to a private meal, while she waited on the holy man with her own hands. At this, one of Gallus' listeners intervened. He asked what had happened to Martin's reputation for never letting a woman near him, and voiced his concern that some who associated too freely with women might draw encouragement from this story. Our passage occurs in Gallus' reply:

Tum Gallus, 'Quid tu', inquit, 'non vides, quod solent docere grammatici, locum, tempus et personam? Propone enim tibi ante oculos captum in palatio imperatoris precibus ambiri, reginae fide cogi, temporis necessitate constringi, ut clausos carcere liberaret, exiliis datos restitueret, bona adempta rehiberet: haec quanti putas constare episcopo debuisse, ut pro his omnibus non aliquantulum de rigore propositi relaxaret? Verumtamen quia occasione huius exempli male usuros esse aliquos arbitraris, illi vero felices erunt, si a disciplina exempli istius non recedant. Videant enim, quia Martino semel tantum in vita iam septuagenario non vidua libera, non virgo lasciviens, sed sub viro vivens, ipso viro pariter supplicante, regina servivit et ministravit edenti, non cum epulante discubuit: nec ausa participare convivium, sed deferebat obsequium. Disce igitur disciplinam: serviat tibi matrona, non imperet, et serviat, non recumbat: sicut Martha illa ministravit Domino, nec

---

[66] Paulinus of Périgueux, *De vita Martini* I, line 134 (*CSEL* 16, p. 24).

[67] Babut's ideas about Sulpicius' general unreliability in his Martinian works, and his theories about hagiography and 'aretalogy' (op. cit. ch. 2), provided a context for his hypothesis that Sulpicius falsified the Martinian chronology. But these wider theories of Babut's have since been rebutted, so isolating his chronological hypothesis.

tamen est adscita convivio: immo praelata est ministranti, quae verbum potius audiebat. Sed in Martino ista regina utrumque complevit: et ministravit ut Martha, et audivit ut Maria. Quodsi quis hoc uti voluerit exemplo, per omnia teneat: talis causa sit talisque persona, tale obsequium, tale convivium, et in omni vita semel tantum.'[68]

As we read this extended explanation, we cannot help noticing its rhetorical nature. Indeed, Gallus' opening advice to recall the circumstances of Martin's action as they would have been analysed in a grammarian's school[69] should forewarn us that what follows is a piece of special pleading—almost, one might venture, akin to those rhetorical exercises which formed the keystone of Roman education. Note the vivid way in which Gallus recreates the scene before our very eyes;[70] and how he spells out the dilemma facing Martin, 'caught' in the palace by the unusual piety of emperor and empress, and by the sorry plight of those unhappy prisoners and exiles whose cause he came to plead. Here is an appeal to our emotions, compelling us to agree that Martin acted rightly. Indeed, Sulpicius' use of the words 'captum', 'cogi', and 'constringi' almost lulls us into thinking that Martin had no option: he did not only what he should, but also the only thing he could.

In addition, note the various stylistic devices employed by Roman rhetoricians. There is alliteration, most notably in the words: 'Martino *s*emel tantum in *v*ita iam *s*eptuagenario non *v*idua *l*ibera, non *v*irgo *l*asciviens, *s*ed *s*ub *v*iro vivens . . .'; and the same passage illustrates another rhetorical figure, that of antithesis. There is the comparison between the empress on the one hand, and Martha and Mary on the other.

[68] *D* II, 7, 2-6. I would like to thank Professor David West for discussing this passage with me, and emphasizing its rhetorical nature.
[69] I.e. the place, time, and person. Traditionally, Roman manuals list seven *circumstantiae* (e.g. *Rhetores Latini Minores*, ed. C. Halm, Leipzig 1863, pp. 103, 141, 220; cf. T. J. Haarhoff, *Schools of Gaul*, p. 73). But our three were mentioned as a trio on their own by Quintilian, in the context of the refutation: *Institutio Oratoria* II, 4, 19 (ed. M. Winterbottom, 2 vols. Oxford 1970, I, 83). Students encountered this method of analysis (viz. with reference to the *circumstantiae*) in the 'progymnasmata', the preliminary exercises, which in the fourth century tended to fall under the *grammaticus*, not the *rhetor*: see H. I. Marrou, *Saint Augustin et la fin de la culture antique* (Paris 1938), pp. 50-2, and cf. p. 10 n. 2; Haarhoff, pp. 72-8.
[70] Such *evidentia* or *sub oculos subiectio* was a rhetorical device strongly recommended by Quintilian: VIII, 3, 61-70; cf. IX, 2, 40-4.

And the last sentence, as well as serving as a summing up (*consummatio*), is a fine example of anaphora, with its constant repetition of the word *talis*.

Given the rhetorical nature of the passage as a whole, it would obviously be rash to extrapolate the words 'Martino ... septuagenario', and to regard these as giving Martin's precise age at the time. Indeed, the very vagueness of the adjective *septuagenarius* prevents this; contrast the precision of the cardinal numbers in the second and third chapters of the *Vita*. The general point that Sulpicius is making is that Martin was an old man at the time he came into such intimate contact with the empress; and his reason for stressing Martin's age was not to help future historians deduce the date of his birth, but because of the common Roman belief that 'old age [is] stronger in repressing desire.'[71] In other words, he emphasized Martin's age, as he emphasized the empress' position as wife, acting under her husband's eye, in order to dispel any suspicion that this dinner party could have been the occasion for improper behaviour between Martin and the empress.

But could Sulpicius have used the word *septuagenarius* if Martin had been only fifty at the time? I do not know. However, we can at least say that gross exaggeration was perfectly acceptable in what was clearly a rhetorical passage. We might compare an earlier chapter where Gallus described some officials' vain attempts to persuade their draught animals to continue with their journey: 'Then all of them together fell to beating [the animals]. The punishment of the mules wore out the Gallic whips. An entire wood that lay nearby was commandeered, and the beasts of burden were belaboured with whole trees; but the savage blows were achieving nothing at all.'[72] Here, the rhetorical nature of 'tota rapitur silva' is obvious, and no one would dream of taking it literally. This should make us think twice about taking the details of the equally rhetorical passage in chapter seven at face value.

A second point worth mentioning is that seventy was then taken as the starting-point for *senectus*, old age. Seventy was

---

[71] Ambrose, *Exameron* I, 8, 31 (*CSEL* 32, i, p. 32).   [72] *D* II, 3, 6-7.

therefore the age at which, traditionally, the fires of desire died down; and, in public life, seventy was the age of retirement.[73] Might this equation between old age and septuagenarians have led to the word *septuagenarius* being loosely applied as a synonym for *senex*, an 'old man'?

That is as far as we can go; and that makes it an appropriate moment to end our exploration, and to try and pull together the threads of our discussion about the date of Martin's birth. First, we may say that the circumstantial evidence points in favour of the 'short chronology': if Martin were born in 336, nothing but the *septuagenarius* passage needs explaining away; whereas if Martin were born *c*.315, a number of points require explanation, and a convincing one is not always forthcoming. Secondly, as regards the two texts: they do conflict with each other, and that is disconcerting; but, as a general principle, we should avoid the temptation to emend or twist either passage to suit our own theory. And so, reluctantly, I feel compelled to reject Griffe's two suggested interpretations of *Vita* 3, 6, as well as Reinkens' unfounded suggestion that the *Dialogues' septuagenarius* is an interpolation.[74]

This leaves us with two possible explanations: one which prefers the *Dialogues'* evidence, and regards the conflicting passage in the *Vita* as deliberate falsification on the part of Sulpicius, for apologetic reasons; and a second which prefers the *Vita* evidence, and regards the *septuagenarius* passage as rhetorical exaggeration in an attempt to make a point. Our detailed examination of the two texts has shown that, although superficially it seems to be just a case of preferring one Sulpician passage to another, at a more fundamental level we are considering two very different alternatives. The *Vita* passage occurs in what purports to be a straightforward historical narrative.[75] Certainly, Sulpicius had good reason

[73] Isidore, *Etymologiae* XI, ii, 6-7 & 30 (ed. W. M. Lindsay, 2 vols. Oxford 1911). Pauly-Wissowa, *Real-encyclopädie der classischen Altertumswissenschaft* (Stuttgart 1894 ff.) I, art. 'aetas', esp. col. 694.

[74] There is no MS evidence to support Reinkens' contention; see Delehaye, 'S. Martin', p. 25.

[75] I refer to *VM* 3, 5-6. *VM* 4, on the other hand, does show clear traces of literary stylization; but, even here, Sulpicius probably does not tell outright lies: see below, ch. 10.

for wishing to play down Martin's years as a soldier; but if that led him to portray Martin staying on in the army for two, rather than twenty-two, years after his baptism, then he was guilty of arrant falsification. Does such evidence as we have about Sulpicius' character warrant this assumption? And, even if this question cannot be answered objectively, is it plausible to assume that Sulpicius could have falsified the Martinian chronology by as much as twenty years, and got away with it? For we must remember that Sulpicius published the *Vita* in 396, when Martin was still alive, and when some people would still be able to think back to Julian's campaign on the Rhine forty years earlier. And, although in some respects the first epistle and the *Dialogues* are evidently replying to detractors of the *Vita*,[76] there is never a hint that such critics found fault with its *chronology*.

The second hypothesis is not as neat; but nor does it make such large assumptions. It only requires us to assume that Sulpicius, in an apologetic and highly rhetorical passage, grossly exaggerated Martin's age. In its context, this would not amount to falsification; rather, it would be exaggeration, or a manner of speaking, that was never intended to be taken as literal truth. As we shall see below in chapter 14, there is plenty of evidence that Sulpicius was prone to heighten and exaggerate real events; but none that he invented them, or calculatingly falsified them.

My own inclination, then, both on the basis of our two texts and on that of the circumstantial evidence, is to regard the 'short chronology' as the more likely option. In other words, I envisage Martin being born in 336, entering the army in 351, being baptized in 354, and leaving the army in 356. However, as my final word I would emphasize that I regard this only as the most likely hypothesis: not as proven fact.

[76] E.g. *ep*. 1, 2-9; *D* I, 26, 4-6.

10

Martin's Movements in 356

One final problem of Martinian chronology still awaits resolution: could Martin have gone and stayed with Hilary at Poitiers immediately after leaving the army, as Sulpicius says?[1] For Martin can scarcely have gained his release before late July or August, 356; and by then, Hilary had already been sentenced to exile in the east because of his forthright opposition to Arianism.

I have deferred this particular chronological question till now as Sulpicius' account of Martin's doings in 356 also raises problems of a different sort. For one thing, what Sulpicius says about the army on the Rhine front that year does not altogether tally with the account given by a contemporary historian, Ammianus Marcellinus. Then again, our doubts are stirred on quite a different score by our realization that Sulpicius has, at the least, dramatized Martin's face-to-face encounter with the Caesar Julian, when he demanded his release from the army; and it can even be suggested that Sulpicius modelled his account of that scene on an existing martyr's passion. Between them, these three points inevitably raise doubts about Sulpicius' narrative for the year 356.

Let us take the chronological problem first. Can we fit in even a short stay with Hilary at Poitiers, given that Martin can scarcely have arrived there before August, while Hilary had been exiled as a result of the synod of Béziers, held at the latest in early June?

---

[1] *VM* 5, 1. Although Fontaine regards this problem as already solved ('Hilaire et Martin', in *Hilaire de Poitiers*, Paris 1968, p. 70), not all scholars would agree: see M. Meslin, 'Hilaire et la crise arienne', in *Hilaire et son temps*, p. 25 and n. 38. In particular, I can see no justification for Fontaine's assurance that we can postpone Hilary's departure 'till the extreme end of 356.' (Fontaine, loc. cit.)

Now, the Caesar Julian's movements provide clues for dating both the synod of Béziers, and Martin's departure from the army. The new caesar had wintered at Vienne in southern Gaul, 355-6. He must have been still in the vicinity when the synod of bishops met at Béziers, for he was in some way involved with Hilary's case, probably through forwarding the synod's conclusions to Constantius in Italy.[2] It seems that Hilary was not directly exiled by the synod, but as a result of biased reporting of its proceedings to the Emperor Constantius.[3] The date of the synod—and probably of the subsequent manipulation of its results by the Arian party— must be set before Julian's departure for Autun and the Rhine frontier, i.e. before 20 June at the very latest.[4]

However, Hilary was not immediately driven into exile. There would have been a time-lag in the transmission of information from Béziers, first to Julian at Vienne, and then to Constantius in Italy; and some delay between Constantius' decision to exile Hilary, and Hilary's actual departure from Gaul. Evidence of such delay is provided by Hilary's publication of the first book of his *Adversus Valentem et Ursacium* between Béziers and his departure for the east.[5] On the other hand, Hilary had already collected the documents, which formed a large part of the book, before the synod met; in which case the final drafting might not have taken more than a couple of months. In any case, there is some evidence that Hilary departed into exile in September 356 at the latest;[6] and, although this evidence is not watertight,

[2] C. F. A. Borchardt, *Hilary of Poitiers' role in the Arian struggle* (The Hague 1966), ch. 2, esp. pp. 28-31; Meslin, art. cit. pp. 23-4; cf. Doignon, p. 465 and n. 4.

[3] Doignon, pp. 467-8; Meslin, p. 24.

[4] Julian reached Autun from Vienne on 24 June 356: Ammianus Marcellinus, *Res gestae* (ed. C. U. Clark, 2 vols., Berlin, 2nd edn. 1963), XVI, 2, 1-2.

[5] Borchardt, pp. 31-3; A. Wilmart, 'L'*Ad Constantium Liber Primus* de S. Hilaire de Poitiers et les *Fragments Historiques*', *Revue Bénédictine* 24 (1907), pp. 149-79, 291-317; Wilmart, 'Les *Fragments Historiques* et le synode de Béziers de 356', *Revue Bénédictine* 25 (1908), pp. 225-9. I find Wilmart more convincing than Griffe, *Gaule chrét.* I, 230-1.

[6] Sulpicius, *Chron.* II, 42, 1-2: Hilary in the fourth year of his exile when the synod of Seleucia met, September 359. Borchardt (p. 31) and Meslin (p. 25) both take this as an absolute; but one could argue, on the basis of *Chron.* II, 39, 6-7, that Sulpicius did not distinguish between those exiled at Milan in 355, and as a result of Béziers, in 356.

we would expect him to have sailed before November, the traditional date for the closure of the Mediterranean for the winter.[7]

Meanwhile, for Martin's movements, we have to go back to Julian's arrival at Autun on June 24. From there, Julian marched some 215 miles to Rheims, where he met up with Ursicinus and the main body of the army. After due deliberation, it was decided to attack the Alamanni by way of the road running from Metz to Saverne, and so on to the Rhine itself. Battle was joined at Brumath, beyond Saverne, and Julian won a decisive victory. The barbarians were cowed and offered no further resistance, so Julian marched north to Cologne, where he terrified the Franks into submission. He then retired to Sens for the winter.[8]

That is the outline of Julian's campaign of 356, as described by Ammianus Marcellinus. Now, Sulpicius sets Martin's release from the army at Worms, where, he says, Julian concentrated his forces.[9] If this geographical indication is correct, it means we must date Martin's discharge after the battle of Brumath: for Worms lies well to the north, and Julian would only have marched through it after Brumath, while *en route* for Cologne. As for the timing: Julian had had to march approximately 215 miles from Autun to Rheims, which he did with commendable speed; then another 220 miles to Brumath, at a rather slower pace;[10] finally, it would have been getting on for another 90 miles from there north to Worms. All in all, it would have been late July, if not early August, by the time Martin was leaving the army at Worms.

After his release, Martin then had to make his way to Poitiers, another 615 miles or so. However, as a *scholaris*, Martin was a cavalryman; and this would have enabled him to cover the distance in perhaps twelve or fourteen

[7] See L. Casson, *Travel in the Ancient World* (London 1974), p. 150; F. Braudel, *The Mediterranean* (2 vols., 2nd edn. ET London 1972-3), I, 246, 248.

[8] Ammianus XVI, 2 and 3; C. Jullian, *Histoire de la Gaule* (8 vols., Paris 1908-26), VII, 187-90.

[9] *VM* 4, 1.

[10] No dallying, Autun to Rheims: Ammianus XVI, 2, 5-8; slower thereafter, because a large army inevitably moves slower, and because Julian was *providus* and *cunctator* after a surprise attack on his rear: ibid. XVI, 2, 10-11.

days.[11] In other words, Martin could have reached Poitiers by mid August; and, if we assume that Hilary only left in September, that would allow for a fortnight or perhaps a month's overlap, which would correspond adequately with Sulpicius' vague expression, 'aliquandiu apud eum commoratus est.'[12] During this period Hilary 'frequently' tried to ordain Martin deacon, but eventually settled for ordaining him to the lowly grade of exorcist. Martin was perhaps reluctant to be tied to Poitiers as a member of its clergy.[13] This short period of discipleship with Hilary was ended not by Hilary's departure for the east, but by Martin's concern to go and convert his parents: a concern prompted by a dream.[14]

In this way, by pushing Hilary's departure as late as is plausible, and by assuming that Julian's army and then Martin himself would have made reasonable speed, it is possible to accept Sulpicius' story of Martin and Hilary meeting—albeit briefly—in 356. Should we accept it? Without being dogmatic about it, I am inclined to do so: partly because Babut's reasons for suggesting that Sulpicius invented this incident are spurious;[15] and partly because it makes better sense of another detail given by Sulpicius, that Martin tried to meet up with Hilary at Rome on the latter's recall from exile in 360, but missed him, and so had to follow him

[11] Martin probably owned his own horse: cf. *C. Th.* VII, 22, 2 §1-2. On speed of travel, see Casson, pp. 188-96, 315; M. Bloch, *Feudal Society* (ET London, 2nd edn. 1962), p. 62. Cf. Braudel I, 362-9.

[12] *VM* 5, 1.

[13] *VM* 5, 2, and Fontaine's notes; cf. Paulinus *ep.* 1, 10. Alternatively, did Sulpicius seek to excuse Martin's lowly grade by inventing the story about the diaconate?

[14] *VM* 5, 3. Cf. Patrick, *Confessio* 23, ed. L. Bieler, *Classica et Mediaevalia* 11 (1950), pp. 70-1. See E. R. Dodds, *The Greeks and the Irrational* (pb. edn. Berkeley, Los Angeles, London, 1971), p. 107.

[15] Babut is plausible in saying that Martin encountered suspicion in his old age, and that therefore it was a skilful move of Sulpicius to present him as a disciple of the great Hilary (*Saint Martin*, p. 72). But I cannot follow him when he says that, if one visit to Hilary was invented, then very probably the second one was also (cf. pp. 72-3, 184-5). Apart from the unlikelihood that Sulpicius, writing before Martin's death, would have invented such a relationship out of the blue, we can point to probable instances of Hilary's influence on Martin (below, ch. 17, notes 57, 65, and cf. Fontaine, 'Hilaire et Martin', pp. 79-84), and to the suggestive results of the excavations at Ligugé, near Poitiers (above ch. 3). And, if Martin definitely enjoyed some sort of relationship with Hilary in the years following 360, Sulpicius had no need to 'invent' an earlier meeting.

to Poitiers.[16] Martin's behaviour here implies that he already knew Hilary.

Let us pass on to a second difficulty raised by Sulpicius' narrative for 356: his account of military matters does not altogether tally with that given by the contemporary historian, Ammianus Marcellinus.

One discrepancy has already been noted: Ammianus makes it clear that a battle was fought near Brumath; and, although Worms figures as one of seven *civitates* held by the Germans, and although Julian doubtless took it in on his march from Brumath to Cologne, Ammianus says nothing of Julian massing his forces there in expectation of imminent battle. Sulpicius, on the other hand, never mentions the battle of Brumath. His account runs: 'Meanwhile, as the barbarians had invaded Gaul, the Caesar Julian drew up his army at Worms, and began to pay out a donative to the soldiers . . .' Battle was expected on the very next day; but, in the event, the barbarians surrendered without fighting.[17] Now, Ammianus was an eyewitness for Julian's campaign that year, and his testimony about the battle at Brumath must be accepted.[18] Presumably, then, Martin's discharge at Worms took place after this battle, which Sulpicius has passed over in silence.[19] Apart from the general reason that biographers then, like local journalists today, felt quite at liberty to keep silent or give a highly distorted view of the general significance of an event, and to focus their attention simply on the men that concerned them, Sulpicius would have had his own particular reasons for silence. He would have preferred not to draw attention to the fact that Martin had taken part in a battle since his baptism, for his military past was something which Martin was never fully able to live down. Years later, a monk in a temper jibed that Martin

---

[16] *VM* 6, 7-7, 1.

[17] Ammianus XVI, 2, 12-3, 2; *VM* 4, §1, §4, §7.

[18] On Ammianus see E. A. Thompson, *The Historical Work of Ammianus Marcellinus* (Cambridge 1947), esp. pp. 4-5.

[19] We cannot assume that Sulpicius simply muddled his place-names, writing 'Worms' for 'Brumath', because Sulpicius insists that there was no battle, whereas Ammianus describes one.

had been 'defiled' by his time as a soldier; and Martin could not deny it.[20]

Despite Sulpicius' silence, however, the battle of Brumath may have been of great significance in Martin's life: for it may have been this experience of actual fighting, coupled with the realization that he could no longer expect to be 'a soldier only in name' if he remained in the Roman army, that prompted him to seek his release at the earliest opportunity. This is guess-work; but it is plausible. Love and peace lie at the heart of the Gospel; and an important strand of Christian thought, before Constantine, insisted that a soldier who became a Christian still remained bound by the basic Christian prohibition against killing, just the same as a civilian.[21] The crucial question is, did Constantine's conversion change this overnight? The answer is not entirely straightforward.[22] In 314, the year after the emperors abandoned persecution and recognized the church, the synod of Arles debarred from communion those 'qui arma proiciunt in pace'. This canon has often been taken to mean that, now that church and state were at peace with each other, Christian soldiers must not leave the army. But a more obvious interpretation is that suggested by Bainton: soldiers must not abandon the army *in peacetime*—the tacit admission being that they may feel obliged to do so in war.[23]

However, Constantine portrayed his wars as Christian wars, and no church leader objected. Indeed, Eusebius set the prevailing tone by hailing Constantine as God's earthly agent for

[20] *D* III, 15, 4. See Fontaine, 'Vérité et fiction', pp. 211–20.

[21] R. H. Bainton, *Christian Attitudes toward War and Peace* (Nashville 1960; pb. edn.), pp. 77–81; C. J. Cadoux, *The Early Church and the World* (Edinburgh 1925), pp. 422–35, 581–7; Siniscalco, *Massimiliano*, pp. 112–20, and cf. 133–6; L. J. Swift, 'War and the Christian Conscience, I', in *Aufstieg und Niedergang der römischen Welt* II, 23, 1, ed. W. Haase (Berlin & NY 1979), pp. 835–68. J. Helgeland's attempt (ibid. pp. 724–834) to argue that no early Christian writer opposed Christian participation in war on the grounds that killing was wrong fails to convince me: e.g. in his treatment of Tertullian and Hippolytus.

[22] Cadoux pp. 588–92 (but note now *The Treatise on the Apostolic Tradition of St. Hippolytus of Rome*, ed. G. Dix, revised H. Chadwick (London 1968); Siniscalco pp. 149–54; Bainton, pp. 85–9. Cf. also W. H. C. Frend, *Martyrdom and Persecution in the Early Church* (Oxford 1965), ch. 16. Note that Martin saw the peace of the church only as a lull before the final persecution: *D* II, 14, 1–4.

[23] Bainton, pp. 80–1; cf. Siniscalco p. 150 and n. 6.

leading men to the Logos.[24] Perhaps the inconsistency can be understood like this: at a formal, intellectual, level, Christians recognized the necessity of warfare, and the more happily identified their emperor's cause with Christianity because his foe was a pagan (or, later in the century, a barbarian heretic); but, in their gut, many Christians still felt uneasy about shedding blood. So, for instance, Basil recognized that killing in battle is not the same as committing murder, but advised: 'nevertheless perhaps it would be well that those whose hands are unclean abstain from communion for three years.' This tallies with the Emperor Theodosius' abstention from communion after shedding blood in battle.[25] If a former general and emperor could feel like that about unavoidable warfare, then we can understand the language of Paulinus of Nola: 'Et qui militat gladio mortis est minister . . . aut enim exitu mortis tenebitur reus aut crimine . . .' I.e. the soldier inevitably has blood on his hands, because either he kills, or he is killed.[26] We can understand, too, that Christians who tried to model their whole lives after the example of Jesus, like Victricius, like Martin, felt compelled to reject the use of weapons designed to kill and maim.[27] Martin's behaviour here accords with the teaching of some pre-Constantinian churchmen.[28] At the same time, he was the forerunner of many medieval ex-soldier saints, who found themselves so sickened by their experience of warfare that they renounced the world and adopted the religious life.[29] Further light is shed on Martin's refusal to wield weapons in war by noting how, later in life,

---

[24] S. L. Greenslade, *Church and State from Constantine to Theodosius* (London 1954), pp. 9-11.

[25] Bainton, p. 78 (Basil); Fontaine *Vie* II, 536 n. 2 (Theodosius).

[26] *Ep.* 25, 3; cf. also 25, 5.

[27] Paulinus *ep.* 18, 7: 'arma sanguinis abiecisti . . . , qui armabaris Christo.' *VM* 4, 5. Cf. also Cadoux, pp. 587, 590-1, and J. Fontaine, 'Le Culte des martyrs militaires', *Ecclesia orans: mélanges . . . A. G. Hamman* (Rome 1980), pp. 141-71. Note too Wulfilas' refusal to translate Kings and Chronicles for the Goths, lest he should stimulate their warlike spirits (D. H. Green, *The Carolingian Lord*, Cambridge 1965, p. 279). Origen shared Wulfilas' distaste for OT wars, but resolved the problem by interpreting them spiritually: Bainton, p. 82.

[28] E.g. Tertullian *De corona* 11, 4-5; ed. with notes by J. Fontaine (Paris 1966), pp. 140-1.

[29] A. Murray, *Reason and Society in the Middle Ages* (Oxford 1978), pp. 376-8.

he followed his master's example in silently submitting to violence, rather than taking the necessary steps to defend himself.[30]

Sulpicius' silence about the battle of Brumath is, then, one point where a comparison with Ammianus suggests that Sulpicius has told us less than the whole truth. Further problems arise over Sulpicius' description of Martin's encounter with Julian. Although Sulpicius portrays the meeting as occasioned by Julian's distribution of a donative to the army, Ammianus explicitly states, apropos of an army revolt in 358, that the soldiers had received neither donative nor pay from the day that Julian arrived in Gaul.[31] It can, however, be argued that this applies only to the common soldiers, and need not preclude a distribution to the *scholae*, to which Martin belonged. Indeed, elsewhere Ammianus mentions that donatives were given to the *agentes in rebus* 'amongst others'.[32] These others might well have included the *scholae*, particularly as this select corps did not come under the authority of the *magister militum*, like the rest of the army, but under that of the *magister officiorum*, like the *agentes in rebus*.[33] True, the pointers to be gleaned from numismatic evidence are not favourable: there appears to have been a lacuna in the striking of money in Gaul between 355 and 358-9. However, this negative evidence cannot rule out the possibility that Julian issued a small-scale donative in 356.[34] This discrepancy with Ammianus is therefore not serious.

The real grounds for harbouring suspicions about the scene between Martin and Julian arise from its 'stylization' after the norms of martyr literature. Sulpicius has cast this encounter into the mould of confrontation between saint

---

[30] *VM* 15, 1-2; *D* II, 3, 4; III, 15, 7. Cf. Matt. 26:51-4; Matt. 5:38-48.

[31] XVII, 9, 5-6.

[32] XVI, 5, 11. Fontaine, *Vie* II, 516-8, revising a suggestion of C. Jullian ('La Jeunesse' pp. 269-70). Both scholars base themselves on Ammianus XVI, 5, 11; but note that Jullian's citation of this passage is highly misleading: Ammianus does not specifically mention the *scholares*, though Jullian misquotes him to that effect.

[33] Jones *LRE* I, 368-9; II, 613. Frank, *Scholae Palatinae*, pp. 49-50, and cf. pp. 123-4.

[34] Fontaine, *Vie* II, 518 n. 1.

and Roman persecutor as portrayed in many acts of the martyrs, especially those of African soldier-martyrs.[35] For instance, the latter provide close parallels for Martin's words to Julian, contrasting service to the emperor with service to Christ.[36] Again, Sulpicius portrays Julian's anger at Martin's request with the words 'tyrannus infremuit'. This suggests the colourful, dramatized language of the literary martyrs' passions.[37] And, if we are surprised at this transformation of the young Caesar Julian (still nominally Christian in 356) into a typical persecuting emperor, then, here also we may see the transforming influence of martyrs' legends at work. For, after Julian became emperor, he not only apostatized himself; he also, when distributing a donative, put pressure on members of the imperial guard to burn incense to the pagan gods. Further, two Christian soldiers who used insulting language were actually martyred. Although this happened in the east, oral accounts might well have reached the west by the time Sulpicius was writing.[38]

Granted, then, that Sulpicius has 'stylized' Martin's encounter with Julian, what are the implications for us? Sulpicius' procedure can be viewed from two angles: the literary cum apologetic angle, and the historical one. From a literary and apologetic stance, the chapter is masterly. Sulpicius, *qua* saint's biographer, had found himself in a difficult position; for Martin's baptism at the age of eighteen manifestly did not mark a break in his life: Martin carried on in the distasteful profession of a soldier, just as before. However, by modelling his account of Martin's departure from the army along the lines of martyr literature, Sulpicius was able to provide his readers with at least the appearance of a dramatic break with the world—and one which came at the end of Martin's military service, and thus signalized the discontinuity between

---

[35] For what follows I am greatly indebted to J. Fontaine's article, 'Sulpice Sévère a-t-il travesti saint Martin de Tours en martyr militaire?', *AB* 81 (1963), pp. 31-58; and to his notes on *VM* 4 in *Vie* II, 509-38.

[36] Below, n. 45.

[37] Fontaine, *Vie* II, 525.

[38] Fontaine, 'Martyr militaire', pp. 49-51. But NB also *Vie* II, 544-5, where Fontaine points out that Julian had just become implicated in Constantius' pro-Arian measures, notably the exiling of Hilary; and this makes *VM* 4's presentation of Julian as a *tyrannus* rather more historical.

his suspect army past, and his subsequent religious life. So Sulpicius was at one stroke seeking to disarm hostile criticism, while at the same time providing well-disposed ascetic circles with the portrait of a saint which they could take to heart: for the military martyr was popular in western circles at this date.[39]

So much we may say in appreciation of Sulpicius' literary skill. But what of the historicity of this episode? One point is that there is nothing intrinsically implausible about the *content* of Sulpicius' account: the actual events which he records could well be true.[40] Another point to be made is that even the stylized manner in which Sulpicius presents the encounter need not necessarily invalidate its essential historicity.

By way of illustration, let us compare Paulinus of Nola's account of how Victricius, once a soldier, later bishop of Rouen, renounced his military career. According to Paulinus, Victricius had gone out on to the parade ground fully armed, for a military assembly. He had then astonished everyone by flinging down his arms at his tribune's feet, determined to exchange his secular military service for service to Christ. A beating and torture failed to shake his resolve; he was condemned to death, and saved only by a miracle: just before the executioner could carry out the sentence, he was struck blind, while the chains dropped from Victricius' hands.[41]

A summary such as this gives no inkling of the elaborate way in which Paulinus tells this story, decking it out with rhetorical language. But even this bare *résumé* reveals an account which is at least as stylized as chapter four of the *Vita Martini*, and probably rather more so: it includes the hagiographical *topos* of the would-be executioner struck blind when he attempts to put a saint to death.[42] Paulinus included this florid passage in a letter he wrote to Victricius

---

[39] I owe these points to Fontaine, 'Martyr militaire', pp. 38–40, 51–2, 56–7. Cf. also Fontaine, 'Le Culte des martyrs militaires'.

[40] Cf. Jullian, 'La Jeunesse', pp. 264–5, 269–70.

[41] *Ep.* 18, 7.

[42] Cf. below p. 201, and Fontaine, 'Martyr militaire', p. 57 n. 1. NB also that while *VM* 4 can be compared to *Passio Typasii*, this account of Victricius can be compared to the *Acta Marcelli* (ed. Musurillo, pp. 250, 254).

in 397; and I regard as plausible Fontaine's suggestion that he was here attempting to outdo his friend's account of Martin and Julian, which had just been published.[43] But there is, surely, one other point to be made. Paulinus' rhetorical, stylized account of Victricius' conversion occurs in a letter written to Victricius himself. This means that it cannot be too far removed from the actual event it describes.[44] And if Paulinus is here simply stylizing a historical event in Victricius' life after the fashion of the *acta martyrum*, then *a priori* it seems plausible to assume that Sulpicius, writing at a time when his account was likely to come to Martin's notice, did the same. At any rate, this shows that the idea of a straight line running from historical accuracy at one pole to literary stylization at the other is so oversimplified as to be downright misleading. Instead we must recognize that the axis which runs from truth to falsehood is not identical with that running from an unvarnished statement to a stylized account. A strong degree of literary stylization does not necessarily exclude substantial historical veracity.

Nor, of course, does it guarantee it. And, in connection with *Vita Martini* 4, there is one further question to be faced: what should we make of the similarities between this chapter and the *Passion of Typasius*, a soldier-martyr who suffered under Diocletian? For there is an undeniable parallelism in the unfolding of events in these two works.[45] In both, the scene is set by the emperor or caesar distributing a donative on the eve of battle. In both cases the saint refuses the donative, and asks to be released for the service of Christ, whose soldier he now is. This naturally angers the emperor/caesar. At this Typasius, who had been warned what would

---

[43] Fontaine, loc. cit. pp. 57–8.

[44] Especially as humility was a Christian virtue which Victricius did not lack: cf. *D* III, 2, 4–5. The same conclusion is reached by F. Heim, 'La Thème de la "victoire sans combat" chez Ambroise', *Ambroise de Milan*, ed. Y.-M. Duval (Paris 1974), p. 268.

[45] There is also a close verbal parallel to Martin's words to Julian: 'Hactenus . . . militavi tibi; patere ut nunc militem Deo . . . Christi ego miles sum: pugnare mihi non licet.' (*VM* 4, 3.) See *Passio Typasii* 5 (*AB* 9, 1890, pp. 120, 121). However, such expressions were a stock-in-trade of the soldier-martyr acts: e.g. *Acta Marcelli*, recension M, chs. 1, 1 and 4, 3; *Acta Maximiliani* 1, 2 and 2, 1 (ed. Musurillo pp. 250, 252, 244). This renders the verbal parallel with *Passio Typasii* insignificant; it is the parallel in the stories which matters.

happen by an angel, prophesies that, if he were released, the emperor would overcome the barbarians in Africa without armed conflict, and Roman armies would be victorious on all sides; whereas Martin, accused of cowardice, expresses his readiness to enter battle unarmed on the following day. In both cases, the emperor/caesar commands that the saint should be kept in custody; and in both, the eventual outcome is the same: the barbarians unexpectedly send envoys suing for peace—though in the *Passio Typasii* this surrender is not immediate, and is precipitated only by the emperor accidentally running through the barbarian lines and routing them while he is out hunting; whereas in the *Vita Martini* it comes, out of the blue, on the very next day.[46]

That there is a parallel here is incontrovertible. Its significance, however, is far from clear, for it is unlikely that Sulpicius could have known the *Passio Typasii* in 396, when he was working on the *Vita Martini*. Monceaux has argued convincingly that the *Passio Typasii* as we now have it is a non-contemporary, composite text: its author, whom he would date to the time of St. Augustine, amalgamated the original written *acta Typasii* with oral legends about the saint which had grown up since his death *c*.300.[47] Now, the significant parallels with the *Vita Martini* occur in the later, legendary part of the *Passio*; and, although Monceaux's dating rests on rather impressionistic grounds, lexigraphical evidence corroborates and refines his *terminus a quo* for the *Passio*'s composition. For the *Passio* says that Typasius built a *monasterium* (chapter 4). This is clearly anachronistic for *c*.300; but the anachronism is revealing, for it would only have been committed at a time when the word *monasterium* had passed into normal use in North Africa. Now, *monasterium* is a Latin neologism first coined by Evagrius of Antioch in his translation of the *Vita Antonii* between 357 and 370. The word was soon taken up by Evagrius' friend, Jerome, and reached Italy in the 380s: it was used by Ambrose in

---

[46] *VM* 4; *Passio Typasii* 2 and 3.

[47] P. Monceaux, *Histoire littéraire de l'Afrique chrétienne* III (Paris 1905, repr. Brussels 1963), pp. 126-31 (which reprints, without alteration, Monceaux's 'Étude critique sur la Passio Tipasii veterani', published in *Revue archéologique* 1904, pp. 267-74).

383, Pope Siricius in 385, and Paulinus in 395.[48] It next occurs in the *Vita Martini*, Sulpicius having probably encountered the word via Martin's Marmoutier. But news of monasticism seems to have come later to Africa, for it was unknown to Augustine's mother before she left for Milan in 385.[49] And, if monasticism itself were not widely known about, neither would the technical term *monasterium* have been. This supposition is strengthened by Augustine's avoidance of the term in 388-9, immediately after his return to Africa. He adopted it for the first time only in 396-7, having founded Africa's first true *monasterium* only in 391.[50] This implies that *monasterium* did not come into common use in North Africa until the late 390s, if not the early fifth century; and this makes it unlikely that the *Passio Typasii* as we know it was written any earlier.

What, then, of the parallels with the *Vita Martini*? If, for reasons of dating, it is unlikely that Sulpicius used the *Passio Typasii* as we now have it, there remain three other alternatives. Either the parallel is largely coincidental, arising from a combination of chance and of an identical request being met by Roman commanders in a similar manner, coupled with the fact that both stories belong in the literary tradition of martyr literature.[51] This is possible. Or Sulpicius was influenced not by the written text of the *Passio Typasii* as we now have it, but by the oral legends which the later text incorporated. This again is possible, for we have already seen that Egyptian

---

[48] L. T. A. Lorié, *Spiritual Terminology in the Latin translations of the Vita Antonii* (Nijmegen 1955), pp. 43–51; J. van den Bosch, *Capa, Basilica, Monasterium* (Nijmegen 1959), pp. 108–11; Lienhard, pp. 60–3.

[49] Augustine, *Confessiones* VIII, vi, 14–15. I assume that Monica would have told Augustine about Egyptian monasticism if she had known of it, as Augustine was then (386) living with his mother. Monica's ignorance of monasticism does not preclude knowledge of it having reached some in Africa by that date, but it does suggest that it was not widely known about. Of course, Africa already had men and women dedicated to virginity (Folliet pp. 25-35), but the term *monasterium* would only have arrived with news of the new monastic developments in the east, or in Italy and Gaul.

[50] van den Bosch, pp. 109-10; Folliet, pp. 40-3.

[51] Confrontation sparked off during the distribution of a donative occurs elsewhere in martyr literature, not just in *VM* and *Passio Typasii*: viz. Tertullian, *De corona* 1; note also Julian's attempt to use the donative as a means of suborning his Christian soldiers to offer incense (above, and Fontaine, *Vie* II, 514, 518-19).

tales travelled to Gaul by word of mouth, and African stories could have done the same. In Sulpicius' *Dialogues*, the Aquitanian Postumianus is shown stopping off in Africa, where he paid his respects to the tombs of the saints, especially St. Cyprian, on his way to visit the desert fathers of Egypt.[52] Alternatively, it could have been Sulpicius' work which influenced the compiler of the *Passio Typasii*, not *vice versa*. In some ways this seems more likely, for Typasius' cult never attained popularity outside the neighbourhood of Tigava in Mauretania Caesariensis, where he was martyred. Even his name was forgotten until 1890, when his *Passio* was published from a single manuscript.[53] The *Vita Martini*, on the other hand, rapidly achieved popularity and a wide circulation, and it was definitely known to Augustine's circle in Africa by 422.[54] This, then, is perhaps the most likely alternative; but any of these options is possible, and none is provable.

Where does this leave the question of the historicity of the events recounted in *Vita Martini* 4: Martin's encounter with Julian, refusal of a donative, request for release, and lucky escape from having to keep his promise to enter battle unarmed? The outer limits at least are clear: on the one hand, Sulpicius has definitely stylized Martin's confrontation with Julian after the pattern of the soldier-martyrs' acts and legends; on the other hand, Martin did gain his discharge from the army that year. Now, if Martin was indeed only twenty at the time, doubtless there was an angry scene with his commander; and, as the *scholares* were so closely associated with the person of the emperor or caesar, this probably did bring Martin face to face with Julian. We may further note that the actual circumstances which secured Martin's release, unlike those in the *Passio Typasii*, are not improbable, nor overtly miraculous—something which Sulpicius was

[52] Above, ch. 5; *D* I, 3, 1-2. Cf. Fontaine, 'Martyr militaire', pp. 45-6; *Vie* II, 510-12.

[53] See *AB* 9 (1890), p. 109. Since then, his name has been found in association with other Mauretanian martyrs in one inscription from Oppidum Novum, near Tigava; but that is all: Monceaux, III, 126, 127; E. Diehl, *Inscriptiones Latinae Christianae Veteres* (3 vols., Berlin 1925-31), I, no. 2067.

[54] This is apparent from the deacon Paulinus' preface to his *Vita Ambrosii*, cit. above p. 99. Sulpicius claims that his *VM* was known in Africa by *c.* 400: *D* I, 23, 5.

uncomfortably aware of, and apologized for.[55] This, coupled with the fact that Sulpicius is unlikely to have read the *Passio Typasii* by 396, suggests that we should not make too much of the parallels with that work. Direct plagiarism is unlikely. More than this—for instance, whether the donative story is literally true, or a literary artifice—we cannot know.[56]

This chapter and the last have surveyed some of the most telling evidence which can be levelled against Sulpicius' accuracy. In an area where other sources are few, it is hard to prove any interpretation right, or wrong; much rests on our judgement. We can certainly see how a Babut can perform a sledge-hammer job, and argue that Sulpicius is wholly untrustworthy; but whether a sledge-hammer is an apt instrument to apply to something as sophisticated as Sulpicius' Martinian writings is another matter. Detailed study suggests that we need a more subtle approach: that Sulpicius, for instance, misleads us over Martin's military career not by telling blatant lies about how long Martin stayed in the army, but simply by keeping quiet about a battle in which Martin presumably took part.

These chapters have involved us in evaluating most of Sulpicius' account of Martin's early life, which is told in a straightforward, narrative fashion. However, by far the greater part of the Martinian writings is taken up with miracle stories illustrating Martin's achievements as monk-bishop of Tours. It is to these that we must now turn.

---

[55] *VM* 4, 7-9. This suggests that he was not copying a more miraculous source.
[56] Cf. Fontaine's summing up, 'Martyr militaire', pp. 52-5.

11

Vir Deo plenus: Sulpicius' Presentation of Martin

After Sulpicius had described Martin's election as bishop and foundation of Marmoutier, he abandoned his chronological narrative. The rest of the *Vita* and the second and third *Dialogues* are taken up with stories illustrating Martin's remarkable powers as a monk-bishop. In the *Vita*, these stories are grouped thematically; in the *Dialogues*, their ordering is more random. But in both works, the approach is the same: Martin is viewed primarily as a man of God, a transmitter of God's grace who wields authority over the natural world and over the forces of evil—not as a busy bishop carrying out the everyday pastoral, liturgical, and administrative duties of the fourth-century episcopacy. This chapter, then, seeks to outline Sulpicius' portrayal of Martin as he appears in the Martinian works: i.e. as 'a man filled with God' (*Vita* 3, 1).

At the outset we should note one feature which is remarkable in the life of one born to pagan parents: there is no moment of conversion for Martin, either in the sense of conversion from paganism to Christianity, or of conversion to the ascetic ideal. Instead, Martin is shown as an *anima naturaliter christiana*—and, indeed, *ascetica*. Martin's yearning for God remains constant from his childhood right through to his death: even as a boy, he was already a monk or priest in his mind's eye; while a soldier, he behaved as though he were already a monk; and even after he became a bishop, he still remained a monk, both in externals such as dress, and in his general outlook.[1]

It is true, of course, that Sulpicius' narrative implies two turning-points in Martin's life: his break with the Roman

[1] *VM* 2, 2-8; *VM* 10, 1-2.

army, and his election as bishop. But although Martin's break
with the army is, as we have seen, dressed up as a break with
the world after the pattern of martyr literature, the surrounding chapters belie this interpretation: viewed in context,
Vita Martini 4 simply marks the point where Martin's natural
bent, deflected by his forcible conscription into the army a
few years earlier, is able to reassert itself. As for the change
caused by Martin's consecration as bishop: the appearance
of a caesura here arises from the fact that Sulpicius, following
the Suetonian pattern of biography, has chosen this event
to conclude the *Vita*'s chronological section before passing
on to Martin's achievements as a bishop. But Sulpicius
himself is adamant that Martin's new role as bishop was
simply added on to Martin's role as a monk; it in no way
superseded the latter.

By way of illustration, let us look at two of Sulpicius'
stories. The first is the famous tale of Martin's charity
at Amiens. This occurred when Martin was still only a
catechumen, though Sulpicius already describes him as 'vir
Deo plenus'. Martin's compassion was stirred when he met
a naked beggar, shivering in the cold. Martin responded
immediately by dividing his cloak between himself and the
beggar. This provoked a varied response: 'Some of the
bystanders laughed at the sight of Martin's mutilated clothing
(*deformis . . . truncatus habitu*); but many who were sounder
in their reasoning (*mens sanior*)' regretted their own inaction.
That Martin's deed was in reality performed for Christ was
made clear by his dream the following night when he saw
Jesus calling the angels to admire the cloak which Martin
had given him.[2] It was as a result of this that Martin was
baptized; and even then he remained a soldier, a suspect
profession for a baptized man.

The parallels between this story and the account of
Martin's election to the see of Tours are interesting. In the
latter case, the multitudes who gathered to choose a new
bishop were miraculously united in their opinion that Martin
was highly suitable for the episcopate. 'But a few, including
some bishops . . . , impiously objected, saying that he was a

[2] *VM* 3, 1-4.

contemptible character, and that a man of abject bearing, wretched dress, and with mutilated hair (*crine deformem*) was unworthy of the episcopate. This madness was ridiculed by the people holding a sounder opinion (*sententiae sanioris*) . . .'; and through God's will the objectors were confounded by the chance reading of a text which the people took as an oracle from heaven.[3] Thus the bishops' protests were overruled, and Martin duly consecrated bishop.

In comparing these two stories, the parallels in content go beyond the slight verbal similarities. In both instances, Martin's religion makes him appear somewhat 'non-U'. In the former case this merely arouses ridicule; in the latter, there is a strong feeling that this disqualifies Martin from the office of bishop. In both instances opinions differ, with the 'sounder' ones supporting Martin's position. More important, in both there is direct contact between the divine and terrestrial realms;[4] and it is this which is the telling factor, not the sacrament of baptism (which came after Martin's charity and vision of Christ), nor that of episcopal consecration (which perforce followed on the *fait accompli* of his popular election). Further, in neither case does Martin make any break with his old way of life: he behaved like a monk before the encounter at Amiens, and baptism did not cause him to leave the army. Similarly, episcopal consecration did not lead him to abandon his ascetic way of life, as Sulpicius stresses: 'For he continued most constantly just the same as before, with the same humility in his heart, the same meanness in his dress. And thus, full of authority and grace (*gratiae*), he fulfilled the eminent office of bishop without abandoning the profession or the virtue of a monk.[5] At first he used a cell next to the cathedral. When this afforded him too little peace he founded the monastery of Marmoutier just across the river from the city, while at the cathedral he set apart

---

[3] *VM* 9, 3-7.

[4] By admitting Martin to heaven in his dream (*VM* 3, 3); and by God's will making itself felt on earth: *Domino volente* (*VM* 9, 4); *divino nutu* (*VM* 9, 7).

[5] *VM* 10, 1-2. *Gratia* cannot be adequately translated: classical authors often paired it with *auctoritas* (as here), to mean 'influence, prestige' (Fontaine, *Vie* II, 663-4). But *plenus gratiae* has definite NT connotations: see John 1:14; cf. Luke 1:28.

a special vestry where he could be alone while business was being conducted by the other clergy in a different room.[6]

The significance of Martin's continuing asceticism in Sulpicius' presentation of him cannot be doubted. Although Sulpicius devotes only one chapter specifically to the monastic life of Marmoutier, references to Martin's ascetic habits recur continually. We hear of the scarcity of food and clothing amongst the monks of Marmoutier.[7] Martin ate fish at Eastertide, seemingly as a treat, while wine was allowed only for monks in ill health.[8] Martin's dress was the *cilicium*, hair shirt; and at night he just lay down on the bare ground with this over him, winter though it might be.[9]

Another aspect of Martin's asceticism was his horror of women and his praise of virginity. His teaching that marriage is 'pardonable' implies that it is a falling away from perfection, albeit a forgiveable one. He resolutely refused to let a married man who had become a monk return to his wife and live in chastity with her, although family monasticism was then widespread. (Think, for instance, of Paulinus and Therasia at Nola.) For Martin, a woman's greatest virtue lay in not letting herself even be seen.[10]

Just as Martin excluded feminine company in order to preserve his chastity, so he spurned the presents of secular potentates to preserve his poverty,[11] and refused to let them dine with him to preserve his humility.[12] This emphasized the fact that he stood outside the normal ties of society; indeed, 'having transcended human nature', he was in direct relationship with the spiritual world.[13] Sulpicius saw a causal link between Martin's asceticism and the miracles he wrought: Martin's 'habitual weapons' were not merely the sign of the cross, but also his harsh garb, fasting, and prayers. With these

[6] *VM* 10, 3; *D* II, 1, 2.

[7] *D* III, 14, 6. For the monastic life of Marmoutier, see also above, ch. 3.

[8] *D* III, 10, 1-4; *VM* 10, 7.

[9] *Ep.* 1, 10-11; cf. *ep.* 3, 14.

[10] *D* II, 10, 4-12, 6.

[11] *D* II, 5, 10; cf. *D* III, 14, 5-6. But NB in Gregory's day Tours boasted a paten which was said to have been given to Martin by the Emperor Maximus: Gregory, *De virt. S. Mart.* IV, 10.

[12] *D* I, 25, 6. But NB *VM* 20 and *D* II, 6, 4.

[13] *D* II, 4, 2; cf. *VM* 2, 7 and 27, 1. See also below, n. 18.

he healed the sick, cast out demons, compelled obedience, and commanded the elements. The explanation for this is Sulpicius' contention that Martin's asceticism, triumphantly pursued amid hostile surroundings, brought him beyond the ordinary human level and close to God, just as the apostles, prophets, and martyrs were close to God; and, *vice versa*, that Martin's thaumaturgical powers proved his special relationship to God.[14]

This latter explains the importance attached to Martin's first miracle at Ligugé. While Martin was absent, one of his disciples had caught a fever and died before he had even been baptized. When Martin learnt of this he prostrated himself on the body in prayer, and eventually succeeded in resuscitating the catechumen. Afterwards the latter described how he had been brought before the Judge's tribunal and already sentenced to the underworld when Martin intervened with his prayers and gained his release. This miracle showed that Martin's holiness was genuine since his prayers clearly carried weight on a supernatural level: 'From this time the fame of the blessed man first shone forth: he who had already been regarded by everyone as a holy man was now held to be also endowed with power, and truly apostolic (*potens etiam et vere apostolicus*).'[15] A story in the *Dialogues* makes a similar point. While Martin was *en route* for Chartres, many pagans crowded out from their village to see him, because they had heard that he was a 'great man'. Martin began to preach to them, but it was only after he had authenticated the crowd's belief that he was a 'friend of God' by restoring a dead child to life that the crowd acclaimed Christ as God.[16]

In the literary setting of the *Dialogues*, this story was taken as proof of Martin's superiority over the ascetics of Egypt: it placed him on a level with the apostles and prophets.[17] Sulpicius also represents Martin as being on familiar terms with the ascetic heroes SS. Agnes and Thecla, with the apostles Peter and Paul, with St. Mary, and with the angels, who delighted in coming to see him.[18]

[14] *Ep.* 2, 8–13; *D* II, 5, 1–2. Cf. below chs. 16–17. [15] *VM* 7.
[16] *D* II, 4, 4–9. [17] *D* II, 5, 1–2. [18] *D* II, 13, 6–8; II, 12, 11; I, 25, 3.

The fact that Martin already within his lifetime existed on such a spiritual plane gave him also superhuman powers of perception. Whatever he was doing, 'he never slackened his spirit from prayer.'[19] So it is not surprising to find Sulpicius acclaiming his ability in expounding scripture, once even likening him to Solomon in his wisdom.[20] His spiritual discernment also enabled him always to expose evil for what it was. For instance, when rumours were flying that barbarians were about to invade Trier, Martin restored confidence by compelling a demoniac to confess that these were disseminated by demons.[21] Similarly, his prayers enabled him to call up and question the shade of a dead man who was popularly honoured as a martyr, but on interrogation was shown up as a brigand.[22] It also meant that Martin would refuse to be swayed by demonically-inspired arguments against his admitting those who had sinned after baptism to his monastery; and, likewise, he would refuse to take action against the insolence of Brice since here, also, he could perceive the demonic instigation behind the man's taunts.[23] In Sulpicius' eyes this gift was particularly valuable since Martin had foretold the imminent end of the world, when false prophets would abound.[24] He thus relates at length the story of Anatolius, who claimed to be a virtue of God; and that of the devil masquerading as Christ before Martin. In neither case could the devil deceive Martin.[25]

This ability to pin-point the demonic was obviously connected with Martin's powers as an exorcist. When entering a house in Trier he stopped because he could *see* a demon in the *atrium*. At his command to be gone the devil seized the cook who promptly went berserk, but perforce obeyed Martin's commands and was powerless to hurt him.[26] Martin's normal treatment of demoniacs was in fact markedly un-theatrical. He would order every one else out of the church and, with the doors made fast, he would pray alone: 'clad in his hair shirt, sprinkled with ashes, he would pray stretched out on the floor.'[27] Thus here again it is Martin's asceticism

---

[19] *VM* 26, 3.   [20] *VM* 25, 6-8; *D* II, 6, 6-7.
[21] *VM* 18, 1-2. Rousseau, 'Spiritual Authority', p. 410.   [22] *VM* 11.
[23] *VM* 22, 3-5. *D* III, 15, 6-7.   [24] *D* II, 14; *VM* 24, 1-3. Cf. *VM* 22, 6.
[25] *VM* 23; 24, 4-8.   [26] *VM* 17, 5-7.   [27] *D* III, 6, 3.

which is emphasized as well as his prayers, with the implication that it was this which made his prayers so efficacious.

Exorcism of demoniacs was only one form of healing
miracle that Martin performed, although it should also be
said that it was the commonest. In addition Martin healed
a leper, a dumb girl, one with acute paralysis, one with
quartan ague; Paulinus from eye-trouble; a woman from a
haemorrhage; a boy from a snake-bite, while he himself was
healed by an angel from bruises gained through falling
downstairs.[28] At times Martin seems to have used the same
means in healing as in other instances of his use of prayer.
He persisted for a week in prayer and fasting in order to
free Lycontius' household from disease;[29] here he was not
even physically present. But at other times he would touch
the affected part of the body, and sometimes anoint it with
holy oil.

This was a mode of treatment for the sick which, like
exorcism, was officially recognized by the church. Another
sphere of activity which was patently bound up with his
position as bishop was his handling of paganism, though
here he certainly went beyond the official norm. Martin saw
paganism as the work of the devil: he would often recognize
his old enemy under the guise of Jupiter, Mercury, Venus,
or Minerva.[30] In his travels, Martin came across peasants who
were still largely heathen. Sulpicius tells us that Martin would
usually win them over by his teaching so that they demolished
their temples of their own accord.[31] However, since Sulpicius
was concerned to demonstrate Martin's *virtus*, it is only those
occasions where Martin was miraculously saved from death
or sought visible assistance from heaven which he describes.
Thus we hear how the pagans in one village stood by while
Martin demolished their temple, but could only be induced
to agree to the felling of their sacred pine by Martin's readiness
to stand where they put him, so that they could cut the tree
down on top of him.[32] Martin was miraculously saved by
making the sign of the cross at the tree as it was falling on
him, thus changing the direction of its fall. On other occasions

---

[28] See appendix.   [29] *D* III, 14, 3-5.
[30] *VM* 22, 1; *D* II, 13, 6; III, 6, 4-5.   [31] *VM* 15, 4.   [32] *VM* 13.

Martin gained his ends by fasting for a length of time in his hair shirt, covered with cinders, as he prayed God for divine aid. At Levroux this came in the form of two armed angels who provided a bodyguard for Martin while he destroyed the temple. At Amboise, a violent storm did his work for him. On another occasion a column came hurtling down from heaven and smashed the offending idol into smithereens: 'Assuredly, it would have been too little a thing if he had made use of the heavenly powers (*caeli virtutibus*) invisibly, unless those very powers could be seen with the human eye to be subject to Martin.'[33]

Here we see the elements of a gratuitous control over nature. Sulpicius' Martin certainly could control fire, water, and the weather; also snakes, animals, and birds. Sometimes this is in answer to prayer or to prevent damage being done, like flames from a burning temple igniting a neighbouring house. But only on one occasion where Martin uses this power to order the hounds off a hunted hare is there any suggestion of kinship between the saint and the natural order. Essentially these miracles show us Martin exercising power over nature, not sympathy with it. Perhaps the strangest case is that where Martin compares birds fishing in the Loire with demons fishing for the souls of men, and then commands them with his 'powerful word' to seek arid and deserted regions, 'using on those birds that authority with which he was accustomed to put demons to flight.'[34]

Again we are brought back to Martin's power to command, his authority. Another aspect of this is stressed when Sulpicius tells of Martin's dealings with secular potentates. Of all the bishops gathered around the Emperor Maximus, Martin alone would command, not fawn; hence 'Martin alone retained apostolic authority.'[35] On the occasion of a feast given by Maximus, Martin's disregard for social conventions when he passed the cup to his priest rather than the emperor appears to have earned him respect. It is true that at the time of the Priscillianist affair Martin's intransigence got him nowhere,

[33] *VM* 14, 3-7 (Levroux); *D* III, 8, 4-7 (Amboise); *D* III, 9, 1-2 (column from heaven).

[34] *Ep.* 3, 7-8. For other cases cited, see appendix.

[35] *VM* 20.

and he was forced to compromise his ideals;[36] but this appears as an admission of Sulpicius' rather than as the image of Martin which he was striving to portray. The latter is better exemplified by Martin's visit to Valentinian I when the emperor ordered the gates to be barred against the bishop. Martin reacted by wrapping himself in his hair shirt, sprinkling himself with ashes, and then fasting and praying for seven days. At the end of this time an angel told him to proceed to the imperial palace. He did so, and found he could enter unmolested. When Valentinian saw him he ground his teeth in rage, but was then compelled to rise and greet the saint by the divine application of fire to his bottom.[37]

This gives us a brief sketch of the salient points in Sulpicius' portrayal of Martin. Sulpicius' foremost concern was to represent Martin as wielding an exceptional power and authority which both stemmed from and testified to his relationship with God. But the Martinian writings are full of action rather than theorizing, and, apart from the historical setting of the opening chapters of the *Vita*, Sulpicius' narrative consists basically of a series of stories: above all, miracle stories. That this emphasis on the miraculous was due to intention can be seen by Sulpicius' apologies for intruding non-miraculous stories, and his desire to give events as miraculous an interpretation as possible.[38] Martin of Tours was very much more than a wonder-worker, but this was how the casual reader of Sulpicius would have seen him. The reason for this stress on the miraculous lay in Sulpicius' belief that a real holy man should be not merely 'sanctus', but also 'potens . . . et vere apostolicus'. It was important to stress Martin's *virtus* since it was this which proved his particular relationship as a friend of God, and his authenticity as a true follower of Christ; a contemporary version of the prophets, apostles, and martyrs, a Gallic version of the Egyptian hermits.[39] Sulpicius did indeed revere Martin as a 'saint', even within the latter's lifetime.

However, this portrayal of Martin did not win universal acclaim. It was rejected by many of the Gallic episcopate,[40]

---

[36] See below, ch. 20.   [37] *D* II, 5, 5-10.
[38] *VM* 4, 7-9; 20, 1; 21, 5; 22, 6; *D* III, 3, 6; III, 11, 1.
[39] *D* II, 4, 6 and 5, 1-2.   [40] *D* I, 26, 3-6; cf. *VM* 27, 3.

and certain aspects were ridiculed even by monks from Martin's own monastery, and within his lifetime. Some of the Marmoutier monks refused to believe in the reality of Martin's spiritual visitors, saints, angels, and demons; and that Brice may have been speaking for the majority when he asserted that Martin, 'as regards his worthless superstitions and his hallucinations of visions, with his ludicrous nonsense, had gone completely senile', is suggested by the fact that he was elected bishop of Tours after Martin's death.[41] Another anonymous sceptic asked how it was that a man who could raise the dead to life and prevent flames from burning a house down had himself recently been burnt by fire, and Sulpicius felt obliged to answer this critic by describing the whole incident.[42] Nor did matters rest there. The first *Dialogue* refers to an allegation that Sulpicius 'had told many lies in that book of yours' (i.e. the *Vita Martini*), and the last book of the *Dialogues* has further references to doubters.[43] Sulpicius now gives the impression of being on the defensive towards them: they have caused him to cite witnesses for the most recent stories he is retailing about Martin.

These sceptics, both bishops and monks, would have known Martin personally, and therefore been in a position to evaluate him for themselves; equally, they belonged to a culture which accepted the possibility of supernatural intervention in the world and the working of miracles. This combination of circumstances means that we cannot either dismiss their scepticism as groundless, or treat it in the same way as we might treat the scepticism of a twentieth-century reader of the Martinian stories by 'demythologizing' Sulpicius' account, and arguing that really Martin was (in our terms) a good man who did much to convert the Gallic countryside and had a gift for healing; and that in late antiquity this meant that he could be viewed as Sulpicius presents him.[44]

---

[41] *D* II, 13, 7; III, 15, 4.

[42] *Ep.* 1, esp. §2.

[43] *D* I, 26, 4; III, 5.

[44] Fontaine, *Vie* I, ch. 5, is excellent on the complexities and the possibilities of interpreting *VM*, especially its supernatural elements. But, while this deals adequately with many of Babut's criticisms, it does not resolve the problem posed by the sceptics of AD 400.

Instead, we must take seriously their claim that the *Vita Martini* contained lies. And it was not such matters as the chronology or Martin's relationship with Hilary that aroused contemporary disbelief: it was the supernatural element in the Martinian writings. Were these fourth-fifth century critics right to disbelieve Sulpicius' thaumaturgical presentation of Martin? At this juncture we cannot say for sure, but we must recognize that they may have been.[45] True, we have seen that the *Vita* and *Dialogues* belonged to the new genre of hagiography, not a non-existent genre of 'aretalogy'. But the inclusion of a centaur and a satyr in Jerome's *Vita Pauli* shows that, right from the beginning, hagiography was open to influences from wholly non-historical spheres: in other words, that saints' lives could contain an admixture of fable.[46] We might add, too, that Sulpicius' knowledge of at least one apocryphal work bodes ill; for the apocryphal gospels and acts contain many miracle stories which are presented as though they actually happened, although in reality they have no historical basis: they are nothing but fables, whose 'truth' lies in the sphere of allegory, not history.[47]

Given this dubious context, given Sulpicius' heavy emphasis on the supernatural, and given the scepticism of at least some of those who knew Martin, it becomes necessary to look further at the issues posed by the supernatural and thaumaturgical elements in the Martinian writings.

[45] Note that H. Chadwick describes Sulpicius' work as 'a largely fictitious biography', 'historical novel' (*The Early Church*, Harmondsworth 1967, pb. edn. p. 182); and Voss dubs the *Dialogues* as a 'Wundertatenbericht' (above, ch. 8, n. 65).

[46] *V. Pauli* 7 and 8. On this work see the excellent discussion by Hoster, pp. 52-65; also below, pp. 197-8.

[47] See R. L. P. Milburn, *Early Christian Interpretations of History* (London 1954), ch. 7, esp. pp. 122-5.

12

Sulpicius and the Oral Tradition

There is one approach to the Martinian writings which would allow of an explanation for the scepticism of some contemporaries without compelling us to relegate the *Vita* and *Dialogues* to the doubtful status of Jerome's *Vita Pauli*. We might assume that Sulpicius simply wrote down what he was told about Martin's life in all good faith; and that the responsibility for the miracle stories he tells lies not with him, but with his informants. Some contemporaries, however, were not as credulous as Sulpicius, hence their scepticism.

This suggestion was originally made as a way of explaining the resemblances of some Martinian miracle stories to those which appear in popular folk-tales.[1] In order to test its validity, we must find out how far Sulpicius was but a redactor of existing traditions, or how far he may be regarded as the true author of the Martinian writings. The related question of whether Sulpicius had the ability to sift out the most reliable information will be left to the next chapter.

A first stage is to trace the links in the transmission of stories about Martin whenever possible. In the *Vita*, Sulpicius says: 'In part I enquired from [Martin] himself, in so far as one could question him; and in part, I learned from those who had been present or who knew [what had happened].'[2] In the *Dialogues* he is even more explicit, often mentioning his source and naming eyewitnesses. On the basis of the available evidence, we may apportion responsibility for Martinian miracle stories roughly as shown in the accompanying table.[3]

---

[1] C. Jullian, 'Notes gallo-romaines, 93', *REA* 24 (1922), pp. 45–7.

[2] *VM* 25, 1.

[3] For details and references, both here and elsewhere in this chapter where they are not specified, see appendix.

Individual/group concerned	No. of occasions when source is mentioned explicitly	Probable no. of further occasions for that source	Total
Monks, priests, Marmoutier tradition	21	11	(32)
Martin (sometimes via monks)	7	7	(14)
Prominent personages (often via monks)	3	2	(5)
The people	3	1	(4)
Sulpicius	2	–	(2)
Unnamed man to monk to Sulpicius	1	–	(1)
Sulpicius' *puer*	1	–	(1)
Wholly unknown	–	–	(4)

Although there is room for difference of opinion over some cases, there can be no doubt about the general picture. This reveals the major role played by the monks of Marmoutier, who generally accompanied Martin on his travels, while next in importance comes the testimony of Martin himself. Popular attestations are seldom evoked; and, even when they are, not in support of folklore-type miracles.

These negative implications as regards assigning popular responsibility for many Martinian miracle stories are confirmed when we approach the problem from another angle: namely, that of the purpose lying behind them. Now, although Sulpicius tends to heighten the miraculous, it is noteworthy that he comparatively seldom uses the word 'miracula' in this context.[4] It was not so much miracles in themselves that he was concerned with, but rather 'virtus', a word which recurs constantly throughout his writings. Here, we may refer to a distinction which Professor Lampe makes when discussing the miracles in the Acts of the Apostles. Lampe distinguishes between irrelevant conjuring tricks such as the *Acta Petri* story of Peter throwing a sardine into water

[4] Only six times apropos of Martin (*VM* 13, 9 and 22, 6; *D* II, 2, 7; III, 9, 4; III, 11, 1; III, 14, 7), and thrice apropos of Egyptian ascetics. Contrast the ubiquity of *virtus*.

and making it swim and eat bread, and miracles which are directly related to God's work: 'focal points at which the continuous activity of God becomes manifest both to his people and to their oppressors.'[5] *Mutatis mutandis*, Professor Lampe's paper reads astonishingly like a commentary on Sulpicius' Martinian works. He brings out the importance of the word *dynamis*, the Greek equivalent of *virtus*, 'with its close association with the concept of the divine Spirit. . . .Jesus is a man attested by God in works of power (*dynameis*, the concrete expression of the *dynamis* that has been bestowed upon him), in wonders and signs.'[6] It is the divine *dynamis* which gives authority to Jesus' words (compare Martin's *potens verbum*); and, as with Martin, healing miracles are closely linked with evangelism. Finally, he sums up Luke's approach:

Miracles are, therefore, in Luke's understanding of the matter, part and parcel of the entire mission of witness. The whole is miraculous, in so far as it is a continuous mighty work of God. By the divine power the gospel is preached, converts are made, the Church is established in unity and brotherhood, the opposing powers, whether human or demonic, are conquered, persecution . . . is turned to good account for the furtherance of the gospel, and judgment overtakes the persecutors. The whole mission . . . is seen in terms of miracle: that is to say, as effected by supernatural power . . .'[7]

Now almost all the miracles wrought deliberately by Martin are just such focal points of God's activity as Lampe describes. Martin's miraculous activities arise either through his solicitude for the people he comes across, healing them, warding fire off from their houses and storms from their crops; or else through his warfare against evil in the forms of error, paganism, and demons. Such stories are too close to the genuine concerns of a fourth-century bishop to make it likely that they have been borrowed from the pool of popular Gallic folk-stories. Further, they are told not simply as *miracula*, stories to arouse wonder, but primarily as stories to demonstrate the *virtus* of God working through Martin.

[5] G. W. H. Lampe, 'Miracles in the Acts of the Apostles', in *Miracles*, ed. C. F. D. Moule (London 1965), pp. 165–6.
[6] Lampe, p. 167.
[7] Lampe, p. 171.

We may, then, defend most of the Martinian miracle stories from the charge that they really belong to a substratum of Gallic tradition, and that the figure of Martin has simply displaced that of an earlier folk-hero. But although the perspective of 'focal points of God's activity' and the few references to popular attestation means that large-scale interference from popular Gallic folklore can be ruled out, we still have to assess the role of Martin and of Sulpicius' Marmoutier informants; for either of these might have been responsible for shaping (and, in the case of Marmoutier, creating?) an account of Martin's deeds that presented them to Sulpicius as 'a continuous mighty work of God'.

Something along these lines has in fact been suggested with regard to Martin by Professor Fontaine. He points to the fact that Sulpicius sought information from Martin himself, and proposes that we should therefore see Martin as the first interpreter, as well as the protagonist, of his life. Martin would have imitated biblical and Christian holy men, and he would have interpreted his own life retrospectively in the light of the Bible, of biblical typology, and of his own ascetic ideal. So when Sulpicius portrays him as the successor of the prophets, apostles, martyrs, and Egyptian ascetics, Fontaine thinks that Sulpicius is simply accentuating and making explicit that which was already implicit in Martin's life. And so 'the problems posed by the work are, in a way, those of an autobiography collected at the level of oral communication.'[8]

Much of this is timely and perceptive. Stray remarks suggest that Martin did indeed interpret some of his acts of healing (and possibly other deeds) as gifts of grace: i.e. as wrought through him by divine power.[9] But we must be wary of jumping from here to the assumption that the Martinian writings therefore reflect Martin's own interpretation of his life. For their general tenor is to present Martin as a man attested by God through miracle-working; and to suppose that Martin saw himself like this, or ranked himself

---

[8] J. Fontaine, 'Alle fonti della agiografia europea: storia e leggenda nella vita di San Martino di Tours', *Rivista di storia e letteratura religiosa* 2 (1966), pp. 196-9.

[9] *D* II, 4, §1 and §7; III, 13, 5. Babut, p. 267.

alongside the prophets, apostles, and martyrs, would accord ill with the humility and unassuming nature that appears as one of his chief characteristics.[10] What is more, the stories which Sulpicius tells on Martin's authority are not very miraculous in bent, and taken by themselves they do not add up to the picture which Sulpicius gives us in his Martinian writings.

This last point about those stories which are told on Martin's authority requires further elaboration. First, what sort of an authority would Martin have been? As portrayed by Sulpicius, Martin appears 'uneducated', but not uncritical in terms of his age towards manifestations of religious devotion. Naturally, the criteria by which men of this period assessed the authenticity of religious cult differed from our own.[11] But Martin did in fact refuse to accept the popular tradition about the burial-place of a local 'martyr' about whom there was no definite information, although he was quite ready to foster the cult of genuine martyrs;[12] and whereas a Spanish bishop could be misled into believing in the reappearance of Christ on earth, Martin refused to be taken in by the devil making similar claims.[13] We may conclude that while Martin, like his contemporaries, believed in the reality of supernatural beings and their intervention in this world, he recognized the need for discernment between genuine spiritual experiences and diabolical hoaxes. He may have interpreted events from a religious angle, but he was not wholly uncritical.

As for the individual stories which probably rest upon his authority: first, we may assume that Martin was Sulpicius' source (either directly or through someone else) for the events of his early life, including his charity at Amiens, with the vision of Christ which followed; his release from the army; his encounter with the devil when travelling from

---

[10] *VM* 1, 7; 10, 2; 25, 2-3; *D* II, 1, 3-4; II, 4, 1-2; III, 2, 4-5. And NB esp. the indirect evidence of *D* II, 3 and *VM* 24, 7. Cf. Ward and Russell, *Lives of the Desert Fathers*, pp. 12-13.

[11] See H. Fichtenau, 'Zum Reliquienwesen im früheren Mittelalter', *Mitteilungen des Instituts für österreichische Geschichtsforschung* 60 (1952), pp. 64-6.

[12] *VM* 11; above ch. 6, n. 56. Cf. H. Delehaye, *Les Origines du culte des martyrs* (2nd edn. Brussels 1933), pp. 88, 90.

[13] *VM* 24; cf. Rousseau, 'Spiritual Authority', pp. 414-15.

Poitiers beyond Milan, on his way home; and his recovery from eating poisonous plants when living as a hermit on Gallinara.[14] Presumably Martin was also responsible for telling others of the times when he had been healed or comforted by angels. Of the occasions when Sulpicius explicitly refers to Martin as his source, one was the similar case of his being visited by SS. Agnes, Thecla and Mary, when he also admitted to seeing SS. Peter and Paul and to being able to recognize each demon and denounce it by name. The other cases are those where Martin realized there were demons at work: when a peasant was gored to death by an ox, when the devil appeared as Christ, and when Martin saw two demons goading on Brice. Perhaps we should also include here Martin's sight of the devil as he himself lay dying. The only other instances where Sulpicius refers directly to Martin's authority are in his account of how Martin was burnt, though not killed, by a fire which broke out when he was asleep; and how Martin sensed that he would be able to restore a dead child to life for the sake of an expectant crowd of potential converts. Note, however, that the latter story was told by Gallus from his own first-hand experience.

What stands out about all these stories told on Martin's authority is the slightness or non-existence of the thaumaturgical element, and the overwhelming preponderance of stories concerned with supernatural beings in the form of angels, saints, and devils. For myself I can well believe that Sulpicius drew most of this latter material from Martin himself;[15] and the comparative frequency with which these stories are cited on Martin's authority contrasts significantly with the virtual absence of any reference to his authority for the more numerous stories illustrating his miraculous powers over nature or in the art of healing. This suggests that the source

---

[14] *VM* chs. 3, 4, and 6. For references to the following incidents, see appendix.

[15] Cf. C. G. Jung, writing in his eighties: 'In the end the only events in my life worth telling are those when the imperishable world irrupted into this transitory one. That is why I speak chiefly of inner experiences, amongst which I include my dreams and visions. . . . Recollection of the outward events in my life has largely faded or disappeared. But my encounters with the "other" reality, my bouts with the unconscious, are indelibly engraved upon my memory.' *Memories, Dreams, Reflections* (ET pb. edn. London 1977), p. 18.

for the latter was not Martin himself; and this tallies with our evidence about Martin as one to whom boasting would be unthinkable. We may conclude that Sulpicius' presentation of Martin did not come, in the main, direct from Martin himself.

Another point is relevant here: that whereas virtually all the miracles deliberately wrought by Martin are 'focal points' of God's activity in Lampe's sense,[16] in the miracles attributed to Martin's *virtus*, but whose occurrence Martin does not actively desire, we can see different influences also at work: notably a stress on Martin's sanctity, power, and inviolability as a man of God. Thus members of Martin's congregation might see a ball of fire rising from his head, or his hands as clothed with jewels, when he was celebrating the eucharist. Men who wronged him were forced to amend their ways and apologize, like the soldiers who had beaten him up or Valentinian I who had excluded him. Or Martin's *virtus* could be demonstrated in little things, such as the potency of his blessing which could impart miraculous qualities to the object blessed: for instance, unbreakability.

This perception of Martin is that of his ardent admirers. The globe of fire round his head was seen not by the whole congregation, nor the archdeacon he had just annoyed; but only by one virgin, one priest, and three monks. The jewels on his hands were noted by Arborius, a senator who had caused his daughter to take the virgin's veil from Martin's own hands.[17] The story of the glass container of oil blessed by Martin not breaking owes its interpretation as a Martinian miracle to Sulpicius himself, while the other incidents were attested by some of the 'faithful' Marmoutier monks. It is surely such sources as these which are responsible for portraying Martin as *potens et vere apostolicus*.

In Sulpicius' *Dialogues* we glimpse these faithful admirers at work in developing the oral tradition as they gather at Primuliacum to swop stories about Martin. Some five or six of them appear to have been disciples of Martin himself, and

[16] Possible exceptions occur in *ep*. 3, 7–8 and *D* III, 9, 4. But on the birds, see below ch. 17, n. 8, and cf. Rousseau, 'Spiritual Authority', p. 412; while the snake, a *mala bestia*, was very possibly poisonous.
[17] *VM* 19, 1–2.

to this number we may add Victor, who had been baptized by him.[18] Not all of these lived permanently at Primuliacum; but some did, and others visited there. As has been pointed out, at a time when Brice, a former critic of Martin, had succeeded him at Tours, Primuliacum had become a place where those Marmoutier monks who remained most faithful to the tradition of Martin could congregate.[19] There, they found a sympathetic audience for reviving their happy memories of their old master.

We may catch the atmosphere by picking up some of the asides made in the *Dialogues*. For instance, Sulpicius remarks on the pleasure to be gained from going over all the Martinian stories again, even when they are already known: partly because the more witnesses there are of the original act, the more its truth is assured—and so the happier one feels; and partly because Martin's deeds impress him so much that they always seem new to him.[20] Postumianus talks of the interest to be found in even the most trivial of Martin's doings.[21] And Gallus stresses the wickedness of ever disbelieving any story told of Martin: it is a crime even to think 'that it is possible for anybody to tell lies of Martin.' He therefore applauds the exclusion of *infideles* from their session because they had come out of 'curiosity' rather than 'piety'; only those who 'believed' were worthy of admission.[22]

Here, in the expressed delight in telling Martinian miracle stories over and over again, we see the oral tradition at work. And here, in the insistence that every story must be accepted in pious belief, is a warning that those responsible for telling these stories saw their role as one of unquestioning exultation at Martin's powers—not the sifting out of the true from the legendary. Indeed, for them, the bigger the miracle, the better.[23] They represent the minority who could see the

---

[18] Gallus, Postumianus, Refrigerius, Evagrius, Aurelius; and Sabbatius, if we identify the one in *VM* 23, 7 with that of *D* III, 1, 4. On Victor's baptism, see Paulinus of Nola, *ep*. 23, 3.

[19] Rousselle-Estève, 'Deux exemples', p. 96.

[20] *D* III, 1, 2-3; cf. also I, 22, 6.

[21] *D* II, 5, 3.

[22] *D* III, 5, 4-6, 1; cf. III, 1, 6. NB also I, 26, 4-5; *ep*. 1, 2-7.

[23] E.g. see *D* II, 5, 1-3.

globe of fire around Martin's head; not the majority, who noticed nothing unusual.

Even apart from the desire for glorification, stories are liable to become distorted as they pass from mouth to mouth. A possible example of such distortion is the tale of how fire compelled Valentinian I to rise and greet Martin. This definitely came via the Marmoutier oral tradition, not direct from eyewitnesses; and it could be that its miraculous aspect has arisen from a garbled version or a literal-minded interpretation of a story that was originally told in language intended metaphorically.[24]

Distortion could also give rise to a further feature often encountered in orally-transmitted material: the occurrence of 'doublets', i.e. two versions, told as two separate stories, of what is in origin one event. The most likely candidates in the Martinian writings are two stories where Martin is shown healing a girl in the presence of other bishops. In both cases Martin blesses oil, and then pours it into her mouth; and in both cases, this cures her, and she is able to speak. The interesting point is that in the *Dialogues* version, located at Chartres, the girl is said to be dumb from birth, so speech is an obvious sign of her cure. But in the *Vita* version, located at Trier, the girl is suffering from paralysis. Here, the restoration of her speech is a prelude to her total cure; but the fact that it is mentioned at all suggests that the version describing the girl as dumb is the original one, and that the *Vita* version, despite its marginally earlier written date, is a doublet which strays further from the actual happening. The greater accuracy of the *Dialogues* version is also suggested by other pointers: by the fact that the bishops in the *Dialogues* story are named, as is a witness; and, on the other hand, by the fact that the illness of the girl in the *Vita* story is greatly emphasized—a typical sign of a more developed version of a story.[25]

Other possible (albeit unprovable) doublets are the two cases where a pagan attempts to attack Martin with drawn

---

[24] 'Ipse non vidi . . . sed factum celebre est, fidelium fratrum, qui interfuerant, sermone vulgatum.' (*D* II, 5, 4.) Cf. below, ch. 14, n. 49. For parallels cf. Lotter, pp. 152-4.

[25] *VM* 16; *D* III, 2, 3-8. Babut, pp. 268-9; Lotter, pp. 144-5.

sword or knife, but fails; and the two cases where Martin's prayers succeed in obtaining the destruction of a pagan statue without the need for human intervention.[26]

In addition to these complications of distortion and doublets which occurred unintentionally in the course of oral transmission, there was also scope for distortion of a semi-purposive kind. I refer to the tendency to present Martin's achievements against the yardstick of earlier Christian heroes, and so to stylize his deeds after their model. In a sense, this is an occupational hazard of all Christian hagiography. But if we recall the ascetic milieu discussed above in chapter 5, we will see that such groups as Martin's disciples and admirers were exposed to its influence in a particularly forceful way. For it was not simply a matter of all ascetics everywhere looking back to the Bible and interpreting contemporary events after biblical models. We must also remember that the frequent personal, literary, and oral contacts between east and west meant that ascetics everywhere were open to influence from the examples provided by contemporary holy men elsewhere. And this was particularly so since instruction often took the form of relating the experiences of older, well-tried ascetics. This shared ascetic milieu provides an essential background for Sulpicius' Martinian works, as the *Dialogues* make explicit. For there, Sulpicius is deliberately comparing the stories told of the Egyptian monks with those told of Martin;[27] and this means that he was, at least in part, telling the sort of stories about Martin as were already being told about other famous holy men. This oral background helps to explain why many Martinian miracles have parallels in the Bible or in contemporary monastic literature. It is probably not a question of deliberate borrowing, but rather of the selection and stylization of real deeds after a hagiographical canon.[28] Such stylization could have been the work of Marmoutier monks as well as of Sulpicius himself, particularly as they were nurtured in an ascetic milieu where the

---

[26] *VM* 15; *D* III, 8, 4-9, 2.

[27] E.g. *D* I, 25, 1-4; II, 5, 1-2.

[28] Cf. Lotter, p. 139; Fontaine, *Vie* I, ch. 3, esp. pp. 98, 101-1. Below, ch. 14, pp. 187 ff. Sample parallels are listed below in the appendix.

achievements of other holy men were proferred as examples
to be followed.[29]

Can we differentiate between the role of Sulpicius and
that of the Marmoutier monks in the touching up and re-
telling of Martinian stories? Inasmuch as all are disciples of
Martin, while the oral tradition of Marmoutier continued
to develop at Primuliacum, this is not always possible. And
yet, certain features can be ascribed to oral transmission,
such as the doublets; while, as we shall see, there is other
evidence which points to the shaping hand of Sulpicius.

Stylistically, there can of course be no doubt that the
work is all Sulpicius'. The Martinian writings are no artless
prose, set down the way people spoke. Instead, as we have
seen, they are highly polished literary compositions, with
their rhythmical *clausulae* carefully worked out, and with
frequent echoes of classical and Christian literature.

From such literary echoes we pass over into cases of
literary elaboration. A good example to take is Sulpicius'
description of Marmoutier, since this is something he was
definitely describing from first-hand knowledge, while we
ourselves also know a certain amount about the site from
our own direct experience. In general terms, Sulpicius'
account is reasonably accurate: a level site enclosed by a
cliff on one side, and by a curve of the river on the other.
But Sulpicius elaborates on this to give a far more dramatic
and romanticized picture, with a feel of the wilderness of the
Bible and the deserts of the eastern monks in his *praecisa
montis excelsi rupe* (there is indeed a cliff at Marmoutier,
but nothing remotely resembling a high mountain!); while
at the same time, his description carries distinct Virgilian
echoes.[30] A further twist has been added by the current
archaeological excavations, which reveal that Marmoutier was
founded upon an earlier Roman site—something which we
would never have guessed from Sulpicius' description, which
makes it sound very remote.[31] This instance, then, reveals

---

[29] See *VM* 25, 5. Cf. Fontaine, *Vie* I, 187-8.

[30] *VM* 10, 4, with Fontaine's illuminating notes ad loc.

[31] M. Ch. Lelong, who is in charge of the excavations at Marmoutier, has kindly
told me of his relevant findings to date in a letter dated 8 Feb. 1982. To summarize briefly: there was a Roman building there *s.* I-II, though its exact location

that at base, Sulpicius' account is moderately accurate. But he has invented one detail; and, more than this, he has skillfully created an atmosphere by the words he has chosen, and by his selection of what information to include, and what to omit.

As regards the stories told of Martin, we have no objective account against which to set Sulpicius'; nor can we be certain, where stylization is obvious, whether it arises from Sulpicius, or from his informants. But if we take the most prominent example of stylization, Martin's confrontation with Julian and departure from the army, we can at least say that it has every appearance of being a literary elaboration, not an oral one.[32] The obvious parallel is Paulinus' account of Victricius' discharge, which is definitely a literary composition. Also, Sulpicius' source for this incident was probably not the Marmoutier monks, but Martin himself; and we can be fairly sure that Martin would not have cast himself as a virtual military martyr. On top of this is the skilful presentation of this incident as Martin's break with the world—a brilliant literary device which suggests careful planning on the part of his biographer. For these reasons we may feel fairly certain that the extensive stylization of this episode is Sulpicius' own work. And this implies that Sulpicius felt no qualms about treating very freely an event for which Martin himself was probably the source, which is an interesting reflection.

We may conclude, then, that Sulpicius would have been ready enough to shape the oral traditions which reached him, though with this proviso: that the two cases discussed above were ones deliberately chosen because literary elaboration and dramatization were obvious. So we should not draw general conclusions from these two about the amount of stylization to expect from Sulpicius. Rather let us heed

has yet to be revealed. This was probably wiped out as a result of the third-century invasions; but the site was certainly reused in the fourth century, and this fourth-century building was itself burnt at the end of the fourth century: this can be dated by coins of Constantine, Valens, and Gratian. How this ties in with Martin is perhaps best left open till the excavations have progressed further; but it does suggest that there was rather more to Marmoutier's site than a 'locus tam secretus et remotus' (*VM* 10, 4)—though, of course, its earlier history might not have been visible to Sulpicius' eye in the 390s.

[32] See above, ch. 10.

the conclusions of Fontaine, *doyen* of this aspect of Sulpician studies: that Sulpicius began by choosing the most vivid incidents for inclusion; and to some of these he simply gave permanent form by setting them down, 'fixing' them as one might fix a charcoal sketch. But others he reworked, super-imposing on them biblical and classical reminiscences which have transformed them into types.[33]

Besides literary stylization there are other indications that Sulpicius took an active part in shaping the Martinian material. We have already seen how carefully he planned the structure of the *Vita Martini*, grouping the stories relating to Martin's achievements as monk-bishop under four heads: the combat against false religion, healings, Martin's gift of seeing through the wiles of the devil, and his forthright approach when dealing with the emperor. Clearly this arrangement was deliberate, imposed by Sulpicius on his material. Another author might have made a different selection, with different emphases.

Particularly noteworthy is Sulpicius' omission of a section on Martin as monk and abbot, though there was sufficient material for this had Sulpicius desired it.[34] Parallel with this we should note the interesting fact that less than a quarter of the miracle stories with known locations can be assigned to Marmoutier, and the majority of these came to Sulpicius not via the Marmoutier tradition, but from Martin himself.[35] Thus such evidence as we have with regard to the influence of Marmoutier interests is wholly negative. We would expect its monks to be particularly interested in Martin's own life as a monk; but instead we see far more of his pastoral activities, with him visiting his diocese, healing the sick, destroying pagan temples, and visiting nobles and the emperor himself. There is no trace of ill-feeling at the amount of time that Martin was absent from his monastery, nor of jealously towards the diocese.

Note, also, that while Sulpicius does not include a section on Martin as abbot, he does find the space to describe his

---

[33] *Vie* I, p. 98. See further ch. 14 below, pp. 187–90.

[34] E.g. *VM* 22, 3; 24, 4–8; *D* II, 10, 4–6; II, 11; III, 14, 7–9; III, 15. Contrast Possidius' life of Augustine: Brown, *Augustine*, pp. 143, 409.

[35] See appendix.

dealings with the emperor, for all that there were few traces of the miraculous here.[36] His insistence that Martin was almost the only bishop to retain his apostolic authority because the others were too subservient to the emperor is obviously aimed at bishops; and its inclusion suggests that it is a concern dear to Sulpicius' own heart—a supposition that can happily be confirmed by referring to Sulpicius' *Chronicle*.[37]

Indeed, the personal concerns of the author of the Martinian works visibly coincide with those of the author of the *Chronicle* on a number of occasions: for instance, in condemning the secular government's interference in church affairs,[38] and in the interest shown in Antichrist.[39] Further, the underlying ideals of the Martinian works correspond exactly to the 'vices' and 'virtues' briefly depicted in the *Chronicle*, where lust, avarice, and ambition are set over against chastity, asceticism, poverty, and humility;[40] and both times, the bishops are singled out for blame.[41]

There is thus a fundamental similarity of approach and concern in Sulpicius' *Chronicle* and in the Martinian works, and this confirms that both are the product of the same mind. It is true that Sulpicius' ideals may well have been inspired by Martin, but this is different from asserting that Martin was the real 'author' of the *Vita Martini*, and Sulpicius nothing but a credulous amanuensis. Rather, the implications of the similarities between Martinian works and *Chronicle*, as of much else we have discussed, are that Sulpicius did not blindly write down whatever he was told about Martin; but that he selected and shaped the material that came to him in accordance with his own designs.

---

[36] Cf. *VM* 20, 1, and *D* III, 11, 1.
[37] See van Andel, pp. 94-5.
[38] *Chron.* II, 49, 9 and 50, 5; *D* I, 7, 2.
[39] *VM* 24, 3; *D* II, 14; *Chron.* II, 33, 3 and cf. II, 29, 6.
[40] E.g. *Chron.* I, 23, 4-6; II, 17, 5; II, 46, 4-5.
[41] *Chron.* I, 23, 5-6; II, 32, 4; *D* I, 21, 1-4.

13

Sulpicius as Historian:
the Evidence of the *Chronicle*

We have left till now one important question raised at the beginning of the last chapter: granted that Sulpicius felt free to select and touch up the Martinian material that he gathered, was he equipped to assess this material critically, from a historical point of view? Happily, Sulpicius has left us not only his Martinian writings, but also a historical work, his *Chronicle*; and this enables us to gauge Sulpicius' qualities as a historian.

First, Sulpicius definitely had some conception of 'truth'; or perhaps we should say, he had two rather different conceptions of truth. On the one hand there was the Christian idea: Jesus had (according to John's Gospel) proclaimed himself as 'the truth', and the early church had soon tried to embody that truth in a body of writings which, as interpreted by the bishop, were held to constitute the church's faith. By the late fourth century the biblical canon was almost established, and Christianity had long since been transformed into 'a religion of the book'. The Bible was inspired writing and as such incapable of error: when Sulpicius found chronological inconsistencies within it he attributed this to careless copyists rather than countenance the idea that a biblical writer had erred.[1] Through the divine inspiration which guaranteed its veracity—and which enriched it with hidden meanings—the Bible was *sui generis*, different in kind from the writings of secular historians. Indeed, it was entirely separate from them, for God's spirit had ensured that it should be 'uncontaminated' by secular writers, 'corrupt mouths, or those mingling truth with falsehoods'.[2]

[1] *Chron.* I, 40, 2.
[2] *Chron.* II, 14, 7-8, on which see van Andel, pp. 60–8; cf. above, p. 41.

Thus from Christianity Sulpicius derived the idea that there was one true account; any deviation from this text was error. It is easy to see how he could pass from this belief in the inherent truth of the Bible to belief in the inherent truth of the Nicene creed. He therefore accused the Arians of deliberately subverting the truth, the Christian faith contained in that creed: by the addition of one letter, 'they had obscured the truth.'[3]

Over against this Christian idea of truth as something revealed and guaranteed by authority lay the classical idea that man could utilize his reason to establish the truth of what happened. And, when we find Sulpicius unable to make the chronological reckonings in the Bible tally with each other, we should remark not so much his protestation of biblical infallibility, but rather how he reacts to this, dismissing the figure of 440 years given in Kings as inaccurate (thanks to scribal corruption, he suggests), and himself supplying the figure of 588 years, derived from his own calculations.[4] Note that Sulpicius has so much faith in his own ability to comprehend a text that it does not occur to him that his own understanding may be deficient, and that beneath this apparent discrepancy there is some deeper mystery which is known to God, even if incomprehensible to man. In this he differs markedly from his contemporary, Augustine, who felt that it was better for a man to pass over what he could not understand than to prefer his own predilections and interpretations to the biblical truth.[5]

Classical literary criticism, in fact, was rather subtle as regards its attitude towards truth. Victorinus' *Explanationes in rhetoricam M. Tullii Ciceronis* recognized that a man's methods of arguments would vary in accordance with his aim, which might be that of *aequitas*, *utilitas*, or *honestas*. However, even the latter was not as straightforward as it might appear, for it could easily become contaminated by

[3] *Chron.* II, 40, 1.
[4] *Chron.* I, 40, 1-2; Prete, p. 61.
[5] Augustine, *ep.* 28, 4 (*CSEL* 34, i, p. 110). Cf. A. Momigliano on Eusebius' *HE*: 'It was founded upon authority and not upon the free judgement of which the pagan historians were proud.' *Essays*, p. 117.

utilitas.[6] Now although the task of a historian was to relate what happened truthfully, clearly, and briefly, his ultimate aim (*telos*) was that of teaching what to pursue and what to avoid, and of fostering eloquence.[7] It was thus likely that the *honestas* of the historian's narrative would be subject to interference on account of his ultimate aims, which were didactic and literary: i.e., those of *utilitas*. That Sulpicius himself was fully aware of how a statement masquerading as one's 'true opinion' might in fact have been subverted by some extraneous aim (such as the desire to flatter) is shown by his account of Nebuchadnezzar. According to Sulpicius, the king refused to tell his dream to the wise men because he was afraid 'lest, as in the way of men, they should infer from the dream something that would please the king: not the truth.'[8]

As a historian in the *Chronicle*, Sulpicius appears to have been more influenced by the classical conception of rational man's ability to discern the truth of what happened rather than by the Christian emphasis on divine authority and mysteries beyond the reach of historical interpretation. Thus, despite his regard for the Bible, we sometimes find Sulpicius acting as a historian and not simply copying his source. One illustration of this is his discussion about which reigns the deeds of Esther and Judith should be attributed to.[9] Esther was said to have lived under King Artaxerxes, but there were two kings of that name. Sulpicius reasons that she was unlikely to have been the wife of the earlier Artaxerxes since Esdras chronicles that reign and makes no mention of her. Further, the earlier Artaxerxes forbade the rebuilding of Jerusalem, and it is doubtful whether Esther would have allowed this had she been married to him; she was therefore probably the wife of the later Artaxerxes.

When trying to fix the period to which Judith belonged Sulpicius goes further. The Bible unequivocally sets Judith's doings in the reign of King Nebuchadnezzar, but Sulpicius

[6] Ibid. II, 51-2; ed. Halm, *Rhet. Lat. Min.*, p. 301. Although Victorinus was discussing forensic oratory, there was no significant difference between this and non-forensic oratory, of which history was one branch.

[7] Anon. fragment *De historia*, ed. Halm p. 588.

[8] *Chron.* II, 2, 1. The Bible has simply, 'Ye have prepared lying and corrupt words to speak before me' (Daniel 2:9).

[9] *Chron.* II, 12, 1-2.

rejects out of hand the idea that this could be the king of that name who captured Jerusalem.[10] However, he had been unable to discover any Persian king Nebuchadnezzar with a reign falling after the captivity. In this predicament Sulpicius followed Eusebius' suggestion that the 'Nebuchadnezzar' referred to in the book of Judith must at best be a Jewish nickname, and that the king's true name must be sought outside the Bible. But he rejected the opinion of 'many' that the king in question might have been Cambyses,[11] since the latter reigned for only nine years, and the Bible says that Judith's deeds took place in the king's twelfth year. Instead he compared the biblical account with those of secular historians, and noted that the eunuch Baguas occurs as the servant both of the King Nebuchadnezzar of Judith and the King Ochus of other writers. He therefore concluded that the deeds of Judith should be attributed to the reign of King Ochus, and it is a tribute to his historical procedures that at least some twentieth-century biblical scholars follow him.[12] Such evaluations were rare amongst ancient historians, and Sulpicius' procedure is correspondingly praiseworthy.

It is perhaps significant that both these pieces of historical argument stem from a chronological basis; for it was his desire to get the chronology straight which led Sulpicius to compare biblical and secular writers,[13] and he appears to have undertaken a fair amount of research to that end. He drew up an entire list of the consuls of Rome from the beginning down to the consulate of Stilicho in 400 AD;[14] and he includes within his *Chronicle* a list of the kings of Syria from the death of Alexander the Great so that their succession can be followed right down to the Roman occupation and the coming of Christianity.[15] This was all in

---

[10] *Chron.* II, 14, for this and what follows.

[11] 'Plerique' could include Eusebius (*Chron.* tr. Jerome, *PL* 27, col. 435), and Julius Africanus (van Andel, p. 147, n. 101).

[12] Prete, p. 58.

[13] *Chron.* I, 1, 4; cf. II, 5, 6-7.

[14] *Chron.* II, 9, 7. I do not know whether he had access to the compilation of the Chronographer of 354, which includes the consular *fasti* up to that year (ed. Mommsen, *Chronica Minora* I (*MGH, AA* IX), pp. 50-69).

[15] *Chron.* II, 19, 1-5.

accordance with his purpose to establish the sequence of events,[16] and he had both Christian chronographers and also secular historians to help him. We even find him writing to his friend Paulinus for help in resolving knotty chronological questions.[17]

It will repay us to look more closely at the *Chronicle*'s relationship to classical historiography. In the opening chapter, Sulpicius undertakes to narrate the course of history from the creation of the world down to his own times, compressing the entire Bible into two books and including nearly all the facts, though leaving aside the biblical *mysteria*. He also explains that, where necessary for clarifying the sequence of events, he has supplemented his biblical sources with information taken from secular historians. From our own observation we can add that, for post-biblical history, Sulpicius restricts himself to the sort of topics covered by Eusebius' *Ecclesiastical History*: viz., church–state relations, and heresies. He omits, for instance, any mention of monasticism. When we recall that the *Chronicle* and *Dialogues* are roughly contemporaneous, this appears as a striking example of a self-imposed limitation—presumably because Sulpicius felt that an account of monasticism would be out of place in a history whose contents were selected and told in a classicizing manner.[18]

It is interesting to compare the *Chronicle*'s opening sentence with that of a contemporary secular equivalent, Eutropius' *Breviarium*:[19]

---

[16] *Chron.* II, 7, 6.

[17] Paulinus, *ep.* 28, 5. The care which Sulpicius lavished on straightening out biblical chronology is an additional reason for my reluctance to interpret *VM* 3, 5 as chronological falsification on his part.

[18] Persecutions and heresies—the church's external and internal conflicts—correspond considerably more to the military and political history covered by secular historians (below, n. 23) than would monastic history. Cf. Theodoret's division of subject-matter between his *Ecclesiastical History* and his *Religious History*.

[19] Sulpicius, *Chron.* I, 1, 1. Eutropius, *Breviarium*, preface; ed. F. Ruehl (Leipzig 1897), p. 1. Prete (p. 9 n. 18) thinks that this proves Sulpicius' knowledge of Eutropius; but the similarities could simply be due to the common historiographical tradition.

Sulpicius	*Eutropius*
Res a mundi exordio sacris litteris editas breviter constringere et cum distinctione temporum usque ad nostram memoriam carptim dicere aggressus sum.	Res Romanas . . . ab urbe condita ad nostram memoriam . . . per ordinem temporum brevi narratione collegi . . .

Sulpicius may have been consciously echoing Eutropius' opening; certainly he appears to have regarded his task as historian in the same terms as his older contempoarary and compatriot.[20] There is nothing to surprise us here. We might compare the way in which Christian writers like Cyprian and Hilary had talked of Christ's *verba* and *facta*, while a pagan counterpart could write of the *Facta et dicta memorabilia urbis Romae*.[21] Sulpicius would have imbibed the classical approach to historiography at the Gallic schools; and, since he wished to appeal to the Christian *literati* who did not know their Bible, his task was clearly that of transposing the biblical narrative into something that they could recognize.[22] The influence of classical historiography shows interestingly in his assumption that wars are what the historian should write about. He enumerates the length of two rulers' reigns, adding: 'It being a time of peace, they performed nothing that history mentions.'—a comment that has no biblical foundation whatever.[23]

There are other modes of thought which Sulpicius derived not from the Bible but from his Roman heritage, such as his contempt for the common people, or his view that peace led to corruption and factions.[24] We also find examples of typically Roman terminology, as when Sulpicius uses the verbs 'constituere' or 'condere' to describe God's creation of the world.[25] However, most fundamental is the general

---

[20] Cf. also F. Murru, 'La concezione della storia nei *Chronica* di Sulpicio Severo', *Latomus* 38 (1979), p. 963 n. 13, who suggests Nepos' lost *Chronica* as a model for Sulpicius'.

[21] Doignon, pp. 231, 234.

[22] Cf. A. G. Amatucci, *Storia della letteratura latina cristiana* (2nd edn. Turin 1955), p. 263.

[23] *Chron.* I, 26, 7; cf. Judges 12:11-15. For war and politics as the subject-matter of classical historiography cf. Momigliano, *Essays*, pp. 141-2, 165.

[24] Cf. *Chron.* I, 32, 3; van Andel, pp. 23-4, 69-72.

[25] Prete p. 15, esp. n. 50.

historical approach underlying his narrative. As Prete says, 'From the classical historians . . . he took not his historical material so much as the practice of narrative prose.'[26] The very idea of composing continuous narrative history where people and events are set in a causal framework comprehensible to man's reason is an aim foreign to that of most biblical writers.[27] Further, in its concentration on *res gestae* and exclusion of the religious and spiritual dimension of the Old Testament, Sulpicius' narrative lacks any idea of progress culminating in the Incarnation.[28] He often neglects the supernatural dimension or transforms it into human terms, with the result that the history of the Israelites is wholly 'externalized'. Sulpicius and the Bible may talk of the same people and events, but their ethos is entirely different.

For instance, in his account of Moses and the burning bush, Sulpicius leaves out everything which in Exodus serves to heighten the holiness, the otherness, of God: the command that Moses should put off his shoes, for the ground was *holy*, and how Moses hid his face, 'for he was *afraid* to look upon God.'[29] Instead, Sulpicius introduces a Virgilian note with his mention of 'flammis . . . innoxiis', 'harmless flames'.[30] Everything that is frightening and irrational is softened, if not ironed out altogether. And he will give a *reason* for why the raven sent out by Noah did not return to the ark: it was feeding on corpses drowned in the flood.[31] Similarly, when describing Antiochus Epiphanes' end, Sulpicius prefers to represent him as dying from grief rather than being struck down by God for his persecution of the Jews—an interesting choice from the hagiographer of St. Martin.[32]

[26] Prete, p. 14; cf. Amatucci, p. 263.

[27] See E. Auerbach, *Mimesis* (ET pb. edn. Princeton 1968[2]), ch. 1, esp. pp. 8–12. By contrast, for the way in which an educated Roman viewed the importance of a temporal sequence, see Jerome, *ep*. 58, 8, 2. Cf. also Doignon, pp. 234 ff. 252, 256 n. 2.

[28] Cf. Prete, pp. 32–3; Murru, p. 972.

[29] Exodus 3:1–6; *Chron*. I, 14, 1–2. This feeling of awe and dread is what Rudolf Otto characterized as 'das Heilige': see M. Eliade, *The Sacred and the Profane* (ET pb. edn. New York 1961), pp. 8–10.

[30] Cf. *Aeneid* II, lines 680–4; van Andel p. 25.

[31] *Chron*. I, 3, 3. No reason is given in Genesis, but Sulpicius' surmise was apparently common in biblical exegesis: Prete, p. 43, n. 105.

[32] II Maccabees 9, verses 5 and 8. Cf. Sulpicius *D* III, 4, 2–6. See further van Andel, pp. 22–3, 50–1.

All this indicates that Sulpicius was perfectly capable of applying the principles of classical historiography, even to material that was presented to him in terms of God's ways with man; even to the sacred scriptures themselves. While including a certain number of supernatural interventions, he presents these in a very matter-of-fact way, and there are fewer than in the Bible.[33] More than this, he clings to the classical idea that events can be presented in a coherent chronological sequence; and when he cannot discover something from his main source, the Bible, he turns elsewhere for information. When he draws a blank, he is prepared to say that he does not know something, rather than fob us off with his own guesswork.[34] He is aware that the truth could be altered in its transmission by the desire to curry favour, or by carelessness on the part of copyists.[35] He shows a fair amount of independence from his sources, and never slavishly follows any one.[36] For instance, he takes much material from Eusebius-Jerome, but he often prefers the chronology of Hippolytus. Even more striking is his open-mindedness about setting aside something he has read in the Bible itself: he can treat the biblical name of King Nebuchadnezzar as no more than a nickname, and turn to secular historians and use his own reasoning powers to establish the king's true identity; or he can prefer his own chronological reckonings to those he finds ready-made in the Bible. And while he makes no secret of his own strongly-held views, he does not let them colour everything he writes, and his *Chronicle* does not appear to suffer from grave disproportions of bias.[37]

If Sulpicius were able to display this limited, but real, historical ability in his *Chronicle*, then presumably he would have been capable of doing the same with the material about Martin had he so wished. As it is, however, we can but be struck by the contrast between the two sets of writings.

[33] See A. Lavertujon, *La Chronique de Sulpice Sévère* (2 vols., Paris 1896-9), I, pp. 202, 275-6, which is not entirely disposed of by Prete, pp. 74-5. See also van Andel, pp. 50-1. However, NB below n. 38.

[34] E.g. *Chron.* II, 4, 6; Prete, p. 60.

[35] Cf. Prete, pp. 61-2.

[36] See, for example, van Andel, pp. 16-21, 26, 30-1, 36, 49-51, 53. Prete, pp. 112-19.

[37] Prete, pp. 62-71, 95, 119. Murru, p. 977.

In the Martinian works Sulpicius offers no chronological framework for Martin's life as a whole, nor does he tie it in to the general Roman chronological system based on consuls or on the regnal years of emperors. Even more obvious is the fact that, whereas in the *Chronicle* supernatural intervention is played down or rationalized, in the Martinian writings it is heavily emphasized.[38] Nor can we see any signs of Sulpicius using his powers of reasoning to query any of the Martinian stories he has been told. Instead, he insists that everything about Martin must be believed, not questioned.

At this point it becomes apparent that we must enlarge our horizons if we are to understand aright Sulpicius' procedure in his Martinian writings. Whereas we think of ascertaining an author's reliability by investigating him as a person, trying to assess how skilful as a historian, how detached, and how truthful he was in other contexts, when we seek to understand an antique author we have to' bear in mind their accepted literary conventions: for instance, when falsehoods were permissible, and what was expected in the various literary genres. It is to these matters that we must now turn.

[38] Sulpicius' account of miracles wrought in the Holy Land in his own century, where he draws on a letter from Paulinus (*ep.* 31, 4-5), is in part atypical of his *Chronicle*. Here (*Chron.* II, 33, 6-34, 5) Sulpicius tends to heighten the miracles which Paulinus records, especially when he says that Christ's footprints remain the same, *although faithful pilgrims daily carry off portions of the sand which Christ trod* (*Chron.* II, 33, 8, italicizing Sulpicius' addition to Paulinus' account). Cf. below, ch. 14, n. 1. But NB also below, ch. 14, n. 67.

14

Literary Complexities

Historians in the ancient world viewed their task rather differently from their modern namesakes. Although some rated truth higher than literary embellishment, this was by no means the rule; and the desire to spin a memorable story, or to encourage readers to follow good examples and warn them off from the bad, could easily interfere with the accuracy of what was recorded. A tale might well be touched up in the telling, and the reader would expect as much. What is more, biography was even more at risk than straight history.

Against this background, one aspect of the Martinian writings stands out clearly: they are the work of a veritable artist. The *Vita Martini* in particular is superbly written. It still remains fresh and alive after much study; it reads well aloud; it forms a coherent whole, while each scene is vividly depicted; and it is only after attempting to paraphrase Sulpicius' narrative that one fully appreciates his skill, precision, and economy of expression. I suspect that the desire to say something neatly (when the pen has a tendency to run away with itself) and the desire to make a good story out of an incident contribute as much to any minor inaccuracies in the Martinian writings as do more deliberate attempts to stylize Martin's deeds. Heightening details for the sake of literary effectiveness could easily lead to fanciful evocations, not matter-of-fact descriptions: we have already encountered examples in Sulpicius' elevation of the cliff above Marmoutier into part of 'a lofty mountain', and in his hyperbolic account of how some pack animals refused to move although whips were worn out on them, and so a wood was torn up and the unfortunate animals were belaboured with whole trees![1]

At times, the hyperbole is so obvious that it misleads no one. But on other occasions, it could give rise to misunderstandings. For instance, in Sulpicius' first epistle he talks of how St. Peter, 'powerful in faith', had overcome the laws of nature by treading the insubstantial waters underfoot. Here, we would scarcely recognize the biblical Peter who panicked and started to sink, and had to be saved by Jesus who asked him, 'Why did you hesitate? How little faith you have.'[2]

This shows that Sulpicius could easily get carried away when he had his pen in hand. And where does one draw the line between heightening a description, and misrepresentation? Between exaggeration, and lying? Significantly, Paulinus of Nola accuses his friend of exaggerating his praise for him up to the point of lying: Sulpicius is wrong to pile up the praises of Paulinus while slandering himself with vituperative remarks, and is mistaken in his belief that Paulinus is a holy man. Paulinus blames Sulpicius' 'excessively passionate affection' for him, 'inasmuch as your great love sweeps you as far as the sin of lying.'[3] Now, Sulpicius' overwhelming affection for Martin is incontestable; and if he was guilty of *mendacium* about Paulinus, what might not his enthusiasm for Martin lead him to? It is sobering to recall that the fictitious *Acts of Paul* had been written by a priest out of love for Paul, in an attempt to honour him.[4]

The priest responsible for this was punished; but not all types of lying were condemned in the ancient world. For this is where a writer's didactic aims could take over from his literary ambitions and derange the truth still further. Of course there were some Christians, of whom Augustine is the most notable, who adamantly refused to countenance

---

[1] Above, pp. 170, 131. Similarly, Sulpicius adds a vivid touch to Paulinus' account of how the earth trod by Christ rejected any paving by adding that the marble was cast up *into the faces of those laying it down*: *Chron.* II, 33, 7; cf. Paulinus, *ep.* 31, 4.

[2] *Ep.* 1, 6; Matt. 14:28-32.

[3] 'quod te multa dilectio usque ad mendacii peccatum trahit'. *Ep.* 24, 1. Cf. also *ep.* 32, 2-3.

[4] Tertullian tells us that the priest responsible, 'quasi titulo Pauli de suo cumulans, convictum atque confessum id se amore Pauli fecisse loco decessisse'; *De baptismo* 17, ed. E. Evans, London 1964, p. 36.

lying under any circumstances.[5] But this uncompromising attitude was not shared by all his contemporaries, and probably not by a majority of them. Jerome, for instance, would argue that even the apostles had practised lying and dissimulation.

It was this which sparked off Augustine's treatise *On Lying*. Augustine had been profoundly disturbed[6] by Jerome's explanation of Galatians 2:11–14, where Paul reprimanded Peter for his inconsistency and weak-minded deference to the Judaizers, a scene which Jerome (following Origen and others) interpreted as a put-up job prearranged between the two apostles, the more pointedly to condemn the Judaizers.[7] Jerome's own point of view appears later in the same commentary, when expatiating upon how St. Paul became all things to all men: 'after the fashion of actors . . . he used to alter his appearance and language into various forms. Not that he was what he pretended to be; but that he might simply appear to be what benefited others.'[8]

Jerome here typifies an attitude towards lying which was then widespread: if a man lied in order to benefit others, his action should be condoned, or even praised. This view had been expressed by Quintilian in his influential *Institutio oratoria*,[9] and it is found in the Alexandrian Christian tradition, which was so heavily influenced by platonism.[10] Of course, some Christians thought otherwise.[11] But Jerome's standpoint was taken up by Cassian,[12] whose *Conlatio*

[5] Not even to preserve oneself from bodily defilement, e.g. rape: Augustine, *De mendacio* xix, 40–xx, 41 (*CSEL* 41, pp. 460–3).

[6] Augustine, *ep.* 28, 3 (*CSEL* 34, i, pp. 107–8).

[7] Jerome, *Commentarii in Epistolam ad Galatas* 2, 7–14 (*PL* 26, cols. 336–42). See J. B. Lightfoot, *Saint Paul's Epistle to the Galatians* (7th edn. London 1881), pp. 128–32.

[8] *In Gal.* 4, 20 (*PL* 26, col. 387).

[9] *Inst.* II, 17, 18–36 (ed. Winterbottom, I, pp. 117–19).

[10] E.g. Origen (Lightfoot, loc. cit.); Synesius of Cyrene, *ep.* 105 (*PG* 66, cols. 1485–8; ET by A. FitzGerald, *The Letters of Synesius of Cyrene*, London 1926, pp. 200–1). Synesius' approach was traditional in pre-Christian Greek thought: e.g. cf. Strabo *apud* R. M. Grant, *Miracle and Natural Law* (Amsterdam 1952), p. 54.

[11] See the *Historia monachorum in Aegypto*, I, 14–15 (ed. Festugière, pp. 13–14; ET Ward and Russell, *Lives of the Desert Fathers*, p. 54).

[12] Although most of the discussion is attributed to Abba Joseph, Cassian accepted full responsibility for his teaching: *Conlatio* XVII, 30, 3 (*CSEL* 13, pp. 499–500).

XVII provides a counter-argument to Augustine's *Contra mendacium*—which was itself occasioned by Augustine's disgust at learning that catholic Christians were practising dissimulation in order to worm out the Priscillianist heresy.[13]

Cassian elaborated upon Jerome's account of how St. Paul became all things to all men[14]—a passage which Augustine contended had nothing to do with authorizing lying.[15] For Cassian, however, such an action as the circumcision of Timothy 'was not lacking in deceit.'[16] Further, he even felt able to argue from biblical precedents in order to justify lying as permissible for his own contemporaries. The example which he gives is particularly pertinent for us as it concerns attributing miracles wrought by oneself to some one else out of humility. As he makes Abba Joseph say:

> For if we would also take account of what we remember to have been the unhesitating practice of our elders—how they used to ascribe to others the marvels of their own spiritual powers or their own deeds when it was necessary to bring these forward in conference for the instruction of the younger men—what else can we consider this but open lying (*apertum . . . mendacium*)? If only we too had anything suitable . . . Indeed we should have no qualms about following them in such fictions.[17]

Thus in antiquity, literary conventions were such as to allow for the heightening of a story for literary ends, and the use of *mendacium* for beneficial ends. With the genre of biography we encounter additional complications, for 'the borderline between fiction and reality was thinner in biography than in ordinary historiography.'[18]

> The Socratics experimented in biography, and the experiments were directed towards capturing the potentialities rather than the realities of individual lives. . . . In Socratic biography we meet for the first time

---

[13] *Contra mendacium* iii, 4 (*CSEL* 41, pp. 475-6).

[14] *Conl.* XVII, 20, 3-10. Cassian probably knew Jerome's work, as his 'nudipedalia non exercere' (XVII, 20, 9) echoes Jerome's 'nudipedalia exercuit' (*Comm. in Gal.* I, 2; *PL* 26, col. 339A): see E. C. S. Gibson's tr. of Cassian's works, *Nicene and post-Nicene Fathers*, 2 ser. vol. 11 (American reprint, Michigan 1964), p. 468, n. 5.

[15] Augustine, *Contra mendacium* xii, 26 (*CSEL* 41, p. 506).

[16] *Conl.* XVII, 20, 9.

[17] *Conl.* XVII, 24, 1-2.

[18] Momigliano, *Development*, p. 56.

that conflict between the superior and the inferior truth which has remained a major problem for the student of the Gospels or of the lives of Saints.[19]

For one major difficulty is that biography was used as a vehicle for expressing philosophical or religious ideals.[20] In this case the figure presented in the biography might bear little resemblance to the historical person of that name. Instead, rival sects or different types of document or men belonging to different periods were able to present conflicting accounts of the same man. For instance, Moses was portrayed primarily as a lawgiver by Greek and Roman literary authors, but in the magical documents as an 'inspired prophet, endowed with divine wisdom and power, whose very name' was magical.[21]

In this context there was certainly scope for Sulpicius' portrayal of Martin to diverge from the historical person; for Sulpicius was concerned to emphasize similarities between Martin's life and that of Jesus and other biblical and post-biblical holy men, prophets, apostles, martyrs, and monks.[22] Naturally this led to a certain amount of literary stylization: for instance, Martin heals a woman from haemorrhages and foretells to his disciples a catch of fish in the same way that Jesus had.[23] He confronts those hostile to him with a firmness of faith and refusal to compromise reminiscent of the martyrs; and throughout his life he fights against the devil and his emissaries of spiritual wickedness, as had the martyrs and their successors, the monks of Egypt. What is more, Sulpicius explicitly draws out the similarities to Christ, and to the prophets, apostles, martyrs, and Egyptian ascetics.[24] All this

---

[19] Ibid. pp. 46–7.

[20] Cf. Momigliano on Xenophon's *Cyropaedia*, ibid. pp. 55–6, and cf. also pp. 46–7. I return to this point at the beginning of ch. 22 below.

[21] J. G. Gager, in his unpublished Harvard dissertation quoted by D. L. Tiede, *The Charismatic Figure as Miracle Worker* (Montana USA 1972), p. 104.

[22] Though such an emphasis might well have had a historical basis, in that Martin himself would have sought to imitate Jesus, and would have been open to influence from the examples of the prophets, apostles, martyrs, and monks: see above, ch. 12, n. 8.

[23] *D* III, 9, 3; III, 10. Also, Martin's healing miracles are generally in the tradition of Jesus: e.g. *VM* 16; cf. Fontaine, *Vie* II, 809, 813 ff.

[24] E.g. *ep.* 1, 5–7; *ep.* 2, 8–13; *D* II, 5, 1–2; III, 17, 6–7. For Christlike examples, see previous note.

is perfectly understandable, and the question to be asked is not whether or why there was literary stylization of this kind, but rather, how far it was carried. There is a crucial difference between Sulpicius fixing upon a genuine trait of Martin's and conveying this in biblical language; and, on the other hand, Sulpicius simply attributing such traits (along with stories to illustrate them) to Martin out of a desire to prove his resemblance to earlier Christian heroes.

On the whole, the evidence suggests the former procedure. Let us take an instance where literary stylization is obvious, the passage crediting Martin with virtual martyrdom in Sulpicius' second epistle.[25] Beneath the rhetoric, all it amounts to is asserting that Martin will now be second to none amongst the apostles and prophets; that he would have undergone various torments for the sake of Christ had he lived in time of persecution; and that although he did not, 'he none the less achieved martyrdom without shedding his blood' by undergoing a perpetual struggle for Christ throughout his life. For he suffered hunger and nakedness, he watched and fasted, he bore insults and persecution, he cared for the sick and for those in danger; he sorrowed with the sorrowful; he was wounded when some one caused offence; he groaned when some one perished. In addition he strove each day against human and spiritual evils which he overcame by his fortitude, his patience, and his equanimity. Religious feeling, pity, and love increased in him up to the end of his life.

Now, although most of this catalogue is given in the words of St. Paul,[26] the interesting thing is that individual details and stories elsewhere in Sulpicius' writings fully corroborate this picture: Martin frequently besought God with vigils and fasting;[27] he was naked except for his cloak when he met the beggar at Amiens, and so was able to give only half of it away;[28] he healed the sick; he was insulted by his disciple, Brice, and beaten up by imperial officials;[29] he was accused of partiality to the Priscillianists by other

---

[25] *Ep.* 2, 8-14. See Fontaine's notes ad loc. (*Vie* III, 1207-41, esp. pp. 1216 ff.); and F. R. Hoare, *The Western Fathers* (London 1954), p. 47.

[26] II Corinthians 11:27-9.   [27] E.g. *D* III, 14, 4; *VM* 14, 4.

[28] *VM* 3, 2.   [29] *D* III, 15, 4; II, 3, 4-5.

bishops, who nearly persuaded the Emperor Maximus to take action against him;[30] he would intercede on behalf of prisoners and exiles, for those whose goods had been confiscated and for those who were threatened with persecution, even at the risk of his own reputation and safety.[31] He turned aside to see if he could help when he heard lamentations coming from a house, and wept at the sorrow and anxiety felt by his followers when they realized he was dying.[32] He did not exclude sinners from his mercy, upholding against the devil the possibility that men who had sinned after baptism could wipe out their former sins through their subsequent way of life, and even promising that if the devil would repent, he would find mercy.[33] He struggled against the forces of human and spiritual wickedness, compromising his own peace of mind in order to save lives,[34] and showing up the wiles of the devil for what they were.[35] His last act was to journey to Candes to settle a squabble amongst the clergy,[36] and his entire life was marked by fortitude, patience, and equanimity.[37]

Thus in this case, at any rate, Sulpicius appears to have been using biblical words to describe real Martinian traits; for most of the stories cited above to corroborate Sulpicius' general portrait are non-glorificatory and individualistic enough to indicate that they are based on historical incidents.[38]

The most problematical instance of stylization is, of course, *Vita Martini* 4, describing Martin's encounter with Julian and the events leading up to his release from the army. We have already discussed this chapter at some length, and concluded that Sulpicius undoubtedly stylized this scene after the pattern of martyr literature; as for whether he invented the

---

[30] *D* III, 12, 2. [31] *D* II, 7, 3; III, 4; III, 11, 3 & 8-9.
[32] *VM* 8, 1-2. *Ep*. 3, 10-11. [33] *VM* 22, 3-5. [34] *D* III, 13.
[35] *VM* 18, 1-2; *VM* 22-4. [36] *Ep*. 3, 6.
[37] E.g. *D* III, 15, 3 & 6-7; *D* II, 1, 9; II, 3, 4.
[38] Martin's willingness to pardon the devil, his involvement in the Priscillianist affair, and Brice's taunts, are not the sort of things which Sulpicius would have invented. Nor is the story of how Martin gave away *half* his cloak (cf. below ch. 21, and notes 5 and 6). Nor how he interceded for Narses and Leucadius, who would have been well-known figures; while instances of Martin fasting, keeping vigils, and healing are so frequent that they could not all have been invented, or contemporaries would have pointed this out. In general, see below, ch. 22.

donative incident: that, we have no means of knowing.[39] However, we can parallel from elsewhere Martin's bold and unwelcome way of speaking to an emperor; for later Martin told the Emperor Maximus that he would not eat with him, because Maximus was responsible for Gratian's death and Valentinian II's loss of Gaul.[40] We can also illustrate Martin's courage from elsewhere: both his moral courage, as shown by his readiness to speak out against Maximus' anti-Priscillianist measures, and his physical courage, best revealed by his fearlessness in face of pagan attempts to kill him.[41] It is quite plausible, then, to think in terms of a forthright encounter between Martin, a *scholaris* demanding his release, and the Caesar Julian, his commander. Sulpicius has indubitably stylized the story, heightening the details, and possibly adding the touch about the donative; but we have no reason to assume that he invented the whole incident.

Stylization apart, there might be other factors at work in a saint's life which could intervene between the narrative and the events on which it was based; and one which we should consider here is the use of extended metaphor. Now, it is undeniable that the Bible describes many miraculous happenings, which modern readers cannot accept at their face value. These often provided the inspiration for miracle stories in fourth- and fifth-century hagiography; or, at least, both sets of writings contain accounts of events which are similar, and equally miraculous, such as the heavenly provision of bread in the wilderness for God's servants.[42] The Bible was regarded as the work of the Holy Spirit, so it was inconceivable that it should contain 'lies'. Still, fourth- and fifth-century Christians did not take it all as though it were a simple historical narrative. Instead it was recognized that the Hebrews, like the Greeks, had their *fabulae*;[43] that some passages of the Old Testament—and perhaps of the New also—should be interpreted allegorically, and not given a

[39] See above, ch. 10.
[40] *VM* 20, 2.
[41] *D* III, 12. *VM* 13, 3–8; 15, 1. Cf. also *VM* 5, 4–5.
[42] I Kings 19:6; *D* I, 11, 4–6.
[43] E.g. Jerome, *Commentarii in Esaiam prophetam*, ch. 27, v. 1 (*CCSL* 73, p. 346). Cf. also Isidore, *Etymologiae*, I, 40, 6.

literal meaning at all;[44] and that elsewhere the biblical language was symbolic, or metaphorical.[45]

It is the latter, the metaphorical use of language, that concerns us now. Let us begin with a sermon of Pope Leo I's about the account of Pentecost given in Acts 2:1-4, where there appeared to the apostles 'tongues like flames of fire (*linguae tamquam ignis*), dispersed among them and resting on each one.' Leo comments:

> Dear friends, although the appearance of what happened was truly miraculous—and let there be no doubting the presence of the Holy Spirit in all his majesty at that joyful outburst of all human languages— yet no one should think that the divine substance was visible in what was seen by corporeal eyes. . . . For just as human sight cannot reach either the Father or the Son, neither can it reach the Holy Spirit.[46]

In other words, the tongues of flame are a visible sign of the presence of the Holy Spirit; but they are not themselves the Holy Spirit.

It is a short step from here to a purely metaphorical use of 'fire' to express the presence of God's Spirit.[47] We meet this, for instance, in a homily attributed to Maximus of Turin about St. Laurence, 'in whose breast burnt the unquenchable flame of the Holy Spirit.'[48] It may well be that the story already mentioned about how fire compelled Valentinian I to rise from his seat and greet Martin has its origin in the use of such metaphorical language.[49] Valentinian

---

[44] E.g. see J. Daniélou, *Gospel Message and Hellenistic Culture* (ET London 1973), pp. 282-8; *The Cambridge History of the Bible* vol. I, ed. P. R. Ackroyd and C. F. Evans (Cambridge 1970), ch. 13 and pp. 538, 543. This approach was adopted largely to explain away passages of the OT which, taken literally, were most unedifying; not to explain away miracle stories, which were generally accepted as historical events, at least by Latin authors: see Grant, chs. 12 and 13.

[45] *Cambridge History of the Bible* I, 447-8, 451-2.

[46] Leo, *Sermo 1 de pentecoste*, § 3 (*SC* 74, p. 146). I would like to thank R. McKitterick for this reference.

[47] Nor need we be restricted to fiery metaphors: cf. Maximus of Turin's interpretation of the cloud which received Jesus at the Ascension as not a real cloud, but God himself, on the analogy of God speaking in the cloud at the Transfiguration: *sermo* 44, 3 (*CCSL* 23, p. 179).

[48] Maximus, *hom.* 74 (*PL* 57, col. 410B).

[49] *D* II, 5, 4-10. Babut also felt that Sulpicius would have known that educated men would not have taken the story of Valentinian's fiery seat literally: *St. Martin*, pp. 107-8. For parallel cases of metaphorical language mistakenly being taken literally in the NT and in a saint's life, see Lotter, pp. 152-4, esp. p. 154. A. Loyen has suggested a similar origin for *VM* 19, 3: Martin 'opened

refused to stand 'until flames covered the royal chair and fire touched the emperor himself on his bottom.' Obviously these details imply genuine fire. However, the story had reached Sulpicius from oral tradition,[50] and the embroidery of detail may derive from this or from Sulpicius' own work where he, or earlier tellers of the story, may have let the metaphor run wild and assume a reality of its own, in much the same way that animals originally suggested in Merovingian manuscripts by the application of eyes to a letter took on a life of their own until it becomes hard to say whether creatures are being formed from letters, or letters from creatures.[51]

Should we interpret in the same way the fiery ball glowing from Martin's head as he celebrated, regarding it as only a metaphorical way of expressing the presence of the Holy Spirit in Martin, particularly on that day when he had just given away his own tunic to a beggar?[52] Perhaps; but a similar story told about Ambrose suggests that people then really believed they saw flames around a holy man's head. Paulinus of Milan, disciple and biographer of Ambrose, described how, while Ambrose was dictating the psalms, 'suddenly a flame shaped like a short shield covered his head and gradually entered through his mouth, like a householder going into his home'. Paulinus was so amazed that he was unable to take down Ambrose's dictation till the vision passed. He consulted the deacon Castus, who 'explained, by his reading of the Acts of the Apostles, that I had seen the coming of the Holy Spirit upon that man.'[53] Now, if all Paulinus was trying to express was that he had been aware of the Holy Spirit descending on Ambrose, why did he not say so straight out, instead of expressing his bewilderment, and how Castus explained it to him? Similar stories are attested from widely different times

---

Paulinus' eyes' to the truth; *BLE* 73 (1972), pp. 152-3; cf. Fontaine, *Vie* II, 885-8. But cf. A. Rousselle, 'Du Sanctuaire au thaumaturge', *Annales* 31 (1976), esp. pp. 1095-6.

[50] 'Verum id, quod dicturus sum, ipse non vidi . . . sed factum celebre est, fidelium fratrum, qui interfuerant, sermone vulgatum.' (*D* II, 5, 4).

[51] Cf. A. Grabar and C. Nordenfalk, *Early Medieval Painting* (New York 1957), p. 129, and the illustrations there.

[52] *D* II, 2, 1.

[53] Paulinus of Milan, *Vita Ambrosii*, 42 (*Vite dei Santi* III, p. 108).

and places: from nineteenth-century Russia comes one of St. Seraphim of Sarov, while from the wholly different culture of the Oglala Sioux Indians in America comes a similar perception of Black Elk.[54] We might do worse than follow a recent historian, who has written of medieval men: 'accepting a more inclusive concept of reality, they saw more than we do.'[55]

This discussion of the possible perception and understanding of fire may not have 'proved' anything; but it does illustrate the complexity of evaluating Sulpicius' Martinian works in historical terms. At that period men did not think that the everyday world was the only reality. On the contrary, events in this everyday world were readily interpreted as external manifestations of deeper realities, and consequently men tended to be more interested in the underlying originators of events than in their immediate external causes, more concerned with inner significance than with the superficial course of events. It is not that men saw things in 'allegorical' terms, but rather, in 'symbolic' terms. For instance, they might be well aware that 'fire' is not identical with the Holy Spirit; nor were they simply using one term (fire) to stand for another term (the Holy Spirit), as in straightforward allegory, which is perfectly logical and rational. No: 'To bring symbolism into play was not to extend or supplement a previous act of the reason; it was to give primary expression to a reality which reason could not attain and which reason, even afterwards, could not conceptualize.'[56] The distinction between the three states of mind is clearly made by Roger Hinks, following Edgar Wind:

Wind emphasizes the importance of the three stages in the history of the symbol: the magical stage (identity of image and meaning) and the rational stage (intellectual differentiation of image and meaning), with the intervening stage (the decisive one, for our purpose) in which the

[54] V. Zander, *St. Seraphim of Sarov* (ET London 1975), p. 90. J. G. Neihardt, *Black Elk Speaks* (pb. edn. London 1974), p. 45: 'I could see a power like a light all through his body.' Pagan Roman authors also describe appearances similar to Martin's: see above, p. 60.

[55] C. Erickson, *The Medieval Vision* (pb. edn. New York 1976), p. 29; see also ch. 2.

[56] M.-D. Chenu, 'The Symbolist Mentality', *Nature, Man, and Society in the Twelfth Century* (ET Chicago & London 1968), p. 103.

original identity, without being formally operative, still retains a power over the imagination of the beholder. It is this suggestive power of metaphor which underlies the whole of civilized art.[57]

I would regard this 'intervening stage' not as a short-lived transitional phase, but as something that persisted for most of Antiquity and the Middle Ages,[58] including the period when Sulpicius was writing.

A specific instance of this mentality is the attribution of something to the devil, when the writer was well aware that it was a human agent who was immediately responsible for the deed in question, and is simply using 'devil' as a shorthand for 'a man acting under demoniacal inspiration'. A clear example comes in one of Augustine's sermons where he is quoting from the account of one of the Cappadocian children, describing how their mother was brought to curse them. The eldest child had struck the mother, and she was hastening on her way to the baptistery to call down a curse on her son. As she went, 'she met some demon, as it is understood, in the likeness of our uncle' (*ei nescio quis in patrui nostri similitudine, ut intelligitur, daemon occurrit*). 'That enemy' then 'persuaded her to curse all [her children]. And she, roused by the serpent's advice, . . . demanded this most strongly from God'.[59] One scene in the *Vita Martini* is particularly reminiscent of this, when Martin 'encountered a devil on the road, in human guise, who asked him where he was going.'[60] The story ends differently with the devil vanishing when Martin professes his faith in God; but the analogous case from Augustine's sermon suggests that we really are dealing with a human being here, despite the similarity of its 'statim . . . inimicus evanuit' with a similar routing of the devil *qua* devil in the *Vita Antonii*, and also later in the *Vita Martini*.[61]

---

[57] R. Hinks, *Myth and Allegory in Ancient Art* (London 1939), p. 18, n. 1. Note also Creuzer's observation 'that a symbol is *bedeutsam*, whereas an allegory *will deuten*'; ibid. p. 15.

[58] Cf. Hinks, pp. 17–18.

[59] Augustine, *sermo* 322 (*PL* 38, col. 1443). The prosecuting Roman official might be addressed as the 'devil' in the *acta martyrum*: Frend, *Donatist Church*, p. 107, n. 6.

[60] 'Diabolus in itinere, humana specie adsumpta, se ei obvium tulit . . .' *VM* 6, 1.

[61] Cf. *V. Ant.*, tr. Evagrius, ch. 4: 'Et statim . . . phantasma quod videbatur evanuit.' (*PL* 73, col. 130). *VM* 24, 8: 'statim ut fumus evanuit'.

A case which is clearly presented as the work of a human acting under demoniacal instigation is Brice's outspoken attack on Martin. Here, Martin explains that he has seen two demons egging on Brice.[62] Such instances support Fontaine's suggestion that the 'demon' who argues with Martin about his admission of post-baptismal sinners to Marmoutier might in fact be a human being in diabolical guise.[63] Indeed, this 'devil' who was so reluctant to forget another's past sins sounds very like the Brice who claimed that Martin was defiled because he had originally been a soldier—and after his baptism!

If 'devils' could thus appear in human guise, what of 'angels'? Fontaine has suggested that the two armed angels who came to dispel the crowd and give protection while Martin destroyed the temple at Levroux might in reality have been Roman soldiers, *protectores*, sent by a sympathetic Roman official.[64] This is plausible, and it may well be that the whole incident is a great deal more historical than Sulpicius' narrative suggests at first sight.

A similar type of explanation may apply to other miracle stories, also; for one noticeable feature of the Martinian writings is Sulpicius' concern to give events as miraculous an interpretation as possible. Thus, when Martin offered to testify to his faith by entering battle unarmed, but was never called upon to do so because the barbarians sent envoys to make peace, Sulpicius interprets this outcome as a deliberate act of God.[65] Similarly, when a glass vessel containing oil blessed by Martin fell on to a marble floor without breaking, Sulpicius concluded, 'this should not be put down to chance, but rather ascribed to the *virtus* of Martin, whose blessing could not perish.'[66]

In other words, whereas Sulpicius' *Chronicle* had sought to provide this-worldly, 'rational' explanations, in the Martinian writings Sulpicius deliberately emphasized the role of divine

[62] *D* III, 15.
[63] *VM* 22, 3-5; Fontaine, *Vie* III, 986-7.
[64] *VM* 14, 3-6; Fontaine, *Vie* II, 783-6.
[65] *VM* 4, 5-9.
[66] *D* III, 3, 5-6. Cf. also how Sulpicius ascribes the destruction of a pagan idol by a storm to Martin's prayers: *D* III, 8, 4-7.

intervention, frequently ascribing what happened to divine or demonic causation, and interpreting as 'miracles' events which might have been passed over as coincidences by another observer—or, we may suspect, by Sulpicius himself in his *Chronicle*.[67]

So far, we have looked at the many literary factors which could interpose themselves between Sulpicius' knowledge of an event, and his description of that in the Martinian writings; and, so far, we may say that Sulpicius embellished and heightened his stories, was ready to stylize Martin's deeds, probably used metaphorical language, and certainly presented things in miraculous and supernatural terms, stressing the role of demons or angels where we would see human or natural causation. All this renders Sulpicius' account rather different from that which we might have produced, had we been present; but it still remains well within the bounds of a late antique 'biographer's licence'; or, to put it another way, none of this implies deliberate deception on Sulpicius' part. However, one important question has yet to be faced: did Sulpicius attribute to Martin stories with a purely literary provenance, which bear no recognizable relationship either to any historical event in his life, or to a heightened, supernaturalized, or metaphorical rendering of such an event?

It is a question that has to be put, for biography could on occasion undergo influence from other genres further removed from history: for instance, from collections of miracle stories.[68] What is more, there are cases of miracle stories from the pre-Christian Greek world reappearing in stories told of saints, and some miracles in the collections devoted to eastern saints have traits whose origin is, in all probability, purely literary.[69]

---

[67] Cf. *Chron.* II, 34, with its source, Paulinus, *ep.* 31, 5. While admitting that Sulpicius 'improves' on his source by having a funeral procession pass at the right moment (according to Paulinus, a corpse had to be sent for), note that Sulpicius attributes their plan to human counsel (*capiunt deinde consilium*), whereas Paulinus attributes it to God (*dominus ... huius consilii lumen infudit*). See van Andel, pp. 50-1.

[68] Cf. Theopompus' *Philippica* (Momigliano, *Development*, p. 56); Apollonius' *Historiae Thaumasiae* (Tiede, p. 18); Valerius Maximus' *Facta et dicta memorabilia* (cf. above, pp. 60-1).

[69] H. Delehaye, *The Legends of the Saints* (4th edn. ET London 1962), pp. 122-4, and cf. pp. 21-5. Delehaye, 'Les Recueils antiques de miracles des saints', *AB* 43 (1925), at pp. 23-4, 66-72.

As an example of a miraculous story which at a literary level appears to have passed from one work to another, let us take the tale of how a holy man was able to swim among or ride upon crocodiles. In Lucian's *Philopseudes* this practice is attributed to Pancrates: 'At first I did not know who he was, but when I saw him working all sorts of wonders whenever we anchored the boat, particularly riding on crocodiles and swimming in company with the beasts, while they fawned and wagged their tails, I recognised that he was a holy man.'[70] Similar feats were ascribed to the usurper Firmus by the pagan *Historia Augusta*, and to the monk Helles by the Christian *Historia monachorum in Aegypto*.[71] In this case the 'miracle' itself is implausible enough to make us reasonably certain that it never actually happened, and specific enough to make us reasonably certain that the three different authors would not have hit upon the same story independently of each other. Further confirmation for envisaging its origins as lying in a collection of miracles is the fact that it is clearly all of a piece with other miracle stories which demonstrate the holy man's command over animals;[72] and this would appear to be its *raison d'être*, for authority over the animal world proved a man's claim to holiness.

It is, of course, possible that the crocodile story occurs in the *Historia monachorum* through popular (oral) attribution of an Egyptian tale to a Christian hero, not through literary borrowing on the part of the author. However, literary borrowing appears to be the origin of at least some stories which recur in Christian saints' lives: Delehaye has pointed to the two persecution tales which Jerome tells at the beginning of his *Vita Pauli*,[73] and the same is surely true of the 'hippocentaurus' and the satyr which make their appearance later in the same work; such creatures belonged to the world of fable, as that student of antiquity, Isidore of Seville,

[70] Ch. 34; ed. & tr. by A. M. Harmon (Loeb series, London & New York 1921), pp. 372-3.
[71] R. Syme, *Ammianus and the Historia Augusta* (Oxford 1968), p. 83.
[72] Cf. L. Bieler, Θεῖος 'Aνήρ: *das Bild des 'göttlichen Menschen' in Spätantike und Frühchristentum* (2 vols. 1935-6, repr. Darmstadt 1967), I, pp. 104 ff. esp. 109.
[73] *V. Pauli* 3 (*PL* 23, cols 19-20); Delehaye, *Legends*, p. 25.

knew full well.[74] We should perhaps view such stories as literary forms which served both to entertain and also to delineate the godlike nature of the hero of whom they were told.[75] In Momigliano's terms, they provide us with cases where the 'inferior truth' has been sacrificed in the interests of the 'superior truth'.

Thus there are cases of stories from *mirabilia* collections appearing in *some* hagiographical works, namely some of those about Egyptian monks, and, of Jerome's writings, the *Vita Pauli* at the least. However, it is not always easy to determine whether similar stories crop up in various literary works through literary borrowing, or simply through the occurrence of similar events which were then interpreted along the same lines. For instance, the story adduced by Sir Ronald Syme to illustrate Christian borrowing from pagan *mirabilia* is Augustine's tale of how Curma the decurion lay all but dead for several days, and on eventually being restored to consciousness recounted his experiences. He had been brought to the place of the dead, but heard a voice dismissing him and asking instead for Curma the smith. The decurion was therefore sent back to earth, while simultaneously the smith from the same town died. Before he returned to earth, Curma the decurion saw amongst others a priest from his district who told him to be baptized, and he had then seen himself baptized by Augustine at Hippo. He was also shown paradise, and told to get baptized in reality if he wished to come back there. He then returned to his body and came to, while simultaneously Curma the smith died.[76]

Now, this story bears obvious similarities to Plato's tale of Er, which was openly recognized as 'fabulosa': i.e. although it was told to edify and its underlying theme was true, the immediate presentation was fictitious.[77] Even more striking

---

[74] *V. Pauli* 7 & 8; cf. Isidore, *Etymologiae* I, 40, 5 (and cf. XI, 3, 39); XI, 3, 21.

[75] It was Philip Rousseau who first suggested to me that miracle stories might be no more than literary forms.

[76] Augustine, *De cura pro mortuis gerenda* xii, 15 (*CSEL* 41, pp. 644-7). Syme, p. 118, n. 2.

[77] See Macrobius, *Commentaria in somnium Scipionis* I, 9 and II, 7-12; ed. F. Eyssenhardt (Leipzig 1868), pp. 467-8, 469-71. Clement and Origen knew the story, and suggested that it might be 'a symbol of the resurrection': Daniélou, *Gospel Message*, p. 127.

is the parallel with stories in Lucian and Plutarch, which include the feature of the mistaken identity: the dreamer has been wrongly taken from this world because of confusion over his identity; and so the dreamer is sent back to his body, while simultaneously a fellow-citizen dies.[78]

How should we interpret these recurring vision stories? Certainly, there are patterns of vision or dream experience which do recur quite genuinely; and accounts of how a man lay at death's door for some time, and on his return to consciousness recounted how he had been transported to a spiritual world, occur in wholly different cultures.[79] We may accept that much of Curma's vision. However, the repetition of mistaken identity in Plutarch, Lucian, and Augustine's stories—a feature which is not found in the visions from other cultures—looks very dubious, and strongly supports Syme's case.

And yet, Augustine told the story on his own authority: he had first heard of Curma's vision through a mutual friend, and had then got Curma himself to tell him his own story direct, in the presence of trustworthy witnesses from his home town who attested both Curma the decurion's lengthy sickness, and also the circumstances relating to the smith.[80] Also, the part of Curma's vision relating to baptism rings true. In view of all this, and of Augustine's whole-hearted abhorrence of lying under any circumstances, I cannot believe that Augustine borrowed the whole story from oral or literary tradition. Rather, the explanation offered by Dulaey appears plausible:[81] that Curma did indeed have a serious illness, during which he had a vision of visiting the otherworld, and it was as a result of this dream that he sought baptism. But that in the two years that elapsed

---

[78] Lucian, *Philopseudes* 25 (ed. & tr. Harmon, pp. 358-9). Plutarch, *De anima* (*apud* Eusebius, *Evangelica praeparatio* XI, 35-6; ed. & tr. E. H. Gifford [4 vols. in 5, Oxford 1903], II, 136-7; III, 610-11; and cf. IV, 412).

[79] E.g. to Black Elk amongst the Oglala Sioux Indians: Neihardt, pp. 26-47, 169-74, and cf. 160-2. For a well-attested medieval example, see Erickson, p. 41. For contemporary European examples, see J. C. Hampe, *To Die is Gain: the Experience of One's Own Death* (London 1979), ch. 3.

[80] Augustine, loc. cit. (pp. 646-7).

[81] M. Dulaey, *Le Rêve dans la vie et la pensée de saint Augustin* (Paris 1973), pp. 205-10. Even Babut rejected the idea that Augustine deliberately borrowed the story from literary tradition: *St. Martin*, p. 85, n. 3.

between this and Augustine's investigation of the event, Curma's actual dream experience became confused with the folk-tale motif of the mistaken identity.

The issues with the Curma story may seem annoyingly obscure, but it is valuable for that very reason. Augustine was unusual in going to such lengths to try and establish the truth, and in giving us such a detailed account. The apparent merging of a real vision with a folklore motif warns us against jumping to a simple either/or conclusion where our information is less. It is from this viewpoint that we should probably regard the somewhat similar story in *Vita Martini* 7, where a catechumen fell sick and was assumed to have died, but was then restored to life through Martin's prayers. After his recovery the man told how he had been taken before a judge and was on the point of being condemned 'to gloomy regions and vulgar crowds', when Martin's prayers ensured his restoration to life. Here, the theme of judgement, which does not appear in Augustine (nor in modern analogues), links this tale with those told by Plato, Plutarch, Lucian, and Jerome.[82] This does not negate the possibility (or even probability) that the catechumen fell sick, appeared dead for some time, and, on regaining consciousness, told of some visionary experience in another world. But it does suggest that either Sulpicius or the previous oral tradition had shaped this experience after the model of current stories and assumptions such as are reflected in Plato's and Jerome's tales. On the other hand, this story is unlikely to be wholly fictional since Sulpicius makes it clear that this was a well-known Martinian miracle: indeed, the one which first gave him a reputation as a powerful healer.[83] At the same time, the very fact that it had occurred so early in Martin's career and had become so widely known would have allowed much scope for oral elaboration before the story reached Sulpicius. My inclination, then, is to view this tale as an example of oral or literary shaping, rather than literary borrowing.

Another possible candidate for literary appropriation is Sulpicius' account of how two would-be assassins were

---

[82] As above, n. 78, and Jerome, *ep.* 22, 30 (*CSEL* 54, pp. 189-91).

[83] That Martin had such a reputation at Ligugé would also fit with the building sequences excavated there: see above, ch. 3, and below, ch. 24, pp. 359-60.

stymied in their attempts on Martin's life: one found himself flat on his back, while the weapon of the other vanished mysteriously.[84] Such a fate for attackers was regarded in antiquity as a hallmark demonstrating the invulnerability, hence the godlike nature, of the man attacked. This is shown by Eusebius' defence of the evangelists' accounts of Jesus just because they included material that would be highly inconvenient for anyone wishing to interpret Christ as a Hellenistic Θεὼς ἀνήρ (divine man). To clinch his point, he argued:

Why, then, did they not lie, and say that Judas who betrayed Him with a kiss, when he dared to give the sign of treachery, was at once turned into a stone? and that the man who dared to strike Him had his right hand at once dried up; and that the high priest Caiaphas, as he conspired with the false witnesses against Him, lost the sight of his eyes? And why did they not tell the lie that nothing disastrous happened to Him at all . . . ?[85]

There is a biblical precedent for this quality of the holy man,[86] as well as pagan precedent, but even here it is hard to be sure that Sulpicius is taking a story from a literary source rather than giving us a miraculous version based on a real event. The fate of the three Christian missionaries in the Tridentine Alps shows that Martin was only too likely to be attacked by outraged pagans when bent on destroying their temples.[87] Therefore, in this case again, we cannot assume that Sulpicius is ascribing miraculous stories derived from literary or oral sources to Martin's account simply in order to prove that he was a 'holy man', when it is highly likely that (non-)miraculous events of such a kind did indeed occur to Martin, and that Sulpicius would have done his best to present such happenings as miraculous.

The same sort of problems arise when we turn to other stories which at first we might take for literary borrowings. Even with the most suspicious ones of all, the 'fixation

---

[84] *VM* 15.
[85] *Demonstratio evangelica* III, 5, 123c–d; ed. I. A. Heikel (Leipzig 1913; GCS vol. 23), p. 129; ET by W. J. Ferrar, *The Proof of the Gospel* (2 vols., London & New York 1920), I, 142.
[86] I Kings 13:4.
[87] Below, p. 331.

miracles', it is impossible to tell from the text itself whether the unacceptably miraculous traits denote a borrowing from the *mirabilia* tradition, or simply that Sulpicius has here been at work, rewriting the story so as to present it in as miraculous terms as possible. Thus we cannot gauge the historicity of Sulpicius' Martinian works by examining the text in itself; nor, thanks to the wide variations within biography and hagiography which we have discussed,[88] can we gauge it by the literary genre to which they belong.

[88] In ch. 8 above as well as in this chapter.

PART III
THE THOUGHT-WORLD

15

Differing Perceptions of Reality

The flexibility of the literary conventions with which Sulpicius worked has this consequence: it means that they can provide little guidance about the extent of the liberties he would have taken with historical truth. In this predicament, there are two possible ways of obtaining a clearer picture: one might christen them the 'external' and the 'internal' approach. The former, attempted below in part V, involves looking closely at the Martinian writings to see how far Martin is portrayed in ideal terms, or how far his activities as described by Sulpicius fit into the imperfect world of reality, and the particular world of fourth-century Gaul. A second line of approach lies through an attempt to understand Sulpicius and what he thought he was doing in his Martinian works.

Much has already been said of Sulpicius' aims and the circumstances in which he wrote; but his Martinian writings present particular problems, being full of miracle stories. This has led convinced rationalists to conclude that they are full of lies, or, at most, childish fables. Such attitudes still persist, although we are now less able to dismiss out-of-hand such events as healing through non-physical means than was the case some fifty years ago. However, the problems posed by these miracle stories must not be brushed under the carpet, for the question of whether or not we believe in Sulpicius' sincerity will inevitably be affected by whether or not we think Sulpicius believed in the stories he told, whether or not he intended his contemporaries to believe them, and whether or not his contemporaries would have been likely to do so.

For the sake of clarity I have grouped Sulpicius' miracle stories in an appendix under five headings: healing miracles, exorcisms, encounters with supernatural beings, miracles where power over nature was exercised, and lastly such cases as second sight, predictions, dreams, and visions. Obviously these categories are not watertight: for instance, resurrections are classed with healing miracles although they also provide a dramatic example of the saint's power over nature, while exorcisms have good claims to be considered as a specific form of healing. However, this five-fold classification provides a basic framework for discussion.

Now, if we were able to assess these miracle stories at their face value, we would probably accept or reject them on the basis of two general criteria: we would reject them if we thought that such occurrences were *a priori* impossible, thanks to our knowledge—or assumptions—about what has or has not occurred in comparable cases in the past, and what is ruled out by the findings of modern science;[1] alternatively, we might reject them if we felt that the evidence for this particular saint performing this particular action was shaky, even though we considered such actions perfectly possible. On the other hand, if both these criteria were met, we would probably accept such stories as being historically valid.

It is the first criterion which concerns us here. However, we cannot proceed by examining each story in turn and adjudging it 'possible' or 'impossible': for one thing, the last chapter has shown the folly of taking Sulpicius' words at their face value; for another, members of different cultures do not necessarily construe the same events in a single way, nor express their own concepts and interpretations in identical terms. In other words, before we can begin to grasp how Sulpicius and his contemporaries would have understood the miracle stories he tells, we must look at how fourth-century men viewed the world around them and the relationship between the natural and the supernatural, and we must try to ascertain how well equipped they would have been to assess Sulpicius' miracle stories critically.

First, we must realize that not all sharing the same culture construe things in the same way, nor does every individual

[1] In general see E. & M.-L. Keller, *Miracles in Dispute* (ET London 1969), esp. part II, ch. 4.

regard things in the same way all the time. An anthropologist has characterized four major perspectives from which the world can be viewed: the commonsensical, the scientific, the aesthetic, and the religious.[2] The first of these probably remains constant, but this particular classification is not otherwise applicable to the fourth century AD. Then, the 'scientific spirit' common today was unknown, their 'science' being wholly different from ours.[3] It consisted of detailed studies of natural phenomena, but did not include general theories of physical laws or the principles upon which the universe as a whole runs. That belonged to the domain of 'philosophy',[4] a sphere which also included much that we would nowadays associate with religion: it required commitment to certain basic propositions, and often to a way of life which made moral demands upon those who pursued it. Adepts were acclaimed as 'godlike men', the pagan equivalent of saints.[5]

An example of the limitations arising from this affiliation of 'laws of nature' with philosophy is Plotinus' treatment of the proposition, 'Are all Souls One?' Plotinus argued that 'if we reject that unity, the universe itself ceases to be one thing and souls can no longer be included under any one principle';[6] as this would have been contrary to the doctrine he derived from Numenius that with incorporeal bodies 'all is in all . . .',[7] Plotinus does not pursue that train of thought; he simply concentrates all his attention on showing how all souls *are* one. His closing words would have had little comfort for those who refused to accept his premises: 'It is our feebleness that leads us to doubt in these matters; the body obscures the truth, but There all stands out clear and separate.'[8] Or, as it was commonly put, 'The mind

---

[2] C. Geertz, 'Religion as a Cultural System', *Anthropological Approaches to the Study of Religion*, ed. M. Banton (pb. edn. London 1968), p. 26.

[3] Marrou, *Saint Augustin*, 'retractio' pp. 678 ff.

[4] Grant, p. 78.

[5] See Nock, *Conversion*, ch. 11, pp. 167–176.

[6] *The Enneads*, IV, 9, 1 (ET by S. MacKenna, revised edn. London 1956, p. 365; Greek text ed. P. Henry and H.-R. Schwyzer (Oxford Classical Texts, Oxford 1964 ff.), vol. II, pp. 178–9).

[7] R. T. Wallis, *Neoplatonism* (London 1972), pp. 33 and 69.

[8] *Enn.* IV, 9, 5 (MacKenna, p. 368; Henry and Schwyzer, p. 183).

sees, the mind hears, but everything else is dumb and blind.'[9]

Given the tendency for men in late antiquity to think in these terms, the comparative lack of interest taken in technical science (apart from medicine and warfare) becomes understandable. Quintilian's recommendations on education allot all set periods to literary studies, relegating science to odd moments.[10] At most, a student might read various introductory manuals which would probably have left him in doubt as to the validity of their theses, since he would find himself presented with many conflicting conclusions based upon inadequate scientific proof.[11] Impatience or boredom with the inconclusive nature of these studies encouraged men to abandon them in favour of philosophical or theological theories which at least claimed to serve a practical purpose, that of revealing how happiness (the 'beata vita') was attained.[12] Irenaeus and Tertullian stressed the inconclusiveness of science in order to demonstrate the futility of such endeavours as measuring the earth or investigating the cause of tides.[13] Such matters were known to God alone, and for men it was faith which mattered, not curiosity; they therefore preferred to put their trust in the authority of the Bible, rather than in the reasoning power of man.

Medicine might have fared better if Galen's insistence upon the priority of practice over theory and the regularity of natural processes had been taken to heart.[14] But although medicine continued to be studied, there does not appear to have been any organized system of instruction in fourth-century Gaul;[15] and if Marcellus' *De medicamentis* is any indication of the way the subject was tackled, the approach took account of popular beliefs as well as scientific remedies.[16] This might be partially due to the agony inflicted upon a

---

[9] A maxim attributed to Epicharmos: Grant, p. 75; cf. Tertullian, *De anima*, 18, 1 (ed. J. H. Waszink, Amsterdam 1947, p. 24 and cf. p. 256).

[10] Marrou, *History of Education*, pp. 281–2; cf. pp. 183–5. Haarhoff, p. 58.

[11] Grant, pp. 79–80.

[12] One of Augustine's surmises as to why Socrates turned from the physical sciences to the improvement of morals: *De civitate Dei*, VIII, 3 (*CCSL* 47, p. 218).

[13] Grant, pp. 80–81, 103, 112.

[14] Grant, pp. 12, 86, 129–130.

[15] See Haarhoff, pp. 87–8. Rousselle, 'Du sanctuaire', pp. 1088–92.

[16] See Rousselle, pp. 1089–90, 1093–5.

patient by the use of surgery and cauterization when anaesthetics were not used; in such circumstances a sufferer
might well prefer more humane, albeit less 'scientific' treatment.[17]

In any case, the view that diseases were caused by demons
was widespread. It was common amongst the Jews of the
inter-Testamental period, and so passed into the New
Testament and the Christian tradition.[18] In late antiquity
pagans likewise attributed sickness to demons. This is
implicit in Marcellus' approach, and explicit, for instance,
in Apollonius of Tyana's deliverance of the Ephesians from
plague: Apollonius was able to localize the evil in a demon
disguised as a beggar, whom he ordered the citizens to
stone.[19] There were occasional dissidents: Plotinus denied
that intelligent people could be persuaded that disease was
caused by demons, and not by natural causes;[20] and according to Philostorgius a doctor named Posidonius, who lived
under Theodosius, denied that delirium was caused by
demons.[21] However, the same passage of Plotinus testifies
to widespread popular support for the idea that diseases are
caused by spiritual beings, and elsewhere Plotinus himself
admits that death and disease can be caused by a magician
whose incantations operate upon the natural sympathies
and forces of the universe.[22] As for Posidonius, Philostorgius
was only citing his opinion as a paradox.[23]

[17] Hilary of Poitiers has a clear reference to the use of anaesthetics during
surgery: *De Trinitate* X, 14. But Augustine, *De civitate Dei* XXII, 8, and
Vindicianus' letter to Valentinian I, §§8-10 (*Corpus Medicorum Latinorum* V,
ed. M. Niedermann [Leipzig and Berlin, 1916], pp. 24-5) imply that they were
not used.

[18] G. Vermes, *Jesus the Jew* (London 1973) ch. 3, esp. p. 61. J. Tambornino,
De antiquorum daemonismo (Giessen 1909), pp. 97-8.

[19] Rousselle, 'Du sanctuaire', pp. 1094-5. Philostratus, *Life of Apollonius* IV,
10 (ed. and tr. F. C. Conybeare, Loeb series, 2 vols. London & New York 1912,
I, pp. 362-7). Gerhard Delling, 'Zur Beurteilung des Wunders durch die Antike',
Studien zum Neuen Testament und zum hellenistischen Judentum (Göttingen
1970), p. 62. I am grateful to Professor C. F. D. Moule for drawing my attention
to Delling's essays.

[20] *Enn.* II, 9, 14 (*Against the Gnostics*), tr. MacKenna p. 146; ed. Henry &
Schwyzer, I, pp. 223-4.

[21] Babut, p. 256, n. 2.

[22] *Enn.* IV, 4, 40-3 (MacKenna, pp. 323-5; Henry & Schwyzer II, pp. 106-10).
There is a helpful discussion of this section by E. Bréhier in his edition: Plotin,
Ennéades IV (Collection Budé, Paris 1927), pp. 46-57.

[23] Babut, loc. cit.

Thus, apart from occasional exceptions, men were unlikely to turn to science to provide them with explanations of things which lay outside the bounds of common sense. At the same time, science in the late empire was not capable of providing men with a coherent system for the universe, a framework within which individual problems could find a satisfactory answer.

Before leaving this discussion of science and the scientific outlook in late antiquity, it is worth considering the latter in a wider context: viz. that of literary scholarship, of what modern historians mean by treating history 'scientifically'. The great exponent of this approach was Porphyry, whose *Against the Christians* cut so near the bone that it was still in need of refutation *c.*400 AD, both in Africa and in Gaul. Jerome himself at one time appears to have contemplated undertaking this task.[24] Porphyry's attack was based partly on the inconsistencies and absurdities of Christianity: e.g. 'why does Christ assign the unfaithful to eternal punishment, while he also says "For with the same measure that ye mete withal it shall be measured to you again"?'[25] Here, Porphyry's approach is akin to that of the grammarians and rhetoricians who set out to prove a story fictitious by examining its *locus, tempus, causa, persona, modus,* exposing the improbabilities or impossibilities involved, and drawing the conclusion that the whole story is false.[26] At times such an approach, based on historical principles, produced impressive results.[27] But when Porphyry shifts his ground to *a priori* arguments about what is and what is not possible, we are back with the limitations of philosophy discussed above in connection with Plotinus. Porphyry is quite prepared to accept that Christians have worked miracles, since on his premises it is perfectly possible to work miracles through the

[24] Courcelle, *Late Latin Writers*, pp. 209-11, 74, 226.
[25] Courcelle, p. 211.
[26] Grant, p. 59. Cf. above, ch. 9, n. 69.
[27] E.g. Porphyry's dating of Daniel to the Maccabean period: see P. M. Casey, 'Porphyry and the Origin of the Book of Daniel', *JTS* 27, (1976), pp. 15-33. And, for Porphyry as a historian, W. den Boer, 'A Pagan Historian and his Enemies: Porphyry against the Christians', *Classical Philology* 69 (1974), pp. 198-208.

magical arts; what he denies is that the Christians are the only ones to be able to perform them.[28]

A 'scientific outlook', therefore, is unlikely to have played any part in leading Sulpicius' contemporaries to question the authenticity of the miracles he tells about Martin. A more important role was probably played by the 'commonsensical' outlook which will be operative in different ways within any culture, and is based upon the 'self-evident'[29] regularity of natural processes. Roman authors used to cite lists of *adynata*, things that were impossible: rivers cannot flow uphill, the sun cannot be stopped in its course, night always follows day, and the seasons follow each other; 2 and 2 cannot equal 100.[30] There are thus some 'facts' which are commonly accepted by a whole people. In addition, there are some individuals in whom an inherent human tendency to believe only that which they themselves have experienced is dominant; such people have no use for any abstract theories, whether these are based on a reasoned case or on pure hypothesis. It was probably one or other of these factors, and not scientific expertise, which motivated the sceptic who, in the sixth century, refused to believe that oil blessed by Martin could have increased, or that a vessel falling on to a marble floor could have remained intact.[31] Gregory of Tours himself, who concludes that the sceptic must have been demonically inspired, likewise had his doubts about the oil which was said to brim over from the oil lamps placed before the fragment of the true cross at Poitiers, until he saw it happening 'with my own eyes'.[32]

Common sense, then, could have raised doubts in some people's minds as to the authenticity of some of the miracles which Sulpicius tells about Martin. However, the role of

[28] *Apud* ps. Jerome, *Breviarium in psalmos*, ps. 81 (*PL* 26, col. 1066 D), which is perhaps a Gallic work: see *Clavis Patrum Latinorum* (*Sacris Eruditi* 3, 1951) no. 629.

[29] In inverted commas because from the same happenings different things will appear 'self-evident' to people from different cultures; cf. J. Beattie, *Other Cultures* (pb. edn. London 1966) pp. 75-6.

[30] Grant, pp. 57-8, and cf. p. 131. Often this 'common-sense' observation will overlap with 'scientific' observation, but not always: e.g. optical illusions.

[31] Gregory of Tours, *De virt. S. Mart.* II, 32.

[32] Gregory, *In gloria martyrum* 5 (*MGH, SRM* I, ii, p. 40).

common sense will obviously be influenced by the sort of
intellectual and religious ideas held. Thus, for instance, in a
society which believed in the existence of spiritual beings and
their power to affect or determine such things as the weather,
the harvest, and the health and fertility of man and beast,
'common sense' could be used to explain why a farmer who
had neglected the customary sacrifices to the appropriate
spirits should find his crops blighted.

At this point we must ask whether the variety of religious
and social groupings within fourth-century Gaul does not
preclude generalizations about 'common-sense' attitudes.
There were the peasants, as yet virtually unaffected by
Christianity, who still retained a natural religion showing
many Celtic traces. There was the aristocracy, nurtured on
Virgil and the classics, whose paganism would have been
very different—intellectual and cultural, not crudely materi-
alistic—and many of whom had in any case lapsed into
Christianity by the end of the century. Different again was
the urban population amongst whom a variety of religions
flourished, though Christianity predominated by the end of
the century. The religions represented range from the pre-
Roman worship of springs and trees, through the official
Roman cults to the oriental mystery religions, including
worship of Cybele and of Mithras, and so to Judaism and
Christianity (including Priscillianism). Obviously a pagan
peasant's religious outlook was far removed from that of
an educated pagan senator's, while a Christian's differed
from both.

None the less in certain key respects, which we shall look
at in the following chapter, peasant, aristocrat, and townsman
all shared a common set of quasi-religious assumptions about
the universe they lived in. Nor should we read too much into
their religious differences; for the majority of human beings
tend to accept the world going on around them for what it
is, and get on with the task of extracting a living and as much
enjoyment as possible out of it. Traditional paganism could
accept such a state of affairs as the norm. In theory, Christianity could not, for it is precisely in its stress upon the need
to live a specifically Christian life *in* the world that this
religion differs from paganism, including the mystery

religions.[33] But in practice, it is normally only a minority within society who approach life from the specifically Christian angle seven days a week.[34] Added to this, by the end of the fourth century the government's support for Christianity and prohibition of paganism had led many to conform to Christianity just because it was the simplest thing to do. Such people saw no necessity to change their old way of life. Augustine had to warn his congregation in a sermon: 'Let no one say: "Of course I visit idols, and I consult inspired men and soothsayers. But I do not leave the church of God; I am a catholic." '[35] Such an attitude tallies exactly with Nock's definition of 'adhesion',[36] and probably many of the 'conversions' to Christianity from the fourth and subsequent centuries would be better classified as 'adhesions'. Conversion proper involves the complete reorientation of an individual's life, but most people are only brought to such a step by encountering exceptional problems or miseries within their world of everday experience.

In addition to the existence of this pragmatic common-sensical outlook which was widespread amongst both pagans and Christians, we must recognize that in more purely religious terms, as well, intellectual paganism and Christianity shared much common ground in late antiquity. E. R. Dodds has pointed out that the Christian–pagan debate was not a question of monotheism versus polytheism, nor one of the nature of the supreme God, nor of Christian ethics versus pagan laxity, nor of faith versus reason, of miracles versus natural laws;[37] in fact, the tenor of his discussion, as of his whole book, is to draw attention to the fundamental similarity of the two religious viewpoints. This enables us to treat together the religious outlook of Sulpicius' educated

[33] Nock, *Conversion*, pp. 12–14; D. Bonhoeffer, *Letters and Papers from Prison*, letter of 27 June 1944 (ET pb. edn. London 1959, pp. 112–13).

[34] Cf. Geertz, p. 43, n. 3; A.-J. Festugière, *La Révélation d'Hermès Trismégiste* (4 vols., Paris 1944–54), IV, pp. 261–2; A. Murray, 'Piety and Impiety in thirteenth-century Italy', in ed. G. J. Cuming & D. Baker, *Popular Belief and Practice* (Cambridge 1972; *Studies in Church History* 8), pp. 83–106.

[35] *Ennarrationes in psalmos*, ps. 88, *sermo* II, 14 (*CCSL* 39, p. 1244). See also *De catechizandis rudibus* VII, 11, 3 and XVII, 26, 1–3 (*CCSL* 46, pp. 132, 151–2). F. Van der Meer, *Augustine the Bishop* (ET London 1961), ch. 4, pp. 46 ff.

[36] *Conversion*, p. 7.

[37] *Pagan and Christian in an Age of Anxiety* (Cambridge 1965), pp. 116–26.

contemporaries, both Christian and pagan; and this will prove sufficiently important for understanding how fourth-fifth century readers would have understood Sulpicius' miracle stories to merit a chapter to itself.

16

The Cosmos and its Denizens, Divine, Daemonic, and Human[1]

The educated Greek or Roman saw the earth as the centre of the universe. Around it lay the seven concentric spheres of the 'wandering stars', the planets, from the moon through to Saturn. Beyond Saturn was the sphere of the fixed stars which daily revolved around the earth. Between the earth and the moon everything was subject to change and imperfection; but beyond the moon order, stability, and eternity prevailed, and it was to these spheres that souls were thought to rise after death.[2]

Within this general framework there was much divergence,[3] but it is the features held in common which concern us. Most striking is the absence of any division into a 'natural' and a 'supernatural' realm: there was but the one universe which embraced all beings with rational souls, stretching from earth, the abode of man, upwards through air, the abode of daemons, and beyond the firmament into the heavens, the abode of the gods. This geographical continuum was also matched on a personal plane: there was no simple antithesis between 'God' on the one hand and 'man' on the other, each confined to his own respective sphere.[4] On the

---

[1] I use 'daemonic' in a neutral pagan sense for the spiritual beings intermediary between man and God, and 'demonic' in the pejorative Christian sense (and 'angelic' in the favourable Christian sense) when I wish to classify these beings as 'bad' (or 'good').

[2] All this was commonplace: see Dodds, *Pagan and Christian*, p. 6; P.-M. Duval, *La Vie quotidienne en Gaule pendant la paix romaine* (Paris 1952), ch. 8, esp. pp. 302-3, 318-19.

[3] Basically between the 'optimists' who stressed the continuity and links between earth and the celestial regions, and the 'pessimists' who stressed the contrast. Dodds, pp. 6-17 and Festugière, *La Révélation* II, esp. pp. x-xv.

[4] Delling, pp. 57, 59. P. Brown, *The Making of Late Antiquity* (Cambridge Mass. & London 1978), pp. 12 ff., esp. p. 17. Cf. Theodoret's description of the

contrary, spiritual beings were associated with every aspect of human life, and each individual had his own guardian spirit(s).[5] Correspondingly, humans could to some extent participate in the divine sphere: the human mind or soul (or at least that part of it which comprised the *intellectualis anima*) was regarded as belonging to the realm of immortality,[6] and its eventual abode was generally envisaged as lying in the supercelestial spheres of the gods.

Within Gaul, the cult of the *Dii Manes*, the divine souls of the dead, was particularly flourishing. This may owe something to Celtic concepts of a continued real existence after death, and to their belief that graves provided one entrance to the otherworld.[7] Gallic pagans were accorded a tomb, sometimes resembling a temple or an altar, where the dead man's family would gather on certain specific days to make libations and sacrifices, and to celebrate a funeral banquet. Much the same rites continued for a time amongst Christian families, under Christian guise.[8] It has been said that the only factor which differentiated the cult of the dead from that of the pagan gods was the fact that the dead were not attributed any power over the elements of the natural world and over the lives of men.[9] With the coming of Christianity even that changed, as the Christians begged those who had passed on, and particularly the martyrs, to intercede with God on their behalf. By the late fourth century the cult of the martyrs was

martyrs as 'divine men': Delehaye, *Les Origines*, p. 114; Festugière, *La Révélation* III, pp. 139-40. And, for the Celts, A. Ross, *Everyday Life of the Pagan Celts* (1970, pb. edn. 1972), p. 174.

[5] Apuleius, *De Deo Socratis* XV (ed. P. Thomas, Leipzig 1908, p. 23); Ammianus XXI, 14, 3-5 (ed. Clark, I, pp. 244-5); and for Gaul, Jullian, *Histoire*, VI, pp. 70-2. For Christians, Cassian *Conlat.* VIII, 17 (*CSEL* 13 pp. 233-4). Brown, *Making*, pp. 68-72; Brown, *Cult*, pp. 51-7.

[6] It was on the grounds of the mind's participation in the *mens mundi* that Ammianus gave an explanation of the workings of prophecy, *Res gest.* XXI, 1, 11 (ed. Clark 1, p. 218); in general see Festugière, *La Révélation*, III.

[7] S. Piggott, *The Druids* (pb. edn. Harmondsworth 1974), pp. 72-3, 102-4, & cf. also pp. 57-67. Duval, pp. 317-29. A. Grenier, 'Sanctuaires celtiques et tombe du héros', *Comptes rendus de l'Académie des inscriptions et belles-lettres* 1943, pp. 360-71, and Grenier, 'Sanctuaires gallo-romains et tombe du héros', ibid. 1944 pp. 221-8; A. Ross, *Pagan Celtic Britain* (pb. edn. London 1974), pp. 65-70. P. Mac Cana, *Celtic Mythology* (London etc. 1970), pp. 123-9.

[8] Duval, pp. 322-9; Delehaye, *Les Origines*, ch. 2, esp. pp. 27-33.

[9] Jullian, *Histoire* VI, p. 252.

well under way. Their prayers were invoked to drive out demons and to secure health, and even their physical remains were thought to possess supernatural powers. Hilary of Poitiers had already claimed that the tombs of the apostles and martyrs proclaimed Christ through the miracles wrought there.[10] His disciple, Martin, shared in the current enthusiasm for the physical remains of the martyrs, though with discretion. Attempts such as his to ascertain the authenticity of relics were not uncommon, but critics of the whole practice of honouring and invoking martyrs in this way were rare, or else have been effectively silenced by subsequent oblivion.[11]

The dead and the martyrs were by no means the only beings intermediary between God and man, for the whole universe was conceived in animate, not inanimate, terms. Thus, even when the discussion is about a word such as 'caelum', this can signify the principle which animates the heavens, their 'soul', rather than a geographical location.[12] On the one hand there was the Stoic conception of the material elements of the universe permeated with divine powers which were invoked under different names, as Demeter on the earth or Poseidon in the water, but all of which were aspects of the *summus deus*; on the other hand the Platonic tradition, resting upon an interpretation of the *Timaeus*, held that there were lesser gods and daemons to act as intermediaries between God and men, and that some of these controlled the elements.[13] However, in the event the Stoic and Platonic traditions often appear to have been assimilated to each other by the fourth century: the supreme God's 'δυνάμεις' (subordinate deities or daemons) enter into God, and thus constitute part of his 'δυνάμεις' in the sense of 'virtues'.[14]

Simultaneously with these developments within paganism, Jewish-Christian theology had been developing its doctrine

---

[10] Delehaye, *Les Origines*, ch. 4, esp. pp. 116, 119.

[11] Above, ch. 12 and notes 11-12; Fichtenau, pp. 65-6. On Vigilantius see below, pp. 274-5.

[12] See Festugière, *La Révélation*, IV, pp. 176-8.

[13] J. Pépin, *Théologie cosmique et théologie chrétienne* (Paris 1964), pp. 286-7 and 307 ff. Festugière, *La Révélation*, III, pp. 162-3. S. Dill, *Roman Society in the Last Century of the Western Empire* (2nd edn. pb. reprint New York 1958), pp. 92-111.

[14] Festugière, *La Révélation* III, pp. 153, 158 ff.; cf. Pépin, pp. 374-5.

of angels along similar lines. Whereas the original Hebrew of Deuteronomy 33:2 read: 'Jahweh came from Sinai; from his right side streamed forth jets of light,' the Septuagint version reads: 'Angels accompany him at his right hand'; and the *Book of Jubilees* and Josephus represent angels as the intermediaries between God and man in delivering the Law to Moses.[15] This is but one example of the way in which the idea of direct intervention by God was replaced by the image of a distant God surrounded by a court of innumerable powers whom God employed for the administration, protection, and chastisement of the world he had made—tasks which now appeared incongruous with the dignity of God.[16] Thus the book of Revelation frequently refers to angels in charge of the earth, waters, fire, and winds, and this conception is taken up and affirmed along with angelic control over the heavenly bodies by Athenagoras and Origen of Alexandria.[17]

By the fourth century there was thus much common ground between Stoics, Neoplatonists, Jews, and Christians in the way they visualized the working of the cosmos.[18] Of course, their views are those of the more educated; how far they impinged upon the thought-world of the Gallic peasant is another question. Doubtless the more intellectual aspects, such as the concentric spheres around the earth, or the conception of divine powers not as individual deities but merely as aspects of the supreme god, went unknown or unheeded by him. More important, however, is the fact that the peasant, too, believed that the denizens of the otherworld acted within this one, and could be induced to help or harm by his performance or neglect of certain rituals. And so he practised lustration processions around the fields to

[15] J. Daniélou, *Les Anges et leur mission* (2nd edn. Paris 1953) p. 14. This view was shared by St. Paul: see J. L. Houlden, *Paul's Letters from Prison* (Harmondsworth pb. 1970), pp. 164, 166, 186.

[16] So Philo: Pépin, p. 375.

[17] Revelation 7:1-2; 14:18; 16:5, etc. Pépin, p. 309; Daniélou, *Les Anges*, p. 11. Cf. also Daniélou, *Gospel Message*, pp. 462-3.

[18] In the Latin west, Tertullian had rejected most Jewish-Christian angelology: J. Daniélou, *The Origins of Latin Christianity* (ET London 1977), pp. 142-3. But by the later fourth century, Latin theologians were becoming strongly influenced by Greek Christian thought, and by neoplatonism.

protect his crops, he venerated holy trees, he made offerings to the goddess of a source in his quest for fertility or healing; in short, he continued to practice a natural religion, based on the assumption that supernatural beings influenced every human activity, and could be humoured, cajoled, or antagonized by his own actions.[19]

This means that, despite the differences between them, the Christian, the educated pagan, and the illiterate peasant all shared certain basic assumptions about the world they lived in. This was at the furthest possible remove from the eighteenth-century mechanistic model, where the relationship of God to the world could be conceived after the analogy of God as a watchmaker who, once he had created the world, simply left it to run as regularly as a machine, determined by the principles of Natural Law.[20] In late antiquity the workings of the whole cosmos were commonly seen as effected by animate beings, not determined by impersonal laws or mechanistic forces.[21] Thus whereas Cicero had been able to maintain that events came about either because they were willed, or because of fate, or chance, or through natural causes, Augustine will go back a stage further and argue that all events (ultimately) depend upon the will of God, and that all efficient causes derive from beings with wills: 'material causes' are wholly subject to the wills of spiritual beings.[22] Nor was this trend confined to the Christians: in *The Golden Ass*, Apuleius attributes to Isis control over fate, the seasons, the weather, spiritual beings, and the whole animate and inanimate world.[23] However, not all pagans shared his belief that everything was subject to the direct control of the one omnipotent Deity. More common amongst them was the idea that a determinative power was wielded by the intermediary daemons, such as those who animated the stars; and

[19] On the Celtic otherworld, see Mac Cana, pp. 123-7. In general see T. G. E. Powell, *The Celts* (pb. edn. London 1963), pp. 115-21; H. Leclercq, 'Paganisme', §xxix, in *DACL* XIII, i, cols. 311-29. Chadwick, *Priscillian*, pp. 51-4, 195.

[20] So William Paley's *Natural Theology* (1802): see L. C. Birch, *Nature and God* (pb. edn. London 1965), pp. 20-1.

[21] Though note that Plotinus saw its workings in terms of natural sympathies between parts of a living whole: *Enneads* IV, 4, 39-42.

[22] *De civitate Dei* V, 9 (*CCSL* 47, pp. 136 ff.).

[23] *Metamorphoses* XI, 25 (ed. R. Helm, Leipzig 1913, pp. 286-7).

just as they believed that these beings could act without the express command of the *summus deus*, so they believed that they could be approached directly by men.

This was one of the real differences between most forms of paganism on the one hand and Judaism and Christianity on the other, the latter admitting the role played by intermediary spiritual beings in the natural running of the world, but firmly insisting upon their subordination to God.[24] The pagans, however, approached the relevant gods or daemons directly with invocations, adjurations, and sacrifices, whereby they sought to win them over in order to gain their own objectives; hence the role of magic, white and black. It is in fact difficult to distinguish between the objectives of traditional pagan religion, which worked on a reciprocal 'do ut des' assumption, and the objectives of 'magic'. Thus Ammianus can explain one form of divination like this: 'The spirit in charge of all the elements . . . gives us a share in the gifts of divination; and the intermediate powers (*substantiales potestates*), won over by various rites, supply prophetic words to humankind, as from ever-flowing sources . . .'[25] His 'ritu diverso placatae' gives no hint that the *potestates* were *compelled* to accede to the request. Admittedly, the whole passage is designed to defend the practice of pagan divination; but it does illustrate the practical impossibility of drawing the line between 'magic' and 'religion'.

Apart from the savage persecution of 371, emperors up to Theodosius proscribed only 'black' magic: i.e. that which was practised with hostile intent. In fact, both 'black' and 'white' magic operated according to the same principles: people turned to the spirits intermediary between man and the gods, the *daemones*, the *elementa*, and even the spirits of the dead (*manes*). Through magical arts these spirits could be conjured to intervene on behalf of the magician: either in a good cause, such as promoting health and warding off storms; or in a bad cause, such as raising storms, perverting men's minds, or otherwise bringing about their ruin.[26]

---

[24] Clement of Alexandria was atypical in allowing the spiritual beings animating the stars a role in weaving astrological conjunctions: Pépin, pp. 375-6.

[25] *Res gest.* XXI, 1, 8 (ed. Clark I, p. 217).

[26] See *C. Th.* IX, 16, 3 and 5.

The underlying assumption that intermediary spiritual beings had an important role in such matters was shared by Christians, too. Whether or not Paul's mention of 'the elements of the cosmos' in Galatians 4:3 originally referred to spiritual beings, it could certainly be taken like this in the fourth century: 'Some think that they [i.e. the *elementa mundi*] are the angels, who have charge of the four elements of the cosmos: viz. of earth, water, fire, and air'.[27] In the same tradition Origen could explain the cry of Jeremiah, 'How long shall the earth mourn, and the herbs of every field wither, for the wickedness of them that dwell therein?' (12:4):

As if the earth were an animal . . . Nor does our understanding allow us to believe that an insensate body has feeling, unless we realize that angels control everthing, earth and water as well as air and fire: i.e. they govern the elements, and by this arrangement they reach all animals, every green thing, even to the very stars in heaven. Another angel is set over the lands; and so all these angels with whom we have to do on earth rejoice when we do right, and mourn when we sin.[28]

This is the context for understanding Sulpicius' story of how Martin's prayers prevented hailstorms from destroying crops in the neighbourhood of Sens for the rest of his life. And, Sulpicius continues, proof that this was due to Martin's influence, and not to chance, comes from the fact that, 'in the year that he died, once again the storm revived and fastened on [the district]: thus the very cosmos felt the passing of the man of faith, so that, as it rightly rejoiced at his life, so it mourned his death.'[29] The common idea of the earth or cosmos 'rejoicing at' or 'mourning' man's doings needs no elaboration; but what *is* interesting is the specific case which Sulpicius is talking about, the protection of a region from hailstorms. I know of no biblical parallel, but there is a contemporary secular parallel: a law of 321 AD explicitly states that *suffragia* in order to protect the grape harvest from hailstorms are perfectly allowable, and not to

---

[27] Jerome, *In ep. ad Gal.* ch. 4, 3 (*PL* 26, col. 371). Cf. also below n. 42.

[28] Origen, *Homiliae XIV in Jeremiam*, VIII, translated by Jerome (*PL* 25, col. 676).

[29] *D* III, 7, 3. Cf. *D* I, 24, 2 'caelo tantum adque angelis testibus', and also *D* II, 4, 2: Martin 'caelo teste frueretur'.

be confused with invocations made through magical arts in order to harm other people.[30] In other words, both the pagan ceremonies and Martin's intervention had the same objective, the protection of crops; and lying behind both is the assumption that the weather is controlled not by impersonal forces such as air currents, but rather by spiritual beings operating them. The difference is that Martin achieves his request through prayer, not magical rites. Presumably Martin was envisaged addressing his prayers to God, who then directed his angels accordingly;[31] he did not appeal straight to the angels. As Paulinus of Périgueux expressed it in the 460s, when describing how the invocation of Martin's name had stilled a storm at sea:

> Spes est una Deus solus. Quaecumque creavit,
> Et regit. Imperium servant elementa creantis.
> Ad nutum Domini raptim commota quiescunt,
> Insuetos motus propere torpentia discunt,
> Dispositisque prius rebus dat iussio legem.[32]

Seen in this context of a world ruled by spiritual beings, Martin's 'nature miracles' take on a rather different complexion. The clearest instance of Martin's using the spiritual beings in control of the natural world to achieve a 'miracle' is the story of how he overthrew an idol set on a great column:

Then he turned to prayer, as was his wont. It is certain that a rather similar column was seen rushing from heaven, which hit the idol and reduced that whole indestructible mass to dust. Indeed, it would be too small a thing if he should use the heavenly *virtutes* invisibly, unless rather those very *virtutes* should be seen visibly, with human eyes, to serve Martin.[33]

The 'virtutes' of this passage are the spiritual beings elsewhere called 'potestates' or 'elementa'. Hilary of Poitiers, when describing the angelic hosts who will surround God in eternal

---

[30] *C. Th.* IX, 16, 3; see Chadwick, *Priscillian*, p. 195. Cf. *VM* 12, 2.

[31] Here Sulpicius simply says 'facta oratione'; but cf. *VM* 14, 4–5 where Martin prayed to God, who then sent two angels.

[32] *De vita Martini* VI, lines 435–9 (*CSEL* 16, p. 156). Cf. also Constantius' *Vita Germani* III, 13 where a similar storm at sea is stirred up by demons and stilled by prayer and holy oil: ed. R. Borius (*SC* 112, 1965), pp. 146–8.

[33] *D* III, 9, 2.

blessedness after the end of this world, referred to them as a 'chorus cælestium virtutum potestatumque', and then a few sentences further on as the 'creationum elementa'.[34]

A similar conception of spiritual beings as controllers of the elements probably lies behind another 'nature miracle' told of Martin, when the fire from a blazing temple, fanned by the wind, threatened to engulf a neighbouring house. It was only warded off by Martin climbing on to the roof of the threatened building, and opposing himself to the oncoming flames. 'Then indeed, in a wonderful way, you would see the fire twisting back against the force of the wind, with the result that the elements seemed to be in a kind of conflict, fighting between themselves. So by the power (*virtus*) of Martin the fire was active only where he commanded it.'[35]

So much by way of a general framework showing how the human and divine were seen interacting with each other, and how the whole cosmos was envisaged in personal terms, factors which together enable one to make sense of Martin's exercise of *virtus*. For a fuller understanding of what might be called the mechanics of miracle-working, let us turn to Augustine's writings. Augustine, unlike most of his contemporaries,[36] cared about understanding how the different pieces of knowledge, learning, and theology which he possessed fitted together into a coherent whole, and in his voluminous writings he hammered out a system which explicitly discussed things which most people took for granted.[37]

Augustine's general theology of miracles, developed with regard to those in the Bible, has been discussed by

---

[34] *Tract. in psalm.* 148, 2 (*CSEL* 22, pp. 859-60).

[35] *VM* 14, 2.

[36] E.g. Hilary of Poitiers simply insists on the superiority of faith to reason, and the fact that the NT miracles *did* happen, even if they cannot be explained: Grant, pp. 211-12. Similarly, Tertullian: Grant, pp. 193-6.

[37] Of course, Augustine's theological ideas evolved considerably; but even the *Epistolae ad Galatas expositio* (AD 394-5) and *De diversis quaestionibus LXXXIII* (AD 388/96) contain in embryo those ideas about the role of spiritual beings and the impotence of man which Augustine later expanded in his *De civitate Dei*. I have deliberately avoided using Augustine's later anti-Pelagian writings.

others.[38] In the six days of creation God created the world and all that is in it from nothing; and this creation contained the potentialities ('seeds') for all that lay in the future, including 'miracles'. Thereafter, God is but drawing out and realizing what was already there in embryo. As God is omnipotent, *all* that comes about (miracles included) does so in accordance with his will. 'Miracles', then, are not contrary to the totality of the created order: they are just unusual happenings whose causes are not known to man, although they have causes. They are no harder for God to perform than are many of the marvels of nature which we take for granted: e.g. the resurrection of some one who has died is less astonishing than the creation of a wholly new human being, though we do not see it that way because we are so habituated to birth.

It was along these general lines that Augustine defended the historicity of biblical miracles. More pertinent for us, however, is Augustine's explanation of the role which men and spiritual beings (demons and angels) play in the actual bringing about of a miracle. Of course, Augustine heavily stresses the omnipotence of God. God is not only the original creator of all things: he is also their sustainer and governor; and thus all that takes place does so by his will, 'whose power reaches out irresistibly over all'.[39] However, in his government of the universe God also makes use of angels and demons, and he allows the latter power over men in accordance with their deserts.[40] Now, as a result of Adam's fall, man's ability to choose freely has been vitiated:[41] the Jews were given the Law, but the rest of mankind was handed over to the rule of the devil and his angels.[42] Escape from their

---

[38] See D. P. De Vooght, 'La Théologie du miracle selon saint Augustin', *Recherches de théologie ancienne et médiévale* 11 (1939), pp. 197–222; cf. Grant, pp. 217–19.

[39] *De civ. Dei* V, 8 (*CCSL* 47, p. 135). On God's responsibilities for the earth's fertility, for control over the elements, for prophecy, healing, and the course of wars, see ibid. VII, 30 (pp. 211–12).

[40] Ibid. VII, 35 (pp. 215–16); *Ad Gal. expos.* 32 (*CSEL* 84, pp. 100–1).

[41] See J. Burnaby, *Amor Dei* (London 1938), pp. 187–8.

[42] *Ad Gal. expos.* 29 and 32, explaining the 'elementa huius mundi' to which we were enslaved—on Paul's analogy, the equivalent of a minor's stewards and overseers (Gal. 4:1–3)—as the devil and his followers (*CSEL* 84, pp. 94–5, 99–101). Augustine is here following Irenaeus and other writers who had conflated two

power is only possible through Christ; and whereas baptism alone is sufficient for children, those who have reached the years of discretion must also conquer their own desires for evil, something which can only be achieved through the gift of God's love shed abroad through the Holy Spirit; for this is the only thing able to rescue man's freedom of will in his fallen state, and enable him to delight in righteousness.[43] God helps us to do right not by dinning his precepts in our ears; rather, 'he gives the increase inwardly, by pouring charity into our hearts through the Holy Spirit who is given to us.'[44]

When considering the problem of how Pharaoh's magicians had been able to work miracles as well as Moses, God's servant, Augustine gave the following explanation.[45] Every visible thing in the world has a spiritual being in charge of it, and every soul is governed by two principles: in part it enjoys a measure of freedom, just as a private citizen has some say over his own affairs; but in part it is coerced and ruled by the force of the *lex universitatis*, which is identical with the wisdom (i.e. providence) of God. The latter is the more important since the soul's responsibility for itself can operate only within the limits allowed it by the *lex universitatis*. Now, to the extent that a human soul chooses to neglect God and concentrate on its own satisfaction,[46] the divine laws hand it over into the power of those *potestates* who seek their own ends and desire to be honoured as gods, i.e., to the

originally quite separate Jewish traditions: that of the fall of the Watchers, a rank of angels; and that of the idea that God had appointed certain angels to the task of presiding over the earth; see J. Daniélou, *The Theology of Jewish Christianity* (ET London 1964) pp. 187-9. See also Augustine *Enarr. in ps.* 136, 7 (*CCSL* 40, p. 1968).

[43] See *De civ. Dei* XXI, 16 (*CCSL* 46, pp. 782-3); *De spiritu et littera*, ch. iii (5) (*PL* 44 col. 203); Burnaby, pp. 187-9, 221-2; Brown, *Augustine*, pp. 154-5.

[44] *De spiritu et littera* xxv (42) (*PL* 44 col. 226); also v (7) (col. 204). On Augustine's identification of the Holy Spirit and love, see Burnaby, pp. 173-7.

[45] *De diversis quaestionibus LXXXIII*, quaest. 79 (*CCSL* 44A, pp. 225-31), q.v. for this and the following paragraph.

[46] This is obviously one facet of Augustine's teaching on man's freedom of will after the Fall: it is only when man lives in harmony with God's purposes that he possesses 'free will'; if his will turns from the unchangeable good which is God to any other concern, then he sins, and is handed over to the devil's sway; see *De lib. arb.* II, ix, 53, quoted by J. Hick, *Evil and the God of Love* (pb. edn. London 1968) p. 66.

demons.[47] If, on the other hand, the soul tries to act in accordance with the *lex universitatis*, then the latter overcomes the soul's self-concern, and the soul is purged through its life of goodness; then that man becomes the temple of God, and as such may sometimes work miracles:

So it comes about that holy servants of God [have] this gift, when it is helpful. Then, in accordance with the public and, so to speak, imperial law—i.e. the power of the most high God—they command the lowest powers so that they perform certain visible miracles: for it is God, whose temple they are, who commands in them; and him they love most fervently, disdaining their own private rights.[48]

Thus, what actually happens when a saint performs a miracle is that God is speaking through the saint; and, since God is omnipotent, all things are possible. However, at least in the *De diversis quaestionibus LXXXIII*, the way the 'miracle' is actually performed is not 'miraculous'. It is simply a question of God directing the lesser spirits, who perforce obey him; for, like his contemporaries, Augustine in his maturity portrayed what happened outwardly in this world as deriving from spiritual beings whom he generally called 'potestates'.[49]

This, indeed, was how he accounted for the fact that even pagan *magi* could work miracles. In the case of magical petitions, the *potestates* would concede what the magician wanted in order to subjugate him to themselves, and there was thus a kind of pact between magician and *potestas*. In those cases where the magician appeared to command, not beg, the *potestates*, his commands were operative because he terrified the lower powers into carrying out his wishes through invoking the names of superior powers. The result is the performance of things which appear miraculous to man, and God allows the *potestates* this power over those men who, having neglected God and preferred their own concerns, have been handed over to the rule of these *potestates*. Augustine also allowed pseudo-Christians and heretics the faculty of working miracles, although this time the rationale was that their invocation of Christ terrified

[47] E.g. see *De civ. Dei* VII, 33 (*CCSL* 47, p. 213).

[48] *De div. quaest.*, *quaest.* 79, 1 (pp. 226-7).

[49] 'Every visible thing in this world has an angelic power in charge of it': *quaest.* 79, 1 (p. 225).

the lower powers into obedience in much the same way as the invocation of the emperor terrified land-holders into submission, even when invoked by erring soldiers whom the government itself disowned.[50]

There were thus three different ways in which the end result of a miraculous happening could be brought about, and all operated through the intermediary spiritual beings directly concerned with the running of the world. The crucial difference lay with the man directing the *potestates*: if he did it for the sake of his own glory, he was a magician or false Christian; but if he did it for the sake of God's glory, then, inasmuch as he was preferring God to God's creatures, or the *lex universitatis* to his own private desires, he was acting in accordance with God,[51] or through divine inspiration, so that one could say that God was acting through him. At the same time, Augustine makes it clear that thaumaturgical gifts are not necessarily proportionate to sanctity: 'But these things are not granted to all holy men for this reason, lest the weak should be deceived by a most fatal error, and think that such deeds are greater gifts than are works of righteousness, through which eternal life is procured.'[52]

However, with this proviso made, and with recognition given to the fact that appearances are deceptive things and thaumaturgy can be practised by other means than God's gift, one can say that Augustine's theology provides us with a coherent account of the connection between living a holy life and working miracles. For him, living a holy life was only possible through cleaving to God with a closeness which makes it impossible to differentiate the action of God from the action of man; for the latter was flooded by the Holy Spirit, the spirit of love, and therefore he lived righteously and adhered to God; and it was in its turn this adherence to God which enabled him to share in God's grace. This was how a man could become the 'temple' of God, and speak with God's voice, not with his own. Hence his prayers were validated by God's authority, and so obtained their objective.

---

[50] *quaest.* 79, 1 and 4 (pp. 227, 229).   [51] Ibid.
[52] Ibid. 79, 3 (p. 228).

17

Martin's Spiritual Powers

(i) *Virtus Martini* in Action

Martin and Sulpicius would have shared these basic late antique assumptions about the physical layout of the universe, and about the role of man, caught up in the cosmic conflict between God and the forces of evil. In general, men were thought to be enslaved to demonic powers; these demons had been defeated by Christ's crucifixion, and it was at baptism, performed at Easter, that the catechumen renounced the sway of the devil, underwent various exorcisms, and was initiated into the victory of Christ which alone was able to redeem him from the devil's domination.

Martin saw the Christian life as a perpetual battle against the forces of evil:[1] 'Wherever you go or whatever you undertake, you will have the devil against you', warned the devil as the youthful Martin set off to convert his parents;[2] and so it turned out. The devil harassed Martin throughout his life, abusing him, arguing with him, slaying one of his peasant dependants, and tricking him into panic when he awoke midst flames so that he got burnt; finally he turned up at Martin's death-bed.[3] All this gives the devil a very active role. Of course, the devil also tried to wreak harm in a more indirect way by seeking to lure a monk into living with his wife,[4] by goading on the savagery of Count

[1] Perhaps influenced by his years as a soldier: See *D* II, 11, 3-7; *ep.* 3, 13 & 16. Cf. *D* II, 4, 9. But this theme was in any case prominent in Latin Christianity: Daniélou, *Origins*, pp. 422-8, 448-53.

[2] *VM* 6, 2.

[3] *VM* 21, 2-22, 5; *ep.* 1, 12-15; *ep.* 3, 16.

[4] *D* II, 11, 1 ('inimicus'); cf. *D* I, 22, 2.

Avitianus and the insolence of Brice,[5] and by striving to mislead monks into mistaking the forces of evil for the forces of good, most notably when he appeared to Martin in the guise of Christ.[6] Yet the ability of the devil to kill a peasant, apparently out of the blue, is so forceful an indication of his power to act directly rather than through the subordination of men that Sulpicius exclaimed 'You will have seen what a judgement of the Lord it was to give this power to the devil!'[7] Martin had been unable to do anything to prevent or remedy the death. A striking simile of the ways of demons preying on men was drawn by Martin as he watched water-fowl fishing in the Loire: '"That is how demons behave," he said. "They lie in wait for the heedless, they seize them unawares, and, once caught, they devour them; and even this cannot sate them." '[8] Thus Martin saw demons lying in wait for men at every turn, and in a way his whole ministry can be seen as a battle against the forces of evil. In addition to his face-to-face encounters with demons, we must remember that the paganism which he attacked so ruthlessly was in his eyes a form of demon worship;[9] and that in addition to exorcising energumens (i.e. the 'possessed'), there is a strong likelihood that he also saw ordinary illnesses as caused by devils, at least in some cases.[10]

How did Martin set about waging this warfare, and what means did he use? Sometimes prayer alone is mentioned, as when Martin called up the brigand's shade, saved himself from death through eating a poisonous plant or being burnt

---

[5] Avitianus: *D* III, 8, 2-3, and cf. also the description of him as a 'bestia' (*D* III, 4, 2, cf. *ep.* 3, 16); and being 'fugatus' (*D* III, 4, 7). Brice: *D* III, 15.

[6] *VM* 24, 4-8; cf. also ch. 23.

[7] *VM* 21, 4. The rustic was in fact gored by an ox; cf. the demon-ridden cow in *D* II, 9, 1-3.

[8] *Ep.* 3, 7. Cf. Minucius Felix, *Octavius* 27, 1, 'impuri spiritus, daemones ... avium volatus gubernant', (*CSEL* 2, p. 39), though NB the context is one of augury and divination.

[9] *VM* 13, 2; 22, 1; *D* II, 13, 6.

[10] This is implied by the use of similar terminology: e.g. a sufferer can be 'correptus' by a fever (*VM* 7, 1) or a demon (*VM* 17, 1); and in both types of case the ill is 'fugata' (*VM* 19, 1; *ep.* 3, 8); cf. also 'leprosum ... osculatus est atque benedixit. Statimque omni malo emundatus' (*VM* 18, 3). NB also Martin's use of exorcized oil (below n. 14). Cf. Fontaine, *Vie* II, pp. 811-13. I use the terms 'energumen', 'demoniac', and 'possessed man' interchangeably, as Sulpicius appears to have done; see further ch. 18, below.

alive, warded off hailstorms from the crops, or sought supernatural aid for the destruction of pagan temples.[11] At other
times Martin would strengthen the impact of his requests by
accompanying them with fasts and vigils, praying con-
tinuously for three days or a week until an answer came:
this was used to gain admission to a reluctant emperor, to
obtain angels to help him destroy a pagan temple, and to
get remission from disease for a senator's household which
had been smitten 'divino numine'.[12] For healing miracles,
Martin would exclude onlookers and pray, and often there
is mention of him touching the affected part of the body[13]
or anointing it with holy oil.[14] Exorcisms were generally
treated in much the same way, apart from the touching and
anointing, though he occasionally used the laying on of
hands.[15] Where he perceived a demon mounted on some one's
back he might put it to flight by· blowing at it ('exsufflans',
a recognized technique), or simply by commanding it to be
gone with his 'potenti verbo'.[16] Martin would also rebuff
the devil by making the sign of the cross, praying, and
quoting from Holy Writ. He used the sign of the cross along
with his trust in the Lord to protect himself from a pagan
sacred tree which was felled on top of him.[17]

We might delineate as a further category of Martinian
miracle stories those which contain no explicit reference to
prayer. Here, the determining factor appears to be Martin
himself, and God goes unmentioned. Within this general
category there are two groups. In one, miraculous power is
mediated directly by a tangible object: either Martin himself,

[11] *VM* 11, 4. *VM* 6, 5-6; *ep*. 1, 13-15. *D* III, 7, 2. *D* III, 8, 7 and III, 9, 1-2.

[12] See below, n. 74.

[13] As in the resurrections (below, appendix); cf. also *D* II, 2, 5-7, and *VM* 19, 3. Gospel precedents are numerous: J. M. Hull, *Hellenistic Magic and the Synoptic Tradition* (pb. edn. London 1974), pp. 140-1.

[14] *VM* 16, 7; *D* III, 2, 6. On the use of holy oil which has been imbued with Christ's power through being blessed, cf. Mark 6:13; James 5:14; *Historia monachorum* I, 12 & XXI, 17; and see Hull, p. 112.

[15] See below, ch. 18.

[16] *Exsufflans*, *D* III, 8, 2-3; the rationale was that the holy man transferred some of his πνεῦμα: Tambornino, p. 81. 'Potenti verbo', *ep*. 3, 8; cf. *D* II, 9, 3, and Hull, p. 106, p. 155, n. 49.

[17] *VM* 22, 1; 6, 2; 13, 8. Cf. Athanasius, *Vita Antonii* 35, 37, 39-40 etc. (*PG* 26, cols. 893, 897-901).

or some material object which has been in direct contact with him.[18] A dramatic illustration of this is the way in which a possessed man reacted to the touch of Martin's fingers, 'as though he had received white-hot iron in his jaws'; and a similar reaction took place when Martin interposed his body in the path of an advancing fire, an achievement which was directly ascribed to the *virtus Martini*.[19] The same effect occurred in reverse when Martin put his finger on a snake-bite, thus attracting all the poison already in the sufferer's body so that he could squeeze it out.[20] Healing also occurred instantaneously for a woman labouring with a period when she touched Martin's clothes.[21]

More magical still are cases where something which had once been in contact with Martin was later the cause of a miracle, without Martin himself being present or knowing anything about the case. Thus straw which he had bedded down in served to cure a man who was possessed, a letter he had written cured a girl of quartan fever when it was simply placed on her chest, and in general fragments of his clothing proved efficacious in healing the sick.[22] The strangest incidents in this category are those where oil blessed by Martin increased, and where a glass ampulla containing such blessed oil crashed onto a marble floor, but remained intact: a miracle which Sulpicius unhesitatingly attributed to Martin's spiritual power (*virtus*).[23]

Alongside these instances where Martin's *virtus* is tangibly conveyed, we should also consider another group of miracles where again the operative factor appears to be Martin, and God goes unmentioned; but this time the miracles are produced by Martin's word of command. The connection between these and the miracles already discussed is made clear by the fact that in the *Dialogues*, Martin is said to have often 'commanded' fires, while in the specific instance given in the *Vita*, Martin places himself in the path of the oncoming

---

[18] For an interesting discussion of the same concept in Luke–Acts, see Hull, pp. 105–14.

[19] *VM* 17, 7. *VM* 14, 2 (above, p. 223).

[20] *D* II, 2, 5–6.

[21] *D* III, 9, 3.

[22] *D* II, 8, 8–9. *VM* 19, 1. *VM* 18, 4–5; cf. Acts 19:11–12.

[23] *D* III, 3, 3–6.

flames, and their shrinking back is ascribed to Martin's *virtus* linked with his power of command: 'Ita virtute Martini ibi tantum ignis est operatus, ubi iussus est.'[24] This power of command was also exercised over demons and demoniacs, creatures, and the shade of a dead man.[25] But perhaps the most striking instance is that when Martin transfixed to the spot a pagan procession:

He raised the sign of the cross upon those in front of him, and commanded the crowd not to move from the place, and to set down their burden. Then indeed, in an astonishing way, you might see the wretched men at first frozen like rocks. . . . But when the blessed man learnt that the gathering was for a funeral, not for pagan rites, he raised his hand again and gave them the power of moving off and taking up the body. Thus, when he wanted he compelled them to stand, and, when it pleased him, he allowed them to go.[26]

It is true that Martin's use of the sign of the cross here is in some respects tantamount to invoking God, but the last sentence puts the emphasis squarely on Martin's will.

Wherein lay the source of Martin's miraculous powers? Was it a matter of external acts, or inner disposition? Was the charisma bestowed equally on all baptized Christians, or focused on the clergy? or the martyrs? or the monks? Was it mediated through the institution of the church, or did God bestow it directly on individuals?

Some clues lie in the matters discussed above in chapter 11. As we saw, both in connection with Martin's baptism and with his consecration as bishop, the sacrament itself is accorded no importance, but is portrayed simply as a ratification of God's approval, the latter having already been manifested directly. Nor did either sacrament make a significant difference to Martin's subsequent way of life. The charisma, then, certainly did not focus upon the clergy, and was not mediated through the church. A further clue lies in Martin's own avowal that he performed fewer miracles as a bishop than as a simple monk.[27] This suggests that the

---

[24] *D* I, 25, 1. *VM* 14, 2.
[25] *VM* 17, 5-6; 18, 1. *Ep.* 3, 8; *D* II, 9, 2 and 6; III, 9, 4. *VM* 11, 4, and cf. *D* II, 5, 2.
[26] *VM* 12, 3 and 5.
[27] *D* II, 4, 1. Cf. also *D* II, 12, 6.

charisma was particularly bestowed on monks—a point which is further borne out by other evidence discussed in chapter 11 indicating a link between Martin's ascetic practices, and his thaumaturgy.

(ii) The Egyptian Ascetic Background

For the background to the idea of charisma focusing upon the ascetics we should turn to Egypt: particularly as this Egyptian background is presupposed by the plan of Sulpicius' *Dialogues*. The Alexandrian theologians provided a coherent rationale for *askesis*, and the main features may be outlined as they could have influenced Martin and Sulpicius either through Hilary's reading of Origen, or through the *Vita Antonii*.[28] The emphasis lay upon man's potential closeness to God, not upon the gulf between man and his creator. Man's soul had been made in God's image. This was now overlaid with sin, and must be restored to its pristine purity and united with Christ through freeing it from all that linked it to the sphere of change and imperfection: i.e. the physical world in which men lived, with its social pressures and economic incentives, and the fleshly desires arising from the body in man's post-Fall state. It was the object of ascetic practices to liberate the soul from all these hindrances that it might once again be established in the purity in which it had been created. The demons, however, tried to hinder man's return towards God, operating both on a cosmological level and a psychological one:[29] as well as encountering men

---

[28] In general see Athanasius, *Vita Antonii*; Lorié, *Spiritual Terminology*, pp. 108-11; cf. J. Daniélou, *Platonisme et théologie mystique*, revised edn. Paris 1953, ch. 3 (on Gregory of Nyssa). However NB that this rationale, though widespread, was not universal throughout the east, particularly outside intellectual circles. It does not appear e.g. in Pachomius nor in the *Apophthegmata*; see *Théologie de la vie monastique* (Coll. 'Théologie', 49, Paris 1961) pp. 41-2, 65-6, 78-82; A.-J. Festugière, *Les Moines d'Orient*, I (Paris 1961), pp. 19-20, 24-5. And yet, an apparently authentic letter of Antony's suggests that Athanasius' *V. Ant.* does not grossly misrepresent or intellectualize Antony's own views: see *The Letters of St. Antony the Great*, tr. D. J. Chitty (Oxford 1975), ep. 1.

[29] A. and C. Guillaumont, art. 'démon', §iii, *Dict. Sp.* III, cols. 189-212; J. Daniélou, 'Les Démons de l'air dans la "Vie d'Antoine"', *Studia Anselmiana* 38 (1956), pp. 136-47.

directly to subvert them through false promises or threats, they got at them indirectly through playing upon their worries or their physical desires. Hence the ascetic's struggle to subject his own body and to ward off demonic attacks are two aspects of the same thing; and this explains the connection between visitation by the devil and the unsettled feeling that this brings to a monk.[30]

However, through prayer and ascetic practices, the monk co-operates with the Holy Spirit. His body is purified from fleshly desires, and his mind or heart (the two are not differentiated in Coptic) is also restored to purity; and so 'the eyes of his heart' are opened, and he receives the gift of spiritual perception. This might enable him 'to see the unseeable God in the purity of his heart, as in a mirror'; or his purified soul 'to see more and further than the demons, as it has the Lord revealing things to it'; or 'to see the many hidden malignities which the evil spirits pour upon us daily in this present time.'[31] The same gift, then, bound up with the ascetic's purity of heart and closeness to God, accounts for his clairvoyance, and also his ability to discern spirits: to see through outward appearances and diabolical hoaxes. So, for instance, Antony knew than an unpleasant smell betokened the presence of a demon, and was not just due to rotting fish; and his disciple Paul the Simple had 'this grace given him by God, that he could see each man's soul, just as we, in turn, see our faces; but also he saw everyone's angel rejoicing over them.'[32]

This eastern ascetic background is certainly relevant for some parts of the Martinian writings:[33] in particular, the stories concerned with angels and demons. One pertinent passage occurs in Rufinus' *Historia monachorum*, describing the ascetic's achievement:

[30] Lorié, pp. 111, 116 ff.

[31] *Vita prima S. Pachomii*, ch. 22, ed. F. Halkin, Brussels 1932, p. 14. (On the mirror image, cf. Matt. 5:8; A. Louth, *The Origins of the Christian Mystical Tradition* (Oxford 1981), pp. 79, 91-3. Hamilton in *Vigiliae Christianae* 34 (1980), pp. 14-18.) Athanasius *V. Ant.* 34 (*PG* 26, col. 893), and cf. ch. 22. Antony, ep. 6 (ET Chitty, *The Letters* p. 18, & cf. pp. 2 & 23. Also Rousseau, 'Spiritual Authority', pp. 385-6.

[32] *V. Ant.* 63. *Verba seniorum* XVIII, 20 (*PL* 73, col. 985). Cf. Rousseau, 'Spiritual Authority', pp. 383, 385-7.

The purer he grows in heart, the more God reveals to him, and shows him his secrets. For he has already become the friend of God, . . . and all that he has sought from him, God grants him, as to a beloved friend. The very angelic powers, and all the divine mysteries, love him as a friend of God, and comply with all his requests.[34]

This, surely, is the context in which to view the angels and saints who came to see Martin out of affection for him, and also Martin's gifts of foreseeing future events or sensing what was happening elsewhere.[35]

The eastern ascetic background also illuminates Sulpicius' chapters 'on the devil and his wiles', and, in particular, the claim that Martin 'held the devil so visible and subject to his eyes, that he recognized him under any guise, whether he was in his own form, or whether he had transformed himself into various figures of spiritual wickedness.'[36] Two illustrative stories are especially relevant. The first is that of Anatolius, who had joined the brothers grouped around Clarus, one of Martin's disciples.[37] Anatolius initially claimed that angels spoke with him; then, that he was a 'virtus Dei', and that God would give him a gleaming white garment to prove his claim and convict those who disbelieved in him. In the night the earth seemed to shake, bright lights shone, and a murmuring of voices was heard. Then Anatolius emerged, clad in a tunic, which was examined by all. Clarus, however, remained suspicious, and urged the brothers to pray for guidance. At dawn he tried to take Anatolius to Martin, 'well aware that that man could not be deceived by the devil's artifice'; but Anatolius resisted, and in the ensuing struggle the garment 'vanished', a happening which Sulpicius ascribes to Martin's *virtus*.

The second story tells that as Martin was praying in his cell, the devil appeared to him decked out in imperial regalia,

---

[33] Cf. Rousseau, 'Spiritual Authority'.

[34] Ch. 1 (*PL* 21, col. 398A).

[35] Visits of saints and angels: *VM* 21, 1; *D* II, 12, 11; 13, 5-8. Foresight, telepathy: *VM* 20, 8-9; 21, 5; *D* III, 14, 8-9. His ability to converse with angels and demons was one way in which Martin gained his praeternatural knowledge (*VM* 21, 2-5; *D* II, 13, 8).

[36] *VM* 21-24. *VM* 21, 1. (Fontaine's edn. accidentally omits 'spiritalis'; cf. Halm's edn. *CSEL* 1, p. 130).

[37] *VM* 23. Cf. *V. Ant.* 40 (= Evagrius, ch. 20), where a demon claims to be a δύναμις τοῦ θεοῦ, which both Latin translations rendered as 'virtus Dei'.

impersonating Christ. Martin was at first 'hebetatus', and stayed silent. The devil urged him to believe:

'Martin, why do you hesitate? Trust your eyes! I am Christ.' Then Martin, prompted by a revelation of the Spirit to perceive that it was the devil, not the Lord, said: 'The Lord Jesus did not predict that he would come clothed in purple, and wearing a glittering diadem. I shall not believe that Christ has come unless he does so in the clothing and appearance of his passion, bearing the marks of the cross.'

At this utterance he vanished instantly, like smoke. He filled the cell with such a stench that the signs left no doubt that he was the devil.[38]

These stories, particularly the latter, are clearly related to stories told of eastern monks to illustrate their gift of discerning between good and evil spirits. This was of great importance, for it was believed that visions could be sent by God to instruct or encourage an ascetic, or by demons to deceive him.[39] Great importance was attached to those visions believed to come from God. Cyril·of Alexandria recommended an Egyptian ascetic, who believed that Melchizedek was a son of God, to seek a ruling from God in a vision. By this means the old man was convinced of his error, and it is implied that Cyril's own authority would not have been so decisive in convincing him.[40] However, such beliefs were fraught with danger, as Cassian was at pains to point out. His second conference, devoted to *discretio* (discernment), tells that Antony insisted that this was the key virtue for the monk, without which he would indubitably go astray.[41] Amongst the cautionary tales included to illustrate this is one of a

[38] *VM* 24, 4-8. See Fontaine's notes ad loc.; and, for the Egyptian dimension, see *Hist. monach.* II, 9-10, and Studer (art. cit. above, ch. 5, n. 23), pp. 354-60. However, I find Studer's theory that this story has an anti-Origenist and anti-Priscillianist slant far-fetched: see G. K. van Andel, 'Sulpicius Severus and Origenism', *Vigiliae Christianae* 34 (1980), pp. 283-4; and NB that Priscillian appears to have accepted the resurrection of the body (Chadwick, *Priscillian*, p. 62). Cf. below, n. 65.

[39] *V. Ant.* 66; 31-40. Another, earlier, tradition found in Tertullian included a third source of dreams, those arising from the soul itself. But by *s*. IV those dreams not sent by God through his angels all tended to be regarded as sent by demons; see Dulaey, pp. 56, 129-31.

[40] Cyril had diplomatically pretended that he did not know the answer; *Verba seniorum* XVIII, 4 (*PL* 73, col. 980).

[41] *Conl.* II, 2, 3-6 (*CSEL* 13, pp. 41-2).

Mesopotamian monk, who was inveigled into believing visions sent by the devil. For a long time, these were perfectly true; but finally the devil showed him the apostles and martyrs in squalor, and the Jews in joy and light, and thus tricked him into embracing Judaism.[42]

These stories reveal the ambivalence of dreams and visions, hence the crucial need to adopt a reliable means of determining their source. For Augustine, with his strong theology of the church, the determining point was whether the dreams arose within the bosom of the catholic church, or outside it.[43] For Cassian, the crux was the individual's humility and willingness to submit all to the scrutiny of a group of older, well-tried ascetics.[44] However, the *locus classicus* for the rules governing the discernment of spirits is Athanasius' *Vita Antonii*, particularly chapters 35-7:[45] the appearance of evil spirits can be recognized by the confusion and noise which accompany them, and by their harmful effects on the ascetic, confusing his thoughts, and interrupting his soul's stable possession of purity. How far are these aspects reflected in the Martinian writings?

The number of ascetic 'technical terms' in Sulpicius' writings is not large. A recent study has listed only six: *monasterium, eremus, cellula, propositum monachi, anachoreta*, and *eremita*.[46] We might add *hebetatus*, the word used to describe Martin's initial reaction to the devil masquerading as Christ: Evagrius had rendered Athanasius' τοῦ ἤθους ἀκαταστασία by *cordis hebetatio*; also *fantasia*, a Greek word taken over to denote diabolical hallucinations.[47] There are also certain traits mentioned apropos of demonic appearances, which have some relevance: noise is one,[48] and the confusion (*turbatio, turbare*) people were thrown into,

---

[42] Ibid. II, 8; cf. *Dict. Sp.* III, cols. 192-4.

[43] Dulaey, p. 147.

[44] *Conl.* II, 10; and cf. Rousseau, *Ascetics*, pp. 187-93.

[45] Analysed by Lorié, pp. 116 ff., q.v. The teaching derives from Origen: see G. Switek, '"Discretio spirituum"', *Theologie und Philosophie* 47 (1972), pp. 36 ff, esp. 42-4.

[46] Gribomont, 'L'influence', pp. 137-41, 144-5.

[47] *Hebetatus*: Lorié, pp. 117-19. *Fantasia*: below, ch. 18, n. 41.

[48] *VM* 21, 2; 23, 6; cf. *V. Ant.* 36; but neither Latin translation uses the same word as Sulpicius, 'fremitus'; see Lorié, p. 116.

another;[49] while Martin is said to have remained unmoved, 'mente tranquilla'—except when caught off his guard.[50] Also, the sign of the cross and citations from scripture had an instantaneous effect in routing the devil, as in the east.[51] Taken together, this evidence confirms that Martin's encounters with devils and angels should be seen in the context of eastern ascetic teaching.

This, however, does not preclude influence from elsewhere. Indeed, when we look at them closely, we perceive that even the chapters devoted to Martin's encounters with the devil contain a number of features which are idiosyncratic, or have western, not eastern, parallels. For instance, *Vita Martini* 21 tells how the devil killed one of Martin's household. It is a remarkable story, for it portrays a concrete instance where Martin is powerless against the devil. This time, it is the devil who is alloted *potestas* by God, and he could well ask, 'Where is your power (*virtus*), Martin?'[52] As Fontaine has suggested,[53] the context for Martin and Sulpicius was probably that leading up to the end of the world as depicted in Revelation, where authority is given to the horsemen and angels to destroy great numbers of men. This means that it fits well with their views on the imminent end of the world; I know of no parallel in eastern ascetic writings.

In the following chapter, the devil's ability to transform himself into diverse guises is fully reminiscent of the *Vita Antonii*;[54] but his appearance in the form of pagan deities is not typical of Egyptian tradition, the gods and goddesses themselves are amongst those popular in Gaul at the time, and the actual phrase, 'mille nocendi artibus', is Virgilian in origin, and was current amongst western ascetic circles *c*.400 AD.[55]

---

[49] *VM* 17, 5; 18, 1-2; *ep* 1, 14; *turbare* or its compounds was used in this context by the pre-Evagrian Latin tr. of *V. Ant.* and by Jerome, Augustine, Cassian, and Benedict (Lorié pp. 116, 121).

[50] Unmoved: *D* III, 15, 3, apropos of Brice's demonically-inspired attacks; cf. *VM* 22, 2; 27, 1. Caught off guard: *ep*. 1, 12 & 14.

[51] Cf. *V. Ant.* 6 and *VM* 6, 2; also *V. Ant.* 35; *VM* 22, 1. Daniélou, 'Les Démons', pp. 143 ff.

[52] *VM* 21, 2 and 4. Contrast and cf. *V. Ant.* 28-9.

[53] *Vie* III, 961; cf. also Job 1:12.

[54] E.g. *V. Ant.* 9.

[55] Below, ch. 23; Fontaine *Vie* III, 964 n. 1.

The next story again has no precise connection with the ideas underlying eastern asceticism. Martin is seen arguing with the devil, who had objected to his admitting to the monastery some who had sinned after baptism.[56] Martin insisted that 'through the mercy of the Lord, those who had desisted from their sins ought to be absolved'; and even went so far as to say that if only the devil himself would repent, 'I . . . would promise you mercy.' As has been pointed out,[57] Martin's humane attitude towards penitent wrongdoers is identical with that of his master, Hilary, and probably reflects his influence. An interesting feature is Martin's readiness to argue with the devil, and various details suggest that Martin's questioner was in fact human, albeit wrongly—or 'diabolically'—motivated.[58]

This chapter is followed by two more containing stories which are linked by the common theme of how men were misled, or narrowly escaped being misled, into believing false claims of spiritual authority.[59] It is here that we find the parallels with the east to which I have already drawn attention: the story of Anatolius, and of the devil masquerading as Christ. The eastern element in this theme of diabolical illusions is further emphasized by the fact that between those two longer stories, there are two thumb-nail sketches: one of a youth in Spain, whose miracles encouraged him to claim that he was Elijah, and then Christ himself; the other, a report that *in the east* a man was boasting that he was John, i.e. the Baptist.[60] Alongside these four stories, which are here grouped together, we might also consider two from elsewhere in the *Vita*: one telling of how Martin exposed a false martyr, the other, of how he compelled a demoniac at Trier to confess to the illusory nature and demonic origin of the rumours he was spreading.[61]

One might spell out the common theme of these stories

[56] *VM* 22, 3-5. Fontaine, *Vie* III, p. 970. Gribomont, 'L'Influence', p. 138 n. 18.

[57] Fontaine, *Vie* III, 976 and n. 1. On the Origenist undertones, see van Andel, 'Sulpicius Severus and Origenism', pp. 278-87.

[58] Cf. Fontaine, *Vie* III, pp. 951-2, 970-1, 985-7, and above, ch. 14, pp. 194-5.

[59] *VM* 23 and 24.

[60] *VM* 24, 1-3.

[61] *VM* 11, and 18, 1-2.

like this: the demons were active in their attempts to delude men, as was prophesied of the last age which would culminate in Christ's second coming. Martin, however, was able to see through the devil's wiles and to expose fraud for what it was. If we try to pin-point the source of Martin's ability to discriminate rightly between the claims which were made, we will probably think of 'that spiritual insight typical of ascetical leaders in Egypt',[62] which we discussed above. And we would be right. However, even here, some details suggest a Latin and martyr-literature context, rather than a Greek ascetic one. The reluctance of a fraudulent man of the spirit to submit to judgment was nothing new in the annals of the church,[63] and the idea of God confirming Anatolius' claim to be a *virtus Dei* by clothing him in a shining white garment is reminiscent of a martyr's dream. Here, Christ raised up the future martyr and, in place of his lowly human chlamys, he pinned on him a new one made of silk, and glistening with light.[64] On another point of detail, we should surely connect the fact that the devil was replete with the imperial regalia when masquerading as Christ with Hilary's outspoken denunciations of the Emperor Constantius as Antichrist, who wrecked Christianity by subverting it, bribing the bishops with gold and concealing all under a fair exterior.[65]

Thus, even in those parts of the Martinian writings which show Egyptian ascetic influence most clearly, individual details reveal that Sulpicius' presentation of Martin's *virtus* was not a straight reflection of eastern concepts. Sulpicius, Martin himself, and Martin's spiritual mentor, Hilary, all belonged to the Latin Christian tradition; and it would be

---

[62] Rousseau, 'Spiritual Authority', p. 410; cf. p. 414.

[63] Cf. H. von Campenhausen, *Ecclesiastical Authority and Spiritual Power* (ET London 1969), p. 185.

[64] The martyr was Polyeuctus, companion of Nearchus. Despite the Greek name, this story apparently comes from a Latin MS, Paris Bibl. nat. fonds latins no. 5278: E. Le Blant, *Les Persécuteurs et les martyrs aux premiers siècles de notre ère* (Paris 1893), p. 93.

[65] Hilary, *Contra Constantium Imperatorem*, esp. §5 (*PL* 10 col. 581-2). Cf. Fontaine *Vie* III, 1022 ff.; above, n. 38. Perhaps also M's insistence on the humiliated, crucified Christ (*VM* 24, 7) owed something to Hilary's spirituality: Hilary often mentions Christ 'in forma servi', e.g. *De Trin.* XI, 48 and 49, an image taken from Phil. 2:7.

rash to assume that the nascent asceticism of the Latin west is but a pale imitation of that of Egypt. The way in which Sulpicius perceived the connection between Martin's asceticism and his miracles may not have been identical with the way in which it would have been understood in the east. We should, then, complement our study of the Egyptian background to Martin's *virtutes* by also looking at the African, Latin, understanding of ascetic practices.[66]

(iii) The Biblical and African Background

The Gospels and the Acts of the Apostles provide so obvious a background for most of the healing miracles told of Martin that detailed discussion would be superfluous.[67] However, as regards the specific role of ascetic practices in these and other miracle stories, we need to look outside the pages of the New Testament.

In the Old Testament there are various cases of fasting to strengthen prayers to God, as when David fasted, lying on the ground for a week, to try and touch God so that He should spare his child.[68] Similar practices occur in IV Esdras, a Jewish-Christian work, which, despite Jerome's rejection of it as apocryphal, was being read and quoted as part of the Bible in southern Gaul *c*.400 AD.[69] In this book prayer accompanied by mourning, fasting, and chastity are clearly depicted as touching God's heart, and bringing an angel to the prophet. As the angel explained:

If therefore you ask again, and again you fast for seven days, I shall again declare to you by day greater things than these, since your voice has been heard by the Most High. For the Mighty One has seen your

[66] Cf. Fontaine, 'L'Ascétisme chrétien', pp. 90–1, 96–8. Martin's concept of the Christian life as a perpetual battle against the devil to be waged through asceticism, and his belief in the imminent end of the world, may owe more to Cyprian than Antony: cf. Daniélou, *Latin Christianity*, pp. 422–4, 443, 448–53.

[67] Cf. above ch. 14, n. 23; ch. 17, §i; and below, appendix. I include resurrections, though here see also I Kings 17:19–24; II Kings 4:33–5.

[68] II Sam. 12:15–23. Cf. the MS variant on Mark 9:29 and below n. 75.

[69] IV Esdras at the end of (some) Vulgates = II Esdras in the apocrypha of Anglican Bibles, *alias* 'The Apocalypse of Esdras'. It was used by Vigilantius: Jerome, *Contra Vigil.* §6 (*PL* 23 cols. 344–5).

righteousness and taken note of the chastity which you have kept since your youth. And therefore he has sent me to show you all these things . . .[70]

That this sort of attitude lived on in the Latin church of the west is shown by Tertullian's writings, where it is assumed that God sent aid to Daniel as a result of penitential fasts performed by the latter:

Daniel alone, trusting in God and knowing what he should do to merit God's grace, asked for a space of three days, and fasted with his companions. And when he had thus commended his prayers, he was instructed in every respect as to the arrangement and meaning of the dream . . .[71]

What is significant is that the Bible itself makes no mention of such penitential fasts. Tertullian has simply assumed them. The passage is valuable as illustrating the difference between the orthodox biblical and Latin attitude, where fasting simply recommends prayers to God,[72] and, on the other hand, the approach of some Greek writers who thought that fasting was directly related to receiving visions as it rendered the soul lighter and more spiritual.[73]

If we now return to our examination of the Martinian writings, it will be clear that various stories demonstrate the idea of penitential fasting strengthening Martin's prayers to God. It is particularly mentioned apropos of three difficult cases: to gain divine aid for destroying the temple at Levroux, whence Martin had already been repulsed by angry pagans; to gain admittance to the Emperor Valentinian, whose heart had been hardened against Martin by his Arian wife; and to ward off a grave pestilence which had smitten Lycontius'

[70] IV Esdras 6, 31-3; ed. B. Violet, *Die Esra-Apokalypse* (Leipzig 1910, GCS 18), pp. 108-10. See R. Arbesmann, 'Fasting and Prophecy in Pagan and Christian Antiquity', *Traditio* 7 (1949-51), pp. 57-9.

[71] *De ieiunio* VII, 7 (*CCSL* 2, p. 1264), referring to Dan. 2:16-19; and presumably making inferences from Dan. 1:16-17. See Arbesmann, p. 63 and n. 65. (*De ieiun.* falls in T's Montanist period, but similar ideas are found in his nonpolemical tract *De anima* 48, 3-4, ed. Waszink, q.v. at pp. 66-7, 512-3.)

[72] The Montanists, who thought that dreams could be extorted from God through fasting, pushed this idea to a (heretical) extreme.

[73] An attitude common to the pagan *Life of Apollonius* and the Christian John Chrysostom; see Arbesmann, pp. 25-30, 55-7, 67-8; H. Musurillo, 'The problem of ascetical fasting in the Greek patristic writers', *Traditio* 12 (1956) pp. 13-17.

household, a case which Martin felt to be especially difficult.[74] The Levroux fast lasted three days, the others, seven days. It is perhaps significant that Tertullian assumed that Daniel's fast was for three days, while the angel prescribed a seven-day fast for Esdras. Certainly the way in which the holy man's fast relates to divine intervention appears to be conceived in identical terms in all these works. What is more, another passage of Tertullian links together rigorous fasting and humiliation of the body in sackcloth and ashes as a way of recommending our prayers to God.[75] Now these are precisely the aids which Martin adopts in the cases mentioned above: he wraps himself in his hair shirt, covers himself with ashes, and fasts, praying continually to God.

Other passages within the Martinian writings also point to common theological ground with African Christianity, rather than with Egyptian asceticism. For instance, despite Sulpicius' praise for monks and virgins, and his strictures against contemporary bishops, some details suggest that holiness was not simply a matter of the individual's purity of heart. So, after Priscillian's death Martin communicated with those bishops whom he held responsible in order to get the witch-hunt after other possible victims called off. However, he was worried by his action—and rightly so, according to an angel. Further, it permanently impaired his thaumaturgical powers:

But when he cured some of the possessed less quickly than usual and with less grace, he immediately acknowledged to us, with tears, that he felt a loss of spiritual power; and that this was because of the evil of that act of communion, in which he had shared of necessity, not in spirit—and that, just for a moment.[76]

Martin only came into contact with the Ithacian bishops *externally* ('non spiritu miscuisset'), yet this was enough to affect his thaumaturgical gifts for life. Alongside this story we might place that told earlier in the *Dialogues* of an Egyptian hermit renowned for his powers of exorcism which

[74] *VM* 14, 3-4; *D* II, 5, 5-7; III, 14, 3-4.
[75] 'This opens the ears of God, dissipates his sternness, calls forth his mercy.' Tertullian, *De patientia* xiii, 2-3 (*CCSL* 1, p. 314). Arbesmann, p. 68. NB prayer accompanied by fasting, sackcloth, and ashes occurs in the OT: e.g. Daniel 9:3.
[76] *D* III, 13, 5. Cf. Pacatus: below, ch. 20, n. 10.

continued unabated despite the growth of the sin of vanity within him.[77] Both stories make the same theological point, that the impairment of thaumaturgical gifts is a matter of external rather than internal contamination. There is a similarity here to the ideas of the 'purists' in Africa. The idea of the contagiousness of sin is prominent in Donatist theology of the fourth century, along with the link between personal righteousness and the power of the Holy Spirit.[78] However, the real link is not so much with the theology of the Donatists, who stressed the role of the ecclesiastical hierarchy and the sacraments, as with the ideas lying behind the *acta martyrum*. Those imprisoned for their faith were regarded as imbued with the Holy Spirit from the moment they entered prison,[79] and this enabled them to perform miracles: when threatened with being burnt alive, the confessors in the *Passio SS. Montani et Lucii* turned to God, and prayed; and immediately, the flames were quenched.[80] For the martyrs and confessors, the church's sacraments were of secondary importance by the side of the pouring out of God's spirit upon them, where no mediation was required; Perpetua saw only martyrs in Paradise—not bishops.[81]

This links up with Sulpicius' portrayal of Martin: on the one hand, the latter's ascetic practices, compassion, and endurance of adversity qualified him to rank amongst the martyrs; on the other hand, asceticism, particularly fasting, played an important part in the religion of the African purists.[82] We know that Sulpicius had read some of the *martyrum passiones*, and their influence on his portrayal of Martin's discharge from the army has already been recognized; but parallels with other aspects of Martin's life can also be found. Most relevant here is the vocabulary used to express the presence of charisma, and the way this is

---

[77] *D* I, 20, esp. §5.

[78] Frend, *Donatist Church*, pp. 120, 318. It has a respectable ancestry: see Frend, *Martyrdom*, p. 419.

[79] Frend, *Donatist Church*, p. 116 and n. 8.

[80] Ch. 3, 3; *Acts of the Christian Martyrs*, ed. Musurillo, pp. 214-16. Cf. Sulpicius *D* I, 18, 4-5.

[81] Frend, *Donatist Church* pp. 116-17; *Martyrdom*, pp. 364-5.

[82] Sulpicius *ep*. 2, 8-13. Frend, *Donatist Church*, pp. 113-14.

connected with the performance of miracles. Thus the martyr Phileas, answering his judge's question about St. Paul, explained: 'Homo similis nobis sed spiritus divinus erat in eo, et in spiritu virtutes, signa et prodigia faciebat', while a prison official was prepared to grant the favour of visitors to Perpetua and her companions, 'intellegens magnam virtutem esse in nobis'.[83] By way of comparison, let us take two Martinian stories. One tells how Martin was *en route* for Chartres, when the pagans of a village he was passing through crowded round to see this famous man. 'Martin sensed what had to be done, and, with the Spirit addressing him, he groaned deeply, and in more than mortal tones he began to preach the word of God to the pagans . . .'[84] The other is the story of Martin's resuscitation of the catechumen at Ligugé. Martin, 'his heart wholly filled with the Holy Spirit' (*tota sanctum spiritum mente concipiens*), excluded the onlookers, and stretched himself out on the lifeless body in prayer. After a time 'he sensed through the Spirit that the power of the Lord was present', and stood up.[85] Within a couple of hours the dead man had revived, and lived to tell the story of his experiences.

In these two cases it is made clear that Martin is acting under the guidance of the Holy Spirit;[86] one might almost say that he becomes a 'medium' for the Holy Spirit. The more general tendency, however, is for Martin to be portrayed as a person who retains his individuality over against God, but whose prayers carry weight with the divinity. This is the procedure implied by the resuscitated man's account of how he had been brought before the heavenly Judge's tribunal when two angels brought word that he was the man that Martin was praying for.[87] It is also implied by the words of the pagan woman in the village: 'We know that you are a

---

[83] *Passio beati Phileae* 5, 3; *Passio SS. Perpetuae et Felicitatis* 9, 1; *Acts*, ed. Musurillo, pp. 350, 116.

[84] *D* II, 4, 5. Cf. Virgil, *Aeneid* VI, line 50, where *nec mortale sonans* describes the sibyl's utterance.

[85] *VM* 7, 3.

[86] Cf. also 'intellexit vir Deo plenus' (*VM* 3, 1); and 'revelante sibi spiritu ut intellegeret diabolum esse' (*VM* 24, 7). The same idea lies behind Martin 'exsufflans' at Avitianus' demon (above, n. 16).

[87] *VM* 7, 6.

friend of God; restore my son to me . . . '; and by Sulpicius himself writing immediately after Martin's death, expressing the hope 'that what we cannot obtain by ourselves, we may at least obtain with Martin praying for us.'[88] Amid a world beset with snares of the devil and presided over by a God who was so distant that his normal contact with men occurred through the medium of angels, and even demons, an *amicus Dei* who could put in a word in one's favour was highly sought-after.[89] Theoretically, the way this power-structure should work was that Martin's influence with God would lead to God deputing his angels to go and answer Martin's prayers, as happened with the catechumen restored to life at Ligugé, and the destruction of Levroux temple, when two armed angels appeared 'saying that they had been sent by the Lord'.[90]

Yet, as we have seen, in addition to miracles wrought by Martin acting under the Holy Spirit's inspiration or through influencing God with his prayers, there is one category of miracles which is directly ascribed to Martin's own *virtus* and his power to command animals, demons, or even fire. The narrow line of demarcation between a miracle ascribed to Martin and one ascribed to God can be illustrated by comparing the request of a father that Martin would heal his daughter, 'pleading that the blessed man would loose her bound tongue by his holy merits', with Martin's response in a similar, if not the very same, situation: Martin, confused, 'drew back saying that this was not within his own power (*virtus*); the old man was wrong; he was not worthy to be one through whom the Lord might show a sign of his power.'[91] Another example is that of the resurrections: in each individual instance, prayer is explicitly mentioned; but when Postumianus is comparing Martin's powers to those of the Egyptian anchorites he simply says, 'Martin . . . commanded the dead.'[92]

---

[88] *D* II, 4, 6. *Ep.* 2, 18.

[89] As was Martin, *VM* 9, 1–3; cf. P. Brown, *The World of Late Antiquity* (pb. edn. London 1971), pp. 101–3.

[90] *VM* 7, 6. *VM* 14, 5.

[91] *D* III, 2, 3 and *VM* 16, 5. See above, ch. 12, p. 168.

[92] *D* II, 5, 2.

However, we cannot overlook the fact that Sulpicius certainly narrates some miracles as though Martin were himself a bearer of spiritual power: for instance, when the demoniac reacted to Martin's hand as to white-hot iron. Further, this power apparently flowed from Martin into things which had been in contact with him: a letter, clothes, or straw. The underlying concept here appears to owe more to the widespread pagan concept of *mana* than to Christianity, though we should note that ideas of this kind occasionally occur in the New Testament: in Mark and Luke, where the woman suffering from haemorrhages touches Jesus, who remarks that 'power' (δύναμις) has gone out of him; and in Acts, where clothes which had been in contact with Paul's skin were efficacious in healing the sick.[93] The same idea of Martin as a bearer of God's power also appears unmistakably in his fixation of the pagan funeral procession, and is implied elsewhere where he issues commands, not prayers.

It looks, then, as though we have the distinction which Gregory the Great was later to make between miracles wrought through prayer, and those wrought through the power (*potestas*) of the holy man.[94] And yet, this is in some ways a false distinction with Sulpicius' Martin; for Martin, whatever he was doing, never slackened from prayer, and so he customarily lived on a higher plane than ordinary people, continually engaging with God and the spiritual world.[95] A saint who was free from all corporeal desires and spent his time in single-minded concentration upon God was as it were 'plugged in' to the divine source of all power, and so long as his feet did not touch the ground and he remained oblivious to the material world, material forces such as fire could not hurt him. Thus Martin could be burnt by fire when he was trying to fight it or escape, but it lost its power to harm him once he concentrated his whole being upon God.[96] Here the *virtus* of Martin is identical with Martin's purity of soul and

---

[93] Above, notes 18-23. Mark 5:25-34; Luke 8:43-8; Acts 19:11-12. See Hull, pp. 105-14.

[94] Gregory, *Dialogues* II, 30-2 (ed. A. de Vogüé, *SC* 260, pp. 220-8; NB p. 223 n. 4): a reference I owe to Lotter, p. 99, n. 52.

[95] *VM* 26, 3-4.

[96] *Ep.* 1, 12-13. Cf. Cassian *Conl.* XV, 10 (*CSEL* 13 pp. 435-6); Vermes, pp. 73-4.

concern with God. However, the 'theorists' in Gaul must have been a tiny minority, and most people would have been concerned with the tangible effects of Martin's *virtus* rather than with its hidden springs. Hence, in the telling of the stories of Martin deflecting the falling tree or transfixing the pagan procession, his use of the sign of the cross may well have been interpreted as a magical symbol, although it was concurrently an outward and visible sign of Martin's faith in Christ's power to save.

But this may present the matter in too complex a manner by drawing a false distinction between the *divina virtus* and the *virtus Martini*. In time of war issues appear straight forward; what matters is the distinction between friend and foe, which overshadows any differences between members of the same side. Martin lived in an embattled world. Far from envisaging a steady consolidation of Christianity through the auspices of Christian emperors, he was convinced that the storm would shortly break: Nero and Antichrist would seize control of the empire and compel the worship of idols, and the reign of Antichrist would only be ended by the advent of Christ at the end of the world. Already the number of false prophets showed that the end was not far off; already, Antichrist was born.[97] Meanwhile, the devil was everywhere, lying in wait for the unwary, and trying to deceive the good by masking his own evil schemes under a virtuous exterior. Men were caught up in the cosmic conflict between the rival powers: *potestas* was potential power, *virtus*, its outgoing aspect, and its achievements were *virtutes*. Yet the devil also was allotted *potestas*,[98] and its effects were everywhere apparent. In this battle, those who were not of the devil's party were for God. All power, all strength, and all goodness derived from him; and therefore one could say of Martin's *virtutes* as of the Egyptians': 'tua haec virtus, Christe, tua sunt haec, Christe, miracula. Etenim quae in tuo nomine operantur servi tui, tua sunt'.[99]

[97] *D* II, 14. *VM* 24, 3.   [98] *VM* 21, 4.   [99] *D* I, 14, 8.

18

Reactions to Martin's Miraculous Powers, Modern and Ancient

The preceding chapters have shown how great is the difference between our thought-world, and that of antiquity. By the same token, we must recognize that our reading of Sulpicius' miracle stories will be very different from theirs. Whatever the original event, for fourth-century man it could easily take on the hue of miracle, of something brought about by supernatural agency. We, however, prefer to concentrate all our attention on a natural cause; and, even when we do not yet understand how such a cause operates, we assume its existence.[1] So, when Martin became aware of what was but then decided by a synod at Nîmes, hundreds of miles away, we would talk in terms of telepathy, where they talked of revelations from an angel. Or we would say that it was their uncle who persuaded the mother of the Cappadocian children to curse them, while they blamed a demon.[2]

Provided we realize what we are doing, and do not forget the gulf which separates us from the thought-world of late antiquity, there is nothing to prevent us from looking at Sulpicius' miracle stories in our own, critical-historical way. Indeed, it may clarify the issues to do so briefly.[3]

[1] Cf. Lotter, pp. 94–7.

[2] *D* II, 10, 8. Above, ch. 14, p. 194. This last instance illustrates that one perception of causality does not necessarily preclude the other: one can be simultaneously aware of the demonic and the human agent.

[3] Especially as the ghost of Hume lives on. While NT 'scholars are generally agreed that Jesus healed the sick and "expelled demons"' (Keller, p. 227), and medievalists who have studied the matter would agree that saints and their shrines fulfilled the same role in the middle ages (e.g. Rousselle, 'Du sanctuaire'; Lotter, pp. 93–5; R. C. Finucane, *Miracles and Pilgrims*, London etc. 1977, ch. 4); despite this it is still possible to find a contemporary historian lumping together all the miracles told in Augustine's *De civitate Dei* XXII, 8, as 'childish fables' (J. Sumption, reviewing P. Brown's *The Cult of the Saints*, *Times Lit. Sup.* 1 May 1981, p. 479).

Interestingly, once we have made due allowance for the tendency of both oral tradition and of Sulpicius himself to heighten the miraculous and to touch up and stylize stories, we will find that many of Sulpicius' Martinian tales are not as 'incredible' as they first appear.

As far as the healing miracles are concerned, there are at least some cases where Martin appears to act more as a doctor than as a thaumaturge: when he healed a boy from a snake-bite, when he cured Paulinus' eye-trouble, and, possibly, in the story of how he cured the raving cook at Trier and how he resuscitated the catechumen and Lupicinus' slave.[4] It has recently been suggested that Martin might have gained some medical expertise during his years in the army, which he continued to put to good use.[5] Also, of course, we should adjust our ideas of 'health', 'illness', and 'cure' to those of the period we are studying.[6] In some cases the illness might well have run its course, and the patient would get better on his own; but, if a saint's aid had been sought, then the cure would be attributed to the saint. This might apply, for instance, to the cure of the fever which gripped Arborius' daughter.[7] In other cases of chronic illness, such as rheumatism and arthritis, there might be a temporary improvement, a remission; and, where follow-up was lacking, this 'cure' alone would be noted, and not any subsequent relapse.

However, most important of all for our understanding of Martin's healing miracles is the realization that some physical disabilities, such as blindness, paralysis, and loss of speech, can result from psychological rather than physical causes: i.e. the diseases are 'functional' rather than 'organic'. Such

---

The story of the ring found in the fish's belly is indeed a folk-tale (*CCSL* 48, p. 821: see K. H. Jackson, *The International Popular Tale and Early Welsh Tradition*, Cardiff 1961, pp. 25–9); but e.g. the healing of the two palsied Cappadocian siblings (*CCSL* 48, pp. 825–7) is not, and it almost certainly happened. Cf. Keller, pp. 64–5, 201–3.

[4] See Rousselle, 'Du sanctuaire', esp. pp. 1095–9. However, as regards Martin's use of holy oil, the context is surely Christian, not that of classical medicine. Why, otherwise, does Martin bless it with the prayer of exorcism (*D* III, 2, 6)? Cf. above, ch. 17 n. 14.

[5] Rousselle, 'Du sanctuaire', pp. 1095–1100. C. Donaldson independently hazards the same guess, *Martin of Tours* (London 1980), pp. 29, 99–100.

[6] Finucane, pp. 71–82.

[7] *VM* 19, 1.

cases may be susceptible of cure through faith-healing or through hypnosis, and these cures are explained by specialists such as those representing the British Medical Association as being due to suggestion.[8] As far as we know all the diseases which Martin healed could have been 'functional'[9] with the single exception of the snake-bite where, as we have seen, Martin acts more as a 'doctor' than a 'faith-healer'. Even with the 'resurrections', it could simply be a case of faulty diagnosis of death, and resuscitation.[10]

Now, in the anxiety-ridden atmosphere of the fourth century, it is easy to see that many people could have been afflicted with psychogenic disorders. Further, a recent study has shown why a holy man such as Martin should have been so effective at combating them: at a time when men felt bewildered and insecure, they needed to put their trust in a *person*, a 'friend of God', who then became responsible for curing them. This was preferable to seeking healing in the traditional pagan way, where the onus lay on the sufferers themselves to establish a right relationship with the divine.[11] What is more, Christianity offered them firm assurance that Christ had defeated the forces of evil through his crucifixion, and that the believer could share in Christ's victory. Martin's deep-rooted conviction that certain illnesses were brought about by demons and that Christ was strong to save men from their snares would have communicated itself to those whom he met; and this expectant atmosphere would have been favourable to faith-healing.[12]

---

[8] E.g. see L. Rose, *Faith Healing* (ed. B. Morgan, pb. edn. Harmondsworth 1971), ch. 5 and p. 176.

[9] See ibid. p. 115. See Finucane, p. 105 and L. D. Weatherhead, *Psychology, Religion and Healing* (2nd revised edn. pb. London 1963) pp. 52-3 on 'leprosy' being used as a term to cover a wide variety of skin diseases in the ancient world; Weatherhead p. 54 on painful menstruation (as opposed to menorrhagia) being due to muscle-spasms which are affected by suggestion. For physiotherapeutic treatment of functional dumbness cf. *D* III, 2, 6-7 and Hull, p. 74.

[10] *Exanimis*, a poetic term (Fontaine, *Vie* II, 616 & n. 2), is used not only of a 'dead' person (*VM* 7, 2 and *D* II, 4, 6), but also of the sick (*VM* 16, 5 and *D* II, 2, 4). Cf. Delling, *Studien zum NT*, pp. 67-8; Finucane, pp. 73-5.

[11] Rousselle, 'Du sanctuaire', esp. pp. 1094-5, 1104-5; Brown, *Cult*, ch. 6, esp. pp. 113-18. Cf. Brown, *Making*, pp. 12-13, 91-101.

[12] E.g. *D* II, 4, 6-8; cf. T. K. Oesterreich, *Possession, Demoniacal and Other* (ET London 1930), p. 105.

The same explanation goes for Martin's treatment of the 'possessed' (with whom the epileptics were unwittingly grouped): the 'demoniacs' or 'energumens'. The instances where Martin saw Avitianus and Brice being goaded on by a demon outside them are only cases of incipient possession, if that.[13] But the majority of cases described are those where, in modern language, either the patient is an epileptic; or he is in a hysterical state, and suffering (or well on the way to suffering) a state of mental dissociation. When the patient is in such a hysterical state he becomes very suggestible; and if people around him assume (as was readily done in the fourth century) that he is 'possessed by a demon', or if he himself puts the idea into his head, then he will accept such a belief, and behave accordingly.[14] In the early centuries of this era people believed in the reality, the ubiquitousness, and the hostility of demons, and such beliefs led to frequent cases of spirit possession. Whereas pagans attributed epilepsy and some cases of spirit possession to the gods, the Christians diagnosed them all as cases of demon possession, to be treated through exorcism.[15] They allowed sufferers to congregate in church, where exorcists would frequently attempt to exorcise them; we might recall that Martin had been ordained exorcist for the church at Poitiers.

It is against this background that we should view Sulpicius' account of Martin's dealings with demoniacs. In the *Vita* Sulpicius describes two cases where Martin succeeded in 'driving the demon out' of a 'possessed' man. In the first case the man became violent at attempts to bring him to Martin, so Martin went to him and cast out the demon by

[13] Cf. *D* III, 8, 2 with I. M. Lewis, *Ecstatic Religion: an Anthropological Study of Spirit Possession and Shamanism* (pb. edn. Harmondsworth 1971), p. 58.

[14] For examples, see Oesterreich, pp. 91–9, 110–17. For an anthropologist's approach, see Lewis; for a psychiatrist's approach, see W. Sargant, *The Mind Possessed* (pb. edn. London 1973), esp. pp. 53–7.

[15] See A. Harnack, *The Expansion of Christianity in the First Three Christian Centuries* (2 vols., ET London & New York 1904–5), I, pp. 152–80. Although he questioned it, Hippocrates bears witness that epilepsy was commonly attributed to the gods (cit. by B. Farrington, *Science and Politics in the Ancient World*, 2nd edn., pb. London 1965, pp. 64–5); and this fits with Martin's testimony that the demoniacs confessed to being gods like Jupiter or Mercury (*D* III, 6, 4). Cf. Rousselle, 'Du sanctuaire', p. 1103.

laying his hands on the man. In the second case a demon seized a cook, who went berserk and started gnashing his teeth. Martin put his hand in his mouth, saying: 'If you have any power, devour these!' The demon reacted to Martin's fingers as to white-hot iron, and was then compelled to leave, being expelled through a flux of the belly. Both these are cases of a man in the throes of 'possession', where the patient is in a fury, and then is suddenly cured: a phenomenon understood by contemporary psychiatrists.[16] There follows, in the *Vita*, an account of Martin interrogating a possessed man in a church at Trier about rumours of a barbarian attack. Here, there is no suggestion that the man was raving, and no mention of any cure.

The *Dialogues* give a general description of what happened when Martin visited his cathedral to pray for the energumens who frequented it. When he set out, 'you might see the energumens roaring all over the church'. Sulpicius continues:

At Martin's approach I have seen one snatched into the air, and suspended aloft with his hands stretched out, so that his feet did not touch the ground. But when Martin had the task of exorcizing demons, he laid hold of no one with his hands, he rebuked no one with his tongue, the way the clergy generally roll out a flood of words. But, when the energumens had been brought forward, he used to command everyone else to leave, and the doors were made fast. Then, clad in his hair shirt, sprinkled with ashes, he would pray in the middle of the church, stretched out on the ground. Then in truth you might see the wretches oppressed, with a diverse outcome: these with their feet carried up aloft, as if hanging from a cloud—nor did their clothes drape down over their faces . . . ; while elsewhere you would see some being tormented without any interrogation, and confessing their crimes. Indeed, they produced their names without being asked: this one said he was Jupiter, that one that he was Mercury. Finally you would see all the servants of the devil being tortured, along with their leader.[17]

As far as we can see, these 'energumens' in the church were not in a state of constant possession. Rather, they were in a

---

[16] *VM* 17; cf. Sargant, p. 45. Rousselle gives an alternative explanation for the raving cook: 'Du sanctuaire', p. 1098.

[17] *D* III, 6, 2-5. See Brown, *Cult*, p. 109: 'The demons in the possessed, therefore, were not being punished by torture: they were confessing the truth under torture.' Note that Martin's eschewal of whirling words, and his reliance instead on prayer, strengthened by asceticism, fits in with the advice given in the pseudo-Clementine epistles *De virginitate*, cit. Harnack, I, 163-4.

disturbed mental state, and it was Martin's prayers that brought about their actual 'possession'—a phenomenon which has been observed elsewhere.[18] Although Sulpicius' description may appear bizarre, and although some minor details are literary borrowings from other works,[19] his general picture of contorted and unnatural bodily movements is doubtless true, as it can be paralleled many times over; while the fact that the possessed named themselves as pagan gods also rings true.[20] Sulpicius does not say anything about the success or otherwise of Martin's methods here, though such a technique (viz. inducing possession in the highly disturbed) can bring about relief in at least some cases.[21]

Bound up with Martin's role as exorcist is his belief in the external reality of demons, angels, and saints, and his own conviction that he was visited by them. This is where Martin's lack of education shows: for, while Augustine was inclined to regard visitations of the souls of·dead people as something that only took place in the mind, Martin saw them as beings external to himself.[22] We should no more doubt Martin's sincerity than we should that of, say, Joan of Arc, another pious but uneducated Christian who claimed that she saw and heard the voices of SS. Catherine and Margaret, and St. Michael.[23] Martin's 'séance' with the dead brigand's shade also belongs here: Martin went to the grave and by prayer was able to summon up the shade (*umbra*) and question it. Martin's companions saw nothing, though they were able to hear the shade's voice; it was Martin who explained that he had seen the brigand's shade. This instance is not wholly unlike the widely-attested experiences of spirit mediums.[24]

[18] Brown, *Cult*, p. 111; Lewis, p. 45; Oesterreich, pp. 96-8; Sargant, pp. 45-7, 143-4.

[19] viz. the clothes that do not hang down: a detail borrowed from Hilary's *Contra Constantium* (Delehaye, *Les Origines*, pp. 119-20; cf. above, ch. 6, n. 53).

[20] Oesterreich, pp. 18, 22-5, etc. Above, n. 15.

[21] Sargant, pp. 45-7, 126-32, 142-4.

[22] *D* II, 13, 5-6; Augustine, *De cura pro mortuis gerenda* XII (14) (*CSEL* 41, p. 643). Cf. Dulaey, p. 111, and below, n. 42. Origen commented that exorcists were generally uneducated people: *DACL* V, i, col. 965.

[23] *The Trial of Joan of Arc*: ET of the verbatim report in Orleans MS 518, by W. S. Scott (London 1956), pp. 77-9, 85-6, 88, 140.

[24] *VM* 11, 4-5. See Fontaine, *Vie* II, pp. 700 ff., esp. 710-12. Cf. Oesterreich, pp. 372-3.

We may perhaps interpret all these 'encounters' as projections from Martin's own mind; but we must recognize that they can appear as objective realities to the people concerned, and it was natural for Martin to take them like this. What is more, this belief would have made Martin a very effective faith-healer and exorcist: he was himself a master of the spiritual world, and so he was well able to diagnose and treat others whose problems lay in this sphere.[25]

Apart from these cases there is little stress on the para-normal in Sulpicius' works: two predictions and one 'oracle', which could be accounted for by common sense and coinci-dence; and two instances of telepathy.[26] We know too little about such matters to be able to convict Sulpicius of fabri-cation on these counts.

The real stumbling-blocks for a twentieth-century reader are the nature miracles. Some of these are explicable in non-miraculous terms, or at least could have been due to chance, such as the storm which razed a pagan monument at Amboise shortly after Martin had prayed for its destruction.[27] Others may be due to Sulpicius' heightening of the miraculous: for instance, the story of a column from heaven smashing a similar pagan column in answer to Martin's prayers[28] might simply be a more miraculous version of the Amboise story. At other times, the miracles told by Sulpicius may have been described in language which was originally intended meta-phorically, not literally.[29] There are a few nature miracles, however, for which we are unlikely to be able to find any underlying rationale: notably the fixation miracles, and the story of how oil blessed by Martin increased.

Yet this does not necessarily mean that Sulpicius and his contemporaries deliberately invented such stories, or regarded them as inventions; for it is here that the distinction between our world-picture and theirs becomes so important. Let us therefore leave aside our twentieth-century outlook, and

[25] Cf. Lewis, pp. 51 ff., 57, 69–70.

[26] *VM* 20, 8–9; *D* III, 10, 1–4; *VM* 9, 4–7; *D* II, 13, 8; *D* III, 14, 8–9. See appendix.

[27] *D* III, 8, 4–7; perhaps also *D* III, 3, 7–8; III, 9, 4; III, 7; III, 3, 5–6; III, 14, 2; *VM* 14, 1–2; *ep.* 3, 7–8.

[28] *D* III, 9, 1–2; perhaps also *VM* 13; *VM* 15, 1–3; *ep.* 1, 13.

[29] E.g. perhaps *D* II, 5, 4–10: above, ch. 14, pp. 191–2.

concentrate for the rest of this chapter on how Sulpicius' contemporaries would have understood his presentation of Martin's miraculous powers, and the grounds for their doubts.

Now, given their understanding of the spiritual universe, men of the fourth and fifth centuries would have seen nothing inherently impossible about the claim that a man with access to the supernatural powers of God and his servants could, through these powers, prevent an inferior being from moving. Their perception of such events is therefore likely to have differed from ours. Perhaps the only miracle which we would have thought appeared as 'impossible' to them as it does to us is that of the increasing oil. And yet, we have a first-hand account of how Gregory of Tours also refused to believe in a miracle of this kind until he saw it happening with his own eyes.[30]

But in this case, why did Sulpicius' contemporaries decry his portrayal of Martin?[31] One point is that his emphasis on Martin's thaumaturgical gifts may have made some Christians uneasy. Vigilantius, an Aquitanian contemporary whom we have already encountered as a pilgrim to the Holy Land, would appear to have protested about the miracles wrought at the martyrs' tombs, saying that they occurred for the benefit of unbelievers, not believers.[32] That miracles had occurred in the early church in order to bring unbelievers to Christianity was an old, widespread belief, which by the fourth century was usually coupled with an explanation of why such miracles were not still wrought: Christianity having spread throughout the empire, such miracles were no longer needed.[33] We find this explanation in Gregory of Nazianzus, John Chrysostom, and Augustine's earlier writings, and this is probably the context for Vigilantius' remarks. For churchmen who belonged to this traditional school of thought, the fourth-century upsurge in the cult of the martyrs and its accompanying miracles was perhaps as disturbing as is the charismatic movement for many traditionally-minded Christians today. Asceticism and its attendant miracles was

---

[30] Above, ch. 15, n. 32.
[31] Above, ch. 11.
[32] Jerome, *Contra Vigilantium* 10 (*PL* 23, col. 348).
[33] Delehaye, 'S. Martin', pp. 73 ff., esp. 75.

frequently linked to this new cult of the martyrs with their miracles, as in the persons of Ambrose and Victricius of Rouen. To confirm their general feeling of uneasiness, churchmen could see many abuses accompanying popular fervour for miracles. Thus Cassian, some twenty-five years later, warned against equating holiness with thaumaturgical gifts: the sick could be cured through their own faith, not that of their healer; or demons might allow a sinful man to work miracles just to lead people astray into copying his sins; what is important for all to copy is the humility of Christ, not his miracles.[34]

However, apparently Sulpicius' detractors were not questioning the potentially harmful side-effects of his thaumaturgical emphasis, but, rather, the truth of his portrayal. Interestingly, of the five cases where scepticism or intimations of it are mentioned apropos of a specific event, only one concerns a nature miracle. Here the sceptic asked 'why Martin himself, who had raised the dead and repulsed flames from houses, had been exposed to a dangerous experience when recently he was burnt by fire.' This sounds like the objection of hard-headed common sense, and there may well have been more of this around than we customarily assume.[35] However, the other references to or intimations of 'scepticism' are quite different: there is one case of men doubting Martin's ability at scriptural exegesis,[36] and three cases relating to Martin's visions.

The first of these comes after the story of how Satan appeared as Christ to Martin, where Sulpicius concludes, 'lest perchance anyone should think it a yarn (*fabulosum*), I learnt of this incident, as I have recounted it above, from the mouth of Martin himself.'[37] The second follows Sulpicius' account of how he and Gallus had kept watch outside Martin's cell for some hours, and been aware of great awe and dread. On Sulpicius' insistence Martin had finally revealed that this was because he had even then been receiving a visit

---

[34] *Conl.* XV, esp. chs. 1 and 7. NB the interesting parallels given by Alardus Gazaeus, *PL* 49, cols. 991 ff.

[35] *ep.* 1, 2. Cf. above, ch. 15, n. 31; Gregory, *In gl. confess.* 80.

[36] *VM* 25, 6-7.

[37] *VM* 24, 8.

from SS. Agnes, Thecla, and Mary. At the same time he admitted that he had also seen SS. Peter and Paul quite frequently, and the demons Mercury and Jupiter. Sulpicius then adds: 'These things appeared incredible even to the majority of those in the same monastery. Still less would I expect that all who hear of them will believe them. For had it not been for the superlative life and virtue of Martin, by no means would we ourselves hold him to have been endowed with such honour.'[38]

Further light is cast upon this by the third instance, Brice's enraged outburst to Martin:

With trembling lips and disturbed mien, his face white with rage, he rolled out words of sin. He asserted that he was the holier one, in that he had grown up in the monastery from his earliest years in the holy discipline of the church, under the guidance of Martin himself. But Martin was filthied from the beginning by his performance of military service—something which he himself could not deny; and now, as regards his worthless superstitions and his hallucinations of visions, with his ludicrous nonsense, he had gone completely senile' (*et nunc per inanes superstitiones et fantasmata visionum ridicula prorsus inter deliramenta senuisse*).[39]

This outburst illustrates the real grounds for contemporaries' mistrust of the claims made about Martin: how were they to know that his so-called visitations by saints, angels, and demons were not mere illusions? How, for instance, could they distinguish between the claims of Martin, and those of Anatolius, who 'said that angels were accustomed to talk with him'? Sulpicius had designated the Anatolius affair as a diabolical *fantasia*, a word which had a special meaning in contemporary ascetic literature: it denoted a hallucination or empty appearance such as the devil created to deceive men.[40] The word *fantasmata*, which Brice used of Martin's visions, was closely related.[41] Martin's claims to have been visited by former mortals would definitely have been rejected

---

[38] *D* II, 13, 1–7.
[39] *D* III, 15, 4.
[40] *VM* 23, 11. Dulaey, p. 95.
[41] Augustine, following Stoic practice, differentiated between *fantasia* and *fantasmata*, but this distinction was not universal; and, when it was used, *fantasmata* denoted a totally imaginary picture, as opposed to *fantasia*, an imaginative evocation in the memory of something once perceived: ibid. 93 ff.

by some churchmen, who did not think that saints could revisit men on earth;[42] and even his claims to have been visited by angels and demons, although they might be allowable in theory, would lay him open to suspicion. As a parallel to the doubts expressed about Martin's claims, we might recall Pachomius' summons to the synod of Latopolis, where he was questioned about his gift of τὸ διορατικὸν, his spiritual insight or clairvoyance.[43] Pachomius cleared himself partly by emphasizing the God-given nature of his gift: he did not obtain visions whenever he wanted them, but when God entrusted them to him; and partly, by pointing to the blameless nature of his life as one who loved God, and cared for his monks.

It was here that Martin was vulnerable. Gifts such as he claimed were a weighty matter, and many felt suspicious, with even Sulpicius admitting the difficulty of believing Martin's claims: 'nam nisi inaestimabilem vitam adque virtutem Martinus egisset, nequaquam apud nos tanta gloria praeditus haberetur.' Yet, for all his brave words, Martin's life was not above suspicion. In some people's eyes he remained smirched by the period he had spent in the army after baptism, 'which he himself could not deny'. It is precisely from the years of Martin's episcopate that we have the ruling of a Roman synod that 'if any one, after remission of his sins [i.e. baptism], shall have worn the belt of the *militia saecularis*, he should not be admitted to the clergy'; and of a papal letter to Gallic bishops (in answer, probably, to questions raised by them), that 'he who, once baptized, has participated in the service of the state (*qui fidelis militat saeculo*) is not free from wrong-doing.'[44] In view of this coincidence between Brice's accusations and the issues in the mind of the Gallic

[42] Jerome held the same views as Sulpicius' Martin (*Contra Vigil.* 6), but was opposed by Vigilantius (ibid.); while Augustine showed himself very reserved in answer to Paulinus' queries (*De cura pro mortuis* X (12) ff.; *CSEL* 41, pp. 639 ff.), wondering whether to consider such appearances as the work of angels (ibid. XIII (16), XVI (19-20)).

[43] *V. Pach.* 112; ed. Halkin, pp. 72-3; Fr. tr. by Festugière, *Les Moines d'Orient* IV, 2, pp. 219-21.

[44] Cited and discussed by Fontaine, 'Vérité et fiction', pp. 209-17, esp. 212-13. *Militia* includes service in the Roman civil service as well as in the army. Here, *militia saecularis*, service to this world's rulers, clearly implies a contrast with the *militia Dei*.

bishops, it is interesting to note that it was Brice who succeeded Martin as bishop of Tours.

Martin's life as a bishop was purer, more ascetic than Brice's;[45] but it was still open to criticism from extreme ascetics, such as Jerome, who felt that the cares of the clergy were incompatible with the utter withdrawal essential for the realization of the monk's goal.[46] Thus, for instance, Abba John of Lycopolis distinguished between monks in the world, and those wholly withdrawn from it. Although those monks who remain in the world and undertake works of hospitality, visiting, and so on, are highly to be commended, none the less all their activities relate only to earthly, perishable matters. This makes them far inferior to the contemplative who concerns himself with heavenly and timeless things. The contemplative, having left behind all earthly cares, 'stands unimpeded in the presence of God, without any anxiety holding him back.'[47] Sulpicius was perfectly well aware of such opinions, as is shown by his report of the Egyptian anchorite who avoided men on the grounds that 'he who is frequented by men cannot be frequented by angels', and his insistence that Martin deserved greater honour because he achieved the same heights although surrounded by throngs of people and hostile clerics.[48] However, the pressing circumstances of Martin's life might well make some strict ascetics doubtful of the genuine nature of Martin's saints, angels, and devils.

On the other side, it was Martin's very asceticism which could render him suspect: particularly in an atmosphere coloured by Priscillianism, by the extravagant claims of other would-be God-inspired men, and by Martin's own expectation of the parousia.[49] Ithacius, bishop of Ossonuba in Spain, accused Martin of being a Priscillianist;[50] and one has to admit that Martin's claims to experience visions and his emphasis on continual prayer, with no manual work save writing for the

---

[45] Cf. *D* III, 15, 2; below ch. 20, n. 38.
[46] Below, pp. 299–300.
[47] *Hist. monach.* I, 62–3; ed. Festugière, p. 34; ET Ward & Russell, p. 62.
[48] *D* I, 17, 5; 24, 2–5.
[49] *VM* 23–4.
[50] *Chron.* II, 50, 4; *D* III, 12, 2.

juniors, is strongly reminiscent of Messalianism which was then rife in Asia Minor, and news of which may well have reached Gaul.[51] Theodoret was to say of the Messalians that they mistake the presence of a demon for the Holy Spirit, and that, rejecting manual labour, they give themselves over to sleep, calling their φαντασίαι, prophecies.[52]

Seen against this background, the scepticism of Martin's contemporaries takes on a new meaning. They would not have denied the possibility that angels and demons might visit a man; but they would have scrutinized any such claims, assessing their validity on the evidence of whether or not the visionary was unassailably orthodox, and of blameless life and character. Something of the doubts they might have entertained on that score has already been said, but to understand their hostility fully it is important to look carefully at the Gallic church of the later fourth century. It is time, then, to pass from the sphere of intellectual history to more mundane and concrete matters.

[51] *VM* 10, 6; 26, 3–4; *D* III, 14, 6. Cf. P. Canivet, 'Théodoret et le Messalianisme', *Revue Mabillon* 51 (1961) esp. p. 27. On widespread acceptance of manual work for monks, e.g. by Jerome and Augustine, ibid. 30 ff. On the role of Messalianism within the ascetic movement of Syria and Cappadocia see J. Gribomont in *Texte und Untersuchungen* 64 (1957) pp. 400–15, and in *Studia Monastica* 7 (1965) pp. 18–19. Its influence could have been mediated to Martin by Hilary, who was exiled to Phrygia (*Chron.* II, 42, 2); or by other contacts, cf. Chadwick, *Priscillian*, p. 167.

[52] *Hist. Eccles.* IV, 10; *PG* 82, col. 1144 A.

PART IV
THE ECCLESIASTICAL CONTEXT

19

Diversity within the Gallic Church: bishops, traditional ascetics, and new-style ascetics

The problem of deciding who was a true Christian was bound to arise with a religion whose founder had lived a life and told stories to illustrate his ideal rather than drawing up a definite code of belief and behaviour. Christianity rapidly came to be embodied in an organization, the church, with its own holy books and religious leaders. However, the question of the relationship between belonging to the church and being a true follower of Christ remained. Were all members of the church truly holy?

As long as Christianity remained a small sect within a hostile environment, the differences between Christians and non-Christians were so marked that they entirely overshadowed differences between more and less faithful Christians within the church: a member of the church was, *ipso facto*, a follower of Christ. However, this changed during the third century when the rapid growth in numbers together with the problem of Christians who had lapsed during persecution forced many to the realization that the church, like Noah's ark, must contain both the clean and the unclean; no complete segregation from worldly contamination was practicable.

The fourth century brought far more dramatic changes: Constantine not only recognized Christianity, he also provided it with the bases for power and wealth within society. This meant that, at the very time when no outward pressure forced Christians together, the character of the church was being altered. Whereas previously ecclesiastical authority had been a concern of Christians alone, now it was formally recognized within society. Church property-owning was relegalized, bishops were given extensive judicial functions which could be exercised even over non-Christians, and the decrees of episcopal councils were enforced with secular sanctions.

The new position of the church can be clearly seen in the role of the episcopacy. In the third century the behaviour of a bishop like Paul of Samosata who modelled his episcopal style of life on that of secular potentates, imitating the practice of magistrates in possessing a throne and audience-chamber and in seeking popular applause, clearly scandalized other bishops.[1] However, with the development of 'l'épiscopat monarchique',[2] such behaviour had become less exceptional by the end of the fourth century. The bishop had long been the key figure within the Christian community, and his authority was further emphasized in the struggle against heretics and schismatics. As *sacerdos*, he alone could confirm, reconcile penitents, give the veil to virgins and widows, and consecrate new churches, and in this way he retained responsibility over his whole diocese. As the direct descendant of the apostles he was the guardian of the true faith, responsible both for teaching his flock and for confounding heretics and pagans; in the frequent synods of the fourth century he played an important part in defining doctrine.

In addition to these spiritual functions he was also the administrator of all wealth bequeathed to the church under his charge. Indeed, as the idea of bequeathing land to a corporate body was foreign to people at that time, the bishop was often acknowledged as the titular owner of church land. Apart from alienating it he could treat it as he liked, and he alone was responsible for apportioning the church's income between the conflicting claims of the clergy, the poor, and ecclesiastical buildings and furnishings. The resources of each diocese varied greatly, but the bishop of Rome was proverbially rich by the mid-fourth century when Ammianus contrasted him with some of the poor bishops in the provinces. Within Gaul Sulpicius frequently castigated the bishops for their worldliness: as soon as

---

[1] F. Millar, 'Paul of Samosata, Zenobia and Aurelian', *JRS* 61 (1971), p. 13.

[2] See the section thus entitled in Gaudemet's *L'Église dans l'Empire romain*, pp. 322–68, for this and the following paragraphs. Note also the interesting study by Rousselle, 'Aspects sociaux', which shows why nobles were likely to be recruited as priests and bishops in the fourth century.

anyone became a cleric, he immediately changed his life-style. 'Hitherto he was content with a small, mean hut, but now he raises lofty panelled ceilings, he builds many rooms, he sculpts entrances . . .'[3] However, Sulpicius was probably exaggerating to make his point, and he was certainly taking up an extreme position when he argued that fourth-century bishops should model themselves on the biblical Levites who possessed no property of their own.[4]

The fact that bishops could now behave and dress as members of the aristocracy inevitably had its effects in a society where the classes were as clearly stratified as in the late empire, and more especially in a society where social prestige and connections were responsible for obtaining favours, if not manipulating justice. The Latin fathers at the council of Serdica had no sooner forbidden bishops to journey to court in pursuit of petitions than they subjoined a proviso that, 'if indeed a bishop has friends in the palace', a deacon acting for the bishop was fully entitled to enlist their support provided that it was for a good cause. In this recognized right of *intercessio* the spiritual and material authority of the bishop were fused, and it was this combination which was responsible for much of the bishop's power.

A further example of the bishop's authority within society is that of his role as judge. The bishop had been recognized as an arbiter from New Testament times, and Constantine gave substance to this claim by authorizing episcopal courts as an alternative to state courts. Cases could be brought or transferred there by one litigating party even without the other party's consent, and there was no right of appeal from the bishop's judgement. These tribunals therefore provided a much speedier resolution than the secular courts, and as their services cost nothing they were normally in heavy demand.

In such ways the bishops became entwined with the affairs of the empire, and this *rapprochement* even outlasted the advent of an Arian emperor in the west in 351.

However, perhaps the keynote of Christianity in fourth-century Gaul was not so much worldliness, as diversity. In

---

[3] *D* I, 21, 3-4. Ammianus XXVII, 3, 15.   [4] *Chron.* I, 23, 4-6.

many areas the church was still in its infancy, and as yet no comprehensive body of canon law was in existence to regulate such matters as the way of life to be followed by ascetics and clerics. *Ad hoc* conciliar decrees condemned specific abuses; but apart from the large ecumenical councils, whose decisions would be confirmed by the emperor, local decisions were operative only within the relevant locality, and were not binding upon bishops who had been absent. There was thus much scope for diversity: whether a practice was considered legitimate, or an abuse to be stamped out, rested largely with the individual bishop.

Asceticism was one sphere where variety was particularly in evidence. There was an immense diversity in the lengths to which it was carried and in the sort of practices followed, as also in the way in which these were regarded by other Christians. The origins of bodily abstinence and the preservation of chastity could be sought in biblical accounts of holy men or the teachings of St. Paul, and we have evidence from the early church that some members of the Christian community renounced marriage and lived in chastity for the love of Christ.[5] Such practices occurred in Rome, Spain, and Africa as well as in the east, and may well have been followed by the Christian communities within Gaul.[6] Those who chose to live in this manner did not cut themselves off from involvement in their local Christian community, but remained in their native city or village, often in their own houses, living a life of continence according to the Gospel precepts.[7] They occupied themselves with manual work and gave away part of their earnings, retaining for their own use enought to live on; they also read the Bible, prayed, and visited each other frequently. However, there was no idea

[5] H. Lietzmann, *A History of the Early Church*, IV (ET, pb. edn. London 1961) pp. 124–33; J. Daniélou and H. Marrou, *The Christian Centuries* I: *The First Six Hundred Years* (ET London 1964) pp. 121–4.

[6] G. D. Gordini, 'Origine e sviluppo del monachesimo a Roma', *Gregorianum* 37 (1956), pp. 221–2. J. Perez de Urbel, 'Le monachisme en Espagne'; Folliet, 'Aux origines'; and R. Metz, 'Les vierges chrétiennes en Gaule au IVe siècle'; all in *Saint Martin et son temps*, pp. 25–44, 45–8, 110–11. Fontaine, 'L'Ascétisme chrétien', pp. 90–8, esp. on Ausonius' aunts (pp. 91–2).

[7] See H. Leclercq, 'Sarabaïtes', in *DACL* XV, 1, cols. 757–8, for this and what follows.

of hierarchy, subordination, and obedience among them, nor of renouncing all wealth: those who inherited land were encouraged to farm it honestly and give their profits to the church and to those in need. Those who lived in this manner in Egypt were apparently called 'remnuoth' (or 'remoboth') or 'sarabaïtes'.

St. Antony also began his life of asceticism like this, but he struck out on a new path altogether when he decided to leave the vicinity of his native village and venture out alone into the desert.[8] Eventually, disciples gathered around him there, and a new form of asceticism sprang up characterized by disciples living in their own cells near a holy man from whom they sought spiritual guidance, and coming together for communal worship. At about the same time Pachomius founded the first cenobitic monastery within Egypt (323). Although the amount of subordination involved varied greatly, these new forms of asceticism had in common a complete renunciation of the world, and their adherents tended to pour scorn upon the practices of the original ascetics, the 'sarabaïtes', who in time became displaced from popular regard.[9]

This diversity amongst ascetics is perhaps even more in evidence in the west. The *Consultationes Zacchaei christiani et Apollonii philosophi*, probably written *c*.360,[10] devotes a whole chapter to monks, and explains that their unpopularity is due to the inclusion within their ranks of many who are wrongly motivated.[11] The author himself distinguishes one group of men who merely simulate abstinence and continence in order to deceive women, 'while either they gaze longingly after gifts, and go in search of the vile rewards of their greed, or they get the mastery of women whom they

---

[8] ibid., and cf. *V. Antonii* (Latin tr. by Evagrius) ch. 10: 'rei novitatem' and 'eremi adhuc monachis ignotae' (*PL* 73, col. 133A).

[9] Leclercq, 'Sarabaïtes', col. 759.

[10] Ed. G. Morin, Florilegium Patristicum fasc. 39 (Bonn 1935). On its dating see G. Morin, *Historisches Jahrbuch* 37 (1916), p. 231; F. Cavallera, *Revue d'ascétique et de mystique* 16 (1935), pp. 132-3, and esp. p. 139, n. 31. P. Courcelle's counter-arguments for *c*.412 (*Histoire littéraire des grandes invasions germaniques*, 3rd edn. Paris 1964, pp. 261-75) are effectively rebutted by G. M. Colombás, *Studia Monastica* 14 (1972), pp. 7-15.

[11] *Consultationes* III, 3 (pp. 100-2), q.v. for what follows.

have subjected by guile, and seduce them from their life vowed to chastity'. Another type starts off on the monastic life in all good faith, but lacks the necessary persistence or is turned against it through the criticisms of others. However, even amongst those with a genuine vocation who persist in their aims, there are great differences of degree. Some are content to remain celibate, or not to remarry, but take part in everyday life just as they had formerly done and do not seclude themselves from worldly delights or evils. Their dress is not dishonourable, they frequently eat in common, they do not disrupt their sleep with nocturnal vigils; although they live in fairly remote places, they pass their time in cities; they give to those in need, but not lavishly. One might sum up their way of life in the phrase 'fides calida est, non tamen fervens'. Other genuine monks are more fervent than these: they dress humbly, eat and drink sparingly, fasting up to the evening; they sing the psalms and praise God at regular and fixed hours, including nocturnal offices and vigils. They work throughout the day, and what any of them lacks is supplied communally. Their bed is formed of strewed rushes, and in sleep they are allowed scanty covering. The last and, in the eyes of the author, the highest grade of monks are the hermits who live alone in caves far from civilization, sustained only by bread and water, and clad in skins or sackcloth. These devote their whole lives to prayer, psalmody, and fighting against crowds of demons, 'and their keenness of mind is fired by the exercise of holy delight'. In this way they lead a heavenly way of life while yet dwelling on earth.

Against this background, our sources for Gallic monasticism in the later fourth century fall into place. As our starting-point let us take Jerome's epistle 22 to Eustochium, for although it relates primarily to Rome, Sulpicius thought it peculiarly applicable to the Gaul of his day.[12] In advising Eustochium upon how she should act to preserve her virginity, Jerome had much to say about the practices rife in Rome: how virgins would fall into sin and become pregnant, would eat and drink freely, walk openly in the streets, and ogle

---

[12] Sulpicius *D* I, 8, 4 ff., which contains verbal reminiscences of Jerome's *ep*. 22: above, ch. 6, n. 66.

young men; some, indeed, neglecting their own families, went so far as to live in the same house and sleep in the same bed as young men of a similar profession.[13] Jerome warned off Eustochium from associating with worldly ladies, even those who were virgins or widows if these were still living worldly lives. He had some scathing remarks about the way in which the clergy would visit such widows, kissing their heads and being paid money, while the women in their turn became puffed up with these signs of attention. If we are to believe Jerome, some even sought the diaconate and priesthood in order to gain admission to noble ladies more easily; such men devoted much attention to their dress and their fine steeds, and were the enemies of fasting and chastity. Amongst the other dangers and vices of which Jerome particularly warns Eustochium are vainglory, pious practices aimed at attracting man's approbation, not God's, the frequenting of public places, greed, and avarice.

Jerome also has some interesting remarks about monks, of which he distinguished three kinds: the cenobites, the anchorites, and the 'remnuoth', who appear to correspond to those whose 'fides calida est, non tamen fervens' of the *Consultationes*.[14] While praising the two former types, he is scathing about the latter:

These live together in twos and threes, but seldom in larger numbers, and are bound by no rule, but do exactly as they choose. A portion of their earnings they contribute to a common fund, out of which food is provided for all. In most cases they reside in cities and strongholds; and . . . all that they sell is extremely dear. They often quarrel because they are unwilling, while supplying their own food, to be subordinate to others. It is true that they compete with each other in fasting; they make what should be a private concern an occasion for a triumph. In everything they study effect: their sleeves are loose, their boots bulge, their garb is of the coarsest. They are always sighing, or visiting virgins, or sneering at the clergy; yet when a holiday comes, they make themselves sick—they eat so much.[15]

[13] *ep.* 22, 13-14 (*CSEL* 54, pp. 160-2). For what follows, see ibid. § 8-10, 13-17, 25-33.
[14] ibid. § 34-6 (pp. 196-201). The same conclusion is drawn by Colombás, pp. 13-14.
[15] *Ep.* 22, § 34 (p. 197). ET by W. H. Fremantle, *St. Jerome: Letters and Select Works* (Select Library of Nicene and Post-Nicene Fathers, 2nd series, vol. 6), reprinted Michigan 1954, p. 37.

As Sulpicius remarked, not only did Jerome attack the greed of monks, but

> he left out nothing altogether that he could not revile and tear in shreds and show up. He was especially hard on avarice, and vanity no less. He had much to say about pride, and not a little about superstition. I will truly confess, he seems to me to have painted the vices of many. Besides, how truly and how forcefully he dealt with the familiarity of virgins and monks and even of clergy. In consequence there are some, whom I will not name, who are said not to like him.[16]

Here, certainly, are some of Sulpicius' favourite themes: the avarice, ambition, and vanity of the Gallic bishops of his day; the worldly attitude of the clergy with their delight in dress, fine steeds, society, and the attentions of virgins and widows;[17] the dubiously close relationships that often existed between ascetics of the opposite sex;[18] the gluttony and touchiness of Gallic monks and clerics.[19] However, these criticisms must be set in their context to be understood. Sulpicius, like Jerome and Cassian, was critical of those who were content with a rather moderate or slight degree of abstinence; who remained celibate, but whose lives were not in other respects markedly different from those of other Christians. Yet it was the ascetics *praised* by Sulpicius who were the innovators, the oddity, while those whom he criticized were leading a way of life which had been highly regarded earlier in the church's history.

One particular example of how a traditional custom could cause a scandal in a different age is that of the 'spiritual marriage' between a monk and a virgin. This had at one time been recognized by the church, possibly even by St. Paul himself.[20] The inherent dangers of such a custom are obvious, and Jerome denounced it for its own sake;[21] but we must

---

[16] *D* I, 8, 6-9, 1.

[17] Above, ch. 12, notes 40-1.

[18] *D* I, 9, 1-2; II, 7, 1-8, 4; II 12, 7.

[19] *D* I, 4, 5-5, 1; I, 8, 5; I, 12, 1-2; III, 16, 1-2; cf. also the stress on examples of obedience in *D* I, 10, 1; I, 18 & 19.

[20] I Corinth. 7:36-8; cf. Lietzmann *History* IV, p. 129; Daniélou & Marrou, p. 123.

[21] *ep.* 117, esp. §2: 'me non idcirco scribere, quia aliquid de vobis sinistrum suspicer' (*CSEL* 55 p. 424); in *ep.* 22, 14 Jerome had had no such qualms about assuming the worst motives despite what people involved claimed. See also Lienhard, p. 119.

remember that Jerome, Sulpicius, and Cassian only give us *their* way of evaluating the merits and demerits of various types of the ascetic life at this period. As it happened, the future lay with such strict ascetics; but this was at least partially due to the vicissitudes of history whereby the (eventual) heroes of the Arian controversy were also the patrons of the new monasticism. Around 360 AD the picture must have looked very different, and a more balanced view of the whole question is that put forward by the author of the *Consultationes Zacchaei*, who, while giving the palm to the strict anchorites, allows a share in future glory also to the less fervent ascetics.

We must therefore realize that to demarcate between the 'goodies' and 'baddies' of the fourth-century church along traditional lines is to let our hindsight distort the original scene. Instead, we should realize the variety of ways in which men legitimately set about living the Christian life at this period; for in the fourth century papal decretals and canon law were in their infancy, and individual bishops were therefore adapting themselves to changing circumstances in their own ways.

At one end of the scale, it must be admitted that the lack of a comprehensive system of discipline provided opportunities for charlatans and immoral behaviour.[22] Jerome and Sulpicius' bitter denunciations of the clerics and ascetics of their own day do not stand alone. Within Gaul, the problem of lapsed virgins was dealt with by the synod of Valence in 374 and by two papal directives.[23] Further, one of the reasons for Vigilantius' attack on the practice of nocturnal vigils was the cloak it provided for immorality and adultery.[24] Another problem which cropped up at the synod of Nîmes was that of false pilgrims who battened on the church's hospitality; we might compare Augustine's strictures on hypocrites dressed as monks who wandered from place

---

[22] In general, see Lienhard, pp. 118-21.

[23] Conc. Valentinum, canon 2 (*CCSL* 148, p. 39). Innocent *ep.* 2 to Victricius of Rouen, *Etsi tibi*, §15-16 (*PL* 20, cols. 479-80); also the earlier communication of Damasus or Siricius, *Dominus inter caetera*, = Siricius *ep.* 10, §3-4 (*PL* 13 cols. 1182-4).

[24] cf. Jerome, *Contra Vigilantium* §9 (*PL* 23, cols. 347-8). See Brown, *Cult*, p. 43.

to place exacting money on false pretences of need or sanctity.[25]

Another devotional feature of the age which could be abused was the reverence felt towards the relics of martyrs. Cult of relics and support for monasticism often went hand in hand, which is perhaps not surprising in view of the fact that the monks were the successors of the martyrs. Victricius of Rouen, Ambrose, and Paulinus all helped to promote both the cult of saints and the practice of asceticism, and these were the twin targets now (*c*.403) being attacked by Vigilantius, who must have swung round against them some time after his pilgrimage to the Holy Land in 395. Vigilantius held that the dead existed in another sphere and had no power to intervene in terrestrial affairs: their bodies were now nothing but dust in a coffin, and they could neither visit places and people on earth, nor avail them by their prayers. He therefore opposed all those contemporary practices designed to honour the martyrs' relics and obtain their favour, and in particular he denounced the burning of tapers in broad daylight as a continuation of pagan practice.[26]

Vigilantius had the support of at least some Gallic bishops, and this is arguably the context for the pseudo-Hieronymian letter *De viro perfecto*. This letter has been plausibly attributed to the Gallic priest, Eutropius, who is known to us through Gennadius' *De viris inlustribus*.[27] What has not hitherto been remarked on is that sections xi-xvi of this letter are wholly taken up with rebutting the arguments of an unnamed man who had been questioning and attacking the miracles reputedly wrought through the relics of martyrs: 'For there are some who prefer to sting with slander, rather than receive with reverence, the outstanding heavenly works of power which operate through the relics of the saints, now, virtually in our own times'.[28] This slanderer sounds very like Vigilantius.

[25]Nîmes, can. 5 (*CCSL* 148, p. 50). Augustine, *De opere monachorum* xxviii, 36 (*CSEL* 41, pp. 585-6).

[26]Jerome, *Contra Vigilantium*, §4-6, and §8 (*PL* 23, cols. 342-4; 346-7). Note that the Synod of Elvira, in nearby Spain, had forbidden candles to be lit in cemeteries in daytime (can. 34).

[27]*Inc.* 'Ecce iterum ad te scribo . . .'; = *ep.* 6, *ad amicum aegrotum*, in *PL* 30, cols. 75-104. P. Courcelle, 'Un nouveau traité d'Eutrope, prêtre aquitain vers l'an 400', *REA* 56 (1954), pp. 377-90.

[28]ibid. §xi (*PL* 30, col. 92A).

Further, Eutropius also has some comments on those who attacked the ascetic way of life, which was the other target of
Vigilantius' onslaught.[29] In view of the fact that Courcelle
has on other grounds suggested that this letter was the work
of an Aquitanian priest writing c.400, I think it can reasonably be seen as directed at those who sympathized with
Vigilantius, perhaps specifically at the latter. In all events,
it testifies to the unease which the promotion of the cult
of the martyrs aroused in some people. That there was some
cause for alarm can be seen by a law of 386, forbidding
trafficking in relics; and, even more pertinently, by Augustine's
reference to false monks who 'membra martyrum, si tamen
martyrum, venditant'.[30]

The monks' role in fostering the cult of the martyrs is an
interesting case, as Jerome appears to support it whole-
heartedly, while not denying Vigilantius' point that in
practice it often involved superstition and abuse. This,
however, is only a minor instance of how the trappings of
the extreme asceticism propagated by Jerome and Sulpicius
might well arouse qualms even in sincere Christians;[31] for
the ascetic practices they praised were revolutionary for
orthodox Christians in the fourth century, and must have
smacked strongly of heretical sects. Not unnaturally asceticism
in practice went with a desire to preserve the church from
worldly contamination, hence a refusal to adapt to the
needs of the majority. It is therefore no surprise to find the
Luciferians Marcellinus and Faustinus praising an ascetic
priest in Rome called Macarius, and complaining that he had
been subjected to persecution under Pope Damasus.[32]

More serious was the danger of association with some form
of Gnosticism, which the ascetics' attitude to bodily needs
and sexual relationships was bound to raise. The Romans
may have been moved only by an understandable dislike of
killjoys when they dubbed those who refused to drink and
laugh as 'continentes . . . et tristes',[33] but their outburst of

---

[29] ibid. §ix (col. 90). Cf. *Contra Vigil.* §15 (PL 23, col. 351).
[30] *C.Th.* IX, 17, 7. Augustine, as above, n. 25.
[31] Cf. Lienhard, pp. 119-27.
[32] *De confessione verae fidei*, 78-82 (*CSEL* 35, pp. 28-9).
[33] Jerome *ep.* 38, 5 (*CSEL* 54, p. 293).

anger at the death of Blesilla, a convert to asceticism, was natural enough. She had but recently recovered from death's door, yet Jerome praised her vigils and psalmody through the night which scarcely allowed her to rest even when her neck was tired, her knees weak, and her eyes closing in sleep. Jerome made no allowances: 'He who is a Christian, let him rejoice; he who is angry shows by his anger that he is not a Christian.'[34] At her funeral, however, popular fury made itself felt. When Blesilla's mother fainted, the crowd was heard to murmur:

'Is not this what we have often said. She weeps for her daughter, killed with fasting. She wanted her to marry again, that she might have grandchildren. How long must we refrain from driving these detestable monks out of Rome? Why do we not stone them or hurl them into the Tiber? They have misled this unhappy lady . . .'[35]

Earlier, Jerome had written that the Romans dubbed any woman who looked sad and pale as 'miseram et monacham et Manicheam', regarding fasting as tantamount to heresy.[36] Nor was it just a question of fasting, for his own teaching on marriage was highly questionable: in his *Adversus Jovinianum* he had described the marital union as 'evil', and talked of the *sordes nuptiarum* as something which not even the blood of martyrdom could wash away.[37] It was small wonder, then, that many looked askance at his brand of monasticism, regarding it as a permutation of Manichaeism.

The Roman monasticism inspired by Jerome was by no means the only part of the ascetic movement to arouse such reactions. Between 382 and 392 Filaster, bishop of Brescia, included the following passage in his catalogue of heresies: 'There are others in Gaul, Spain, and Aquitaine, as it were "abstainers", who follow equally the most vile splinter of the Gnostics and the Manichees; they do not hesitate to preach the same things, breaking up marriages by their persuasive powers, and promising abstinence from food . . .'[38]

---

[34] *Ep.* 38, 2 & 4; *ep.* 39, 1 (pp. 290, 292, 294–5).
[35] Jerome, *ep.* 39, 6, 2 (p. 306). ET by Fremantle, p. 53.
[36] *Ep.* 22, 13, 3 (p. 161).
[37] R. F. Evans, *Pelagius: Inquiries and Reappraisals* (London 1968), p. 30.
[38] *Diversarum hereseon liber*, 56, esp. §1 (*CSEL* 38, pp. 45–6); cf. also 33, §5 (p. 32).

The context is that of the Priscillianist affair in Gaul, and of the suspicions and dissensions which it engendered—all of which is very pertinent to our understanding of the Gallic bishops' reaction to Martin himself.[39]

[39] Cf. Sulpicius, *D* III, 12, 2.

20

The Priscillianist Affair
and its Aftermath

The history of church and state in Gaul in the later fourth and early fifth century is peculiarly confused by the interplay of rival political and religious factions. At a political level Gaul was ruled by an emperor or usurper unrecognized by the official emperor for many years (viz. for most of Maximus' reign (383-8), for Eugenius' usurpation (392-4), and for those of Constantine (407-11), Jovinus (411-13), and, for the area around Toulouse, Attalus (414-16)). On the ecclesiastical front, Gallic bishops were concerned with Priscillianism from the synod of Saragossa in 380; the schism resulting from Priscillian's execution lasted from c.385-98, and the bitterness engendered appears to have persisted longer. Meanwhile the redivision of civil provinces, the transference of the pretorian prefecture from Trier to Arles, and finally Pope Zosimus' ill-conceived scheme for giving the ambitious bishop of Arles metropolitan powers over the dioceses within Narbonensis I and II and Viennensis, to the detriment of other bishops' rights, meant that the period was one in which bishops were quarrelling about the extent of their jurisdiction and infringements of their traditional episcopal rights. To confuse matters even more, political and ecclesiastical quarrels became so entangled that it is hard to decide, for instance, whether Priscillian was executed for religious or political reasons (i.e. as a heretic or as a magician); whether Ambrose refused to communicate with the bishops responsible for the execution because it would involve communicating with wrongdoers (i.e. bishops responsible for shedding blood), or because as an ambassador of Valentinian II he did not wish to appear favourable to the advisers of Valentinian's enemy. A further problem is that our knowledge is too incomplete for us to be certain of much that happened, yet we have enough scraps of information to tempt us into assuming that we know how they fit together. I would like to suggest a little shuffling round of these scraps to form a slightly different pattern from the standard one as regards the years following the synod of Turin in 398; but first we must look at some of the dissensions leading up to that attempt at conciliation.

(i) The Priscillianist Affair

The Priscillianist affair was the source from which many of the dissensions sprang.[1] Priscillian himself was a well-educated layman living in the neighbourhood of Cordoba who was attracted by ascetic practices and, apparently, by speculative ideas with Gnostic affinities.[2] This was in the 370s. His influence spread, attracting educated and uneducated people, particularly women, and he even won the support of two bishops, Instantius and Salvianus. However, Hyginus, bishop of Cordoba, was dubious about their practices and reported the whole matter to Hydatius, bishop of Mérida, who exacerbated the situation by harassing Priscillian's followers. Such dissensions finally led to the calling of a synod at Saragossa in 380 where various ascetic practices were anathematized by the assembled bishops, although neither Priscillian nor any of his supporters was formally condemned—at least, not in the official canons.[3]

The next stage began with Priscillian's party making an unsuccessful bid for support against Hydatius in Mérida. This proved a fiasco; but shortly afterwards Priscillian was

[1] In general, see Sulpicius *Chron.* II, 46 ff. and its appraisal by van Andel, pp. 97-115, and by Prete, pp. 76-98; E.-C. Babut, *Priscillien et le Priscillianisme* (Paris 1909); A. d'Alès, *Priscillien et l'Espagne chrétienne à la fin du IVᵉ siècle* (Paris 1936); Chadwick, *Priscillian.*

[2] Babut hotly denied that Priscillian's beliefs were heretical, but my own impression is that Priscillian's teaching does smack of heresy: e.g. on the divine nature of the soul. See Chadwick, *Priscillian* ch. 2, esp. pp. 71, 96-9; also pp. 181, 191-205, 211-15. Van Andel, pp. 109-10.

[3] Sulpicius asserts that they were (*Chron.* II, 47, 2), but Priscillian emphatically denied this, *Liber ad Damasum episcopum* (= *tractatus* II; *CSEL* 18 p. 35). See Chadwick, *Priscillian*, pp. 26-8.

successfully consecrated to the see of Avila by those bishops who supported him (381). The opposing bishops then sought help from the secular government. At first they were successful, but before long the Priscillianist leaders turned the tables. Driven out of Spain, they passed through Aquitaine, where Priscillian acquired quite a following in the area around Eauze (Elusa): a point of great interest when we recall that Primuliacum cannot have lain far away.[4] Priscillian and his supporters then continued to Italy. Although cold-shouldered by Ambrose and Pope Damasus, they gained the ear of Gratian's *magister officiorum*, and a rescript quashing of the government's earlier decrees against them. As a result they were reinstated in their bishoprics, while the ringleader of their opponents, Ithacius, bishop of Ossonuba, was arraigned as a disturber of the church. Ithacius fled to Trier, but his cause was in a parlous state when suddenly the overthrow of Gratian's government by Maximus (383) entirely altered the situation. Maximus sought to gain support by posing as strictly orthodox, in contrast to the legitimate emperors of Valentinian's stock who had Arian leanings.[5] He therefore summoned an episcopal synod to Bordeaux in 384/385.[6] The assembled bishops, who probably included Martin, adjudged the Priscillianists guilty of heresy and Instantius was deposed from his bishopric; but Priscillian tried to protect himself by appealing to the emperor.

This led straight to the fatal *dénouement*. The bishops Ithacius and Hydatius, Priscillian's accusers, went to the emperor at Trier and put their case to him. Martin, however, besought Ithacius to desist from his accusation, arguing that the heretics had already been sufficiently punished by the bishops' sentence expelling them from their churches, and that it would in any case be quite wrong for an ecclesiastical case to be judged by a secular official. Ithacius retorted by

---

[4] Sulpicius, *Chron.* II, 48, 2; above, ch. 4, n. 3; below, ch. 20, iii.

[5] See Maximus' letters to Valentinian II and Pope Siricius, *Collectio Avellana* no. 39 and no. 40 §3 (*CSEL* 35, pp. 88-91).

[6] Prosper, *Chronicon s.a.* 385; Hydatius *Chron. s.a.* 385, which suggests that Martin was amongst the bishops assembled at Bordeaux (ed. Mommsen, *Chronica Minora* I, p. 462, for Prosper; vol. II, p. 15, for Hydatius). Cf. Chadwick, *Priscillian*, p. 45, n. 1. For the date see Matthews, *Western Aristocracies*, p. 165, n. 3.

accusing 'all men, however holy, who were zealous for devotional study (*lectio*), or whose way of life involved striving through fasting, as associates or disciples of Priscillian'; and he even included Martin in this category.[7] However, Martin still had some influence with the emperor: while he was at Trier no action was taken against the Priscillianists, and before he left he obtained Maximus' promise that he would do nothing bloodthirsty against them. But once Martin was out of the way other bishops persuaded the emperor to put Priscillian on trial, and the case was entrusted to the prefect Evodius. Priscillian, on scant evidence, was found guilty of sorcery, a capital charge. Owing to a wide-spread feeling that a bishop should not act as prosecutor in a case that would lead to execution, the case was then retried before the emperor, with a secular official replacing Ithacius as Priscillian's accuser. The sentence was one of capital punishment for Priscillian and some of his adherents, while others were sent into exile.[8]

The severity of this sentence shocked people. Amongst those executed were Latronianus, 'an exceedingly learned man, and worthy to be compared to the ancients in the art of poetry', and Euchrotia, widow of Delphidius, a famous rhetorician of Bordeaux.[9] As portrayed by Pacatus, Theodosius' panegyrist, she was in fact innocent, being reproached only with 'excessive piety, and too assiduous a cult of the divinity', while the bishops responsible for the persecution are portrayed in a manner reminiscent of Sulpicius:

Yes, there was also this breed of informers, bishops in name, but in truth accomplices—indeed, executioners—who were not content to rob the wretches of their ancestral estates, but also falsely accused them up to the point of shedding blood, and oppressed the lives of the accused who were already paupers. Moreover, when they had been party to capital sentences, . . . they came away to the holy mysteries with hands polluted by contact with punishment, and they defiled rites with their presence, which they had dishonoured in their minds.[10]

[7] *Chron.* II, 50, 3. Cf. Jerome, *ep.* 22, 13, 3 (above, ch. 19, n. 36).

[8] *Chron.* II, 50, 6–51, 4. Chadwick, pp. 125–32, 138–45.

[9] Jerome, *De viris inlustribus* 122 (ed. Richardson, p. 53). Prosper, as n. 6 above.

[10] Pacatus, *Panegyricus* 29 (ed. E. Galletier, Paris 1955, Budé edn., pp. 95–6).

While Hydatius, who was less responsible for the turn of events, at some time resigned his bishopric of his own volition, Ithacius clung to his, and, protected by Maximus' authority, was acquitted of any blame by an episcopal synod; only one bishop, Theognitus, stood out against him.[11]

It was at this stage that Martin returned to Trier in order to intercede for some of Gratian's erstwhile supporters, and to try and obtain the recall of those tribunes who had been sent to Spain to ferret out Priscillianist suspects; meanwhile, he held himself aloof from the Ithacian bishops.[12] The latter were dismayed at his arrival and his separation from them, and besought Maximus to proceed against him by force and treat him as though he were a Priscillianist himself. The emperor would not go that far, but he argued with Martin that he should join in communion with the other bishops; and, on Martin's refusal, he appointed executioners for those supporters of Gratian for whom Martin had been interceding. Dismayed, Martin went straight back to the palace as soon as he heard this news, and promised to join in communion with the other bishops if the emperor would rescind the order for the executions and call off the tribunes who were already on their way to Spain. Maximus agreed to this, and the following day Martin joined the other bishops in consecrating Felix as the new bishop of Trier. That done, he departed, ill at ease with himself; and from then onwards he held aloof from all gatherings of bishops.[13]

The whole sorry affair left behind it a fouled atmosphere. Within eighty years of the last persecution by a pagan emperor, a Christian emperor was seen putting to death Christian bishops, priests, deacons, and devout lay people whose only 'fault' in some people's eyes was their zeal for religion, while their accusers were bishops who appeared to be more concerned with vengeance, worldly gain, and self-justification.[14] It had shown that he who had the ear of the

[11] Sulpicius *Chron.* II, 51, 6. *D* III, 12, 1 & 3; III, 11, 2.

[12] *D* III, 11, 3 & 7-9.   [13] *D* III, chs. 12 and 13.

[14] Pacatus, loc. cit. Sulpicius, *Chron.* II, 50, 1-4, and cf. *D* III, 12, 1-2. Note also that Jerome did not dub Priscillian as a heretic in his *De viris inlustribus*; rather, he implied that his sympathies were on his side (ch. 121): cf. the similar language used for Hilary's Arian opponents (ch. 100) with that applied to Hydatius and Ithacius (ed. Richardson, pp. 53 and 47).

secular government could get his way, and that this could be obtained through bribery or flattery;[15] and it had done much to poison relationships between ascetics and easy-going bishops since the former might now be regarded as suspect simply because of their asceticism, while the latter could be regarded as tarred with the brush of greed, self-seeking, and cruelty which Ithacius had displayed. It did not quell the Priscillianist heresy, which flared up again with renewed life;[16] instead it became the cause of over a decade of episcopal strife within Gaul.

(ii) Continuing Dissensions

When Ambrose visited Maximus shortly after Priscillian's death (385/6) on an embassy from Valentinian II, he excommunicated Maximus and refused to communicate with the Ithacian bishops responsible for the executions.[17] He was forcibly expelled. However, in the late summer of 387 Maximus invaded Italy, and this spurred the eastern emperor Theodosius to take action against him. In 388 Maximus was defeated and killed. He was now dubbed a usurper, and his acts were denounced.[18] This laid the way open for those who deplored Maximus' harsh treatment of Priscillian to voice their resentment. It is no fluke that Pacatus' hostile portrayal of Priscillian's episcopal adversaries, quoted above, occurs in his panegyric on Theodosius which he presented to the latter in 389.

Our sources for Gaul over the next two decades are incomplete, but they do enable us to gain some idea of how things shaped there. In the spring of 390 a synod of Gallic bishops met in Milan, and it could have been here that Ithacius was deposed from the episcopate.[19] However, there

---

[15] *Chron.* II, 48, 5–49, 4; *D* III, 11, 2.

[16] *Chron.* II, 51, 7–8. Chadwick, *Priscillian*, pp. 148 ff.

[17] J.-R. Palanque, *Saint Ambroise et l'Empire romain* (Paris 1933), pp. 174–5; on the date cf. above ch. 9, n. 29.

[18] *C. Th.* XV, 14, 6–8. Matthews, *Western Aristocracies*, pp. 222–9.

[19] Ambrose *ep.* 51, 6 (*PL* 16, col. 1161); news of the Thessalonica massacre of spring, 390, came while this synod was meeting. On Ithacius' deposition, Sulpicius *Chron.* II, 51, 5; cf. Chadwick, *Priscillian*, p. 148, who thinks a Spanish synod a more likely venue for the latter.

were apparently many such episcopal synods, for our next piece of information relates to Ambrose's third journey to Gaul in 392, made for the purpose of baptizing Valentinian II, and *not* to attend another synod of Gallic bishops, 'on account of whose frequent dissensions I have often excused myself'.[20] This note is sounded again in the synodal record of the council of Nîmes where the bishops gathered in 394 or (more probably) 396 'ad tollenda ecclesiarum scandala discessionemque sedandam'. Its second canon inveighing against the admission of women to the sacred ministry may well be aimed against Priscillianist practices,[21] and the subscription of a bishop Felix coupled with Martin's abstention suggests that this was a synod held by the Felician party. Finally, another synod was held after the deaths of Ambrose and Martin; this time it was at the instigation of the Antifelician bishops, and met in Turin in September 398.[22] Here, since the Felicians had sent legates to the synod, it was decreed that any who chose to cut themselves off from communion with Felix should be received into communion with the other bishops.[23] A *Vita Felicis*, dating from the late ninth century or later, records that its hero resigned from his episcopate after twelve years, and died shortly afterwards. Despite its late date this piece of information fits perfectly with contemporary evidence, including Sulpicius' high regard for Felix's personal qualities, and should probably be accepted as true.[24] With this, the dissensions which had divided the bishops of Gaul for the last twelve years should surely have died down.

[20] Ambrose, *De obitu Valentiniani consolatio* § 25 (*PL* 16, col. 1367). NB that another ascetic, Aper, stayed in the country, 'iam pene forensibus turbis aemulos ecclesiarum tumultus et concilia inquieta declinans.' (Paulinus *ep*. 38, 10; *CSEL* 29, p. 333).

[21] *Concilia Galliae* (*CCSL* 148), p. 50; for its date, see above ch. 9, n. 6. Cf. Council of Saragossa, can. 1 (*Sacrorum Conciliorum... collectio*, ed. Mansi vol. III (Florence 1759), cols. 633–4). Cf. Chadwick, *Priscillian*, pp. 158–9.

[22] See the synodal preamble and can. 6 (*CCSL* 148, pp. 54, 57–8). For the dating, Palanque, 'Les Dissensions' (cit. above ch. 9, n. 8), pp. 482–4; Chadwick, *Priscillian*, pp. 160–5. As I have dated Martin's death to November 397, not January, the synod of Turin must be dated to Sept. 398.

[23] can. 6 (*CCSL* 148, pp. 57–8). On Felicians/Antifelicians, below p. 317, n. 6.

[24] Palanque, 'Les Dissensions', pp. 483–4; cf. Chadwick, *Priscillian*, pp. 161–2. Sulpicius, *D* III, 13, 2.

However, such evidence as we have suggests that much the same problems beset the Gallic episcopate early in the fifth century as during the last decades of the fourth. In 405 Exsuperius, bishop of Toulouse, sought the Pope's advice about which books were canonical and which should be rejected as apocryphal,[25] which is a sure indication that Priscillianist troubles were not yet over in his diocese; and as late as 417 Pope Zosimus, doubtless acting on the smears of Patroclus of Arles, again raised the Priscillianist bogy apropos of a bishop ordained by Proculus of Marseilles.[26] Patroclus had his own reasons for trying to discredit Proculus' deeds in the eyes of the Pope, and it is most unlikely that the charge was true; but the point is that the designation 'Priscillianist' was still being used as a weapon against (devout) Christians. Nor is this altogether surprising when we recall the tenacity of Priscillianism in Galicia (where it lasted well into the sixth century), and the cultural contacts between northern Spain and south-west Gaul.[27]

Gallic hostility towards asceticism also appears in Vigilantius' attack, particularly in the fact that he had the support of his own bishop, and of others also;[28] it is interesting that Desiderius and Riparius had resort to Jerome in Palestine for a refutation of Vigilantius' teachings. To add to this dossier we have the evidence of Eutropius' epistle *De viro perfecto*, which tells us that men were accustomed to tear in shreds those of God's servants who dressed soberly, ate sparingly, and kept vigils continently.[29] Further, a letter of Paulinus of Nola's tells much the same story. Paulinus is congratulating a friend, Aper, on his conversion to asceticism, and a large proportion of the letter is devoted to the enemies and detractors which this decision of Aper's has made:

[25] The reply of Innocent I is preserved, *Consulenti tibi*, = Innocent *ep*. 6 (*PL* 20, cols. 495-502); see *cap*. vii, 13 (cols. 501-2) for apocrypha. Cf. Chadwick, *Priscillian*, pp. 187-8.

[26] 'Atque utinam in Tuentio pravi tantum mores, non etiam Priscilliana superstitio patuisset!' Zosimus *ep*. 4 (*Cum adversus*), §3 (*PL* 20, col. 664A).

[27] Chadwick, Priscillian, esp. pp. 150-7, 166-9, 174-6, 184-8, 208-17, 222-31. Fontaine, 'Société et culture', *BLE* 1974, esp. pp. 247-56.

[28] Jerome *ep*. 109, 2, 1 (*CSEL* 55, p. 353); *Contra Vigilantium* §2 (*PL* 23, cols. 340-1).

[29] ps. Jerome *ep*. 6, 9 (*PL* 30, col. 90 B). Cf. above, ch. 19, n. 27.

'Justly . . . do you say on this account that you believe you are a Christian, because those who used to love you have begun to hate you, and those who feared you, to despise you'; and it was precisely the ascetic traits of humility and chastity which aroused this hatred.[30]

Perhaps, then, it is not very surprising that clerical celibacy was often not maintained, and that the issue appears to have been a controversial one. It crops up regularly in documents of this period: in the canons from the synods of Valence (374) and Turin (398),[31] and in the papal letters *ad Gallos episcopos*,[32] to Victricius (404), and to Exsuperius (405).[33] The official papal line was that bishops, priests, and deacons must not have married twice, or married a widow; and that while they might live with their wives, they must cease begetting children. 'Be ye holy, for I, the Lord your God, am holy', was reiterated from Leviticus; for the priest must always be ready to celebrate the sacraments, and for that, purity was an essential prerequisite.[34] Hence also the decrees forbidding the ordination of anyone 'qui fidelis militat saeculo',[35] i.e. who had continued in government service after baptism.

However, decrees are one thing, and what actually happened, another. True, there is some evidence from Gaul which tallies with the papal line: the synod of Turin considered the case of those who 'beget children when in the ministry', and decreed that they should not be admitted to the higher grades of ecclesiastical office.[36] This, however, was the decision of the stricter Antifelician bishops, whereas the evidence of the *Contra Vigilantium* suggests that many Gallic bishops had no qualms about ordaining clerics who

[30] *Ep.* 38, 2-7 (*CSEL* 29, pp. 325-31), esp. § 3. The letter cannot be precisely dated.

[31] Valence can. 1; Turin can. 8 (*CCSL* 148, pp. 38-9, 58).

[32] *Dominus inter caetera* § ii, 5, from the pontificate of Damasus or Siricius (i.e. 366/99); given as Siricius *ep.* 10 in *PL* 13, cols. 1181-94, at cols. 1184-5.

[33] *Etsi tibi* and *Consulenti tibi*; see below, n. 34 and above, n. 25.

[34] e.g. Innocent to Victricius of Rouen, *Etsi tibi*, = *ep.* 2, iv-vi and ix (*PL* 20, cols. 473-6; but reading 'viduam' for 'mulierem' in canons iv and v, cols. 473-4, as in notes b and d); see also Griffe, *La Gaule chrét.* III, pp. 67-9.

[35] *Dominus inter caetera* § ii, 7 (*PL* 13, col. 1186), reiterated in *Etsi tibi* § ii, 4, to Victricius (*PL* 20 col. 472). Cf. above, p. 259.

[36] Can. 8 (*CCSL* 148, p. 58).

continued to have conjugal relations with their wives. Jerome refers to the bishops supporting Vigilantius as men 'who do not ordain deacons, unless they are already married: not trusting the chastity of any bachelor, and indeed showing how holy their own lives are by suspecting evil of all; and unless they see clerics' wives pregnant, and babies crying in their mothers' arms, they do not bestow [on them] the sacraments of Christ.'[37] Nor, it would appear, was Jerome's gibe that the Gallic clergy could not believe in the chastity of an unmarried priest wholly groundless: Brice, bishop of Tours, was accused of a sinful way of life at the synod of Turin, and later expelled from his see because of suspected adultery, while another bishop, Remigius, was also apparently deposed on a charge of adultery c. 408.[38]

Thus the dispute between a rigorist, ascetic minority and a laxer majority continued into the fifth century in Gaul, and to some extent it appears to have overlapped with another great cause of dissension amongst the episcopate: that of conflicting jurisdictional claims. Synodal decrees and papal directives are full of prohibitions against bishops ordaining clerics without due authority and receiving into communion those who had been excommunicated by their own bishops. On the first point, the general ruling was that the metropolitan of the province had the ultimate responsibility for ordinations within his province.[39] However, the bishops of Arles and Vienne disputed the title of metropolitan between themselves, while Proculus, bishop of Marseilles, claimed quasi-metropolitan rights over the province of Narbonensis II, although theoretically his see lay within the province of Vienne and was not a metropolitan seat at all.[40] The council of Turin allowed Proculus to exercise the rights he claimed

---

[37] *Contra Vigilantium* 2 (*PL* 23, col. 341A). Cf. also Jerome, *ep.* 69, 2, 2 (*CSEL* 54, p. 680).

[38] Zosimus, *ep. Posteaquam a nobis*, §5 (*CSEL* 35, p. 104); *ep. Cum adversus*, 2 (*PL* 20, cols. 662-3). Gregory of Tours, *Hist.* II, 1 (*MGH, SRM* I, i pp. 37-8). E. Ewig suggests a possible link with the Bacaudae troubles: *Archiv für mittelrheinische Kirchengeschichte* 14 (1962), p. 11. On Remigius, see below, n. 48.

[39] Innocent, *Etsi tibi* i, 3 (*PL* 20 cols. 471-2); Turin can. 2 (*CCSL* 148, pp. 55-6). Cf. in general *Dominus inter caetera* vi, 18 (*PL* 13, cols. 1193-4).

[40] Turin, canons 1 & 2 (*CCSL* 148, pp. 54-6); Palanque, 'Les Dissensions', pp. 485-90.

during his lifetime in recognition of his personal standing, and admonished four bishops, probably from Narbonensis II, for undertaking ordinations without due authority.[41] As for that other *bête noire*, bishops showing no respect for the judgements of their fellow bishops, we have denunciations and prohibitions of the practice of a bishop receiving into communion, ordaining, or promoting either laymen or clerics who had been excommunicated by their own bishops.[42]

Is there anything more to these episcopal dissensions within the church than squabbling and uncertainty about practices where as yet no tradition had become established? Given the exiguous amount of evidence, it would be dangerous to read too much into it. However, it is very odd for bishops to have ordained and promoted men whom they knew had already been excommunicated elsewhere; this suggests that bishops did not see eye to eye with each other. Proculus' consecration of Lazarus, whose attacks on Brice he had rebuffed earlier, at the synod of Turin, is perhaps relevant here.[43] Another point to be made is that there certainly appears to have been a pro-Proculus and an anti-Proculus party in southern Gaul, and it looks as though it overlapped with a grouping of those pro-asceticism and those anti-asceticism.[44] On the one hand there was Proculus, recommended by Jerome as a guide to the youthful monk Rusticus, and consecrator of one bishop who was suspected of Priscillianism,[45] and another who was rigorist enough to accuse Brice of various crimes, and was later found in association with one of Martin's disciples, Heros of

[41] Turin can. 3 names the bishops as Octavius, Ursio, Remigius, and Triferius. Remigius' see was certainly within Proculus' jurisdiction, so it is likely that all four came from Narb. II.

[42] *Dominus inter caetera* vi (*PL* 13, cols. 1193–4); Nîmes 3, and cf. 4; Turin 7 (*CCSL* 148 pp. 50 and 58).

[43] Though note that Lazarus had been censured, not excommunicated, at Turin: Chadwick, *Priscillian*, p. 162. Difference of opinion over suspect Priscillianist ascetics might have been another cause: cf. Sulpicius *Chron.* II, 47, 3, and Chadwick, *Priscillian*, pp. 175–6.

[44] I am here in general agreement with E.-C. Babut, *Le Concile de Turin* (Paris 1904), although I do not accept his date for the council of Turin, nor his manipulation of the text of canon vi (ibid. p. 230). Fundamental is Duchesne, *Fastes épiscopaux* I, esp. pp. 95–112. On Proculus, cf. Rousseau, *Ascetics*, p. 175.

[45] Proculus recommended: Jerome *ep.* 125, 20, 2 (*CSEL* 56, p. 141). Bishop Tuentius suspected of Priscillianism: above, n. 26.

Arles.[46] On the other hand there was Patroclus, who supplanted Heros as bishop of Arles and left a bad reputation as a purveyor of ecclesiastical offices and political influence;[47] Remigius, suspected of adultery, perhaps deposed by Proculus to make way for Lazarus, but certainly back in the graces of Patroclus and Zosimus by 417;[48] while he and three other bishops had joined in usurping Proculus' rights of consecration before the synod of Turin, and previously participated in the Felician synod of Nîmes.[49]

Thus there was certainly open dissension between these two rival groups in the second decade of the fifth century,[50] and the persons of Proculus, Lazarus, and Remigius provide a link with the last decade of the fourth century. This, coupled with our knowledge that in the first decade of the fifth century bishops were still afraid of Priscillianism, and that many of them were opposed to ascetics and willing to ordain clergy who maintained marital relations with their wives, all points to the conclusion that the differences which had divided the Gallic church in the last decades of the fourth century persisted into the fifth.

(iii) Sulpicius' Hostile Environment

This provides us with the background against which the concluding sentences of Sulpicius' *Chronicle* make sense:

[46] Heros and Lazarus are jointly defamed by Zosimus (*Posteaquam a nobis*, CSEL 35, pp. 103 ff.); they turned up together as Pelagius' accusers at the synod of Diospolis in 415. Prosper of Aquitaine describes Heros as 'vir sanctus et beati Martini discipulus', (*Chron. s.a.* 412; ed. Mommsen, *MGH, AA* IX p. 466). On Lazarus, himself probably a product of Marmoutier (NB his attacks on Brice), see further Griffe, *La Gaule chrét.* II, pp. 252-6.

[47] Prosper, loc. cit.; *Chronica Gallica a.452*, ed. Mommsen (*MGH, AA* IX), p. 654.

[48] *Chron. Gallica a.452*: 'Proculus Massiliensis episcopus clarus habetur: quo annuente magna de suspecto adulterio Remedi episcopi quaestio agitatur.' (Edn. cit. p. 652); Babut (*Le Concile*, pp. 235-42) suggests Aix as Remigius' see, and I find his hypothesis plausible despite Duchesne's objections (*Fastes épiscopaux* I, p. 101, n. 2; 'Le Concile de Turin', *Revue Historique* 87 (1905), pp. 296-7). Cf. Griffe, *La Gaule chrét.* II (1957 edn.), pp. 201-5.

[49] Above, n. 41; and for their presence at Nîmes, *CCSL* 148, p. 51.

[50] Prosper, apropos of Patroclus' ousting of Heros: 'eaque res inter episcopos regionis illius magnarum discordiarum materia fuit.' *Chron.*, loc. cit.

But amongst our own people incessant feuding and strife had been kindled, which, after being already tossed to and fro for fifteen years by shameful quarrels, could not in any way be laid to rest. And now, when all was seen to be stirred up and confused, especially by the dissensions of bishops, and everything had been corrupted through them by hatred, bribery, fear, fickleness, envy, factiousness, lust, avarice, conceit, sloth, and idleness, finally the many were striving with mad counsels and obstinate attachments against the few giving good advice; and amidst all this the people of God and all the best men were treated to abuse and mockery.[51]

As Sulpicius' *Chronicle* was written from the standpoint of AD 400, the 'fifteen years' of discord takes us back to 385, the probable date of Priscillian's execution. The puzzle, of course, is that Sulpicius' *Chronicle* was written *after* the synod of Turin of 398, which had supposedly healed the Gallic schism; but that Sulpicius says not a word of the synod, and implies that the church is still as riddled with discord as ever.

We will return to this question shortly; but first, let us look at another Sulpician passage which reveals more of the context of these remarks. At the beginning of the *Dialogues*, which are roughly contemporaneous with the *Chronicle*, Sulpicius asks Postumianus to tell the tale of his pilgrimage, 'how the faith of Christ flourishes in the east, what may be the tranquillity of the saints, the mode of life of the monks', and about their miracles. 'For indeed, because in this area and amid these circumstances in which we live, life itself is burdensome, gladly would we hear from you whether Christians are allowed to carry on with their lives, even in the desert.' Postumianus then asks if all the Gallic bishops were still as they had been when he set out, but Sulpicius begs him to leave this gloomy subject: not only have they become no better, but even the one bishop who had formerly been favourable to them, and stood by them against the persecutions of the other bishops; now even this bishop had become 'harsher than he ought towards us'; and Sulpicius sadly reflects that 'we are almost deprived of the friendship of the wise and religious man.'[52]

Babut originally interpreted this passage to mean that the

---

[51] *Chron.* II, 51, 8–10.   [52] *D* I, 2, 2–5.

last bishop who had been favourable to the Antifelician party of Sulpicius had now turned against them. Palanque offers a similar interpretation: Sulpicius belonged to a rigorist minority which refused to accept the reconciliation with the Felicians provided for by the synod of Turin; his silence about the latter proves nothing, coming as it does from an 'écrivain passionné, demeuré seul peut-être dans son intraitable opposition.'[53]

Now, it is, of course, true that schisms in the west had often resulted from a purist minority of the orthodox refusing to receive back sinners into their own church: the Novatians and Luciferians are examples of this; and, more pertinently, some of the Spanish bishops had refused to accept back repentant Priscillianists on the terms laid down at Toledo.[54] However, it is hard to see what Sulpicius could have objected to: of the two bishops who had prosecuted Priscillian and were therefore in some sense guilty of his blood, one had resigned his bishopric, and the other had been deposed; further, the bishop they had consecrated, Felix, seems to have resigned his bishopric of his own accord. In addition to this, Sulpicius stood in the religious tradition of Martin and Hilary, and it is noteworthy that Martin himself had on occasion communicated with the Felicians, albeit reluctantly, while Hilary had been willing to effect a *rapprochement* with bishops of Arianizing tendencies against the common threat of Eunomianism—much to the disgust of the Luciferians.[55] Sulpicius appears to have continued this tradition. He is fully aware of the need for not losing one's temper and for being forgiving, and a specific instance of this is cited in the *Dialogues*: his reaction of sorrow rather than anger at his freedman's flight from him. One might add, also, his forbearance towards Vigilantius.[56]

In any case, if we look closely at Sulpicius' remarks, we find that it is not a case of Sulpicius himself being high and

---

[53] *St. Martin* p. 157. Palanque, 'Les Dissensions', p. 493.

[54] Chadwick, *Priscillian*, p. 186.

[55] Cf. Marcellinus and Faustinus, *De confessione verae fidei* 24 (*CSEL* 35, p. 12). Also refs. given above, ch. 14, n. 63.

[56] *D* I, 12, 2-4; cf. *D* III, 18, esp. § 2, 'dices tamen illi, sed non aspere, non acerbe, conpatientis alloquio . . .' Babut, 'Sur trois lignes', p. 213.

mighty and cutting himself off from any contact with the bishops; rather, it is the bishops who have been persecuting him; and, from his questions about how asceticism is flourishing in the east, and his hopes that it is at least possible for Christians to live in the wilderness, in contrast with the difficulty of doing so in Gaul, we see that the cause of these persecutions was Sulpicius' practice of the ascetic life. This, indeed, is precisely what is implied by the closing remarks of his *Chronicle* about how the 'plebs Dei et optimus unus quisque probro atque ludibrio habebatur'; and it finds added confirmation in his remarks about the virgin who declined to receive a visit from Martin: 'What bishop, other than Martin, would not have taken this as an affront to himself? How impassioned and angry he would have become towards the holy virgin! He would have judged her a heretic, and ordered her to be anathematized.'[57] The heresy they would have accused her of would have been Priscillianism, for elsewhere Sulpicius writes that Ithacius had regarded all holy men devoted to biblical study and fasting, including Martin, as virtual Priscillianists, while the tribunes hunting out Priscillianists in Spain had been going to rely simply on the outward indications of fasting and dress, which were common to all ascetics.[58]

The implication, then, is that the bishops in Sulpicius' part of Gaul mistrusted and harassed him because of his asceticism. If it is asked why this should be, even after the synods of Turin and Toledo, then the answer surely lies in the evidence discussed above in section ii: viz. in the continuing fear of Priscillianism and mistrust of asceticism, which, as we have seen, lasted well into the fifth century in southern Gaul. The reason why Sulpicius does not mention the synod of Turin might then be, because it had not definitively healed the dissensions arising from Priscillian's execution. Even if all the bishops were now back in communion with each other, problems may still have persisted.

There is some evidence to support this view. Victricius of Rouen, a friend of Martin's and another keen episcopal

---

[57] *D* II, 12, 9.
[58] *Chron.* II, 50, 3-4. *D* III, 11, 4-5; 12, 2.

supporter of monasticism, found himself accused of some sort of heresy, apparently of a doctrinal nature, and had to journey to Rome where he presumably cleared himself with Pope Innocent.[59] Both he and Exsuperius of Toulouse, two bishops of a non-worldly type, made a point of consulting the Pope about matters of church discipline, as though they needed outside support to get the correct course accepted by all.[60] Victricius is particularly charged with getting his fellow bishops to accept the rules which Innocent lays down (§ 1), and Innocent ends the letter by saying that if all the bishops fully observe them,

ambition will cease, dissension will die down, heresy and schism will not arise, the devil will not obtain an entry for raging, unanimity will remain, iniquity, having been overcome, will be trampled underfoot, truth will blaze out with spiritual ardour, and the peace already professed with the lips will be united with the will of the mind.[61]

This is a most interesting passage. It obviously shows that there was no open schism in the Gallic church at the time (*c.*404);[62] but also, it implies that dissensions were still simmering beneath the surface. Peace is professed in word, but as yet this is not matched by any real unanimity of will, nor an end to all the discord.

This means that we should not dismiss the pessimistic end of Sulpicius' *Chronicle* out of hand as evidence of nothing more than Sulpicius' bitter intolerance. Where, surely, Sulpicius misleads us in implying that *all* Gallic bishops at the time of writing were worldly men, hostile to ascetics. We know that this is not true: we have but to think of Victricius of Rouen, Proculus of Marseilles, and Exsuperius of Toulouse to give this the lie. Indeed, a fragmentary letter of Paulinus of Nola's, preserved for us by Gregory of Tours, names eight good Gallic bishops of the early fifth century: Exsuperius of Toulouse, Simplicius of Vienne, Amandus of

---

[59] Paulinus of Nola, *ep.* 29, esp. § 4–7 (*CSEL* 29, pp. 319–23).

[60] See *Etsi tibi* § 1 and *Consulenti tibi* § 1 (*PL* 20, cols. 469–70, 495–6). On Exsuperius' merits see Jerome, *ep.* 123, 15, *ep.* 125, 20 (*CSEL* 56, pp. 92, 141–2), and the Paulinus passaged noted in my next paragraph.

[61] *Etsi tibi* §17 (col. 481).

[62] It is taken in this sense by Babut (*St. Martin* pp. 156–7, 161) and Palanque ('Les Dissensions', p. 491). NB it is virtually contemporaneous with Sulpicius' *Chronicle*.

Bordeaux, Diogenianus of Albi, Dinamius of Angoulême, Venerandus of Clermont, Alithius of Cahors, and Pegasius of Périgueux.[63] But this does not necessarily mean that Sulpicius is insincere in implying that his asceticism has got him into trouble with the bishops; nor that Sulpicius was more extreme and intransigent than Paulinus and the bishops that Paulinus praises. Rather, it may be a matter of geography: of how the bishops in the neighbourhood of Primuliacum regarded the ascetic life.

Unfortunately, the exact location of Primuliacum is unknown.[64] However, we can say in general terms that it lay within striking distance of Toulouse and Narbonne, and was not far off the road from Narbonne to Bordeaux. As we know that Sulpicius' bishop was called Gavidius, we can also state with some assurance that Primuliacum cannot have lain within the dioceses of those cities which we know did not have a bishop Gavidius at this time: Bordeaux and Toulouse for sure, and probably also the other cities listed above in the fragmentary letter of Paulinus'. We can also rule out Narbonne itself. As a glance at map 2 will show, this leaves the diocese of Agen, or some diocese within Novempopulana, as by far the most likely locality. Within this area, it is not very surprising to find a mistrust of asceticism still persisting. In about 381 Priscillian and his episcopal companions had crossed from Spain into Aquitaine, 'where they were splendidly received by ignorant men, and sowed the seeds of faithlessness. And most of all they perverted the people of Elusa, then indeed good and zealous in their religion, by their vicious preaching.'[65] Elusa, or Eauze, was the capital of Novempopulana. Clearly the experience had been an unpleasant one, and it is therefore understandable that the bishops of this area remained jittery about Priscillianists under the beds—especially as they had a long frontier with Spain, and so were liable to renewed infection from Galicia, still strongly Priscillianist.

All this may appear very hypothetical when our information about the bishops of Novempopulana and Agen in

---

[63] Gregory, *Hist.* II, 13 (*MGH, SRM* I, i, pp. 62-3).
[64] For what follows, see above ch. 4, n. 3.
[65] Sulpicius, *Chron.* II, 48, 2.

the early fifth century is so slight. But what we have fits into this pattern precisely, for it was probably in the diocese of Saint-Bertrand-de-Comminges in Novempopulana that Vigilantius wrote, and Vigilantius was supported by bishops.[66] Added interest comes if, as seems plausible, we identify the Desiderius who, along with Riparius, denounced Vigilantius' teachings to Jerome, with the Desiderius to whom Sulpicius dedicated his *Vita Martini*. Desiderius and Riparius were priests, who found 'that their own parishes were contaminated by the proximity of that man' (i.e. Vigilantius), and that his ideas were favourably received by some (or many: *nonnulli*) in the area.[67] Desiderius provides us with one link between Vigilantius and Sulpicius; as we shall see in the following chapter, there was probably a direct one, also.

In conclusion, we may say that Vigilantius' activity is exactly contemporaneous with Sulpicius' composition of the *Chronicle* and *Dialogues*, and in all probability they were living not far apart. So the fact that Vigilantius' bishop gave him a sympathetic hearing may well be the other side of the coin to Sulpicius' diatribe against the bishops for their hostility towards asceticism. Indeed, even the apparent deterioration of Sulpicius' relations with the bishops between his writing of the *Vita Martini* in 396 and his composition of his other main works in the early fifth century may be connected with Vigilantius' activities.

The general context of persistent hostility towards asceticism probably also explains the reception of Sulpicius' Martinian writings within Gaul. In his own lifetime Martin had lived 'amongst clerics who were at variance with him, amongst bishops who raged with anger', and it was specifically his asceticism which the clergy objected to. They were

---

[66] Vigilantius probably came from Calagurris (modern Saint-Martory), in the diocese of St.-Bertrand (Convenae); certainly he lived just under the Pyrenees. See Jerome, *Contra Vigilantium* § 1, § 4, § 6 (*PL* 23, cols. 340, 342, 345); R. Lizop, *Les Convenae et les Consoranni* (Toulouse & Paris 1931; Bibliothèque Méridionale, 2 série, vol. 25), pp. 133–7, 349–50, 352.

[67] Jerome, *Contra Vig.* 3 (col. 341). On Desiderius cf. above, ch. 5. Note that Desiderius and Riparius sent their request to Jerome via Sisinnius, the official Toulouse messenger, which implies that they were from Toulouse or a neighbouring diocese—which strengthens the case for Vigilantius being from the St.-Bertrand diocese.

'hostile towards his *virtus* and life, hating in him what they did not see in themselves, and what they were not capable of imitating'.[68] If the clergy had been so hostile towards Martin within his lifetime, then it is scarcely surprising that they rejected Sulpicius' glorificatory portrayal of him as a 'holy man' as being full of lies, and remained suspicious about his claims to have encountered saints, angels, and devils.

[68] *D* I, 24, 3. *VM* 27, 3. I would accept, with Heinzelmann (op. cit. above, ch. 3, n. 2), that by the mid fifth century there had been a *rapprochement* in Gaul between the aristocratic episcopacy and monasticism; but this did not happen as smoothly or as speedily as H implies. Martin's episcopal colleagues certainly did not regard his asceticism as akin to the traditional virtues of the Roman aristocracy: see *VM* 9, 3.

21

Jerome, Vigilantius, and the *Dialogues*

That the bishops of Gaul should have had no good word to say of Martin is understandable enough, in the light of our last chapters; but what of the silence or veiled hostility shown towards Sulpicius' Martin by the leading Latin propagandist of asceticism, the ready-tongued Jerome? We have already noted the striking coincidences between the ascetic ideals of Sulpicius' Martin and Jerome, and the fact that they both wrote in the same literary genre, both relishing miracles as signs of sanctity. We have seen also that Sulpicius knew of some of Jerome's ascetic writings, while Jerome knew of Sulpicius' *Dialogues* by c.410, and may well have known of the Martinian writings earlier.[1] He had several Gallic correspondents, amongst them Desiderius, very probably the dedicatee of Sulpicius' *Vita Martini*. In view of this, it seems odd that Jerome never refers explicitly to St. Martin, whose way of life, one would have thought, would have made him a suitable paradigm for Jerome's Gallic correspondents.[2]

In fact, Jerome makes one definite reference, and two possible allusions, to Sulpicius' Martinian writings; and none of them is complimentary. When commenting upon Ezekiel 36:1-15, prophesying a future time when the desolate parts of Israel will be settled and fruitful, he rejects the literal interpretation which refers this to the millenium; the time when the new Jerusalem will descend from heaven and end a period of persecution, during which circumcision and sacrifices had been enforced. The latter interpretation, Jerome

---

[1] Above, ch. 6, ii.
[2] Cf. Jerome's *ep*. 125, 20, to Rusticus, commending Proculus and Exsuperius; and *ep* 118, 5 to Julian, commending Pammachius and Paulinus.

continues, had been given by many Latin writers: Tertullian, Lactantius, Victorinus of Pettau, 'and recently our Severus in the dialogue which he has named *Gallus*'.[3] The reference is to *Dialogue* II, 14, 1-4, where Martin expounds his beliefs about the end of the world and the imminence of Nero and Antichrist, the latter of whom would enforce circumcision. That Jerome's criticism hit home can be seen from the widespread omission of this passage in the French branch of manuscripts of the *Dialogues*, while the so-called Gelasian Decree, drawn up around the late fifth century, put the *Dialogues* on its black list.[4]

Another possible reference, this time to the *Vita Martini*, occurs in Jerome's commentary on Isaiah (408/10). Jerome sets alongside Isaiah 58:7, 'if you see a naked man, clothe him', Jesus' teaching in Luke 3:11, 'he who has two tunics, let him give one to him who has none.' Jerome then continues: 'For he did not command that one (tunic) should be cut up and divided, as many do for the sake of popular favour; but that a second one should not be kept'.[5] I find it hard to believe that this is not a covert jibe at Martin's famous division of his cloak outside Amiens.[6]

The third possible allusion occurs in Jerome's eulogy of Nepotian. Like Martin, Nepotian had been a soldier before he became an ascetic and a cleric; but Jerome passed rapidly over his time in the army, although Nepotian was already, apparently, living a model life.

Another, I say, would relate that when he was in the palace guard, his body was chafed by a hair shirt beneath his military cloak and white linen, that his lips were discoloured through fasting as he stood before the secular powers, that while he was clad in the garments of one master, he was serving another, and that he wore the military uniform for this end, that he might succour the widows, the orphans, the oppressed, and the wretched. But I do not like these delays and half

---

[3] *In Hiez.* XI (*CCSL* 75, p. 500).

[4] Halm (*CSEL* 1), p. 197; cf. Babut, *S. Martin*, pp. 301-2. *De libris recipiendis et non recipiendis* V, 7 (ed. E. von Dobschütz, *Texte und Untersuchungen* 38 (1912), p. 56, and cf. pp. 312-13).

[5] *Comm. in Esaiam* XVI, lviii, 7 (*CCSL* 73A, p. 666).

[6] *VM* 3, 1-2. I owe this reference to P. Antin, *Essai sur saint Jérôme* (Paris 1951), p. 215.

measures in the service of God: the centurion Cornelius, a righteous man, as I read, was, I hear, baptized immediately.[7]

Here, the 'another would relate' looks very like an allusion to Sulpicius, who devoted one and a half chapters of the *Vita Martini* to Martin's exemplary life as a soldier.[8] However, as Jerome's eulogy of Nepotian was only written in the summer of 396,[9] at the same time as Sulpicius was completing his *Vita Martini*, we must be wary. It is possible that Jerome had already heard of his work on Martin via an oral source.[10] But we may be reading too much into the 'referret alius', which exemplifies a common literary technique for getting across information which one professes to set at naught.[11] In any case, soldiers who became monks were not rare, and we also know of three other cases of soldiers who acted like monks.[12]

However, Jerome's unfavourable reaction to such an attempt to lead a double life would have been equally applicable to Martin. Indeed, running all the way through Jerome's letters is an insistence that monks should be entirely cut off from the world.[13] They should live in solitude preparing for

[7] Jerome, *ep.* 60, 9, 2 (*CSEL* 54, p. 558). Cf. also *ep.* 60, 10, 2 ('nihil sibi amplius reservavit') with *VM* 2, 8 ('nihil sibi . . . reservare').

[8] It is taken like this by Babut, *S. Martin*, pp. 280-1; and by F. Prinz, *Frühes Mönchtum im Frankenreich* (Munich & Vienna 1965) p. 21 & n. 10. Cf. also Fontaine, 'Vérité et fiction', pp. 216-17 & n. 75.

[9] Nautin, art. cit. (below, n. 20) § viii, in *Revue des Études Augustiniennes* 20 (1974), pp. 280-1.

[10] Viz. Vigilantius, if one accepts the identification of the one who visited Jerome in 395 and the one who brought Paulinus a letter from Sulpicius in 396. See below.

[11] E.g., noble birth. Cf. Jerome, *ep.* 108, 3; Hilary of Arles, *Sermo de vita sancti Honorati*, 4 (*SC* 235, pp. 76-8).

[12] Nebridius (Jerome *ep.* 79, 2); Exuperantius (Jerome *ep.* 145); and the unknown man 'qui saeculum ridet et sub chlamyde monachum gerit' who was one of the petitioners for the Pelagian treatise *De induratione cordis Pharaonis . . .* (preface); ed. G. de Plinval, *Essai sur le style et la langue de Pélage* (Collectanea Friburgensia 31, Fribourg en Suisse, 1947) p. 137.

[13] Rousseau argues that Jerome relaxed his fierce insistence of *ep.* 14 that monks must be utterly cut off from the world (*Ascetics*, pp. 109-12, 115-18, 125-32). I do not think Jerome is wholly consistent, but NB: (1) nearly all his letters praising household asceticism are addressed to women, for whom it would have been wholly impractical to recommend the solitary life in the wilderness. (2) Even *ep.* 66, commending Pammachius' disbursement of his possessions amongst the needy and his adoption of the monastic life, still appears to be urging Pammachius on to perfection, and adjudges him less perfect than Paula

the dreadful judgement to come, and they thus fulfil an entirely different role from that of the clergy; while, similarly, it is impossible to be a true monk while remaining in the world.[14]

This is the main difference between the ascetic ideal of Jerome and that of Sulpicius' Martin, who remained in the army, but behaved so that 'non miles, sed monachus putaretur';[15] and who, even after his final adoption of the ascetic life, was still inveigled into being made a bishop; he thus became subject to all the pressures and compromises that inevitably accompanied life in the world.[16] Jerome, on the other hand, refused to exercise his priesthood. There are a few other things which differentiated Sulpicius' ideals from Jerome's: for instance, the Marmoutier monks undertook no work, except for the copying assigned to the youngest monks, whereas Jerome recommended manual work to Rusticus and the virgin Demetrias.[17] Added to this, Martin held various ideas which Jerome would have regarded as questionable. One is his belief in the imminent persecutions of Antichrist and end of the world, which we have already discussed. Another possible one is Martin's belief in the objective reality of the demons who confronted him and argued with him.[18] A third, which will require more attention,

and Eustochium (§8 and §13). (3) *Ep.* 79, which actually praises Nebridius for carrying out good works while remaining a soldier (§2), was written at a time when Jerome stood in need of patrons, as Rousseau himself points out (ibid. p. 118). (4) While freely admitting that Jerome commended such ascetic virtues as chastity and abstinence as befitting the clergy (e.g. *epp.* 52; 60, 10; 125, 17; *Adv. Jovin.* I, 34-5), I feel that his aim was indeed the 'improvement of standards in the church' (Rousseau, p. 129); but at the same time he maintained that this was different from the solitary life, and that the latter was 'perfection'. For, after telling Rusticus how to live so that he might deserve to be ordained, he then concluded his letter: 'aut, si perfecta desideras, exi cum Abraham de patria et de cognatione tua et perge, quo nescis. Si habes substantiam, vende et da pauperibus ... Nudum Christum nudus sequere. ...' (*ep.* 125, 20, 5).

[14] *Contra Vigilantium* §15 and §16 (*PL* 23 cols. 351-2). *Ep.* 117, 1, 2 (*CSEL* 55 p. 423). *Ep.* 14, 6-8; *ep.* 58, 5 (*CSEL* 54, pp. 52-6, 533-5).

[15] *VM* 2, 7; contrast Jerome *ep.* 118, 6, 1: 'nolim te inter saeculares esse monachum et inter monachos saecularem' (*CSEL* 55 p. 443).

[16] *D* I, 24, 3; cf. *D* III, 11-13.

[17] *VM* 10, 6. Jerome *ep.* 125, 11; *ep.* 130, 15 (*CSEL* 56, pp. 130-1, 195-6).

[18] In *ep.* 125, 9, Jerome says he wishes to see monks 'who cannot think of inventing stories, like some silly people, of demons attacking them, in order to claim a miracle for themselves in the eyes of the ignorant and the crowd, and

is Martin's expressed belief that if the devil would repent, Christ would pardon him. This view is very close to one of Origen's, which was even then being denounced as heretical; and when we recall that the *Vita* was published in 396, and so in the midst of the Origenist controversy, it is easy to grasp the riskiness of this passage in the *Vita Martini*.[19]

Alongside—and probably overshadowing—these theoretical grounds on which Jerome may have conceived an aversion for Sulpicius' Martin, is a very personal reason: Jerome probably first heard of Sulpicius through Paulinus of Nola's communication with him; and his relationship with Paulinus was soured first by a *contretemps* with Paulinus' courier, Vigilantius, and secondly, by Paulinus' friendship with Rufinus, now become Jerome's arch-enemy.[20] And, if we identify this Vigilantius with one of that name who belonged to Sulpicius' community at Primuliacum, then the concatenation of people and circumstances which rubbed up Jerome the wrong way is suddenly given a violent twist, which more than accounts for Jerome's negative attitude towards Sulpicius' Martin.

We have already encountered Vigilantius as a priest, probably in the diocese of Saint-Bertrand-de-Comminges, who in the early fifth century spoke out against abuses accompanying the cult of relics and against the enforced celibacy of the clergy. He also questioned the value of selling all one's goods and giving the proceeds to the poor, of sending money to support the Christian communities at Jerusalem, and of secluding oneself in a monastery. He thought it more worthwhile to look to the needs of the

---

therefrom to get profit.' (*CSEL* 56, pp. 128-9). Rousseau, *Ascetics* p. 122, suggests its relevance for Sulpicius' Martin (though NB I disagree with his translation of the passage, loc. cit. n. 54). However, cf. Jerome, *V. Hil.* 5-8 (*PL* 23, cols. 32-3).

[19] *VM* 22, 5. I owe this point to van Andel, 'Sulpicius Severus and Origenism'.

[20] The principal sources are Jerome's letters 53 and 58 to Paulinus, and 61 to Vigilantius. On these, see P. Courcelle, 'Paulin de Nole et saint Jérôme', *Revue des Études Latines* 25 (1947 [1948]), pp. 250-80; P. Nautin, 'Études de chronologie hiéronymienne (393-397)', an article scattered through *Revue des Études Augustiniennes* 18, 19, and 20, esp. vol. 19 (1973), pp. 213-39. I regret that I have not seen the work of R. Eiswirth cit. by Lienhard, p. 99, n. 82.

poor in one's neighbourhood, and felt they would be better served if well-wishers retained their property and gave away the profits, and if sincere Christians remained in society and tried to benefit it from within, rather than turning their backs on it to live in solitude.[21] It is small wonder that Jerome, when invited, entered the lists against him with such gusto. However, Vigilantius had not always held such views; for, as we may recall, he had himself gone to the Holy Land in 395 as a protégé of Paulinus, from whom he brought a letter for Jerome, and alms for the communities there.[22] At this date, then, he must have been in sympathy with the monastic ideals of Paulinus and Jerome, and willing to distribute alms in the Holy Land.

Vigilantius was unfortunate in his timing. He arrived in the Holy Land in the spring or early summer of 395 to find Jerome's community in Bethlehem at loggerheads with its bishop, John of Jerusalem, and, indeed, excommunicated by him.[23] The controversy concerned Origen, the brilliant third-century theologian whose commentaries on the Bible laid all subsequent generations in his debt, but whose theological system contained some audacious theories extraneous to a Christianity founded upon the Bible: e.g. that the souls of angels, men, and demons had all been created the same, and that the potential was there for passing from one state to another—hence his belief that even devils could, in the end, be saved. Subsequent generations had tended quietly to ignore or reject such speculations, while making full use of his exegetical works and homilies. However in 393 Epiphanius, bishop of Salamis on Cyprus and a fanatical hammer of heretics, instigated a movement to get all Origen's works banned. Jerome readily complied, but his erstwhile friend Rufinus, then living on nearby Olivet, refused, as did the diocesan bishop, John of Jerusalem. Tension gave way to open hostility when Epiphanius rashly ordained one of the Bethlehem community priest, to save them from having to use the local clergy who were loyal to Bishop John.

---

[21] See Jerome, *Contra Vig.* §§13–15 (*PL* 23, cols. 349–51).

[22] Jerome, *ep.* 58, 11, 3; *ep.* 61, 3, 4; *Contra Vig.* §13.

[23] For the general context, see Kelly, ch. 18. On the timing of Vigilantius' visit, see Courcelle, 'Paulin', pp. 261–2; Nautin, *Rev. Ét. Aug.* 19, pp. 221–2, 231–4.

This was an open infringement of John's jurisdiction, and he retaliated by excommunicating Jerome's Bethlehem community (394).

This state of hostility still persisted in 395, when Vigilantius paid his visit; and Vigilantius lacked tact. He asked Jerome about his reading of Origen, apparently accusing him of being an Origenist himself.[24] His questioning of Jerome's attitude towards Origen may well have occurred as a result of conversations with Rufinus and Melania, for Rufinus later aroused enmity by pointing out that up to 393, Jerome had shared his own good opinion of Origen.[25] It may even be that Vigilantius stayed with Rufinus and Melania in their community on the Mount of Olives before visiting Jerome, for Melania was related to Vigilantius' patron, Paulinus, and Vigilantius would naturally have preferred to stay there than with a community which was excommunicated.[26]

The ban on Jerome's monastery probably explains Vigilantius' reluctance to spend much time with Jerome, and his abrupt departure. In the summer or autumn of 395 he returned to Italy and repeated his accusation of Origenism throughout north Italy, this time levelling his attack not only against Jerome, but against other members of the Bethlehem community.[27] Jerome wrote back an angry refutation, and ended by pouring scorn and indignation on Vigilantius' interpretation of a verse in Daniel. This presumably silenced him, and we may conjecture that he returned home to Gaul. Vigilantius' next onslaught, *c.*403, was not to be against Origenism, but, as we have seen, against relic cultus and monasticism. In the intervening years he must have swung round against these practices—partly, perhaps, as a result of what he had witnessed in the Holy Land.

---

[24] See Jerome, *ep.* 61, 1.

[25] Kelly, pp. 231-4.

[26] So Nautin, *Rev. Ét. Aug.* 19, p. 231. In any case, contact between Rufinus and Vigilantius is implied by Jerome, who later accused Rufinus of stirring up Vigilantius against him: *Apologia contra Rufinum* III, 19 (*PL* 23, col. 492).

[27] On Vigilantius' brief stay and abrupt departure, see Jerome, *ep.* 58, 11, 3; *ep.* 109, 2, 5. On his accusations, see Jerome, *ep.* 61. I see no reason to assume that Vigilantius returned via Egypt (so Courcelle, 'Paulin', p. 263, n. 1; Nautin, *Rev. Ét. Aug.* 19 p. 233). The sense of Jerome's 'dimisisti Aegyptum' (*ep.* 61, 1, 3) is surely, 'you have left Egypt out of your accusations' (viz. of Origenism): i.e. why pick just on me?

Now Sulpicius' first letter to Paulinus at Nola was brought by two couriers in the spring of 396; and one of the couriers was called Vigilantius.[28] Is this the same Vigilantius as carried Paulinus' letter to Jerome the previous year? Chronologically, it is quite possible, as it is in any case likely that Vigilantius returned home to Gaul in the autumn of 395 before winter made travelling difficult. Geographically, it is probable, for Primuliacum lay in the same general area as Vigilantius' place of origin, Calagurris, the modern Saint-Martory.[29] Also, Vigilantius was not a common name: it does not occur on any inscription from Gaul or Spain; it features only once in Diehl's collection of Christian inscriptions (at Rome); and once in the *Prosopography of the Later Roman Empire* (relating to a military commander in the west who was assassinated in 409).[30] On top of this, both namesakes belonged to the same religious circles as Paulinus of Nola, were (at that time) in sympathy with the monastic life, and acted as letter-bearers.

The chief argument against identifying the two is that whereas the one who stayed with Jerome was a priest, referred to by Jerome as 'sanctum Vigilantium presbyterum', Paulinus talks about Sulpicius' letter-bearers to him as 'conservi nostri, pueri tui', which makes them sound rather junior and lowly for one of them to have been a priest;[31] and we may further feel that carrying letters between Primuliacum and Nola would not be a very apt use of a priest's time.

However, we must beware of letting our own preconceptions cloud our judgement. In the later Roman Empire the

---

[28] Paulinus, *ep.* 5, 11. On the dating, see Lienhard, pp. 178-82.

[29] Above, ch. 20, iii.

[30] The indices to *CIL* vols. II, XII and XIII list no Vigilantius. For the inscription at Rome see Diehl, *Inscriptiones Lat. Christ.* vol. II, no. 2836 A. For Vigilantius, *magister equitum*, see A. H. M. Jones, J. R. Martindale, & J. Morris, *The Prosopography of the Later Roman Empire* (Cambridge, vol. I 1971, vol. II 1980-vol. II by Martindale alone), II, p. 1165.

[31] Jerome, *ep.* 58, 11 (*CSEL* 54, p. 541). Paulinus, *ep.* 5, §14 and cf. §11 (*CSEL* 29, pp. 32-3). One could also ask why, if the Vigilantius who went to the Holy Land was a member of Primuliacum, he went as a protégé of Paulinus, not Sulpicius. But this is understandable when we realize that Paulinus was already in correspondence with Jerome (accepting Nautin's chronology for Jerome, *epp.* 53 and 58: *Rev. Ét. Aug.* 19 (1973), pp. 213-24).

clergy were recruited from every class of society, including the lowest. Compare, for instance, the case of Sanemarius. He was an ex-slave of Paulinus', whom Paulinus freed and sent to the church at Bordeaux with the request that he should be ordained, so that he could hold services at the tomb of Paulinus' parents.[32] Priests in the brotherhood of Paulinus and Sulpicius, then, could well have had the lowly origins implied by the word *puer*;[33] and that Primuliacum should have included priests is not surprising when we recall that boys were trained for the priesthood there, and that there were various priests and deacons amongst the monks who, so it is implied in the *Dialogues*, lived in the vicinity of Primuliacum.[34] As for a priest acting as letter-bearer, it is worth noting that when Paulinus asked the clergy at Bordeaux to forward a letter he enclosed, he hoped the task would be given to one of the clergy.[35] Admittedly, he was probably thinking of one of the lower grades (cf. Cardamas, ordained an exorcist); but if Sulpicius' courier Vigilantius were indeed the man who a year previously had carried Paulinus' letter to Jerome, then Sulpicius would have had a particular reason for sending him. What all this amounts to is showing that although Paulinus nowhere says that the Primuliacum Vigilantius who brought him a letter from Sulpicius was a priest, he could have been.

Did the Vigilantius who had dealings with Jerome come from a lowly enough background to be classifiable as a *puer*? Jerome's vicious slanders need to be taken with a pinch of salt, but it does look as though his Vigilantius was the son of an inn-keeper in Calagurris (Saint-Martory).[36] Jerome also calls him a *portitorem clientulum* of Paulinus; and he

---

[32] Paulinus, *ep.* 12, 12 (*CSEL* 29, p. 83). In general, Jones, *LRE* II, pp. 920–2.

[33] Agewise, *puer* was an elastic term: cf. F. Cavallera, *Saint Jérôme, sa vie et son œuvre* (2 vols., Louvain & Paris, 1922) II, pp. 5–6. But Paulinus' expression 'noster Vigilantius' and 'conservi nostri, pueri tui' shows that here, the term is used to denote members of the Primuliacum household, who had diverse origins: see above, ch. 4, i.

[34] Above, ch. 4, n. 10. *D* III, 1, 4.

[35] *Ep.* 12, 12. On Cardamas, see *epp.* 15, 4 and 19, 4.

[36] Jerome dubs him 'caupo Calagurritanus': *Contra Vig.* §1 & §8. Cf. also ibid. §6 (at end); §10 (at end); §13 (at beginning); and Jerome, *ep.* 61, 3, 2. The *Itinerary of Antoninus* lists a *mansio* here, en route from Saint-Bertrand to Toulouse: Lizop, pp. 118, 349–50.

sneers at his unpolished style and lack of education, bidding him get lessons from the grammarians and rhetoricians, and flaunting his own superior knowledge by studding his letter to Vigilantius with Greek tags. On the other hand, Vigilantius was no fool: he possessed Origen on Job (presumably in Hilary's translation), and he clearly thought and argued for himself, and employed secretaries and copyists.[37] I would read him as a self-taught man from a fairly humble background, who had doubtless been to the grammarian's school, but lacked the literary polish imparted by the rhetoricians; who read his Bible and biblical commentaries, but could easily be outclassed by Jerome's literary brilliance and wide-ranging knowledge. There would be nothing to stand in the way of a great ex-senator like Paulinus calling such a man a 'puer'. The identity of the Primuliacum Vigilantius with the one who visited Jerome is, then, likely; and this likelihood is strengthened by the fact that it was Paulinus, and not the bishop of Saint-Bertrand or one of his neighbours, who recommended Vigilantius to Jerome in 395: this would fit with Vigilantius at that time belonging to the circle of Paulinus' close friend, Sulpicius.[38]

If we accept the identity of the two couriers named Vigilantius, this fully explains Jerome's silence or veiled hostility towards Martin; for it means that Jerome would have been prejudiced against Sulpicius from the very first, through the latter's close association with Vigilantius.

The story does not end here. By c.403 Vigilantius must have broken with Sulpicius' Primuliacum community, and published his attack on monasticism and relic cultus. Meanwhile a bishop who had formerly supported Sulpicius grew decidedly cool, if not openly hostile towards him.[39] Something

---

[37] Jerome, *ep.* 61; *Contra Vig.* §3. Note, however, that Gennadius praised Vigilantius' prose style: *De viris inl.* 36.

[38] Cf. above, n. 31. Fabre (*Essai sur la chronologie*, p. 22, n. 1) and Courcelle ('Paulin', p. 261) link Paulinus' sending Vigilantius to Jerome in 395 with Gennadius' reference (*De vir. inl.* 36) to Vigilantius as a Gaul who was a priest at Barcelona—the place where Paulinus was ordained (Christmas 394) immediately before his departure for Nola. But all Jerome's references to Vigilantius imply that he lived in Gaul, not Spain (*Contra Vig.* §1, §3, §4 & §6). I suggest that he moved to Spain later, perhaps as a result of the barbarian invasions of 407.

[39] Riparius applied to Jerome for help in combating Vigilantius in 404: Cavallera II, 51. Bishop becoming hostile: above ch. 20, iii.

of the hurt that this occasioned Sulpicius can be picked up from the odd bitter outbursts in the *Chronicle* and *Dialogues*, which he was then working on, and from the note of sorrow, smarting, and discomposure, on which both works end.[40] One context for the *Dialogues*, then, is that of Vigilantius' attack and the support which he enjoyed from some bishops: the *Dialogues* represent Sulpicius' reaffirmation and defence of the pro-ascetic views he had originally put forward in the *Vita Martini*.[41]

However, there is also a second context for the *Dialogues*: that relating to Jerome, Rufinus, and the debate over Origen. Since 395, not only had Jerome's excommunication been lifted, but the anti-Origen party had gathered considerable strength with Theophilus of Alexandria's volte-face against Origenism in 399, followed the next year by condemnations of Origen's teaching from the Pope and the bishop of Milan. At the same time the rift between Jerome and Rufinus, temporarily mended, had deepened into bitter animosity, with each defending himself and attacking the other; and Origen still lay at the heart of their dispute. Sulpicius' friend, Paulinus, was naturally drawn more towards Rufinus' party by his kinship with Rufinus' great protector, Melania. And through Paulinus, Sulpicius himself was in touch, at least indirectly, with Rufinus; for, as we have seen, it was to him that Paulinus forwarded Sulpicius' chronological queries when he was doing research for his *Chronicle*, and it is possible that Rufinus used Sulpicius' *Chronicle* when adding an account of fourth-century events to his translation of Eusebius' *Ecclesiastical History*.[42] Conversely, Sulpicius must have read Rufinus' *De adulteratione librorum Origenis* before he wrote his first *Dialogue*, for he reproduces its

[40] *Chron.* II, 51, 8-10; *D* III, 18 (note Babut's addition from the Book of Armagh to Halm's text: 'Sur trois lignes inédites', p. 208). Babut (loc. cit. pp. 209-10) further conjectured that Vigilantius was the unnamed man responsible for luring away Sulpicius' runaway, Pomponius (*D* III, 18, and cf. I, 12, 3-4). His theory is attractive; but it is difficult to see how Vigilantius, now an anti-monastic priest in southern Gaul, should have been to blame for getting Pomponius shipwrecked off Cyrenaica.

[41] Cf. Babut, loc. cit. pp. 212-13.

[42] For general background, see Kelly chs. 20 & 21. On links with Rufinus, see F. X. Murphy, 'Rufinus of Aquileia and Paulinus of Nola', *Rev. Ét. Aug.* 2 (1956), pp. 79-91; and above, ch. 6, notes 76 & 77.

arguments precisely, occasionally echoing its very words.[43] And yet, Sulpicius is careful not to identify himself with Rufinus' views, and goes out of his way to compliment Jerome.

In his *Dialogues*, Sulpicius skilfully puts the narrative into the mouth of Postumianus. He portrays the latter arriving in Alexandria to find a feud going on between the bishops and the monks (shades of Gaul!). In 400 Theophilus had convoked a synod which condemned Origen, and decreed sanctions even against those who read him. He had also called in the civil authorities against the monks (*scaevum exemplum*—remember Priscillian).[44] Postumianus expounded the monks' (i.e. Rufinus') views of Origen, according to which he was an expert commentator on the Bible, the dubious passages had been inserted by heretics, and the faithful would easily be able to discern between the good and the heretical for themselves. The bishops, however, had banned all his works, and one of the heretical passages they pointed to aroused particular resentment: that where Origen had said that, through the cross, Jesus would redeem even the devil. As for Postumianus' own views: despite the bishops' ban, he dipped into Origen's books for himself, and found there much which gave pleasure, but quite a few passages that were clearly reprehensible. He does not seem to have swallowed the argument that all the erroneous passages were interpolated; but he regarded them as mistaken, rather than heretical, as the bishops thought. He was, however, perturbed to find that Jerome, 'vir maxime catholicus et sacrae legis peritissimus', was now condemning all Origen's works indiscriminately, although he was once thought to have been a follower of Origen. Postumianus added that 'praestantissimi . . . viri et doctissimi' (viz. Rufinus) disagreed with Jerome about this blanket condemnation of Origen.[45]

---

[43] Cf. Sulpicius *D* I, 6, 2-7, 1, with Rufinus *De adult.* esp. §1, §7, §16 (*CCSL* 20, pp. 7, 11, 17). I discuss the similarities fully in my 'Sulpicius' Saint Martin', pp. 375-6. Van Andel has independently reached the same conclusion: 'Sulpicius Severus and Origenism', p. 284 and n. 43—though I do not share his view that Sulpicius had also read Origen's *Peri Archon*. He might have done so, but there is no real evidence of it.

[44] *D* I, 6, 1; I, 7, 2. Cf. Guillaumont, *Les 'Képhalaia Gnostica'*, pp. 63-4.

[45] *D* I, 6 & 7. Cf. van Andel, art. cit. p. 279.

The whole passage is a masterly exercise in sitting on the fence, with Sulpicius refusing to identify with either party. On the one hand, his sympathy for the monks, who represent Rufinus' views, is obvious: and it comes out particularly in his uneasiness at the way the bishops have handled the whole affair. However, he does in fact accept that some passages of Origen are mistaken (not interpolated), such as that which holds out hope of the devil's redemption; and I think we should here follow the argument of van Andel, and see this passage as deliberately aimed at correcting any misapprehensions on the part of the anti-Origenist lobby (especially Jerome) as to the soundness of Sulpicius' own views. In other words, whereas in the *Vita* Sulpicius had portrayed Martin's expressed willingness to pardon the devil as an instance of his laudable charity, even towards hardened sinners, by the time he came to write the *Dialogues*, Sulpicius was aware that a similar view of Origen's had been condemned, and he sought to exculpate himself.[46]

But at the same time as showing sympathy with the views of the Origenist monks and Rufinus, and as clearing himself from any suspicion of Origenist views, I would suggest that Sulpicius had also another aim: that of defending Jerome's orthodoxy against Vigilantius, who had not long since accused Jerome himself of Origenism.

This concern becomes even clearer in the following chapters of the *Dialogues* (I, 8 & 9), where Sulpicius expatiates upon Jerome's learning, the appositeness of his writings for Gallic monasticism, and his ceaseless devotion to the catholic faith. His outspoken denunciation of heresy and clerical vices has earned him hatred from some, but all good men admire him: 'for those who consider him a heretic are mad. I can speak the truth: the learning of that man is catholic, his teaching is sound.'[47] This, I feel, was written very much with an eye to Vigilantius and those Gallic bishops who supported him, using the smear of heresy as an excuse for decrying his astringent comments on clerical and monastic abuses. In this context we should also recall the point made above, that the

---

[46] Van Andel, art. cit. Cf. *VM* 22, 5 and *D* I, 7, 1.
[47] *D* I, 9, 4-5. Babut, 'Sur trois lignes', pp. 212-13.

Dialogues are to be seen partly as Sulpicius' defence against Vigilantius' attacks on monasticism and saints' cultus.

However, the main theme of the *Dialogues* is not a defence of Jerome, so much as a defence of Martin, even to the point of providing an *apologia pro Martino* directed at Jerome, as well as at the Gallic bishops. As already indicated, Martin's attempt to live as a baptized Christian while remaining a soldier, and to live as a monk while acting as bishop, would not have commended him to Jerome. Further, Vigilantius' revulsion against asceticism and his link with Sulpicius would have done much to discredit Gallic monasticism in the eyes of Jerome. Surely, then, it is no fluke that all the parallels between Sulpicius' and Jerome's ascetic views occur *in the Dialogues*, as though Sulpicius was consciously trying to bring out the similarities.[48] Jerome's castigation of lax ascetics was taken to heart by Sulpicius to a surprising degree,[49] and Martin was portrayed as a shining exception to the laxity current in Gaul: 'if we would follow the ways of Martin, we would never be defending ourselves from the charge of kissing, and we would be free from the reproaches of silly gossiping.'[50] At the end of the *Dialogues* Sulpicius paints Martin's achievements in even stronger terms. Africa had had Cyprian, Greece, the Apostle Paul, and Egypt has any number of holy men. However, 'Europe will not yield precedence to her [Egypt], nor indeed to all Asia, because of the merits of Martin alone.'[51]

Now Jerome had been at pains to point out in his *Vita Pauli* that Paul rather than Antony was the first monk, and in his *Vita Hilarionis* that Hilarion did all for Palestine that Antony did for Egypt.[52] In this passage of the *Dialogues* Sulpicius is putting Martin also on the spiritual map. In part, he was probably reacting to the claims made for Antony as Jerome had done;[53] in part, I think he was also reacting

[48] Above, ch. 6, ii, esp. notes 60-6.
[49] Surprising because Jerome's *ep.* 22 was concerned largely with abuses rife in Rome, and Pannonia (§34); not Gaul, as one might suppose from Sulpicius' reaction.
[50] *D* II, 8, 2.
[51] *D* III, 17, 5-7.
[52] *V. Pauli*. 1; *V. Hil.* 14 (*PL* 23, cols. 17-18, 35).
[53] Cf. Rousseau, *Ascetics*, p. 144: 'Where Sulpicius followed Jerome most was in reacting *against* the *Life of Antony*'.

towards Jerome himself, in an attempt to show that not all Gallic monks were unworthy of imitation, and that the hero of his *Vita Martini* rivalled, and even surpassed, the level of sanctity attained by the eastern monks.

*   *   *   *   *

These last chapters have revealed a complex background of disagreement within the church as regards the new type of asceticism, such as Martin had adopted. As a result, we can see that Martin could have fallen foul of other bishops and monks on two quite separate scores. On the one hand, the majority of Gallic bishops tended to feel hostile towards Martin's strict asceticism, with its implicit criticism of their own comfortable lives, and its possible links with heresy; and some Gallic 'monks' and virgins may well have shared some of their misgivings (cf. *D* II, 8, 3). These would have been men and women who lived celibate, but made no attempt to adhere to the strictness or the seclusion which characterized the new type of asceticism initiated by Antony, and followed by Martin. On the other hand, those who were thoroughgoing ascetics might also look askance at Martin, as one whose military past and pastoral present inevitably meant that he had remained caught up in the toils of human society, while the perfection sought after by the monk was to be found only in the depths of quietude. Added to this, Jerome had his own reasons for regarding Sulpicius with coolness, thanks to the unfortunate Vigilantius affair.

In view of all this, we can well understand the hostility with which many contemporaries greeted Sulpicius' presentation of Martin as a perfect holy man, and their reluctance to believe that such a one could really have been visited by saints and angels, and was not merely subject to diabolical hallucinations. Martin's dual role as a monk-bishop led to his falling between two stools: he did not fit in with the majority of the bishops or the older type of *continentes*; nor, however, was he a desert hermit in the sense that Antony had been.

This concatenation of circumstances thus accounts for the hostile reaction towards Sulpicius' Martinian works, and for the disbelief with which some contemporaries greeted

Sulpicius' portrayal of Martin. We need no longer assume that such disbelief is necessarily to be accounted for by the fact that Sulpicius' account was untrue.

On the other hand, this does not automatically prove the converse, viz., that Sulpicius' account was 'true'; or, to put it more accurately, it does not help us to penetrate the relationship between Sulpicius' presentation of Martin, and the monk-bishop of Tours whom he knew. Of course, with writings of the Martinian type we can rarely expect to reach certainty as to what happened, or to be able to say that such and such an event took place like this, while that one did not. However, through further study of the Martinian writings and comparison with some other material, we can go a long way towards understanding what kind of a person Martin was, and whether he actually did the sort of things which Sulpicius portrays him as doing. It is to these matters that we shall now turn.

PART V

TOWARDS THE HISTORICAL MARTIN

22

A Saint Grounded in Reality

A hagiographer can derive his inspiration to write from two very different sources: from an abstract idea or ideal, or from a person he knows and admires. In the first case, where an author is concerned primarily with putting over a theme, he is simply using a figure as a peg on which to hang his own ideas. But in the second case the author's starting-point and finishing-point is a historical individual; and, although he may feel that this individual incarnates the Christian ideal and may strive to present him in such terms, he will still find himself continually brought face to face with the intractable events of everyday life which are so full of particular details that they send awry the philosophers' and theologians' attempts to see them in terms of universal principles.

The two approaches, whether one starts from a personified ideal[1] to which one wishes to give historical verisimilitude, or from an individual whom one strives to present in terms of an ideal, can lead to similar results. However, the starting-point is quite different. In the one case, the foremost desire is to show forth and to teach something of God and of the Christian way of life, while the individual through whom God operates, even though he had a historical existence, is of secondary interest. *Vitae* of this kind set out to communicate a religious ideal, not to portray the subject as he actually was.

---

[1] Of course, a hagiographer may not be putting over a *religious* ideal in a *vita*; instead, he may simply be using a *vita* for expressing (e.g.) the claims of his church to land, or for many other purposes. However, this does not affect my basic distinction between (i), lives written primarily to make a point or argue a case; and (ii), lives which grow out of the writing up of an individual. I have here assumed that it was a religious ideal being put over under (i) as this would lead to the closest results with (ii); and also, because this is more to the point when considering Sulpicius' writings.

This was a perfectly acceptable aim for biography in antiquity, and it was taken over by Christian writers: Theodoret of Cyrrhus entitled his account of the lives of Syrian holy men φιλόθεος ἱστορία or Ἀσκητικὴ πολιτεία (*Religious History* or *The Ascetic Way of Life*), and pointed out in his prologue that his concern was with depicting heavenly things, not corporeal ones. Similarly Jerome wrote his *Vita Malchi* as a 'historiam castitatis' for virgins, exhorting them to preserve their chastity.[2]

With the second approach, the author's dominating concern is with one specific individual, the object being to honour him[3] and to present him as a true follower of Christ. To this end the biographer was anxious to endow him with a worthy portfolio, as it were. This might involve ascribing to him traits which were held to be specifically Christian virtues, and also miracle stories, as, for good or ill, people tended to associate a man's holiness with his thaumaturgical powers. In practice, then, there were many factors which could lead an author even with this second approach to depart from historical accuracy. 'Nevertheless it is one thing to extol a dead man with commonplaces, another to set out his own characteristic virtues', as Jerome himself pointed out in his *Life of Hilarion*; and it is significant that this *Life* bears a closer resemblance to biography than either of his earlier *vitae*, which were written more to make a point than to illustrate a personality.[4] The distinction between the two different approaches therefore makes a valid starting-point.

Let us then turn to the Martinian writings to see whether Sulpicius was primarily interested in conveying a message, with Martin as no more than a peg on which to hang his own ideas, or primarily interested in Martin *qua* Martin. The former thesis was strongly argued by Babut in 1912.

[2] Theodoret: *PG* 82, col. 1283. Jerome, *V. Mal.* 10 (*PL* 23, col. 62). Cf. above, ch. 14, n. 20.

[3] True, this was the professed objective of the presbyter responsible for the fictional *Acts of Paul* (above, ch. 14, n. 4); but the difference is that the presbyter never knew Paul in person, and therefore did not draw his inspiration from a living person. NB also that the presbyter was convicted and defrocked on this charge.

[4] *V.Hil.* 1, preface (*PL* 23, col. 29). On Jerome's saints' lives, see Hoster, ch. 3; Rousseau, *Ascetics*, pp. 133–9.

However, his ideas on this subject cannot be divorced from other, more dubious, theories of his; and his thesis is only tenable when taken *in toto*.[5] Babut held that the asceticism of Paulinus and Sulpicius led to their being considered as virtual Priscillianists; while disavowing Priscillian's name, they none the less belonged to a small sect of schismatic Christians whom he christened the 'Antifelicians'. These, he thought, were only reconciled with the church at or after the council of Turin which he wished to date to 417.[6] In the meantime, these schismatics were persecuted by the Gallic episcopal hierarchy, and even Sulpicius' *Chronicle* can be seen as skilful pleading of their case as is shown, for instance, by his attempt to dissociate them from the condemned Priscillian by pretending that the latter's following was essentially a Spanish, not Gallic, phenomenon. Martin, while not being himself a Priscillianist, was an ascetic of such strictness that he might well be suspected of heresy, and would have been included as a victim of the witch-hunt for ascetics advocated by the anti-Priscillianist bishops *c*.386; he escaped only through the personal goodwill of the Emperor Maximus.[7] This, however, meant that he was one of the few clergy, and perhaps the only bishop, who sympathized with the 'Antifelician sect', and it was for this reason that Sulpicius chose him as the hero for his biographical writings. It was a choice forced on him by circumstances and does not imply that Martin was already famous. In reality, Sulpicius did not know Martin very well: he saw him for the first time only in 396, and he pretended to a more intimate knowledge of Martin merely in order to impress.[8]

In other words, Babut regarded Sulpicius' objective as being primarily the 'Antifelician' cause, and he minimized

---

[5] Cf. R. Aigrain's discussion of Babut and Delehaye, *Revue d'histoire de l'église de France* 7 (1921), at pp. 278-9. Babut's views outlined here have been dealt with firmly and justly by Delehaye, 'S. Martin', pp. 60, 66-72.

[6] Babut, *St. Martin* pp. 28-31, 46-7, 110-11, and 155-65. Babut designates as 'Antifelicians' those who refused to be in communion with the bishops who had been responsible for Priscillian's execution and had immediately afterwards consecrated Felix as bishop of Trier, a consecration which these 'extremists' regarded as invalid.

[7] Ibid. pp. 47, 151-4.

[8] Ibid. pp. 110-11; pp. 54-64, and cf. pp. 35 and 81.

Sulpicius' actual acquaintance with Martin. However, in reality it was the 'Felicians', not the 'Antifelicians', who were out of communion with the rest of the church;[9] and there is no evidence that Sulpicius belonged to a schismatic group. True, the bishops tended to suspect him because of his asceticism. However, Babut has it the wrong way round: Sulpicius first became interested in Martin, resolved to write his life, and visited him at Tours; and only after this did he himself embrace the ascetic life.[10] Thus, far from Martin serving only as a vehicle for Sulpicius' arguments, it was in reality Martin who inspired Sulpicius with the ideals he then portrayed in his literary works; and it was Martin, not the 'Antifelicians', whom Sulpicius sought to defend in his writings.

Babut's thesis will find few adherents today; but a more plausible line has been taken by Rousseau, who sees the Martinian writings as an attempt to convey a different ideal: that of the monk-bishop. He argues that Sulpicius purposefully shows us Martin putting to a pastoral use his ascetic gifts of discernment and healing, and throwing himself into pastoral work while continuing his monastic life of prayer and fasting. The Martinian writings, then, represent a deliberate attempt to harness ascetic sanctity to the purposes of the whole church.[11]

In a sense, this is true; for the Martinian writings are, amongst other things, ascetic propaganda, aimed at the Gallic church. However, they are at the same time much more than this, and Martin meant a great deal more to Sulpicius than a convenient peg on which to hang his advocacy of asceticism.[12] Rousseau, like Babut, overemphasizes Sulpicius' 'remoteness' from Martin.[13] Sulpicius was not remote from his subject in the way that Jerome, or even Athanasius, was. He knew Martin for the last three or four years of the latter's life, and visited Tours frequently, drawing his inspiration and many of his ideas from Martin.[14] So,

---

[9] Delehaye, 'S. Martin', p. 68.
[10] Above, ch. 2.
[11] 'Spiritual Authority', pp. 404–19, esp. 419; *Ascetics*, part IV, ch. 1.
[12] Above, ch. 7.
[13] *Ascetics*, pp. 145–6. Contrast above, ch. 7, i, and cf. Brown, *Cult*, pp. 63–5.
[14] *Ep.* 2, 14; *D* II, 13, 3–4; above, p. 31, and ch. 7, n. 32.

while one of Sulpicius' objectives was indeed to provide a model for others to imitate, and while his portrayal of Martin appears to be a portrayal of his own ideals, we must also realize that these ideals derived from none other than Martin. Martin's influence certainly played a part, perhaps an important part, in Sulpicius' conversion, and Primuliacum was inspired by Marmoutier. All this would suggest that Sulpicius had a very real interest in the actual person of Martin.

That Sulpicius' primary concern lay with Martin, rather than with asceticism or the cult of saints in general, is borne out by his predilection for visiting Tours annually, while remaining insensible to the charms of St. Felix and his devotees at Nola.[15] Nor was this due to chauvinism on Sulpicius' part, for he had no qualms about depicting the whole ecclesiastical scene in contemporary Gaul in the darkest colours, with the single exception of Martin.[16]

Sulpicius' particular concern with Martin is also apparent in the *Dialogues*, one of whose objectives was to defend *Martin*—not just asceticism. Indeed, Sulpicius' concern to defend, not simply commend, Martin's asceticism is overlooked by Rousseau. To say that 'Sulpicius was clearly convinced that exact correspondence could be achieved between the demands of spirituality and an ecclesiastical career' is, surely, to fall victim to Sulpicius' brilliant propaganda.[17] In the *Dialogues* Sulpicius did his utmost to show that, despite Martin's entanglement in the world, he still achieved the same heights as the Egyptian hermits. But it is not so much a case of Sulpicius himself being convinced of the excellence of monk-bishops, as of his desire to convince others that, though a bishop, Martin was still a genuine monk.

Sulpicius' particular concern with Martin (rather than with asceticism in general) can also be illustrated in another way in the *Dialogues*, by comparing Sulpicius' treatment of Egyptian ascetics with his treatment of Martin. Although the chapters concerned with the Egyptian ascetics comprise only some twelve sides in Halm's edition,[18] while those concerned

[15] Paulinus *ep.* 17, 4 (*CSEL* 29, p. 127).
[16] *D* I, 26, 3-6; I, 22; II, 8, 1-3; *VM* 20, 1; *Chron.* II, 51, 9-10.
[17] Rousseau, *Ascetics*, p. 150. Cf. 'Spiritual Authority', pp. 407, 409.
[18] *D* I, 10, 1-12, 1; I, 13-20; ch. 22.

with Martin occupy some seventy-two sides, Martin's thaumaturgical powers are only once directly ascribed to Christ
working in him,[19] whereas the miracles of the Egyptian monks
are thrice portrayed as being wrought by Christ through his
servants.[20] Similarly, in the chapters devoted to Martin there
are only three occasions where Sulpicius explicitly draws
attention to a specific deed or trait of Martin which he
recommends for imitation,[21] whereas in the first *Dialogue* the
teaching aim is far more in evidence. Stories are told with a
conscious moral, such as that of the two monks, one of
whom was never gluttonous, the other never angry; or the
obedience of the cenobites is demonstrated by telling of one
monk who entered a blazing oven on his abbot's command,
and another who persevered in carrying out his abbot's orders
to water a stick until it should burgeon.[22] There is also a tale
to illustrate the dangers of vanity, whose relevance to Gaul is
dilated upon for another chapter,[23] and another to illustrate a
mistaken sense of duty, which again is said to be particularly
applicable to the state of Gaul.[24] All in all, barely half the
stories are told simply for the sake of demonstrating the
sanctity of the Egyptian ascetics, or of portraying their
customs,[25] while at least half illustrate the powers of Christ
working through his servants, or the need for specific Christian
virtues. We learn almost nothing about the individuality of
the Egyptian protagonists; they are not even named, and the
stories which are told of them have been selected in order to
make a spiritual point, not to bring out their individual
characteristics.

The contrast which this presents with the way in which
Sulpicius talks of Martin is brought out all the more strongly

[19] *D* III, 10, 5.

[20] *D* I, 10, 4; 14, 6-8; 22, 5; and cf. also *D* I, 15, 6, and I, 2, 2.

[21] *VM* 22, 6; *D* II, 12, 7-10; *D* III, 16. Of other passages, one refers only in
general terms to the educational value of Martin's life—and this in the preface,
where it was a commonplace (cf. *VM* 1, 6 with *V. Antonii* preface); a second
seeks to make the best of an incident which, unqualified, might have paved the
way for laxer principles (*D* II, 7); and in a third (*D* II, 1, 3), the moral is left
implicit.

[22] *D* I, 12, 1-2. *D* I, 18 & 19; cf. also I, 10, 1.

[23] *D* I, 20 & 21.

[24] i.e. a monk abandoning the desert in order to convert his family: *D* I, 22,
1-5. Applicability to Gaul: *D* I, 21, 6; cf. *D* II, 11.

[25] *D* I, chs. 11, 13, 15, 16, and 17.

by the occasions when we can see reality breaking in through Sulpicius' picture. No conscientious hagiographer could have invented the story of Martin cutting his cloak in two so that he could give *half* of it to a beggar, while keeping the other half for his own needs.[26] Nor is it likely that the second story of Martin clothing a beggar is invented either; for in that case there would have been no point in introducing the archdeacon into the story, with Martin delegating to him the task of finding something for the beggar to wear and only giving away his own tunic when the archdeacon did nothing— a story which incidentally reveals the archdeacon's exasperation with Martin.[27] Another very plausible story is that telling how Martin persuaded a former soldier, now a monk, that it would be a mistake for him to start living with his wife again.[28] This he achieved by means of an analogy: the soldier was led to agree that an army drawn up for battle was no place for a woman, and hence, that in the ascetic's warfare against evil, women should be kept separated from men. Martin's argument is given at some length, and introduced by Gallus' promise that he will be repeating Martin's very words. All one can say is that the military analogy seems as eminently suitable coming from Martin, an ex-soldier, as it would be out of character coming from Sulpicius, a writer.[29]

In other places the historicity of an individual incident is yet more firmly attested by the fact that it counteracts a general principle which Martin and Sulpicius wished to uphold. Thus, for instance, Sulpicius inherited the idea of ἀπάθεια, imperviousness to the passions, as a trait of the holy man from the *Vita Antonii*; but although he therefore claimed that Martin was never seen emotionally upset, grieved, or laughing, he still shows us Martin weeping over the sins or fate of others.[30] There are other examples of Martin breaking an ascetic norm: he would not accept gifts

[26] i.e. to cover his nakedness: *VM* 3, 1-3. Cf. above, ch. 21, p. 298, and Babut, *St. Martin*, pp. 179-80.

[27] *D* II, 1.

[28] *D* II, 11.

[29] Note, however, Jerome, *ep*. 22, 21, 8: 'Nemo enim miles cum uxore pergit ad proelium.' (*CSEL* 54, p. 173.)

[30] Babut, *St. Martin* p. 78; Fontaine, *Vie* III, pp. 1103-6. Cf. *VM* 27, 1 with 27, 2, *ep*. 3, 11-12, *ep*. 2, 12-13, and *D* III, 13.

for himself, but he made an exception for those from an outstanding virgin;[31] nor would he allow himself to be in close proximity to the opposite sex, but here again individual circumstances such as the particularly blameless life of a virgin, or the need to avoid offending the empress when he was at the imperial palace to intercede for prisoners and exiles, would lead him to relax the rigidity of his asceticism.[32] All these stories are examples of passages where the particular is portrayed at the expense of general principles, where a historical incident has taken precedence over a timeless ideal.

These cases may not fit with a rigid asceticism, but they are meritorious in their own right; or at least, easily condonable. Other events proved more intractable: most notably the Priscillianist affair and its aftermath.[33] Here, Martin's intransigent stand against those bishops involved with Priscillian's execution cut no ice with the emperor, who retaliated by appointing executioners for those whose cause Martin was pleading. This forced Martin into a compromise: in return for obtaining his own humanitarian requests he reluctantly agreed to take part in the consecration of a new bishop along with those implicated in Priscillian's prosecution. Afterwards Martin felt very unhappy about what had happened and sank down, 'going over the cause of his grief and of what he had done, his thoughts blaming and defending him by turns.' The words of the angel who came to comfort him are striking: 'Martin, you are deservedly stung by your conscience', he said, 'but no other course was open to you. Renew your *virtus*, resume your steadfastness, lest now you risk not your fame, but your salvation.' Striking also is Martin's admission that ever since that evil his thaumaturgical powers had been impaired and he took longer to cure energumens. 'He lived for sixteen years after this; he attended no synod, and kept away from all episcopal gatherings.'[34]

This incident does not stand alone. Martin was also powerless to prevent or remedy the devil's killing of one of the peasants who worked for his monastery, an event which the

---

[31] Cf. *D* III, 14, 6 with *D* II, 12, 6.
[32] *D* II, 12, 1–3; II, 7, 1–3.
[33] *D* III, chs. 11–13; above, ch. 20.
[34] *D* III, 13, 3–6. Cf. above, ch. 17, iii (p. 243).

devil gleefully announced to him, questioning 'where is your *virtus*, Martin?' Similarly, he was caught out by the devil when he woke suddenly in the middle of the night to find himself surrounded by fire and his clothes burning. At first he tried to escape, and got burnt; it was only when he turned to prayer that he was preserved from the flames.[35] On a less miraculous level, Martin is credited with converting only his mother to Christianity: his father remained an obdurate pagan.[36]

In a different context, it is notable that Martin never wholly succeeded in living down his military past. Sulpicius may have passed lightly over his time as a soldier, but he could scarcely have omitted it altogether. The taunt that it had stained him with sin after his baptism was flung in his teeth by none other than a monk who had grown up from boyhood in Martin's monastery, Brice.[37] Nor, it would seem, was this an isolated attack. It was precisely during Martin's episcopate that papal letters were stressing the need for priests to be holy, and ruling out the possibility of ordaining those who had served in the *militia*;[38] and although Brice asked Martin's pardon for this particular incident, he continued to attack him and was elected to succeed him on his death.[39] Again, Sulpicius does not scruple to tell us a story of Martin's charity which illustrates the exasperation that the clergy could on occasion feel for their bishop.[40] He also tells us elsewhere that there were many even at Marmoutier who refused to believe in the reality of Martin's encounters with saints, angels, and demons.[41] This corroborates Brice's outburst, and it also shows that Sulpicius was either unable to suppress mention of opposition to Martin, or was unconcerned about doing so.

There are thus quite a few occasions when Martin and his achievements are seen in the harsh light of mundane reality, not the golden effulgence of otherworldly perfection. In

[35] *VM* 21, 2-5. *Ep.* 1, 11-15.
[36] *VM* 6, 3.
[37] *D* III, 15, 4, quoted above, ch. 18, p. 258.
[38] See reference cit. above, ch. 18, n. 44.
[39] *D* III, 15, 7; cf above, ch. 20, n. 38.
[40] Above, n. 27.
[41] *D* II, 13, 7.

addition, there is one other factor which serves to place Sulpicius' stories firmly in their Gallic context: that is, the naming of witnesses to attest the truth of what he tells.

In the *Vita*, Sulpicius is content with general assertions of his truthfulness; but a crescendo of concern is apparent, culminating in the last *Dialogue* in an explicit policy of naming witnesses for each deed. If we analyse his statements we find that there are two places where Sulpicius simply protests the truth of what he is saying in general terms;[42] six where he swears by God;[43] three where he gives Martin himself as the source;[44] and three where he talks of the added certainty afforded by eyewitnesses.[45] In some cases, these categories overlap. Belief is classified as something that is worthy of reward by God, while disbelief is set down to demonic inspiration, *infirmitas humana*, *incredulitas*, *infidelitas*, or *perfidia*, and classified as a sin.[46] Added to this, there are some ten occasions when Sulpicius explicitly names eyewitnesses. What are we to make of all this?

We should not attach much importance to swearing by God. Augustine's deprecation of the blasphemy and perjury occasioned by this practice shows that some of his contemporaries were quite ready to take God's name in vain, and Jerome appears to have been of their number.[47] This is very relevant in considering Sulpicius' assertions, for the latter's wording appears on occasion to be consciously evoking that of Jerome's *Vita Pauli*.[48] Elsewhere, too, the context of Sulpicius' protestations, whose wording echoes that of John's gospel, does indeed give them the air of a

---

[42] *VM* 1, 9; 27, 6-7.
[43] *VM* 25, 7; *ep*. 1, 14; *ep*. 2, 9; *D* I, 15, 1; II, 13, 4; III, 5, 5.
[44] *VM* 24, 8; *ep*. 1, 14; *D* II, 13, 4.
[45] *D* II, 13, 7-8; III, 1, 2-3; III, 5, 2-3.
[46] *VM* 27, 6-7; *ep*. 1, 2-9; *D* I, 26, 4-6; II, 13, 7; III, 5, 2-6, 1.
[47] Augustine, *Contra mendacium* xviii, 37 (*CSEL* 41, p. 521). Jerome felt free to disregard Paul's 'ecce coram Deo, quia non mentior' (Gal. 1:20), interpreting the Apostle's behaviour as a piece of deliberate deception (above, ch. 14). Cf. Augustine *De mendacio* xxi, 43 (*CSEL* 41 p. 465).
[48] *V. Pauli* 6: 'Quod ne cui impossibile videatur, Jesum testor et sanctos angelos eius ... Haec igitur incredibilia videbuntur his, qui non credunt omnia possibilia esse credentibus.' Cf. Sulpicius: 'Ne cui autem hoc incredibile forte videatur...' (*D* I, 15, 1); 'Quia multos ... incredulos scio ... Jesum testor...' (*VM* 25, 7); 'Haec plerisque ... incredibilia videbantur' (*D* II, 13, 7). Cf. also *D* I, 26, 5 (and cf. also *V. Pauli* 6 and *D* I, 20, 4).

disconcerting 'légèreté'.[49] Of Sulpicius' other practices, some have a dubious rhetorical background. Quintilian says that some classify 'incredibile est quod dico sed verum' as a figure of speech called ἀνθυποφοράν, and this is dangerously close to Sulpicius' 'incredibiliora forte dicturus sum, sed Christo teste non mentior'.[50] Another common rhetorical device was that of citing eyewitness testimony. As Macrobius put it, 'attestio rei visae apud rhetoras pathos movet';[51] and the recognition of this convention means that we cannot necessarily trust Gallus' assertion, 'nor indeed shall I talk about what I have heard from others, but rather what I myself have seen.'[52]

On the other hand, the fact that the invocation of eye-witnesses was sometimes only a literary device does not necessarily mean that it always was. In effect, if one *did* wish to prove the truth of a story and there were no previous written accounts, the naming of eyewitnesses was as good a guarantee as was possible in the circumstances. In the last *Dialogue*, at any rate, Sulpicius sounds sincere in that he names witnesses for each story he tells, and explicitly invites those with doubts to ask these witnesses for corroboration. Martin had been dead for less than a decade, and this meant that most people still remembered the events of his life as something which they themselves had seen. They must not be surprised

that I should append the names of witnesses to each miracle story, and individuals to whom anyone who may be sceptical may refer, as they are still alive. This is necessitated by the lack of faith of many people, who are said to have their doubts about some of the things which were recounted yesterday. Let them therefore accept witnesses who are still alive and well; and, because they doubt our good faith, let them rather trust them.[53]

It is one thing to claim eyewitness testimony in general terms; but it is quite another to name witnesses who would

---

[49] Fontaine, *Vie* III, p. 1227 and n. 1.

[50] Quintilian, *Inst. orat.* IX, 3, 87 (ed. Winterbottom, vol. II, p. 532). Sulpicius, *D* II, 13, 4.

[51] *Saturnalia* IV, 6, 13 (ed. J. Willis, Leipzig 1970, p. 236); cf. E. R. Curtius, *European Literature and the Latin Middle Ages* (ET London 1953), p. 175; Delehaye *Legends*, pp. 55-6.

[52] *D* I, 27, 8.

[53] *D* III, 5, 2-3; cf. III, 7, 4. Similarly, Walter Daniel later listed witnesses to Ailred's miracles, in response to contemporary scepticism: see above, ch. 1, n. 8.

have been well known at the time, and to invite people to question them.[54] Of the named witnesses, Refrigerius, Gallus, Saturninus, Evagrius, and Arpagius make no known appearance outside the pages of Sulpicius' books; although there is no particular reason to doubt their existence, we should not rely on their testimony. On the other hand, several of the personages with whom Martin came into contact were socially or politically important people within the Gaul of his day, and would therefore have been well known.[55] This applies to Arborius, *vir praefectorius*;[56] Lycontius, *ex vicariis*;[57] Taetradius, *vir proconsularis*;[58] Auspicius (and his son, Romulus), *vir praefectorius*;[59] Lupicinus, 'honoratus secundum saeculum vir',[60] and, probably in the same bracket, Evanthius.[61] On the political front, there would have been witnesses enough for Martin's relations with the court at Trier, and particularly with Maximus; while the people of Tours and Marmoutier would have been fully acquainted with Martin's dealing with Count Avitianus, and would have known Dagridus, his *ex tribunis*.[62] Of well-known religious figures, Paulinus of Nola is the outstanding example;[63] but we should also note the presence of bishops Victricius of Rouen and Valentinus of Chartres at one of Martin's healing miracles, while the detail that Marcellus was a priest at Amboise serves to give weight to his testimony.[64]

[54] See Delehaye, 'S. Martin', pp. 37-9.

[55] Cf. Jullian, 'Notes gallo-romaines' §97, *REA* 25 (1923), pp. 49-54; and particularly Matthews, *Western Aristocracies*, p. 78 and ch. 6, esp. pp. 154-6.

[56] *VM* 19, 1-2; *D* III, 10, 6; cf. Jones, Martindale, and Morris, *Prosopography*, I, pp. 97-8, and K. F. Stroheker, *Der senatorische Adel im spätantiken Gallien* (1948, reprinted Darmstadt 1970), no. 28.

[57] *D* III, 14, 3-5; *Prosopography*, I, p. 523.

[58] *VM* 17, 1-4, possibly related to the Tetradius to whom Ausonius addressed a verse epistle (*Prosopography* I, p. 885); cf. Wightman, *Roman Trier*, p. 232, and below, ch. 23, n. 28.

[59] *D* III, 7, 1-5; *Prosopography*, I, p. 141.

[60] *VM* 8, 1; possibly identical with Claudius Lupicinus, for whom see *Prosopography* I, p. 520; Stroheker no. 227.

[61] *D* II, 2, 3.

[62] *D* III, 5, 1; cf. III, 3, 1-4; III, 4; III, 8, 1-3. Ct. Avitianus may be identical with, or related to, Claudius Avitianus, a former vicar of Africa: *Prosopography* I, pp. 126-7. See also F.-L. Ganshof, 'Saint Martin et le Comte Avitianus', *AB* 67 (1949), pp. 203-23.

[63] *VM* 19, 3; cf. Paulinus *ep.* 18, 9 (*CSEL* 29, p. 136).

[64] *D* III, 2, 3-8. *D* III, 8, 4-7.

The significance of these names of Gallic personages is that they provide us with a specific context for Martin's work, both in time and space; and as this context would have been the same as that of Sulpicius' readers within Gaul, it could not have been invented to add historical verisimilitude to his writings. This confirms the point made earlier, that Sulpicius was primarily interested in a historical person; and that although he strove to present Martin in as glorificatory terms as possible, he—like his readers—was so close to the man and the events he was depicting that he was unable to stray away altogether from what actually happened.

23

Martin's Campaign against Paganism

Martin's onslaught against pagan shrines, and paganism in general, is not systematically described by Sulpicius. Rather, it crops up in the course of his narrative for just the same reasons as most of his other activities: because of associated miracle stories. However, by culling all Sulpicius' relevant stories, and supplementing these with information derived from Gregory of Tours and a few gleanings from archaeology, we can piece together a fair picture of Martin's achievements in this sphere. And the interest of doing so is that for this aspect of Martin's work, to an unparalleled degree, literary evidence from elsewhere and archaeological evidence from Gaul itself is sufficiently plentiful to provide us with a context for Martin's activities; and this, in turn, enables us to assess the plausibility of what Sulpicius tells us.

Let us start with Sulpicius' account. In general terms, Sulpicius tells us that Martin usually preached to the pagans so successfully that they demolished their temples themselves; and that wherever he had destroyed pagan sanctuaries, he built either a church or a monastery, so that there was no place devoid of them.[1] The only time he actually shows us Martin preaching to the pagans with such effect is near a village *en route* for Chartres, where the villagers crowded round because they had heard reports of Martin's greatness. Rising to the occasion, Martin preached in an inspired manner, and then crowned all by resuscitating a dead child. It was at this point, when the miracle had proved that Martin was indeed a 'friend of God', that the villagers all desired to become Christians.[2]

[1] *VM* 15, 4; 13, 9.
[2] *D* II, 4. Was this populous *vicus* near the road to Chartres, Saunay? Saunay

But things did not always go so smoothly. In one village he succeeded in destroying the temple, but met with serious opposition when he attempted to cut down a sacred tree. At Levroux, in the diocese of Bourges, he was repulsed by angry pagans and had to retreat for three days until help came in the form of two armed 'angels', who guarded him while he razed the temple and smashed the idols and altars to dust. On both occasions the villagers are reported to have decided to adopt Martin's religion once he had emerged triumphant, and the old gods had shown their inability to look after their own cause.[3] Conversely, the continued existence of an impressive pagan monument at Amboise kept alive a feeling of pagan reverence in that locality.[4] Martin chid the parish priest for not destroying it; but the priest pointed out that 'such a massive structure could scarcely be demolished by a band of soldiers or by the strength of a state labour force'; it was certainly beyond the powers of weakling clergy or monks. Martin solved the problem through prayer, which brought a storm to smash the idol. Elsewhere he resorted to fire as a means of destroying a pagan sanctuary.[5]

The general picture that emerges, then, is one of preaching, coupled with destruction of pagan temples and monuments. And although Martin is said usually to have persuaded his hearers to abandon the pagan gods by preaching alone, there are four specified cases where he met with fierce resistance. We might also note that Martin's missionary activity was not confined to his own diocese. Levroux lay within that of Bourges, and the convent of Clion, which Martin probably founded, looks as though it belonged there also, although Sulpicius claims that it lay on the boundary between Bourges and Tours.[6] What is more, we have a reference to

was one of the *vici* in which Martin founded a church (Gregory: see below, n. 16). It has yielded archaeological remains, including a Roman cemetery, while a Roman road is said to have passed through its territory: Boussard, *Carte*, no. 147 (p. 114), and cf. figures 1 and 2 in my article, 'From Town to Country: the Christianisation of the Touraine 370-600', *Studies in Church History* 16, ed. D. Baker (Oxford 1979), pp. 43-59.

[3] *VM* 13 and 14, 3-7.
[4] *D* III, 8, 4. Cf. *C. Th*. XVI, 10, 16.
[5] *D* III, 8, 5-7. *VM* 14, 1.
[6] *D* II, 8, 7.

Martin destroying a temple in a district of the Aedui, which lay even further away from Tours.[7]

Now, Martin's determined drive to root out paganism and to destroy all pagan monuments, despite fierce opposition, fits into a general pattern of what was going on elsewhere in the Roman Empire at the time. It is true that, magic apart, paganism seems to have been officially tolerated down to Theodosius' drastic laws of 391 and 392, and that even then the official line was still that temples should be preserved.[8] However, in many cases the zeal of individual Christians outstripped legal enactments. Our best evidence for comparing with Martin's activities is the role played by Cynegius, pretorian prefect of the east from 384 down to his death four years later. Although his official mission to Syria and Egypt was to prevent curials from escaping their obligations, he seems to have utilized his stay at Antioch in 385-6 as an occasion for overthrowing pagan sanctuaries by means of bands of monks.[9]

We are well informed on his activities thanks to Libanius' complaint, the *Pro templis*, which he addressed to the Emperor Theodosius. Libanius continually emphasizes that the pagans have kept within the law, and it is those who have demolished shrines who have outraged the law—and with impunity.[10] He makes it quite clear that the destroyers

---

[7] *VM* 15, 1. The old *civitas Aeduorem* was partitioned between three bishoprics: that of Autun, and of the two *castra*, Chalon and Mâcon (Babut, *St. Martin* p. 220, n. 1). There was certainly a bishop of Chalon by 346; the earliest bishop of Mâcon who is reliably attested *floruit c.*540, but the see may well be older: see Duchesne, *Fastes épiscopaux* I, pp. 9, 30; II, pp. 192, 196-7.

[8] *C.Th.* XVI, 10, 10-12; see F. Martroye 'La Répression de la magie et le culte des gentils au IVe siècle', *Revue historique de droit français et étranger* 9 (1930), pp. 669-701. Temples to be preserved: e.g. *C.Th.* XVI, 10, 15 (Spain and Gaul, 399). However, this same year imperial officials demolished temples in Carthage, and *C.Th.* XVI, 10, 16 issued in the east allowed the demolition of country temples. See now G. Fowden, 'Bishops and Temples in the Eastern Roman Empire A.D. 320-435', *JTS* n.s. 29 (1978), pp. 54-5, 65.

[9] See P. Petit, 'Sur la date du "Pro Templis" de Libanius',*Byzantion* 21 (1951), esp. pp. 298-304. Matthews, *Western Aristocracies*, pp. 140-2. Jones, *LRE* I, p. 167. Fowden, pp. 62-4 and cf. pp. 58-61 for earlier (illegal) destruction of temples under Constantius.

[10] *Pro templis* §§ 8, 15-20, 24, 50-1. (Text, *Libanii opera* III, ed. R. Foerster, Leipzig 1906; French tr. with notes by R. Van Loy, 'Le "Pro Templis" de Libanius', *Byzantion* 8 (1933), pp. 7-39, 389-404.)

were primarily monks, although he also mentions the use of soldiers for these ends.[11] The latter occasion probably refers to the destruction of a large temple of Jupiter undertaken by Marcellus, bishop of Apamea, which Theodoret describes in detail. Here, the massive solidity of the temple defeated even the troops, and it was only after a demon had been miraculously expelled that it was finally destroyed by fire.[12] All this is very similar to what Sulpicius tells us of Martin: the role played by monks, the resort to fire, and perhaps to soldiers, and the problems caused by the solidity of some pagan edifices. Also, both in Syria and Gaul, the setting is predominantly rural: it is the religion of the pagan peasants that is being attacked.

Libanius, pleading the cause of paganism, portrays the pagans as essentially peaceful, and accuses the Christians of killing those who resist them. But in many places the outraged pagans had no qualms about attacking their Christian assailants. When the Christians in Colonia Sufetana (Byzacena, North Africa) overthrew a statue of Hercules, the angry pagans killed sixty Christians in reprisal and demanded a new statue.[13] Even more relevant for a comparison with Martin's missionary work is the fate of the three clerics martyred in the Alps in 397. These men had settled in an area where Christians were unheard of; instead they saw the local pagans 'polluting' the area with their lustration ceremonies. Thinking that to do nothing was tantamount to connivance, the Christians built a church at their own expense and tried to convert the pagans through argument—with disastrous results. 'These, inebriated more with fury than wth wine, seized them, and cut them down with most cruel slaughter . . .' To complete their work they tore down the church and out of its beams made a great pyre on which they burnt the Christians.[14]

---

[11] Monks: § 8, § 46. Soldiers: § 43.

[12] Theodoret *H.E.* V, 21 (*PG* 82, cols. 1244–5). On the identification of the incident described by Theodoret and that described by Libanius, see Petit, pp. 301–2. Cf. also Fowden, pp. 64–7.

[13] Van der Meer, *Augustine*, pp. 39–40.

[14] Maximus of Turin, *serm.* 105, 2 and cf. 106, 1 (*CCSL* 23, pp. 414–15, 417). Cf. Martin mistaking a pagan funeral for a lustration ceremony, *VM* 12, 2. I owe my knowledge of this event to Hood, 'Sulpicius Severus', p. 7.

For Gaul, almost our only literary account of the fourth-century warfare against paganism apart from Sulpicius' writings is a short passage in a letter of Paulinus of Nola to Victricius of Rouen. Here, Paulinus praises Victricius for establishing holy choirs in churches and monasteries in the cities, towns, and islands of his diocese of Rouen, which were hitherto outside the pale of civilization. Paulinus congratulates Victricius; but he also lets slip that *such things have been happening throughout Gaul.*[15] Further light is shed by Gregory of Tours' report, and by archaeological discoveries. Luckily for us, Gregory lists all the *vicus* churches founded by his predecessors in the diocese of Tours. Martin was the first bishop of Tours to tackle the question of village churches in the diocese, founding them at Langeais, Saunay, Amboise, Ciran-la-Latte, Tournon, and Candes.[16] But Martin's example was followed by all his successors for the next hundred years, thus indicating that Martin was not unique in his attempts to christianize the country areas of his diocese.

Archaeology has as yet produced little of value from the Touraine itself: a stele depicting a bearded god between two goddesses (?) is said to have come from Langeais, while extensive Roman remains have been found at Candes, which may come from a temple.[17] These two, then, may be sites of pagan monuments destroyed by Martin, which were then replaced with churches. Amboise, as we have already seen, had a sizeable pagan monument. Further, Sulpicius tells us that the monks there lived in a *castello veteri*, and a vast circular camp has been noted with its eastern rampart still preserved.[18]

Archaeological evidence from outside the Touraine does more to corroborate Sulpicius' account. He describes Martin as destroying an 'extremely rich' temple at Levroux (Leprosum),

---

[15] Paulinus, *ep.* 18, 4 (*CSEL* 29, p. 131).

[16] 'In vicis quoque, id est Alingaviensi, Solonacensi, Ambaciensi, Cisomagensi, Tornomagensi, Condatensi ... ecclesias aedificavit.' *Hist.* X, 31, iii, accepting the identifications of the *MGH* editors, who in turn follow A. Longnon, *Géographie de la Gaule au VIe siècle* (Paris, 1878). See also Stancliffe, 'Christianisation of the Touraine', with maps.

[17] Langeais stele: É. Espérandieu, *Recueil général des bas-reliefs, statues et bustes de la Gaule romaine* (15 vols., Paris 1907–66) IV, no. 2988, p. 122. Boussard, *Carte* no. 84 (Langeais) and no. 70 (Candes).

[18] *D* III, 8, 4; Boussard, Carte, no. 112.

a Roman site which has yielded an inscription to Mars Cososus, and a theatre, a building which was often associated with a temple.[19]

Sulpicius also places one of Martin's missionary endeavours in the *pagus Aeduorum*, and here various pagan cult centres have been found which come to an abrupt end in the later fourth century.[20] The sanctuary at the source of the Seine was destroyed during the reign of Magnus Maximus, 383–8. Here, some 120 *ex voto* bronzes and many coins, the latest of which belonged to Maximus' reign, had been collected in a large vase in response to some danger, while statues of the gods had been smashed.[21] Another Aeduan sanctuary which was destroyed during the period covered by Martin's episcopate is that of Mont-Martre, near Avallon. On this site there was a square temple of the normal Celtic kind, with the addition of a large terrace before the entrance. Here again the statues had been deliberately smashed, and the coin series ends with Valentinian I (emperor 364–75), suggesting destruction around that time.[22]

A third case is that of Mont Beuvray in the Morvan, the old pagan centre of Bibracte. Here, popular tradition attributed the destruction of a pagan temple to Martin before ever a temple was discovered. On the top of the hill stood a chapel dedicated to St. Martin, and it was only in the course of excavating this chapel, then in ruins, that a pagan temple was discovered underneath. Its coins stopped short at Valentinian I, and there were obvious signs that the temple had been destroyed by fire. Legend attributes its destruction to Martin himself, who would only have escaped popular vengeance by a prodigious leap on the part of the donkey he was fleeing on.[23]

---

[19] *VM* 14, 3; *CIL* XIII, i, 1353; Fontaine, *Vie* II, 778–80.

[20] *VM* 15, 1. Matthews, *Western Aristocracies*, pp. 157–9, cites the same examples as I do. On the dioceses involved, see above, n. 7.

[21] A. Grenier, *Manuel d'archéologie gallo-romaine* (4 vols., Paris 1931–60): IV, *Les Monuments des eaux*, pp. 608–39, esp. pp. 612–13, 635–9.

[22] Grenier, IV, pp. 709–10.

[23] J.-G. Bulliot & F. Thiollier, *La Mission et le culte de Saint Martin d'après les légendes et les monuments populaires dans le pays éduen* (Autun & Paris 1892) pp. 385–90. There is a helpful large-scale map of the *pays éduen* at the front of the book.

Legend was also at work on stories of Martin's role in overthrowing paganism in Autun itself. By the twelfth century the pagan attack on St. Martin which Sulpicius reports as taking place *in pago Aeduorum* had been localized to the capital city,[24] and up to 1750 it was apparently still possible to see the remnants of a pagan temple which had been modified to form a Christian church. Local monastic tradition attributed this original Christian foundation to Martin, who was said to have built this as an oratory to SS. Peter and Paul; in 602 Queen Brunechildis would have only changed the dedication, attributing this to Martin himself.[25]

In these cases from the ancient *civitas Aeduorum* it is impossible to know whether the Martinian tradition is a genuine one going back to the saint's lifetime, or whether Sulpicius' account has given rise to the identification of the Christian responsible for destroying these temples with Martin. However, that there is some truth in the connection which Sulpicius postulates between Martin and the *civitas Aeduorum* is suggested by the fact that already in the later fifth century, bishop Euphronius of Autun donated some marble for St. Martin's grave at Tours.[26] This means that the link between Autun and St. Martin was already a century old before Brunechildis' veneration for St. Martin led to her munificent patronage in that city of the Merovingian patron saint.

In any case, whether or not we attribute a historical foundation to the Aedui-Martin link, the picture of a bishop in the last thirty years of the fourth century going about destroying pagan temples is corroborated by the archaeology of Gaul as a whole. Some temples were destroyed during the devastating barbarian invasions of the third century; but many were then restored, and the coins found show that these temples often continued to be frequented up to the last quarter of the fourth century. Grenier gives a table of

[24] The story was apparently told in a twelfth-century MS which was hung in the choir of St. Martin's church, Autun; Bulliot & Thiollier, p. 228.

[25] Ibid. pp. 230–1; but see now Prinz, p. 33.

[26] Gregory, *Hist.* II, 15; Prinz, p. 33, n. 81. Part of this carved marble survives, in all likelihood: see M. Vieillard-Troiekouroff, *Les Monuments religieux de la Gaule d'après les œuvres de Grégoire de Tours* (Paris 1976), p. 318 and fig. 65. NB also the popularity of St. Martin's cult in Aeduan territory, to which Bulliot & Thiollier have drawn attention.

the latest coins found in temples in Normandy, which illustrates when the temples fell out of use. Out of the eleven datable cases, there are four from the period 258-73; three from 306-40; and four from 364-88.[27] There are none later than Maximus. This seems to be the general pattern.

Thus, supernatural intervention apart, Sulpicius' portrayal of Martin's warfare against pagan cult sites is very likely. There are indeed two queries which could be raised: how was it possible to achieve all this against the law? And what was Martin doing, destroying temples in the dioceses of Bourges and Autun? Part of the answer may well lie in Martin's friendly relations with the officials and the aristocracy of Gaul. As we have seen, Martin was frequently approached by nobles, not just by peasants: alongside the story of how Martin converted a whole village by preaching and then resuscitating a child, we may place that of how he converted a senator in Trier by expelling a demon from his slave.[28] Friendly support from such upper-class sympathizers contributed in a number of ways to the promotion of Christianity. For one thing, the line between private wishes and official jurisdiction was often blurred, so that if an official were to utilize his public position to further his personal religious commitment, he would probably be able to get his way: witness Cynegius, and also the succession of prefects at Rome.[29] If, then, Martin was on friendly terms with the local officials, and these were Christians, they could be relied upon to turn a blind eye to any infringement of the law on Martin's part, and they may even have provided him with an armed guard on occasion.[30]

[27] Grenier IV, p. 741. For his general conclusions, see p. 950.

[28] Above, n. 2. *VM* 17, 1-4. Taetradius may have founded a church as a result: see K. Böhner, *Die fränkischen Altertümer des Trierer Landes* (2 vols., Berlin 1958), I, pp. 286-8, II, pp. 155-6.

[29] E.g. Gracchus was publicly baptized with the *insignia* of his office while he was prefect of Rome; he also ordered temple statues of the gods to be broken and the closure of a shrine of Mithras: A. Chastagnol, *La Préfecture urbaine à Rome sous le Bas-Empire* (Paris 1960) p. 157. Matthews, *Western Aristocracies*, pp. 22-30, 76-87, 139-45, 159-60, and *passim*. Cf. also J. Percival, 'Seigneurial Aspects of Late Roman estate management', *English Historical Review* 84 (1969), at pp. 470-2.

[30] See *VM* 14, 5 and above, ch. 14, n. 64. Cf. also the reference to *militari manu et vi publicae multitudinis* in *D* III, 8, 6, and Babut, *St. Martin*, pp. 212-17.

Equally important was the role such noblemen could play in the conversion of the peasants on their own country estates. Some villas contained pagan sanctuaries where landowner and *coloni* might come together for religious observances.[31] It made a crucial difference if such pagan sanctuaries were destroyed, and replaced by an estate church; or, alternatively, if the landowner chose to turn a blind eye to the continuance of pagan practices amongst his *coloni*.[32] Now, if a friendly landowner chose to call in the bishop of Tours to christianize his estate, this would have been his concern, not the local bishop's.[33]

However, this can hardly apply to any of the cases described by Sulpicius, because four of the temples (including Levroux) are specified as being in *vici*, not on private estates, while in the remaining two (as well as in some of the *vici* cases) armed resistance to Martin is mentioned.[34] This would seem to rule out a villa setting, as we would expect the estate-owner there to keep his peasantry under control, and not allow them to threaten Martin's life. So in the cases described by Sulpicius it is probably more important to recall that the country areas of Gaul, at least outside Provence, were missionary territory at this time. In this missionary phase, church organization in the countryside would have been non-existent, or at most rudimentary, and so somewhat fluid. Diocesan boundaries, though well known in that they followed the *civitas* boundaries, had not yet hardened into

Soldiers were sometimes used in the east: loc. cit. and above, notes 11 and 12. In general see Fowden, art. cit., who makes the additional point that while officials came and went, the bishop stayed put, so gaining *de facto* influence and power (pp. 57–8).

[31] E.g. Montmaurin (Haute-Garonne): Grenier IV, pp. 544–9 (latest coin is of Magnus Maximus).

[32] The crucial role played by landowners is recognized in a law of 412 (*C. Th.* XVI, 5, 52, 4), which entrusts African landowners with the task of stamping out Donatism amongst their *coloni*; and in the sermons of Maximus of Turin (*serm.* 106 and 107, *CCSL* 23, pp. 417 ff., 420). Cf. in general F. J. Dölger, 'Christliche Grundbesitzer und heidnische Landarbeiter', in Dölger's *Antike und Christentum* (6 vols., Münster in Westfalen, 1929–50), vol. VI, part 4, pp. 297–320.

[33] Babut, *St. Martin*, p. 217, n. 2; p. 221.

[34] *Vici* temples: *VM* 13, 1; 14, 1; 14, 3 (Levroux); *D* III, 8, 4 (Amboise). Armed resistance occurred possibly in the first and certainly in the third instance, as also in those in *VM* 15 (*Aedui*). This leaves only *D* III, 9, 1–2, which I am inclined to regard as a doublet of the Amboise episode.

quite the recognized dividing lines they were soon to become
—or so we might assume from the conciliar and papal exhor-
tations that they should be recognized.[35] In these circumstances Martin's activities in other dioceses become more
understandable.

Further, at least some of Martin's denunciations of paganism may have arisen as casually as that described in *Dialogue*
II, 4, where the crowd of pagans spontaneously flocked
towards Martin, then *en route* for Chartres. Their request to
him to resuscitate a woman's only son provided him with a
challenge to vindicate Christianity, a challenge which he
could hardly have refused. Martin certainly did travel a
considerable amount: north to Chartres, Paris, and Trier;
south, probably, to a synod in Bordeaux;[36] and south-east
to Vienne, where Paulinus remembered meeting him in the
company of Victricius of Rouen.[37] This last journey could
easily have taken him through Aedui country, and his attack
on an Aeduan temple might have been a spontaneous by-
product.

There are, then, no insuperable problems about Sulpicius'
presentation of Martin's onslaught on Gallic paganism.
Indeed, some details add further verisimilitude. One is the
fact that Martin was apparently able to destroy a temple in
one village, but met with bitter opposition when he tried to
cut down a pine-tree sacred to a god ('daemoni dedicata').[38]
Sacred trees are a common feature of Celtic religion, whereas

[35] Council of Turin, can. 1-3 (*CCSL* 148, pp. 54-7). Babut *St. Martin*, p. 221
and n. 4, though cf. also p. 220. Gaudemet, *L'Église*, pp. 323-8. Did the division
of the *civitas* of Autun between two or three bishoprics (above, n. 7) foster
uncertainty over diocesan boundaries in Aeduan territory?

[36] Above, ch. 20, n. 6. On this journey Martin may have participated at the
funeral of a presbyter Romanus at Blaye, on the estuary of the Gironde (Gregory
of Tours, *In gl. confess.* 45, citing a written life of Romanus): see Jullian, *Histoire*
VII, p. 269, n. 3. It is impossible to know whether Martin really visited the other
places named by Gregory, Sireuil near Angoulême, Nieul-les-Saintes (*De virt. S.
Mart.* I, 18 & IV, 31), and Artonne in the Auvergne (*In gl. confess.* 5).

[37] *Ep.* 18, 9. It was presumably also at Vienne that Martin baptized Foedula:
below, ch. 24, n. 60.

[38] *VM* 13, 1-2. On sacred trees amongst the Celts see Powell, *Celts*, pp. 136-7;
J. Zwicker, *Fontes historiae religionis celticae* (pt. I Berlin 1934, pt. II Bonn
1935), *index rerum* under 'arbor'; C. Plummer, *Vitae Sanctorum Hiberniae*
(2 vols., Oxford repr. 1968), I, pp. clii-clv; J. Vendryes, *La Religion des Celtes*
(*Les Religions de l'Europe ancienne* III, pt. 2, Paris 1948), pp. 280-1.

the erection of temple buildings is secondary, stemming from Roman influence. As the prohibitions of church councils were to show, local reverence for such natural features as trees, wells, and stones proved more tenacious than the trappings of pagan cult introduced by the Romans.

Another interesting link between Sulpicius' account and Gallo-Roman paganism should probably be seen in Sulpicius' description of a 'column of massive bulk, crowned by an idol', which Jullian identified as a Jupiter column.[39] Such columns are a speciality of Roman Gaul. The figure on the top is typically a horseman, identified with Taranis-Jupiter, whose horse rests its front legs on a giant with a serpent's tail.[40] Carved quadrilateral and octagonal blocks such as usually composed the lower half of these monuments have been found within the Touraine at Yzeures, on the Creuse.[41]

Owing to the scarcity of archeological finds in the form of temples and dedications in the Touraine,[42] there is little evidence on which to base reflection and comment upon Sulpicius' list of the pagan deities most often encountered by Martin: Mercury ('maxime infestus'), Jupiter ('brutus adque hebes') Minerva, and Venus.[43] However, it is perhaps worth pointing out that this list could scarcely have come out of Sulpicius' library. Caesar had mentioned the first three divinities, together with Apollo and Mars; but prior to Sulpicius I can find no literary references within Gaul to

---

[39] *D* III, 9, 1; Jullian 'Notes gallo-romaines', *REA* 24 (1922), p. 125 n. 3. Cf. also the description in *D* III, 8, 4-5 (perhaps of the same monument: above, n. 34, and cf. ch. 12, n. 26).

[40] Hence their designation as 'Jupiter columns' or 'les colonnes du cavalier au géant anguipède'; Powell, *Celts*, p. 136; P. Lambrechts, *Contributions à l'étude des divinités celtiques* (Bruges 1942), ch. 5 and distribution map vii.

[41] Espérandieu, IV, 2997-9. The octagonal block, perhaps depicting the divinities of the seven days of the week (E's suggestion—the figures themselves are hard to decipher), is typical of these monuments (Lambrechts, p. 83).

[42] The tower of Cinq-Mars may well not be a religious monument (Boussard, *Carte*, no. 86, with photographs). From near Suèvres we have a pair of inscriptions to Apollo (*CIL* XIII, 3073-4). At Yzeures remains of pagan monument(s) were used as the foundation for a Christian church, presumably built by bishop Eustochius (*c*.444-61; Gregory, *Hist.* X, 31, v); an inscription was found there to 'Numinibus augustorum at deae Minervae' (*CIL* XIII, i, 3075). Deities represented on the carvings from Yzeures include Minerva, Jupiter, Mars, Vulcan, Apollo, and perhaps also Venus, Saturn, Mercury (Espérandieu 2997-9); from Archevêché we have carvings including one of Diana (Espérandieu 2991).

[43] *VM* 22, 1; *D* II, 13, 6; *D* III, 6, 4.

Venus.[44] However, her appearance here is plausible enough: while in the first and second centuries AD the Roman goddesses most often depicted were Minerva and Juno, later Venus seems to have taken over from the latter;[45] and the three goddesses who recur most often in the literary sources from the fifth century onwards are Minerva, Venus, and Diana.[46] All these goddesses became assimilated to the Celtic mother-goddesses, which probably explains their popularity.[47] Martin's experience therefore fits well with what we know of fourth-century Gallic paganism.

We can therefore leave Sulpicius' account of Martin's warfare against paganism with the general verdict that, miracles apart, it is much what our literary and archaeological evidence would lead us to expect. What is important is that there is now a sufficient body of other evidence for us to be able to evaluate Sulpicius' account by it, rather than *vice versa*; and, while we cannot locate every individual incident which Sulpicius describes, we can accept the six parishes named by Gregory of Tours as authentic, together with the destruction of the temple at Levroux, not far beyond the boundaries of the diocese of Tours, and some missionary work in the *pagus Aeduorum*. In all this we may agree with Babut that Sulpicius can mislead not by telling us about deeds wrought by Martin which in fact Martin never did,

---

[44] *De bello gallico* VI, 17, 1-2; NB that Caesar agrees with Sulpicius about Mercury's primary role: 'Deum maxime Mercurium colunt'. For Venus, I base myself on the references in the index of Zwicker, *Fontes*. There are also astonishingly few references to Venus in the index of *CIL* XIII, pt. 5.

[45] On a sculpted stele from Dijon (approx. *s.* I *med.* AD), Juno fills the role of goddess with torch and serpents, thus taking the place of the indigenous earth goddess who appeared on the stele of Mavilly (41/54 AD); but on a stele dating from about a hundred years later, found in the church of St. Landry, Paris, it is Venus who is carrying the torch and Juno does not appear; J.-J. Hatt, 'Essai sur l'évolution de la religion gauloise', *REA* 67 (1965), pp. 80-125, esp. pp. 111, 112, and 115. As for relevant finds near Tours: a fragmentary Venus has been found at Orléans (Espérandieu, IV, 2972); she is probably also represented on the damaged octagonal stone from Yzeures (above notes 41-2); and it is possible that the head of a young girl found at Bazoches-les-Hautes (Loiret) should be interpreted as a Venus (Espérandieu IV, 2976). This is little enough to go on, but other deities fare no better in this area: there are no representations of Juno at all.

[46] Hatt, p. 118, confirmed by the index of Zwicker, *Fontes*.

[47] Grenier IV, pp. 940-1, 952-3; É. Thevenot, *Divinités et sanctuaires de la Gaule* (Paris 1968), pp. 178-84.

but simply by spotlighting Martin's achievements and remaining silent about those of other contemporary bishops, an emphasis which gave rise to the idea that Martin was the great evangelist of Gaul. As, doubtless, Sulpicius intended.[48]

[48] *D* III, 17, 6. Cf. Babut, *St. Martin* pp. 229-31—although Martin was in fact going *beyond* the law, not carrying out the law as Babut suggests.

24

Martin, Sulpicius' Martin,
and the Future

Sulpicius was concerned with portraying not the everyday Martin of flesh and blood, but the spiritual leader who inspired him; and in writing the *Life*, letters, and *Dialogues* about Martin there were other subsidiary motives present, particularly literary ambitions, and the desire to defend Martin and his way of life. All things considered, we should not expect strict historical accuracy from Sulpicius.

However, despite all that can be said against the historicity of the Martinian writings, there are two strong arguments in favour of our accepting Sulpicius' account as being based on a real personality, rather than seeing it as a stereotype composed purely for literary or apologetic reasons: first, because only in this way can we make adequate sense of Sulpicius himself; and secondly, because however questionable the stories told of Martin may appear at first sight, on closer examination we find that there are good reasons for accepting some of them, while in general they convey a picture which fits with our other evidence.

To start with Sulpicius: either we must accept his enthusiasm as having a genuine origin in Martin's personality, or we must find some means of explaining it away. Babut sought to do the latter by arguing that what Sulpicius was really concerned with was not Martin, but the fortunes of the small schismatic sect of Antifelicians to which he belonged; and that his adoption of Martin as hero was forced upon him by the absence of any alternative: it was not the result of deliberate choice. A more sophisticated approach would be to interpret Sulpicius as an advocate of the ascetic cause, who wrote brilliant ascetic propaganda, but who remained somewhat distant from the historical

Martin.[1] Either way Martin is simply regarded as a convenient peg on which Sulpicius chose to hang his own message. However, as we have seen, this interpretation is not consistent with the evidence. The *Vita Martini* was not written years *after* Sulpicius' conversion to asceticism—i.e. to promote a cause he had adopted some time previously. Rather, it is a product of 394-6, the very years which saw Sulpicius' conversion.[2] This being so, far from Sulpicius adopting the figure of Martin simply as a mould into which he could pour his own ideas, we must recognize that it was Martin who inspired him with many of his ideas, and, above all, who brought him to the point of putting the ascetic ideal into practice. This does not alter the fact that in the *Vita Martini* Sulpicius idealized Martin, selecting those facets he wished to portray and omitting others, thus distorting the general picture. However, it does mean that the ideal he was trying to portray was essentially the same as the ideal which Martin sought to follow in his own life. After all, had Sulpicius simply required a platform for his own ascetic views, there was no need for him to have adopted the controversial figure of Martin. A little-known eastern monk would have served his purpose adequately, as it did for Jerome.[3]

A different attempt at explaining away Sulpicius' apparent concern for Martin could be made. One might accept that Sulpicius was genuinely involved with the historical Martin, but discount the significance of this by regarding Sulpicius as something of a crank: an extremist, of an unstable temperament, whose enthusiasms had no general application. There is an element of truth in this, as in the other approach. Certainly Sulpicius was a man of strong likes and dislikes, and certainly he took a jaundiced view of the contemporary Gallic church. However, there is no evidence that he was unbalanced; and when we realize the situation in which he found himself, his apparent extremism becomes

---

[1] Cf. Rousseau, *Ascetics*, pp. 145–6, 148 (and see above, ch. 22); though I would not tax him with quite the rigid views I here put forward.

[2] Above, ch. 2, & ch. 7, i.

[3] One can dispose even more rapidly of the view that Sulpicius wrote primarily for literary reasons. Apart from the fact that a less controversial subject (e.g. a martyr) would have made a more straightforward hero, there would have been no need for Sulpicius to have adopted the ascetic life.

explicable.[4] Further, his attitudes and way of life do not show him to have been an isolated crank, or an insincere convert; rather, he fits perfectly with the international circle of ascetics mirrored in Paulinus of Nola's correspondence, a circle which included such figures as Augustine, Jerome, and Rufinus. There is, then, no good reason for dismissing the testimony of Sulpicius.

The second type of corroboratory evidence for Sulpicius' presentation of Martin is basically concerned with the circumstantial plausibility of the stories Sulpicius tells, and, as regards some of them, the unlikelihood that Sulpicius would have invented them. On these grounds, the bare skeleton of Martin's life stands intact. We can accept that Martin was born to pagan parents at Sabaria in Pannonia, and brought up at Pavia, where he probably encountered Christianity. And, because his father was a soldier, Martin was naturally drafted into the Roman army as a young man. We may further accept the story of Martin the soldier giving away half his cloak to a beggar and the subsequent dream which impelled him to seek baptism at the age of eighteen, while yet remaining in the army. For a monk-bishop, this past as a baptized soldier was far too awkward to have been invented by a favourable biographer. Again, we can accept Martin's release from the army in 356; his visit to his parents when he succeeded in converting his mother, but not his father; and a spell in Italy.

How much more of the early chapters of the *Vita Martini* can be relied upon is perhaps best left open. For those, like me, who incline towards 336 as the date for Martin's birth, the idea of Martin hearing and being attracted by reports of monasticism when he was a boy at Pavia is not implausible; and this, in its turn, makes Martin's experiments with the ascetic life in Italy and on Gallinara from 357–60 quite probable. As for Martin's relations with Hilary, I am inclined to accept that they met, albeit briefly, in 356; but there are obvious chronological difficulties involved, which should prevent us from treating this as an assured 'fact'.

However, we get back to firmer ground with Martin's foundation of Liguge, outside Poitiers, soon after Hilary's

---

[4] Above, ch. 4, iii; ch. 20, iii.

return from exile in 360. Here Martin lived as a monk for the next decade, attracting disciples; and it was here, also, that he acquired a reputation as a healer, a holy man whose prayers carried weight in the court of heaven. The stories of the two resuscitations that belong to this period are likely to be based on real happenings;[5] but we can in any case illustrate Martin's reputation as a healer at this time in the classic way, by citing a story whose main point is quite different, but which incidentally evinces widespread recognition of his healing powers. The story is that of Martin's election as bishop of Tours, despite his own reluctance. This was achieved by a citizen of Tours pretending that his wife was sick, and begging Martin to come and cure her.[6] The plan was simply a hoax to winkle Martin out of his monastery and into the town. There was no question of Martin being called upon to demonstrate his healing powers, and therefore no reason for Sulpicius to invent the tale.

Martin was to spend the rest of his life, from his election *c*.371 to his death in 397, as bishop of Tours; and this is the period to which the majority of Sulpicius' stories belong. Although a bishop, Martin remained a monk, at first using a little cell off the cathedral, and then founding the monastery of Marmoutier. Sulpicius knew this monastery at first hand since he visited Martin there. Probably his description of the monastic life there is reasonably accurate, as far as it goes, though it may mislead by being selective; his description of the site is obviously romanticized.[7]

As for Martin's other activities in these years, there can be little doubt that he did do the sort of things which Sulpicius portrays him doing, and the fact that these are so often described in terms of supernatural *virtus* should by now be readily understandable, following our detailed discussion in part III above. For instances of healing, we might single out as particularly well attested the case of the dumb girl cured at Chartres in the presence not only of Evagrius,

---

[5] For *VM* 7, see above, ch. 14, p. 200 and n. 83. For *VM* 8, the naming of the aristocrat Lupicinus is some guarantee: cf. above, ch. 22, n. 60.

[6] *VM* 9, 1.

[7] Cf. above, ch. 3: NB the employment of a peasant to haul timber (ibid. n. 18). On the site, see above, ch. 12, and notes 30–1.

but of the bishops Valentinus (of Chartres) and Victricius (of Rouen).[8] As regards exorcism of the possessed, this was one of the church's recognized tasks; and that Martin may have had special gifts in this direction is suggested by Sulpicius' statement that Hilary ordained him exorcist. In any case, the story involving so distinguished a man as Taetradius would not have been invented.[9] That Martin himself thought he saw and spoke with saints, angels, and devils, is, in my eyes, not open to doubt, although it is clear that some of Martin's own contemporaries had their doubts. Finally, Martin must have had a more general reputation as an *amicus Dei* than simply as a healer and an exorcist, for this alone would explain why the inhabitants of the area around Sens should have sought his help to protect their fields from hailstorms.[10] This was done through Auspicius, an ex-prefect; and the mention of names of the senatorial class, coupled with Sulpicius' forthright invitation for sceptics to ask men in the relevant area, rules out the possibility of literary invention.

Martin's other activities described by Sulpicius would have been normal amongst the bishops of his day. His practice of interceding with the emperor or his officials for prisoners and those condemned was but the normal exercise of episcopal *intercessio*; and even Martin's violent attacks on pagan temples, which were officially illegal and which were presented in such miraculous terms by Sulpicius, even these are only what we would expect from the evidence of literary sources from elsewhere and archaeology within Gaul, while Gregory of Tours' list of the parishes founded by Martin further confirms this aspect of his activities.

Thus, however many doubts we may have about individual stories, we must admit that Martin as bishop did do the sort of things which Sulpicius portrays him doing. Where Sulpicius surely misleads us is in his *omissions*, which are of two kinds: he implies that Martin was the only bishop in Gaul to perform such deeds; and he implies that Martin spent his whole time either living an ascetic life of prayer and austerity, or putting

---

[8] *D* III, 2, 3–8.
[9] *VM* 5, 2; 17, 1–4.
[10] *D* III, 7; cf. also *D* II, 4, §4 and §6.

his *virtus* to pastoral use. Either way, we see virtually nothing of the humdrum affairs of ordinary episcopal life, and there is no attempt to look at events from the point of view of those bishops who conscientiously discharged their responsibilities in this sphere.

It is probably Sulpicius' burning concern with Martin *qua* Martin which leads him to concentrate so exclusively on this figure, and to make his presentation of him all the more striking by portraying his greatness in isolation from other figures. That there were other good bishops within Gaul can be seen by Paulinus' praise of Victricius of Rouen and of eight other early fifth-century bishops.[11] Gregory of Tours also gives us a story about bishop Illidius of Clermont. His fame had reached even the emperor at Trier (presumably Maximus), and the latter had sent for him to come and cure his daughter who was possessed, a deed which Illidius accordingly performed.[12] However, although Griffe has put together a chapter section entitled 'some holy bishops', the material is sparse;[13] there is just enough to show that Martin was not wholly unique, but nothing to undermine Sulpicius' portrayal of the majority of the Gallic episcopate as being worldly-minded.

Sulpicius' omissions about Martin's own life are more interesting. The normal activities of a bishop fell into three categories: liturgical, administrative, and pastoral. Of these, there was no need for Sulpicius to describe the liturgical; this could be taken for granted. We know that Martin celebrated the mysteries, anointed the sick, and bestowed the veil on virgins,[14] and we can safely assume that he also performed the other sacraments and dedicated the churches which he had founded.

The administrative tasks of the episcopate require further consideration. The role of episcopal synods increased considerably during the fourth century when they were used both to define and condemn heresies, and to rectify weaknesses and abuses of practice. Sulpicius never tells us that

---

[11] Paulinus, *ep.* 18 (*CSEL* 29, pp. 128–37); and see above, ch. 20, iii, and n. 63.
[12] Gregory, *Vita Patrum* II, 1 (*MGH, SRM* I, ii, p. 219).
[13] *La Gaule chrétienne* I, bk. 2, ch. 7, §ii.
[14] *D* II, 1, 9-2, 1; III, 10, 6. *D* III, 2, 6. *VM* 19, 2.

Martin went to any synods, but this is perhaps implied for the first part of his episcopate by contrast with the period following Priscillian's death and Felix's consecration, after which 'he attended no synod'; we hear explicitly of his absence from the synod of Nîmes, though we should also note that Martin showed great interest in its decisions.[15] That Martin had been present at the synod of Bordeaux, convened in 384 to hear the cases of Priscillian and Instantius, is implicit in Hydatius' statement that Priscillian had been judged a heretic 'in the same way by St. Martin the bishop and by other bishops'.[16]

Synods met only occasionally. Far more of a bishop's time might be taken up with looking after ecclesiastical property, for which he held all responsibility. The see of Tours is unlikely to have been rich at this period, but already churches were starting to accumulate the vast properties they later enjoyed, and a corresponding amount of attention was needed to administer them. Presumably all such matters were part of the business affairs which Martin delegated to his clergy, along with the practicalities of administering the church's alms to the poor, as we can see from the (second) story of a pauper who asked for clothing: Martin ordered his archdeacon to see to the beggar, and then entered his own private *secretarium* to be alone, as was usual for him. 'For he used to retain this solitude for himself even at church, while the clergy were left free. Indeed, at a time when the presbyters were sitting in another sacristy, either with leisure for the exchange of greetings, or taken up with attending to affairs (*audiendis negotiis*), Martin . . . maintained his solitude.'[17] Babut assumed that the bishop's role as judge for those cases which were brought before the episcopal court was included in the delegated *negotia*, and he was probably right.[18] Certainly Augustine was exasperated at the

---

[15] *D* III, 13, 6; II, 13, 8.
[16] *Chron. s.a.* 385 (*MGH, AA* XI, p. 15).
[17] *D* II, 1, 2.
[18] *St. Martin*, p. 120. 'Negotia' is used in this specifically juridical sense in a letter of 3 Gallic bishops of *c*.453 AD (*CCSL* 148, p. 136), while from the other end of the empire we have evidence from Alexandria Troas that such cases were delegated to clerics, or even laymen (Jones, *LRE* I, p. 480).

amount of time taken up in this way; and, although the citizens of Tours may have been less litigious than the Africans, such matters could scarcely have been to the taste of Martin who moved two miles out of Tours for his monastery because 'he could not bear the disturbance of people visiting him'.[19]

However, it is also worth bearing in mind Sulpicius' apologetic motives in this context. To say that 'the lives of these men [Ambrose, Augustine, Martin] displayed little of the tension and frustration' implicit in their attempt to live as monk-bishops[20] is perhaps to miss the point. Sulpicius, as we have seen, was very sensitive to Jerome's remarks; and Jerome had pointed to the contradiction of living as a monk within the world, where contempt and rudeness led on to vexation, and this in turn tended to divert the monk from his commitment.[21]

Sulpicius himself was fully aware of such assumptions. In his first *Dialogue* he reported the opinion of an Egyptian holy man that 'he who is frequented by men cannot be frequented by angels', and later on he explicitly pointed to the contrast with Martin: while the Egyptian hermits had been free from all hindrances, Martin, 'in the midst of crowds and in the company of people, amongst squabbling clergy and enraged bishops, under pressure of almost daily scandals from this side and that, yet stood firm against everything in the invincible strength of his *virtus*, and accomplished such great deeds . . . '[22] Some of these 'scandals', such as the events concerned with Priscillian's execution, were too well known to be glossed over altogether; here, Sulpicius' narration of the story shows that there were considerable tensions and frustrations involved. This indicates why Sulpicius would have tried to avoid portraying Martin enmeshed in the toils of a bishop's cares; in fact, he may not have escaped them as completely as Sulpicius' narrative implies.

Sulpicius' portrayal of Martin may, therefore, need modification; Martin may have been more involved in the everyday

---

[19] Brown, *Augustine*, pp. 195-6. *VM* 10, 3.
[20] Rousseau, 'Spiritual Authority', p. 407.
[21] *Ep.* 14, 7, 2 (*CSEL* 54 p. 54); cf. above, ch. 21, notes 13 & 14.
[22] *D* I, 17, 5 (cf. above, ch. 18, n. 47). *D* I, 24, 3.

cares of the world than his biographer let on. Further, even as regards Martin's pastoral activities, which are what Sulpicius concentrated on, we are given a very selective picture. As bishop, Martin had general pastoral responsibility for all in his diocese; and this to a far greater extent than a bishop today, for the first moves towards establishing a parochial system in the Tours diocese were taken only by Martin himself. In addition, Martin had particular responsibility for the clergy, both at Tours and elsewhere in the diocese, while he also stood as father to the monks gathered round him at Marmoutier. But Sulpicius' coverage is patchy. He devotes a section of the *Vita* to Martin's onslaught on false religion, including his unmasking of a false martyr's shrine, and his physical assaults on pagan temples. However, it is only *en passant* that we see Martin visiting the churches he had founded, settling church squabbles, egging on the parish priests,[23] while we have to turn to Gregory of Tours to learn the names of the country parishes which Martin founded. What Sulpicius concentrates on is largely Martin's concern for the poor, the sick, and the oppressed, and his readiness both to help them himself and to intervene with the secular powers on their behalf.

It is also interesting to realize that Sulpicius does not give full coverage even to Martin's promotion of monasticism. He mentions Ligugé (although it is not named—its monks may have transferred to Marmoutier when Martin moved there), and there is a whole chapter on Marmoutier itself. But, apart from this, he talks only vaguely of Martin establishing churches or monasteries wherever he destroyed a pagan temple. It is left for us to surmise that the convent of Clion, in which he stayed one night, was founded by him; and to piece together, from a number of stray references, the important role which Martin played as teacher and guide to his monks.[24]

What sort of a picture of Martin can we extract from Sulpicius, reading between the lines where appropriate?

---

[23] *D* II, 3, 1; II, 9, 6; *ep.* 3, 6; *D* III, 8, 5-7.
[24] *VM* 13, 9. Clion: *D* II, 8, 7-8. Reference to a convent, *D* II, 11, 1. Martin as a monastic guide and teacher: *VM* 23, 9-10; 25, 4-5. *Ep.* 3, 7. *D* II, 10 & 11. *D* III, 15, 6.

One striking feature is the way in which Martin stood outside the normal ties of society. By birth he was a foreigner; he had contracted no ties in his adopted province through marriage, and his avoidance of female company would have further isolated him from ordinary Gallo-Romans. Because of his lack of formal education he would have been regarded as an outsider by the upper class, amongst whom a common cultural tradition formed a bond transcending a man's geographical or social origins. It is also interesting to note that the inhabitants of Tours and miracles worked at Tours seldom crop up in Sulpicius' narrative. Instead, the people with whom Martin appears to have associated are the country peasants whom he sought to convert from paganism, several important personages from the senatorial aristocracy and the imperial family itself, and, most frequently of all, the monks of Marmoutier. Martin's deliberate eschewal of the conventions of polite society probably contributed to the respect in which he was held by the upper classes, and perhaps to the impact which he made upon the country peasants; they would have recognized a genuine holy man in him.[25]

However, despite Martin's remoteness from everyday society, he did not live in isolation; rather, he created an alternative society, knit together by the close bonds of the communal life. Martin's commitment to monasticism was fundamental: although Sulpicius focused the spotlight on Martin, we are continually made aware that Martin was not alone, but accompanied by monks. Even on Gallinara he had a priest with him, and he never again attempted to live at any great remove from others: Ligugé was close to Poitiers, and so to Hilary; and from then onwards, Martin drew disciples around him.

Martin clearly did more to foster communities of monks and of nuns in his diocese than Sulpicius explicitly says; but the long-term contribution of Martin to the development of monasticism in Gaul is hard to assess. Indirectly, of course, his influence has been incalculable; for he did much to convert Sulpicius, and, in his writings, Sulpicius has preserved

---

[25] Upper classes: *VM* 20, 7; Sidonius Apollinaris *Epistulae* bk. VIII, no. 3, §5 (ed. P. Mohr, Leipzig 1895, p. 175). Peasants: see *D* II, 4, 4-9. For a possible parallel see M. Douglas, *Natural Symbols* (London 1970), pp. 69-70.

Martin's own exemplary monastic life for all time. But there will have been a direct influence as well. Marmoutier served as a nursery for future bishops, and we can name at least one of these: Heros, bishop of Arles.[26] In a very interesting discussion Professor Fontaine has recently pointed out that Heros might possibly have served as an intermediary between the monasticism of Martin and that of Provence, thinking especially of Cassian, writing in the monastery of St. Victor at Marseilles, and of the famous monastery of Lérins.[27] Was there direct continuity of Martinian monasticism at Ligugé or in the Touraine? For Ligugé, this seems doubtful, as the archaeological evidence suggests that this site was occupied by pagans in the fifth century.[28] Even with Marmoutier, it is difficult to be sure of continuity of monastic life there, although it was certainly a popular pilgrimage spot by the mid-fifth century.[29] One is tempted to blame all on the barbarian invasions of 407-8; but the temptation should probably be resisted. What we can say with some assurance is that by the sixth century, monasticism was flourishing in the Touraine; and it may be that Martin was at least indirectly, and partially, responsible, with his fame attracting people to the religious life in the area.[30] For the question of direct continuity, we must await the results of the current excavations at Marmoutier.

Another aspect of Martin's marginal position in Gallo-Roman society is his identification with other outsiders, as when he kissed a leper at Paris.[31] A most revealing incident is that when Martin was beaten up by some officials, who took Martin for a poor man, if not a tramp, and set about him with whips and sticks. They never guessed from his

[26] Lazarus, bishop of Aix, may be another. See above, ch. 20, ii, esp. n. 46.
[27] 'L'Ascétisme chrétien', pp. 105-13, esp. p. 107.
[28] Coquet, *L'Intérêt*, pp. 12-13; *Revue Mabillon* 44 (1954), pp. 83-9; ibid. 45 (1955), p. 112.
[29] Monastic continuity there is doubted by Babut, *St. Martin* p. 239, n. 2, and by Delehaye, 'S. Martin', p. 100. However, it is affirmed by Marmoutier's current excavator, C. Lelong: 'Études sur l'abbaye de Marmoutier', *Bulletin trimestriel de la Société Archéologique de Touraine* 39 (1980), p. 282. See also the thoughtful remarks of Fontaine, *Vie* I, p. 170.
[30] E.g. St. Leobard: Gregory of Tours, *Vita patrum* 20, 2 (*MGH, SRM* I, ii, p. 292).
[31] *VM* 18, 3.

appearance that he was a bishop, and Martin did not disabuse them.[32] His identification with the poor can be seen in another way in his willingness to share whatever he had with them, as in the famous story where he divided his cloak between himself and a naked beggar—unable to give away his whole cloak because he had already donated his other clothes to those in need; or in the other story where Martin gave his own tunic to a beggar, extracting it from beneath his outer garment.[33] In fastening upon the former story to illustrate the Christ-like qualities of Martin, tradition has for once picked upon a deed entirely typical of the man.

Martin's way of setting himself alongside others, rather than hiding behind his episcopal dignity, comes out in other ways, also. For instance, when a monk came to ask him whether he might resume living with his wife (while remaining faithful to his monastic profession), and was not immediately convinced by Martin's disapproval of the idea, Martin did not react by forbidding it outright or by losing his temper; instead, he used a concrete analogy to get the other man to see for himself that it was not a good idea.[34] At times, Martin's refusal to use his episcopal authority to dismiss any cleric for making personal attacks on him went against the better judgement of others, as in his toleration of Brice. However, he acted from the best intentions. It was not in him to write off any one as beyond redemption, however great and however persistent his sins. Indeed, as we have seen, he was even ready to promise the devil forgiveness, if only the latter would repent.[35]

However, while Martin refused to use his position to protect himself from abuse, he reacted quite differently when it was other people who were at risk. He spared no pains in going to seek out a governor in Tours in the middle of the night in order to plead for prisoners who were to suffer punishment, and he journeyed to the imperial court

---

[32] *D* II, 3, 2-4. NB also *D* II, 1, 3-4: Martin sat on a humble stool, not a grandiose throne.

[33] *VM* 3, 1-2. *D* II, 1.

[34] *D* II, 11. Cf. also Martin's compassionate treatment of the possessed: above, ch. 18, n. 17.

[35] Cf. *VM* 26, 5 and *D* III, 15, 6-7. *VM* 22, 3-5.

at Trier in order to intercede for other unfortunates.[36] The most striking case involved Priscillian and his supporters. Martin's pleas on their behalf placed him in some danger as a presumed Priscillianist sympathizer, while later on Martin had to make the hateful sacrifice of acting in communion with the bishops responsible for Priscillian's death, in order to save the lives of others—a move for which his conscience afterwards tormented him.[37]

This case is interesting as revealing the limits of Martin's influence with the emperor. In the *Vita*, Sulpicius had proudly asserted that Martin was alone among the bishops in retaining his 'apostolic authority' *vis-à-vis* the emperor: he did not fawn upon Maximus, and when he had a request to make, 'he commanded rather than asked'. Up to a point this approach appears to have been highly successful, with Martin's unusual behaviour and his forthrightness winning him respect.[38] But the crucial case of Priscillian shows up the limitations of Martin's influence with the emperor. In terms of political expediency, Maximus may have had no choice,[39] and it is likely that no single bishop could have dissuaded him from proceeding with Priscillian's execution; though, had Martin been able to unite the other bishops behind him, the story might have been different. At the same time we should acknowledge that although Martin failed to protect Priscillian's life and was forced into an act of communion with bishops who had played a part in securing his death, he did achieve something.[40]

Martin's intervention with Maximus reveals also another side of his character: his aggressive courage, and his readiness to fight, single-handed if need be, for a cause he believed in.[41] The same qualities appear in Martin's assault on paganism. He saw this as the work of the devil, not of human beings

[36] *D* III, 4; II, 7, 2 and III, 11, 8.

[37] *D* III, 11, 8–13, 6. Above, ch. 20, i.

[38] *VM* 20; cf. *D* II, 5, 5–6, 3.

[39] He needed to display his punctilious concern for orthodoxy, and he needed the Priscillianists' estates: see Chadwick, *Priscillian*, pp. 120-1, 144.

[40] Cf. Chadwick, *Priscillian*, pp. 134, 146, who highlights the different ways in which Maximus received Ambrose and Martin, making a real attempt to win the latter's support.

[41] Cf. *VM* 4, 2-6; *VM* 13; *VM* 15; *D* II, 5, 5-9; II, 9, 1-2; III, 12.

who thought differently from himself; and therefore he had no qualms about traipsing around the countryside, destroying temples by main force—albeit illegally.

His warfare against paganism is only one instance of his fight against the powers of evil. As indicated above, Martin saw his whole life as a battle against the devil, who continually threatened and tormented him—when he set off to convert his parents, as he sat in his cell, or when he lay on his death-bed.[42] Martin appears to have perceived and interpreted all that happened in terms of the workings of God or the devil: where others saw an angry or wicked man, Martin saw a man goaded on by the devil. Indeed, one might say that he saw devils and angels at every turn.[43] Not unrelated is his expectation of the imminent end of the world and of the second coming of Christ, and his belief that Antichrist had been born in the world, and was now growing up as a boy.[44] The literal way in which he took his visionary experiences and the biblical prophecies of the parousia may be bound up with his relative lack of education. At least we can say that he appears as a man of imagination and feeling, indeed of impetuosity (as in halving his cloak), rather than a man who engaged in rational analysis.[45]

As he journeyed along the roads or down the river with his disciples, Martin would generally be a little apart from the others;[46] but at times he would point to everyday sights, interpreting these as illustrations of the spiritual life in almost parabolic fashion. For instance, he would point to a shorn sheep, saying: 'It has fulfilled the Gospel precept, "he who has two tunics should give one to him who has none"; so should you do, also.' Or he would use the sight of waterfowl pursuing fish to illustrate the activities of demons.[47] We never see Martin crack a joke, nor even engage in casual conversation. The impression is that his mind did not dwell or focus on the surface of what he saw, but always sought

---

[42] Above, ch. 17, i.

[43] *D* III, 8, 2; III, 15, 6; II, 13, 6-8; *VM* 17, 5; *VM* 21 & 22, etc. Cf. above, ch. 17.

[44] *D* II, 14.   [45] Though see above, ch. 12, and notes 12-13.

[46] *D* II, 3, 1; II, 13, 8.

[47] *D* II, 10 (esp. § 2); *ep*. 3, 7-8 (quoted above, ch. 17, i).

the spiritual meaning lying behind it—though we should recognize that he was practical enough in the face of human suffering, and it may be that this lack of attention to surface detail is typical primarily of Martin as an old man, which was how Sulpicius knew him; not of the younger Martin.[48]

The obverse of the picture of Martin as often withdrawn from other company is Sulpicius' statement that his mind was always concentrated in prayer. It was this which made Martin what he was. Sulpicius valiantly tries to capture the inner character of the holy man he visited, but such attempts inevitably fall short of their goal.[49] We are left guessing at the spirit which animated all his work; but one clue lies in Martin's impact upon Sulpicius, which turned the would-be biographer into a disciple. To pick up one detail, Sulpicius felt unable to demur at Martin himself washing his feet, because 'I was so overwhelmed by the authority of that man'; and clearly the conversation they had deeply impressed Sulpicius.[50]

After reviewing the salient points of Martin's life in this way, his sincerity and his concern to live out the Gospel will be apparent. But at the same time we should seek also to understand why some had their doubts about certain of his ideas and practices, if not about his suitability for the episcopate at all. Of course, Martin had an active social conscience, and effectively helped the poor, the sick, and the oppressed. Again, up to the fiasco of Priscillian's death, he appears to have intervened effectively with emperors, while never becoming subservient—something which was a very real danger for bishops at this time. But, naturally, the difference between Martin's approach and that of the other bishops cannot have endeared him to them. Martin also made an impressive beginning in the fight against rural paganism and the task of converting the peasantry; but here he overstepped both the bounds of legality and of his own diocese. Finally, he founded the first monasteries in Gaul (as far as our knowledge goes), and obviously did much to promote the ascetic life in the area; but this in itself

---

[48] Cf. above, ch. 12, n. 15.
[49] See *VM* 25–7; Griffe, *La Gaule chrét.* I, pp. 294–5.
[50] *VM* 25, 2–7.

would have rendered him suspect as a slightly crazy extremist in some eyes, if not (after the Priscillianist affair) an outright heretic.

In addition to these achievements, some of which would not have commended him to the majority of easy-going bishops of his day, we should also recognize that, considered as a bishop, Martin had some less laudable traits. He clearly had the power to attract disciples; but a bishop in fourth-century Gaul was in a position of leadership in an institution, and that required something more than the charismatic power to draw followers. There was a need to relate to everyone within the diocese, and not identify too narrowly with any one party. There was also a need to relate to his clergy and his fellow-bishops.

As regards the need to relate to everyone within the diocese, we can but point to Sulpicius' strange silence about Martin's relations with the citizens of Tours, and speculate about the cause.[51] However, that Martin did not see eye to eye with all his clergy at Tours is apparent in Sulpicius' story of how the archdeacon, an important official, failed to carry out Martin's request to provide clothing for a beggar, and subsequently lost his temper with Martin; while it is even more explicit in the Brice episode.[52] And the fact that Brice was elected Martin's successor is sufficient proof that he must have enjoyed considerable support amongst the clergy, and very possibly amongst the citizens of Tours, also. It may be that Martin got off on the wrong foot with his clergy at Tours because they resented the way in which popular acclaim had foisted him upon them as their bishop; but if Martin failed to sort out this problem in the twenty-six years of his episcopate, it does not say much for his ability to handle tricky problems of human relationships. Sulpicius may praise Martin's patience and love in letting the lowest cleric insult him with impunity, but one must question

---

[51] Cf. Babut, *St. Martin*, pp. 112–21, though he goes much too far. Did Martin find it easier to relate to peasants than to a more sophisticated urban population?

[52] Archdeacon: *D* II, 1; and cf. H. G. J. Beck, *The Pastoral Care of Souls in south-east France during the Sixth Century* (*Analecta Gregoriana* 51, Rome 1950), pp. 67–8. Brice: *D* III, 15.

whether, in a bishop, this does not betoken weakness and lack of leadership.[53]

Similar difficulties may well have cropped up in Martin's dealings with his fellow bishops. He could communicate with those who respected him; he could stand firm against those who opposed him; but could he establish a normal working relationship with a colleague who had a different approach? Certainly Martin may have encountered snobbery and distrust undeservedly, because of his social and military background; but the misgivings of other bishops probably arose at least in part from his idiosyncracies, and they were not entirely groundless. His intervention in other dioceses is likely to have stirred up other bishops' resentment towards him. Further, his asceticism served to place him outside the normal structure of society with which the church as a whole was becoming increasingly involved, while it also rendered him suspect of heretical tendencies. His claims to receive visits from saints and angels, his belief in the imminence of the parousia, and his attempt to protect Priscillianist suspects—all this would have strengthened suspicions of his own unorthodoxy. Again, as a monk-bishop who lived outside his cathedral city in a rural retreat, and who delegated to his clergy all administrative business and social calls, Martin was following norms of behaviour which were at complete variance with those of the majority of the Gallic episcopate. The distance between the two viewpoints is epitomized in Sulpicius' account of Martin's consecration to the see of Tours, when the bishops assembled for the occasion thought that Martin's uncouth appearance as a monk showed that he was unworthy of the dignity of the episcopate. For Sulpicius, however, it was precisely the asceticism of Martin which qualified him supremely well for the episcopate; it served as the basis for his episcopal authority, and informed all his pastoral actions.[54]

By now the limitations of Sulpicius' portrayal of Martin should be apparent. It is not a matter of Sulpicius telling outright lies, or inventing stories about him, as Babut thought;

[53] *VM* 26, 5; *D* I, 24, 3. Cf. Babut, *St. Martin*, ch. 3 and p. 203.
[54] *VM* 9, 3; *VM* 10, 1-2; above, ch. 11.

rather, it is a case of a one-sided presentation of the evidence. There should be no doubt that Martin was an authentic follower of Jesus, in some ways reminiscent of St. Francis. However, when measured against the responsibilities which fell to a bishop, it must be recognized that Martin, though exemplary in some respects, fell short in others.

He was, of course, supremely unlucky in the period in which he lived, for the controversy caused by Priscillian's case ran deep, splitting the church—and splitting it into those for and against monasticism. Further, as Griffe has pointed out, it was the Gallic church's misfortune that at this critical juncture it lacked a leader of the stature and skill of Hilary, who could unite the bishops behind him.[55] Martin took the 'right' line, the same one as Ambrose, and he had plenty of courage; but he was unable to carry the others with him. Had there been another Hilary to provide the leadership, this might not have mattered. But, as it was, it placed Martin in an unenviable position. His decision simply to concentrate on his own diocese, and, for the future, to ignore all episcopal gatherings, was sensible in the circumstances; but it was obviously far from ideal. It is an indication that, however great his pastoral, spiritual, and monastic gifts, Martin felt unable to influence the mainstream of ecclesiastical decision-making in Gaul. His age may be part of the answer (even on the 'short' chronology Martin was then in his fifties); and the problems do indeed seem to have been very intractable;[56] but, in part, we should probably take it as an unfavourable comment on Martin's ability to relate to his fellow-bishops, and on his leadership qualities.

Thus, whereas in happier times these shortcomings would have mattered less, while his explicitly Christian qualities might have won the respect of all, as it was, the episcopate was divided: a minority, who were pro monasticism, respected and revered him; but the majority were suspicious of his strict asceticism and his visionary experiences. In other words, the divisions within the Gallic church which came into prominence through the Priscillianist affair are as

[55] *La Gaule chrét.* I (2 edn.), p. 316.

[56] Ambrose also seems rather to have despaired of the Gallic bishops in these difficult years, and excused himself from various synods: above, ch. 20, n. 20.

essential for our understanding of Martin's position as a bishop as for our understanding of Sulpicius.

If this explains the varying views held about Martin during his lifetime, it also paves the way for our understanding of Martin's reputation within Gaul over the decades following his death. There was neither an instantaneous and widespread cult of Martin as the apostle of all Gaul, nor yet total indifference to his memory such as Babut posited.[57] He received honourable mention in the chronicles of Prosper and Hydatius (*c.*430) and in the *Gallic Chronicle of AD 452*,[58] as also from the author of the *Narratio de imperatoribus domus Valentinianae et Theodosianae*, who appears to have been a contemporary and admirer of Theodosius II (408–50).[59] Contemporaneous with the brief mentions that appear in these literary sources are the first pieces of epigraphic evidence, the Foedula inscription at Vienne, and the Ariomeres inscription at Ligugé.[60]

Even more significant is the testimony of the building sequence at Ligugé revealed by Dom Coquet's excavations.[61] Most securely dated is a remarkable semicircular edifice, which incorporates the modest three-roomed building which lay to the north of the church. The three-roomed building has been plausibly interpreted as Martin's own dwelling place, and it is difficult to see what else the semicircular building could be except for some form of pilgrimage centre or memorial. Happily, the semicircular building can be dated by pottery fragments in its foundations to the late fourth

---

[57] *St. Martin*, pp. 13 ff. On Martin's posthumous fame, see Delehaye, 'S. Martin', pp. 115–36; Prinz, pp. 19–46; E. Ewig, 'Der Martinskult im Frühmittelalter', *Archiv für mittelrheinische Kirchengeschichte* 14 (1962), pp. 11–30.

[58] Prosper *s.a.* 381 (*MGH, AA* IX, p. 461); for Hydatius, the extracts on Martin *s.a.* 405 are interpolations, but NB the special mention *s.a.* 385, 'a sancto Martino episcopo et ab aliis episcopis' (*MGH, AA* XI, p. 15); *Chronica Gallica a.452* in *MGH, AA* IX, p. 650.

[59] ed. Mommsen, *MGH, AA* IX, p. 629, and cf. p. 617.

[60] Foedula, *CIL* XII, no. 2115, noting (*i.a.*) Foedula's baptism by *Martinus procer*. On this title see J. Doignon, '"Procer", titre donné à saint Martin', *Saint Martin et son temps*, pp. 151–8. Ariomeres, see J. Coquet, 'Fouilles de Ligugé: (1) L'Inscription d'Ariomeres', *Revue Mabillon* 51 (1961), pp. 54–70, esp. p. 58; and cf. above, ch. 3.

[61] See above, ch. 3 and n. 7. On the semicircular (or semi-decagonal) building, Coquet, *L'Intérêt*, pp. 11–14; Eygun, in *Gallia* 12 (1954), pp. 380–9.

to fifth century. It had already gone out of use before the end of the fifth century, as some pagan burials had by then been inserted into its floor.

We should probably attribute to the same period the development of a martyrium, just to the west of Martin's original church, centring upon the more westerly of the Roman rooms.[62] This square-shaped room now became the centre of a cruciform building, with arcades opening north, south, and east into square-ended apses or transepts, thus yielding a groundplan similar to that of the mausoleum of Galla Placidia at Ravenna. Two fine ionic capitals, reused elsewhere in medieval rebuilding works, probably belong to this building of *c*.400, and indicate the craftsmanship employed. In the sixth century, a nave with side aisles—or three naves—was added on to the west of this martyrium, thus creating a rectangular basilica with a square-ended apse at the east end. This was presumably the church visited in the late sixth century by Gregory of Tours, who prayed at the screen in front of the corner where Martin was said to have resuscitated the catechumen.[63] What is interesting is that the initial development of this martyrium appears to antedate the great expansion of Martin's cult that occurred in Merovingian times; certainly the semicircular building does so.

At Tours itself there appears to have been an anti-Martinian reaction on Martin's death, or at least a desire for a different sort of bishop; for Martin's old opponent, Brice, was elected to succeed him. However, Brice himself is reported to have built a small chapel over Martin's grave, probably after his return to the city from which he had been driven out on a charge of adultery.[64] Further indications come from the versified *De vita Martini* of Paulinus of Périgueux, written between 462–4. The last book contains posthumous miracles wrought by Martin, which shows that his reputation as a

---

[62] Coquet, *L'Intérêt*, pp. 9–10.

[63] Coquet, *L'Intérêt*, pp. 14–15; Eygun, in *Gallia* 21 (1963), pp. 462–4. Gregory, *De virt. S. Mart.* 30 (*MGH, SRM* I, ii, p. 207).

[64] Gregory, *Hist.* X, 31, iv (*MGH, SRM* I, i, p. 528); ibid. II, 1 (pp. 37–8); cf. above, ch. 20, n. 38, and Palanque, 'Les Dissensions', pp. 494–5. The cult at the grave of St. Médard of Soissons had a similarly modest beginning: Gregory, *In gloria confess.* 93 (*MGH, SRM* I, ii, pp. 357–8). See also Delehaye, 'S. Martin', pp. 115 ff.

holy man lived on in the locality; we also learn that it had become a popular custom to make a pilgrimage to Marmoutier once a year, at Easter.[65] However, the real upsurge in the cult of Martin at Tours was the work of bishop Perpetuus (461-91), who commissioned Paulinus of Périgueux's verses, built a fine new church geared for pilgrims (into which he translated Martin's remains), and elicited dedicatory verses from Sidonius Apollinaris.[66]

However, such signs of honour for Martin all come from places with which either Martin or his disciples had been personally connected. One scholar, who has plotted the beginnings of Martin's cult on a map, has concluded that for the first century after his death Martin's renown as a saint was restricted almost exclusively to Aquitaine; it was only with Clovis' conquest of this area in 507 that Martin's cult achieved a wider dispersion through Gaul, thanks to his being adopted by the Merovingians as their patron saint.[67] This, perhaps, is why Martin goes unmentioned by Cassian and the monks of Lérins, though there may also have been other factors at work.[68] Be that as it may, we have still to explain why St. Martin should have appealed strongly enough to the Merovingians for them to adopt him as their patron saint. Geography does not account for everything,[69] as other saints such as Geneviève of Paris were nearer the heartland of Frankish settlements. Victory over the Visigoths of Aquitaine may have something to do with it;[70] but some part must surely have been played by the existing fame of St. Martin—a fame which had already reached Rome, where Pope Symmachus was even then founding the church of St. Martin *in montibus*.[71]

[65] Babut, *St. Martin* p. 291, n. 3. Paulinus of Périgueux, *De vita Martini* VI, lines 351-68 (*CSEL* 16, pp. 153-4).

[66] Babut, *St. Martin*, pp. 293-6; Delehaye, 'S. Martin', p. 118.

[67] Prinz, pp. 27, 32-3.

[68] Babut's thesis that Cassian and the Lérins monks were actively hostile to Sulpicius' St. Martin is unproven; see Delehaye, 'S. Martin', pp. 133-6. Still, Lérins-Marseilles preferred a theological slant to a thaumaturgical one, and may have felt that Sulpicius' presentation of Martin was liable to mislead men into concentrating on the miracles rather than the Christian virtues which lay behind them. However, cf. also Fontaine, as n. 27 above.

[69] Cf. Prinz, pp. 32-3.

[70] Cf. Gregory, *Hist.* II, 37 (pp. 85-88).

[71] Ewig, 'Der Martinskult', pp. 14-15.

On what was this fame based? In the first place, upon Sulpicius' hagiographical portrayal of Martin, which served as the basis for Paulinus of Périgueux's verses; possibly, also, on local memories of Martin himself; and finally, on the careful fostering of these assets by Perpetuus and later bishops of Tours. What is certain is that in the time of Gregory of Tours when the cult of Martin was in its heyday, it was *Sulpicius'* St. Martin which formed the basis for this cult: when a Spanish couple were trying to obtain healing for their baby through Martin's *virtus*, they pointed out to the saint that they had brought a relic of his all the way from Tours on the strength of the miraculous deeds which they had heard of him; they then went on to cite a list of miracles which was clearly taken from Sulpicius' Martinian writings.[72]

Thus in one sense Babut is right: Martin's posthumous fame rests largely upon the writings of Sulpicius Severus. But instead of this later popularity originating from the fluke of Sulpicius having utilized the figure of Martin for lack of any other suitable candidate to serve as the vehicle for his own religious views, the story appears to have been the other way round; for it was Martin who was instrumental in bringing Sulpicius to adopt those views. So, while we must recognize that Sulpicius' St. Martin is an idealized figure, we must also recall that it is drawn by a man who had been sufficiently struck by the Martin of flesh and blood to adopt his ideal as his own; to break with his old way of life and follow him.

[72] Gregory, *De virt. S. Mart.* III, 8 (*MGH, SRM* I, ii p. 184).

Appendix:
Table of Martinian Miracle stories

Note

The following classification is to some extent approximate. The least satisfactory part is the column headed 'Select Parallels', as there is no obvious criterion for deciding what to include and what to omit. However, for all its inadequacies I hope that it may serve two useful purposes: to illustrate what types of stories have biblical and/or monastic and/or classical parallels, and to signalize any remarkable similarities I am aware of (e.g. between *VM* 12 and *HM* 8, 25-9).

On the question of witnesses and the transmission of stories, I have listed definite witnesses without brackets, while presumed witnesses or line of transmission are put within parentheses when they can be surmised with a fair degree of probability.

I have used standard abbreviations for books of the Bible, and given references as to English Bibles, not the Vulgate. Note also:

Apollon.	Philostratus, *Life of Apollonius*
HM	*Historia monachorum* (Greek text)
Lucian	Lucian, *Philopseudes*
M	Martin
Mar. tr.	Marmoutier tradition
Rufinus	Rufinus' Latin tr. of the *Historia monachorum*, listed with ch. nos. and col. nos. referring to *PL* 21
Valerius	Valerius Maximus, *Facta et dicta memorabilia*
V. Ant.	Athanasius, *Vita Antonii* (ch. nos. refer to the Greek text)
V. Hil.	Jerome, *Vita Hilarionis*
V. Pauli	Jerome, *Vita Pauli*

Nature Miracles

Reference	Description	Location	Witnesses/ Transmission	Select Parallels
VM 12	M transfixes pagan funeral cortège through sign of the cross	Countryside	(?? Mar. tr.)	*HM* 8, 25–9
D II, 3, 6–10	Officials' mules transfixed after beating up M	*En route* in Tours diocese	Gallus	(Cf. the *tabellae defixionum*)
D II, 9, 6	M commands hounds to let a hunted hare go	*En route* in Tours diocese	(Gallus)	
Ep. 3, 7–8	M orders birds away with his *potens verbum*	Loire, between Candes & Tours	disciples (Mar. tr.)	*HM* 4, 3
D III, 9, 4	M commands snake to go away	By a river	(Gallus, Mar. tr.)	
D III, 3, 6–8	Barking dog silenced when abjured in M's name (M not present)	?	Saturninus	
VM 14, 1–2	M deflects fire by interposing his body	a village	(? Mar. tr: monks present on similar occasion)	
Ep. 1, 10–15	M only burnt, not killed by fire	sacristy of church in Tours diocese	M told Sulpicius	Cf. *HM* 10, 31–2
D II, 5, 9	Fire compels Valentinian I to rise & accede to M's demands	Imperial palace, Trier	Mar. tr.	

D III, 7	M frees part of Sénonais from hailstorms	*pagus* of the Sénonais	Romulus to Refrigerius	
D III, 8, 4–7	Storm razed idol in answer to M's prayers	Amboise	Marcellus, priest of Amboise	
D III, 14, 1–2	Storm stilled by evoking 'the God of M' (M not there)	aboard ship in Tyrrhenian Sea	unnamed man had witnessed this, & told Gallus	
D III, 9, 1–2	Column from heaven smashes idol in answer to M's prayers	?	Refrigerius	
VM 13	M deflects tree felled on him by hostile pagans through sign of the cross	a village	Mar. tr.	
VM 15, 1–2	Enraged pagan attacked M with sword, but found himself flat on his back	*pagus* of the Aedui	(??Mar. tr.)	Cf. I Kings 13:4 Valerius 2, 10, 6
VM 15, 3	Knife of attacking pagan vanished	?	(??Mar. tr.)	
D III, 3, 1–4	Oil blessed by M increased	(Tours)	Arpagius (oil blessed for Ct. Avitianus' wife)	I Kings 17:11–16
D III, 3, 5–6	Glass vessel of oil blessed by M did not break when dropped on marble floor	(Primuliacum)	(Sulpicius &) S's boy	II Kings 4:2–7

Healing Miracles

Reference	Disease	Procedure	Location	Witnesses/ Transmission	Select Parallels
VM 16	Girl entirely paralysed	M prayed alone, then blessed oil & poured it into her mouth. Her limbs slowly revived through contact with M	Trier: asked in church, healed in house	the people	For the approach to M cf. Lk. 8: 40–2. For the means used cf. Mk. 6:13 & HM 9, 11
D III, 2, 3–8	Girl of 12 dumb from birth	M excluded crowd; prayed, blessed oil & poured it into girl's mouth while holding her tongue	Chartres	Bishops Valentinus & Victricius; Evagrius (i.e. Mar. tr.)	
VM 19, 1–2	Arborius' daughter had quartan fever	Healed by application of a letter from M (M absent). M then veiled her as a virgin	(Arborius' house)	(Arborius; then prob. to Mar. tr.)	Cf. Apollon. 3, 38; also Acts 19:11–12
D III, 9, 3	Woman with haemorrhage	Healed on touching M's clothes	?	Refrigerius	Mk 5:25–34, etc.
VM 18, 4–5	Unspecified diseases	Cured through touching M's clothes (general statement)			Acts 19:11–12
VM 18, 3–4	Leper	M kissed and blessed him	At gate of Paris	?	Cf. Mk. 1:40–5, etc.
VM 19, 3	The pupil of Paulinus' eye was clouded over	M applied eye-salve (penicillo contigit)	?	(Paulinus)	
VM 6, 5–6	M ate poisonous hellebore	M healed through prayer	Gallinara	(Martin)	

D II, 2, 4-7	Evanthius' slave swollen from poisonous snake bite	M squeezed out the poison	Evanthius' estate	Gallus, who was E's nephew	Lucian 11
D II, 2, 3	Evanthius seriously ill	Healed while M was on his way	Evanthius' estate	(Gallus)	
D III, 14, 3-6	Lycontius' entire household was prostrated by deadly plague	L wrote to ask M's help. M fasted & prayed for a week—was not present	Lycontius' house	(Mar. tr. – cf. §6)	
VM 7	Catechumen died of fever in M's absence; already judged in other-world, but revived through M's prayers	M excluded others, & prostrated himself on the body in prayer. Man revived after 2 hours.	Ligugé	(Ligugé monks. It also became widely known.)	Cf. I Kings 17:17-24; II Kings 4:31-7; and cf. Lucian, Plutarch, & Jerome (above ch. 14, notes 78 & 82).
VM 8	Slave hanged himself	M excluded others & prostrated himself on the body in prayer	Lupicinus' estate	Crowd saw the revived man	I Kings 17: 17-24; II Kings 4:31-7. Matt. 9:18-25
D II, 4 4-9	M preached to pagans; was then asked to revive dead child	M knelt, prayed, & restored the child alive to its mother	outside village *en route* for Chartres	Gallus (§3) (also Martin: §7)	Acts 9:36-42; cf. Apollon. 4, 45.

Demoniacs and Exorcisms

Reference	Description	Location	Witnesses/ Transmission	Select Parallels
VM 17, 1–4	M cast demon out of Taetradius' slave by laying hands on him. As a result, T became a Christian.	Taetradius' house, Trier	?	General remarks: exorcism stories are common in NT and monastic sources, but there are no close parallels
VM 17, 5–7	M saw demon which then entered cook. M put his hand in raving cook's mouth, then forced demon to leave through belly	A house in Trier	?	
VM 18, 1–2	M interrogated demoniac about rumoured barbarian invasion	Church in Trier	Took place in public	
D II, 8, 7–9	Straw slept in by M cures energumen (in M's absence)	Convent of Clion	Nuns (?? who then told Marmoutier?)	(Cf. Acts 19:11–12)
D II, 9, 1–4	Cow goaded to savagery by demon on her back. M commanded demon to be gone	*En route* back from Trier	Gallus	Cf. *V. Hil.* 23
D III, 8, 1–3	M drove off demon from Ct. Avitianus by blowing at it	Avitianus' office, Tours	Gallus ('memini')	

	Description	Location	Witnesses/Transmission	Select Parallels
D III, 6, 2–5	General description of M's treatment of demoniacs: M excluded onlookers & prayed.	Cathedral, Tours	Gallus	Jerome, *ep.* 108, 13. Hilary, *Contra Constantium* 8.
D III, 14, 1	Energumen cured before he entered monastery	Marmoutier	Gallus	

Encounters with Supernatural Beings

Reference	*Description*	*Location*	*Witnesses/ Transmission*	*Select Parallels*
VM 6, 1–2	M meets the devil in human guise	Road beyond Milan	(Martin)	(? cf. *V. Ant.* 6)
VM 21, 2–5	Devil boasts of killing peasant	Marmoutier	Martin told the monks	
VM 22, 3–5	Demon objects to M accepting penitence for post-baptismal sin	Marmoutier	M. tr.	
VM 24, 4–8	Devil appears to M masquerading as Christ	Marmoutier	Martin told Sulpicius	*HM* 2, 9–10 & many others: above, ch. 5, n. 23
Ep. 3, 16	M saw devil as he lay dying	Candes	(M. tr: M was amid his disciples)	
D III, 15	M saw 2 demons goading on Brice	Marmoutier	M explained it to Brice & all the monks	

Encounters with Supernatural Beings (cont'd....)

Reference	Description	Location	Witnesses/ Transmission	Select Parallels
VM 22, 1–2 & D II, 13, 6	M often saw and recognized demons and devil	(Marmoutier)	(M to M. tr.)	V. Ant. 39 & passim
VM 19, 4	Angel tended M's bruises at night as he lay in his cell	Marmoutier	M to Sulpicius (M)	HM 25, 3
VM 14, 3–7	2 armed angels protected M destroying temple	Levroux, Bourges diocese	(? Mar. tr: cf. monks' presence at VM 13, 7)	(cf. II Maccabees 10:24–31)
D II, 13, 8	Angel brought M news of synod of Nîmes	Aboard a boat	Sulpicius & Gallus present	(Cf. V. Ant. 59–60 Apollon. 8, 26–7)
D III, 4, 1–5, 1	Angel awoke Ct. Avitianus to compel him to let M in & heed his requests	Governor's palace, Tours	Avitianus told tribune Dagridus who told Refrigerius	(? cf. Valerius, 1, 7, 7)
D III, 13, 3–4	Angel comforts M after Priscillianist/Felix affair	Nr. Andethanna, en route Trier to Tours	M was alone. (Prob. came from M to Mar. monks: cf. D III, 11, 1 & III, 13, 5.)	Cf. I Kings 19:4–9; Rufinus 1 & 16 (cols. 403 & 439)
D II, 13	M visited by SS. Agnes, Thecla & Mary; and often by SS. Peter & Paul	Marmoutier	Sulpicius & Gallus heard voices; M explained it to them	
VM 11	M calls up & questions a dead brigand's shade through prayer	False martyr's shrine, nr. Marmoutier	M alone saw the shade; monks with him heard voices. I.e. M to M. tr.	(I Sam. 28) Rufinus 28 (cols. 450 & 452); Apollon. 4, 16

Dreams, Visions, Predictions, Telepathy

Reference	Description	Location	Witnesses/ Transmission	Select Parallels
VM 3, 3–4	M dreams of Christ clad in his half-cloak	Amiens	(Martin)	
VM 5, 3	M admonished in a dream to convert his parents	Poitiers	(Martin)	Acts 16:9
Ep. 2, 1–5	Sulpicius' vision of M on M's death	Primuliacum	Sulpicius	*V. Pauli* 14 *V. Ant.* 60
D II, 2, 1–2	Ball of fire shone from M's head as he blessed the altar	Cathedral, Tours	Seen by 1 virgin, 1 priest, 3 monks	Valerius 1, 6, 1
D III, 10, 6	Arborius saw/heard M's hand bejewelled as he celebrated	Church (? Tours cathedral)	Arborius	
VM 9, 4–7	Defensor silenced by biblical oracle	Cathedral, Tours	Congregation (the people)	
VM 20, 8–9	M predicts Maximus' fate if he attacks Italy	Imperial palace, Trier	(? Martin)	(Cf. I Kings 22: 15–38)
D III, 10, 1–4	M predicts Cato will catch fish	Marmoutier	Mar. tr.	Lk. 5:1–11 Jn. 21:4–6
D III, 14, 7–9	M sensed that a monk was exposing himself	Marmoutier	Mar. tr.	

Bibliography

I (a): Primary Sources, Literary

AMMIANUS MARCELLINUS, *Res gestae*, ed. C. U. Clark (2 vols., Berlin 1910-15, 2nd edn. 1963).

ANTONY, *The Letters of St. Antony the Great*, ET by D. J. Chitty (Fairacres publications, 50; Oxford 1975).

ATHANASIUS, *Vita Antonii*: Greek text, *PG* 26, cols. 835-976.

—— *Vita Antonii*: Earliest Latin anon. tr.; critical text, ed. G. J. M. Bartelink, with Italian tr. by P. Citati & S. Lilla: *Vite dei Santi*, vol. I (1974).

—— *Vita Antonii*: Latin tr. by Evagrius, *PL* 73, cols. 125-70.

—— *Vita Antonii*: ET by R. C. Gregg, Athanasius, *The Life of Antony and the Letter to Marcellinus* (The Classics of Western Spirituality; pb. edn. New York & London 1980).

AUGUSTINE, *Confessiones*, ed. P. Knöll, *CSEL* 33 (1896).

—— *Contra mendacium*, ed. J. Zycha, *CSEL* 41, v, iii (1900), pp. 467-528.

—— *De civitate Dei*, ed. B. Dombart & A. Kalb, *CCSL* 47 & 48 (1955).

—— *De cura pro mortuis gerenda*, ed. J. Zycha, *CSEL* 41, v, iii (1900), pp. 619-60.

—— *De diversis quaestionibus LXXXIII*, ed. A. Mutzenbecher, *CCSL* 44A (1975), pp. 1-249.

—— *De mendacio*, ed. J. Zycha, *CSEL* 41, v, iii (1900), pp. 411-66.

—— *De opere monachorum*, ed. J. Zycha, ibid. pp. 529-96.

—— *Epistolae ad Galatas expositio*, ed. J. Divjak, *CSEL* 84 (1971), pp. 53-141.

CASSIAN, *Conlationes*, ed. M. Petschenig, *CSEL* 13 (1886).

—— *De institutis coenobiorum*, ed. M. Petschenig, *CSEL* 17 (1888).

DAMASUS, *Epistolae, PL* 13, cols. 347-76.

FILASTER OF BRESCIA, *Diversarum hereseon liber*, ed. F. Marx, *CSEL* 38 (1898).

GENNADIUS, *De viris inlustribus*, ed. E. C. Richardson, *Texte und Untersuchungen zur Geschichte der altchristlichen Literatur* 14, i (1896).

GREGORY OF TOURS, *Historiae*, ed. B. Krusch & W. Levison, *MGH, SRM* I, i (new edn., Hannover 1951).

—— *Liber in gloria confessorum*, ed. B. Krusch, *MGH, SRM* I, ii (new edn., Hannover 1969).

—— *Liber in gloria martyrum*, ibid.

—— *Libri iv de virtutibus sancti Martini episcopi*, ibid.

—— *Liber vitae patrum*, ibid.

O. Guenther, ed., *Epistulae imperatorum pontificum aliorum . . . Avellana quae dicitur collectio*, *CSEL* 35 (1895).

J. Gwynn, ed., with introduction and appendices, *Liber Ardmachanus: The Book of Armagh* (Dublin & London, 1913).

C. Halm, ed., *Rhetores Latini Minores* (Leipzig 1863).

HILARY OF ARLES, *Sermo de vita Sancti Honorati*, ed. M.-D. Valentin, *SC* 235 (1977).

HILARY OF POITIERS, *Contra Constantium imperatorem*, *PL* 10, cols. 577–603.

—— —— *Tractatus mysteriorum*: Hilaire de Poitiers, *Traité des Mystères*, ed. with Fr. tr. by J.-P. Brisson, *SC* 19 (1947).

Historia monachorum in Aegypto, ed. A.-J. Festugière (Subsidia hagiographica 34; Brussels 1961).

—— —— —— ET by B. Ward (introduction) & N. Russell (tr.), *The Lives of the Desert Fathers: the Historia monachorum in Aegypto* (pb. edn. Oxford & Kalamazoo 1981).

—— —— —— see under Rufinus.

HYDATIUS, *Chronicon*, ed. T. Mommsen, *Chronica Minora* II, *MGH, AA* XI (Berlin 1894).

INNOCENT I (POPE), *Epistolae et decreta*, *PL* 20, cols. 463–612.

ISIDORE OF SEVILLE, *Etymologiae*, ed. W. M. Lindsay (Oxford Classical Texts; 2 vols., Oxford 1911).

JEROME, *Apologia adversus libros Rufini*, *PL* 23, cols. 415–514.

—— *Commentarii in Epistolam ad Galatas*, *PL* 26, cols. 307–438.

—— *Commentarii in Esaiam*, ed. M. Adriaen, *CCSL* 73 & 73A (1963).

—— *Commentarii in Hiezechielem*, ed. F. Glorie, *CCSL* 75 (1964).

—— *Contra Vigilantium*, *PL* 23, cols. 339–52. (This is the edition I cite; but NB in other editions it occupies cols. 353–68.)

—— *De viris inlustribus*, ed. E. C. Richardson, *Texte und Untersuchungen* 14, i (1896), pp. 1–112.

—— *Epistulae*, ed. I. Hilberg, *CSEL* 54, 55, & 56 (1910, 1912, & 1918).

—— *Vita Hilarionis*, crit. edn. by A. A. R. Bastiaensen in *Vite dei Santi* IV (1975); but owing to problems of availability, I have continued to cite from *PL* 23, cols. 29–54.

JEROME, *Vita Malchi, PL* 23, cols. 55–62.

—— *Vita Pauli, PL* 23, cols. 17–30.

—— *Letters and Select Works*: ET by W. H. Fremantle, A Select Library of Nicene and post-Nicene Fathers of the Christian Church, 2nd ser. vol. 6, edd. Schaff & Wace (repr. Michigan 1954).

PSEUDO-JEROME (EUTROPIUS?), *Epistola vi ad amicum aegrotum de viro perfecto, PL* 30, cols. 75–104.

LEO I (POPE), *Sermons*, vol. III, ed. R. Dolle, *SC* 74 (1961).

LIBANIUS, *Pro templis*, ed. R. Foerster, *Libanii opera*, III (Leipzig 1906).

—— *Pro templis*, French tr. with notes by R. Van Loy, 'Le "Pro Templis" de Libanius', *Byzantion* 8 (1933), pp. 7–39, 389–404.

LUCIAN, *Philopseudes*, ed. and tr. A. M. Harmon, Loeb series of Lucian's works in 8 vols., vol. III (London and New York, 1921).

J. D. Mansi, ed. *Sacrorum Conciliorum nova et amplissima collectio*, vol. III (Paris 1759).

MAXIMUS OF TURIN, *Sermones*, ed. A. Mutzenbecher, *CCSL* 23 (1962).

T. Mommsen, ed., *Chronica Minora s. IV–VII*; *MGH, AA* IX & XI (2 vols., Berlin 1891 & 1894).

T. Mommsen & P. M. Meyer, edd., *Theodosiani libri xvi cum constitutionibus sirmondianis et leges novellae ad Theodosianum pertinentes* (2 vols., Berlin 1905), vol. I.

G. Morin, ed., *Consultationes Zacchaei christiani et Apollonii philosophi* (Florilegium Patristicum, fasc. 39; Bonn 1935).

C. Munier, ed., *Concilia Galliae a. 314–506, CCSL* 148 (1963).

H. Musurillo, ed. & tr., *The Acts of the Christian Martyrs* (Oxford Early Christian Texts; Oxford 1972).

PACATUS, *Panegyricus Theodosio Augusto*, ed. E. Galletier (Budé edn.; Paris 1955), pp. 47–114.

Vita prima S. Pachomii, ed. F. Halkin, *Sancti Pachomii Vitae Graecae* (Subsidia Hagiographica 19; Brussels 1932).

—— French tr. by A.-J. Festugière in *Les Moines d'Orient*, vol. IV, 2 (q.v.)

PALLADIUS, *The Lausiac History of Palladius*, ed. with introduction & commentary by C. Butler (Texts and Studies, ed. J. Armitage Robinson, 6; 2 vols., Cambridge 1898 & 1904).

Passio Sancti Typasii Veterani, ed. in *AB* 9 (1890), pp. 116–23.

PAULINUS OF MILAN, *Vita Ambrosii*, ed. by A. A. R. Bastiaensen, with Italian tr. by L. Canali, *Vite dei Santi*, vol. III (1975).

PAULINUS OF NOLA, *Carmina*, ed. G. de Hartel, *CSEL* 30 (1894).

—— *Epistulae*, ed. G. de Hartel, *CSEL* 29 (1894).

—— *Letters of St. Paulinus of Nola*, tr. and annotated by P. G. Walsh (Ancient Christian Writers, vols. 35–6. 2 vols., Westminster Maryland & London, 1966/7, 1967).

PAULINUS OF PÉRIGUEUX, *De vita Martini*, ed. M. Petschenig, *CSEL* 16 (= *Poetae christiani minores*, 1888), pp. 16-159.
PHILOSTRATUS, *Life of Apollonius*, ed. & tr. F. C. Conybeare (Loeb series; 2 vols., London & New York 1912).
PLOTINUS, *The Enneads*, edd. P. Henry & H.-R. Schwyzer (Oxford Classical Texts; Oxford, in progress: vol. I, 1964; vol. II, 1977).
— *The Enneads*, ET by S. MacKenna (London, revised edn. 1956).
PONTIUS, *Vita Cypriani*, ed. M. Pellegrino, *Ponzio, Vita e martirio di San Cipriano* (Verba Seniorum, 3; Alba 1955).
POSSIDIUS, *Vita Augustini*, ed. A. A. R. Bastiaensen, with Italian tr. by C. Carena, *Vite dei Santi*, vol. III (1975).
PROSPER OF AQUITAINE, *Chronicon*, ed. T. Mommsen, *Chronica Minora* I (q.v.).

QUINTILIAN, *Institutio oratoria*, ed. M. Winterbottom (Oxford Classical Texts; 2 vols., Oxford 1970).

RUFINUS, *De adulteratione librorum Origenis*, ed. M. Simonetti, *CCSL* 20 (1961), pp. 1-17.
— (tr.) *Historia monachorum*, *PL* 21, cols. 387-462.

SIRICIUS (POPE), *Epistolae et decreta*, *PL* 13, cols. 1131-96.
SULPICIUS SEVERUS: *Sulpicii Severi opera ad MSS. codices emendata, notisque, observationibus et dissertationibus illustrata*, ed. H. de Prato (2 vols., Verona 1741 & 1754).
— *Opera*, ed. C. Halm, *CSEL* 1 (1866).
— *La Chronique de Sulpice Sévère*, ed. with French tr. and copious notes by A. Lavertujon (2 vols., Paris 1896-9).
— Sulpice Sévère, *Vie de Saint Martin*; ed. with French tr. and introduction (vol. I) and commentary (vols. II & III) by J. Fontaine; *SC* 133-5 (3 vols., Paris 1967-9).
— *Vita Martini*, ed. with commentary by J. W. Smit, and Italian tr. by L. Canali, *Vite dei Santi* IV (1975).
— ET of all Sulpicius' works by A. Roberts, *The works of Sulpitius Severus*, A Select Library of Nicene and post-Nicene Fathers of the Christian Church, 2nd ser. vol. 11, ed. Schaff & Wace (repr. Michigan 1964).
— ET of the Martinian works in F. R. Hoare, *The Western Fathers* (London 1954).
— ET of the Martinian works by B. Peebles in *Fathers of the Church*, vol. 7 (New York 1949).

TERTULLIAN, *De anima*, ed. J. H. Waszink (Amsterdam 1947).
— *De corona*, ed. J. Fontaine (Paris 1966).

VALERIUS MAXIMUS, *Facta et dicta memorabilia*, ed. C. Kempf (Berlin 1854).

VICTRICIUS OF ROUEN, *De laude sanctorum, PL* 20, cols. 443-58.

ZOSIMUS (POPE), *Epistolae et decreta, PL* 20, cols. 639-86.
J. Zwicker, ed., *Fontes Historiae Religionis Celticae* (pt. I Berlin 1934; pt. II Bonn 1935. Fontes historiae religionum ex auctoribus graecis et latinis collectos, ed. C. Clemen, fasc. 5).

I (b). Primary Sources, Epigraphical and Archaeological

Corpus Inscriptionum Latinarum (16 vols., Berlin 1862 ff.).
E. Diehl, *Inscriptiones Latinae Christianae Veteres* (3 vols., Berlin 1925-31).
É. Espérandieu, *Recueil général des bas-reliefs, statues et bustes de la Gaule romaine* (15 vols., Paris 1907-66), vols. III, IV & IX.
E. Le Blant, *Inscriptions chrétiennes de la Gaule antérieures au VIII siècle* (2 vols., Paris 1856 & 1865).
—— *Nouveau recueil des inscriptions chrétiennes de la Gaule antérieures au VIII siècle* (Paris 1892).

II: Select Secondary Sources

R. AIGRAIN, 'Bulletin critique', *Revue d'histoire de l'église de France* 7 (1921), pp. 278-84 (discussion of Babut and Delehaye).
P. ANTIN, 'L'Édition J. Fontaine de Sulpice Sévère, *Vita S. Martini*', *Revue Mabillon* 58 (1970), pp. 25-36.
Antonius magnus eremita, ed. B. Steidle (*Studia Anselmiana* 38, Rome 1956).
R. ARBESMANN, 'Fasting and Prophecy in Pagan and Christian Antiquity', *Traditio* 7 (1949-51), pp. 1-71.
E. AUERBACH, *Literary Language and its Public in Late Antiquity and in the Middle Ages* (ET London 1965).
—— *Mimesis* (ET pb. edn. Princeton 1968²).

E.-C. BABUT, *Le Concile de Turin* (Bibliothèque de la Fondation Thiers, fasc. 6; Paris 1904).
—— 'Sur trois lignes inédites de Sulpice Sévère', *Le Moyen Age* 19 (1906), pp. 205-13.
—— *Priscillien et le Priscillianisme* (Bibliothèque de l'École des Hautes Études: Sciences Historiques et Philologiques, 169; Paris 1909).
—— *Saint Martin de Tours* (Paris n.d. [1912]).
R. H. BAINTON, *Christian Attitudes toward War and Peace* (pb. edn. Nashville 1960).
G. BARDY, 'Copies et éditions au V siècle', *Revue des sciences religieuses* 23 (1949), pp. 38-52.
J. BERNAYS, *Ueber die Chronik des Sulpicius Severus* (Berlin 1861).

L. BIELER, Θεῖος Ἀνήρ: das Bild des 'göttlichen Menschen' in Spätantike und Frühchristientum (2 vols. 1935-6; photographically reproduced Darmstadt 1967).

J. W. BINNS, ed., *Latin Literature of the Fourth Century* (London 1974).

M. BLOCH, 'Saint-Martin de Tours: à propos d'une polémique', *Revue d'histoire et de littérature religieuse* n.s. 7 (1921), pp. 44-57.

C. F. A. BORCHARDT, *Hilary of Poitiers' role in the Arian Struggle* (The Hague 1966).

J. BOUSSARD, 'Étude sur la ville de Tours du Ier au IVe siècle', *REA* 50 (1948), pp. 313-29.

— 'Essai sur le peuplement de la Touraine du Ier au VIIIe siècle', *Le Moyen Age* 60 (1954), pp. 261-91.

— *Carte et Texte du Département d'Indre-et-Loire* (Forma Orbis Romani. Carte archéologique de la Gaule romaine, edd. A. Grenier & P.-M. Duval, fasc. 13; Paris 1960).

P. R. L. BROWN, *Augustine of Hippo* (London 1967).

— *The World of Late Antiquity, from Marcus Aurelius to Muhammad* (pb. edn. London 1971).

— 'The Rise and Function of the Holy Man in Late Antiquity', *JRS* 61 (1971), pp. 80-101.

— *Religion and Society in the Age of Saint Augustine* (London 1972. A collection of articles and reviews).

— *The Making of Late Antiquity* (Cambridge Mass. & London, 1978).

— *The Cult of the Saints: its Rise and Function in Latin Christianity* (Chicago & London, 1981).

J.-G. BULLIOT & F. THIOLLIER, *La Mission et le culte de Saint Martin d'après les légendes et les monuments populaires dans le pays éduen* (Autun & Paris 1892).

A. R. BURN, 'Hic Breve Vivitur: A Study of the Expectation of Life in the Roman Empire', *Past and Present* 4 (1953), pp. 2-31.

C. J. CADOUX, *The Early Church and the World* (Edinburgh 1925).

P. CANIVET, 'Théodoret et le Messalianisme', *Revue Mabillon* 51 (1961), pp. 26-34.

— *Le Monachisme syrien selon Théodoret de Cyr* (Théologie historique 42; Paris 1977).

F. CAVALLERA, *Saint Jérôme, sa vie et son œuvre* (Spicilegium Sacrum Lovaniense, études et documents, 1 & 2; 2 vols., Louvain & Paris, 1922).

H. CHADWICK, *Priscillian of Avila* (Oxford 1976).

O. CHADWICK, *John Cassian* (2nd edn. Cambridge 1968).

A. CHASTAGNOL, 'Le Diocèse civil d'Aquitaine au Bas-Empire', *Bulletin de la Société nationale des Antiquaires de France* (Paris 1970), pp. 272-92.

— 'Le Repli sur Arles des services administratifs gaulois en l'an 407 de notre ère', *RH* 249 (1973), pp. 23-40.

M.-D. CHENU, 'The Symbolist Mentality', *Nature, Man and Society in the Twelfth Century* (ET Chicago & London 1968).

D. J. CHITTY, *The Desert a City* (pb. edn. London & Oxford, 1977).

P. R. COLEMAN-NORTON, 'The Use of Dialogue in the *Vitae Sanctorum*', *JTS* 27 (1926), pp. 388-95.

J. COQUET, 'Découvertes archéologiques à l'Abbaye de Ligugé: un "Martyrium" martinien?', *Revue Mabillon* 44 (1954), pp. 45-94, and plates.

—— 'Les Édifices religieux du haut moyen âge à l'abbaye de Ligugé', *Revue Mabillon* 45 (1955), pp. 75-147, and supplement containing 19 plans and illustrations.

—— 'Fouilles de Ligugé: (1) L'Inscription d'Ariomeres. (2) Pierres à décor mérovingien', *Revue Mabillon* 51 (1961), pp. 54-75.

—— *L'Intérêt des fouilles de Ligugé* (Société des amis du vieux Ligugé; revised edn. Ligugé 1968).

P. COURCELLE, 'Paulin de Nole et saint Jérôme', *Revue des Études Latines* 25 (for 1947, actually published 1948), pp. 250-80.

—— Un nouveau traité d'Eutrope, prêtre aquitain vers l'an 400', *REA* 56 (1954), pp. 377-90.

—— *Late Latin Writers and their Greek Sources* (ET Cambridge Mass. 1969).

J. M. COURT, 'The Philosophy of the Synoptic Miracles', *JTS* n.s. 23 (1972), pp. 1-15.

F. L. CROSS, ed., *The Oxford Dictionary of the Christian Church*, 2nd edn. revised Cross & E. A. Livingstone (London etc. 1974).

A. D'ALÈS, *Priscillien et l'Espagne chrétienne à la fin du IVe siècle* (Paris 1936).

J. DANIÉLOU, *Platonisme et théologie mystique* (revised edn. Paris 1953).

—— *Les Anges et leur mission d'après les Pères de l'Église* (Collection Irénikon, n.s. 5; 2nd edn. Paris 1953).

—— 'Les Démons de l'air dans la "Vie d'Antoine"', *Antonius magnus eremita* (q.v.), pp. 136-47.

J. DANIÉLOU, *A History of Early Christian Doctrine before the Council of Nicaea*, 3 vols: I *The Theology of Jewish Christianity* (ET London 1964); II *Gospel Message and Hellenistic Culture* (ET London 1973); III *The Origins of Latin Christianity* (ET London 1977).

—— & H. MARROU, *The Christian Centuries* (edd. Rogier, Aubert, & Knowles), vol. I: *The First Six Hundred Years* (ET London 1964).

H. DELEHAYE, 'Saint Martin et Sulpice Sévère', *AB* 38 (1920), pp. 5-136.

—— 'Les Recueils antiques de miracles des saints', *AB* 43 (1925), pp. 5-85, and 305-25.

—— *Sanctus. Essai sur le culte des saints dans l'antiquité* (Subsidia hagiographica no. 17; Brussels 1927).

H. DELEHAYE, *Les Origines du culte des martyrs* (Subsidia hagiographica no. 20; 2nd edn. Brussels 1933).
— *The Legends of the Saints* (ET London 1962, from the 4th French edn. of 1955).
— *Les Passions des martyrs et les genres littéraires* (Subsidia hagiographica no. 13B; 2nd edn. Brussels 1966).
G. DELLING, 'Zur Beurteilung des Wunders durch die Antike', *Studien zum Neuen Testament und zum hellenistichen Judentum* (Göttingen 1970), pp. 53–71.
— 'Das Verständnis des Wunders im Neuen Testament', ibid. pp. 146–59.
W. DEN BOER, 'Some Remarks on the Beginnings of Christian Historiography', *Texte und Untersuchungen* 79 (1961, = *Studia Patristica*, ed. F. L. Cross, IV), pp. 348–62.
D. P. DE VOOGHT, 'La Théologie du miracle selon saint Augustin', *Recherches de théologie ancienne et médiévale* 11 (1939), pp. 197–222.
S. DILL, *Roman Society in the Last Century of the Western Empire* (2nd edn. pb. reprint New York, 1958).
E. R. DODDS, *The Greeks and the Irrational* (1951; pb. edn. Berkeley, Los Angeles, & London 1971).
— *Pagan and Christian in an Age of Anxiety* (Cambridge 1965).
J. DOIGNON, *Hilaire de Poitiers avant l'exil* (Études Augustiniennes; Paris 1971).
T. A. DOREY, ed., *Latin Biography* (London 1967).
M. DOUGLAS, *Natural Symbols: explorations in cosmology* (London 1970).
L. DUCHESNE, *Les Anciens Catalogues épiscopaux de la province de Tours* (Paris 1890).
— *Fastes épiscopaux de l'ancienne Gaule* (3 vols., 2nd edn. Paris 1907, 1910, & 1915).
— 'Le Concile de Turin', *RH* 87 (1905), pp. 278–302.
M. DULAEY, *Le Rêve dans la vie et la pensée de saint Augustin* (Études Augustiniennes; Paris 1973).
P.-M. DUVAL, *La Vie quotidienne en Gaule pendant la paix romaine* (Paris 1952).

R. F. EVANS, *Pelagius: Inquiries and Reappraisals* (London 1968).
E. EWIG, 'Der Martinskult im Frühmittelalter', *Archiv für mittelrheinische Kirchengeschichte* 14 (1962), pp. 11–30.
F. EYGUN, summary report on Ligugé excavations in *Gallia* 12 (1954), pp. 380–9; 21 (1963), pp. 461–6; 25 (1967), pp. 260–2.

P. FABRE, *Essai sur la chronologie de l'œuvre de saint Paulin de Nole* (Publications de la faculté des lettres de l'université de Strasbourg, fasc. 109; Paris 1948).
— *Saint Paulin de Nole et l'amitié chrétienne* (Bibliothèque des Écoles françaises d'Athènes et de Rome, 167; Paris 1949).

A.-J. FESTUGIÈRE, *La Révélation d'Hermès Trismégiste* (Études bibliques; 4 vols., Paris 1944-54); esp. vol. II, *Le Dieu cosmique* (1949); III, *Les Doctrines de l'âme* (1953); IV, *Le Dieu inconnu et la gnose* (1954).

—— 'Lieux communs littéraires et thèmes de folk-lore dans l'hagiographie primitive', *Wiener Studien* 73 (1960), pp. 123-52.

—— *Les Moines d'Orient* (4 vols., Paris 1961-5).

H. FICHTENAU, 'Zum Reliquienwesen im früheren Mittelalter', *Mitteilungen des Instituts für österreichische Geschichtsforschung* 60 (1952), pp. 60-89.

R. C. FINUCANE, *Miracles and Pilgrims* (London etc. 1977).

G. FOLLIET, 'Aux origines de l'ascétisme et du cénobitisme africain', *Saint Martin et son temps* (q.v.), pp. 25-44.

J. FONTAINE, ed. and comm., Sulpice Sévère, *Vie de Saint Martin* (SC 133-5; 3 vols., Paris 1967-9).

—— 'Vérité et fiction dans la chronologie de la *Vita Martini*', *Saint Martin et son temps* (q.v.), pp. 189-236.

—— 'Sulpice Sévère a-t-il travesti saint Martin de Tours en martyr militaire?' *AB* 81 (1963), pp. 31-58.

—— 'Une clé littéraire de la *Vita Martini* de Sulpice Sévère: la typologie prophétique', *Mélanges offerts à Mlle Christine Mohrmann* (Utrecht 1963), pp. 84-95.

—— 'Démons et sibylles: la peinture des possédés dans la poésie de Prudence', *Hommages à Jean Bayet* (Coll. Latomus 70; Brussels 1964), pp. 196-213.

—— 'Alle fonti della agiografia europea: storia e leggenda nella vita di San Martino di Tours', *Rivista di storia e letteratura religiosa* 2 (1966), pp. 187-206.

—— 'Hilaire et Martin', *Hilaire de Poitiers, évêque et docteur* (q.v.), pp. 59-86.

—— 'Valeurs antiques et valeurs chrétiennes dans la spiritualité des grands propriétaires terriens à la fin du IVe siècle occidental', *Epektasis: Mélanges patristiques offerts au Cardinal Jean Daniélou*, edd. J. Fontaine & C. Kannengiesser (Paris 1972), pp. 571-95.

—— 'L'Ascétisme chrétien dans la littérature gallo-romaine d'Hilaire à Cassien', *La Gallia romana* (Accademia Nazionale dei Lincei: Problemi attuali di scienza e di cultura; Rome 1973), pp. 87-115.

—— 'Société et culture chrétiennes sur l'aire circumpyrénéenne au siècle de Théodose', *BLE* 1974, pp. 241-82.

—— 'L'Affaire Priscillien ou l'ère des nouveaux Catilina; observations sur le "Sallustianisme" de Sulpice Sévère', in *Classica et Iberica* (= Festschrift in hon. of J. M.-F. Marique), ed. P. T. Brannan (Worcester Mass. 1975), pp. 355-92.

—— 'L'Aristocratie occidentale devant le monachisme aux IVème et Vème siècles', *Rivista di storia e letteratura religiosa* 15 (1979), pp. 28-53.

—— 'Le Culte des martyrs militaires et son expression poétique au IVe

siècle: l'idéal évangélique de la non-violence dans le christianisme théodosien', *Ecclesia orans: Mélanges patristiques offerts au Père A. G. Hamman* (= *Augustinianum* 20; Rome 1980), pp. 141-71.

G. FOWDEN, 'Bishops and Temples in the Eastern Roman Empire A.D. 320-435', *JTS* n.s. 29 (1978), pp. 53-78.

W. H. C. FREND, *The Donatist Church* (Oxford 1952).

—— *Martyrdom and Persecution in the Early Church* (Oxford 1965).

F.-L. GANSHOF, 'Saint Martin et le Comte Avitianus', *AB* 67 (1949), pp. 203-23.

J. GAUDEMET, *L'Église dans l'Empire romain (IVe-Ve siècles): Histoire du Droit et des Institutions de l'Église en Occident*, ed. G. Le Bras, vol. III (Paris 1958).

C. GEERTZ, 'Religion as a Cultural System', *Anthropological Approaches to the Study of Religion* (A. S. A. monographs, ed. M. Banton, no. 3; pb. edn. London 1968), pp. 1-46.

D. GORCE, *La Lectio divina des origines du cénobitisme à saint Benoit et Cassiodore: I, Saint Jérôme et la lecture sacrée dans le milieu ascétique romain* (Wépion-sur-Meuse & Paris 1925).

G. D. GORDINI, 'Origine e sviluppo del monachesimo a Roma', *Gregorianum* 37 (1956), pp. 220-60.

R. M. GRANT, *Miracle and Natural Law in Graeco-Roman and Early Christian Thought* (Amsterdam 1952).

F. GRAUS, *Volk, Herrscher und Heiliger im Reich der Merowinger* (Prague 1965).

A. GRENIER, *Manuel d'archéologie gallo-romaine* (4 vols., Paris 1931-60); esp. vol. IV, *Les Monuments des eaux* (1960).

J. GRIBOMONT, 'Le Monachisme au IVe siècle en Asie Mineure: de Gangres au Messalianisme', *Texte und Untersuchungen* 64 (1957, = *Studia Patristica*, edd. Aland & Cross, II), pp. 400-15.

J. GRIBOMONT, 'L'Influence du monachisme oriental sur Sulpice Sévère', *Saint Martin et son temps* (q.v.), pp. 135-49.

—— Le Monachisme au sein de l'église en Syrie et en Cappadoce', *Studia Monastica* 7 (1965), pp. 7-24.

É. GRIFFE, 'La Chronologie des années de jeunesse de saint Martin', *BLE* 62 (1961), pp. 114-18.

—— 'La Pratique religieuse en Gaule au Ve siècle: *saeculares et sancti*', *BLE* 63 (1962), pp. 241-67.

—— *La Gaule chrétienne à l'époque romaine* (3 vols., 2nd edn. Paris 1964-5). Occasionally, where expressly stated in the notes, I have used the 1st edn. This comprises vols. I and II only (Paris & Toulouse, 1947, 1957). All other references are to the 2nd edn.

A. GUILLAUMONT, *Les 'Képhalaia Gnostica' d'Évagre le Pontique et l'histoire de l'Origénisme chez les Grecs et chez les Syriens* (Patristica Sorbonensia, 5; Paris 1962).

—— with C. GUILLAUMONT, 'Démon' §iii; in *Dict. Sp.* III, cols. 189-212.

T. J. HAARHOFF, *Schools of Gaul* (Johannesburg 1958²).

M. HADAS & M. SMITH, *Heroes and Gods: Spiritual Biographies in Antiquity* (New York 1965).

C. P. HAMMOND, 'The Last Ten Years of Rufinus' Life and the Date of his Move south from Aquileia', *JTS* n.s. 28 (1977), pp. 372-429.

J.-J. HATT, 'Essai sur l'évolution de la religion gauloise', *REA* 67 (1965), pp. 80-125.

Hilaire de Poitiers, évêque et docteur (Études Augustiniennes; Paris 1968).

Hilaire et son temps (Actes du colloque de Poitiers 29 sept.-3 oct. 1968; Études Augustiniennes; Paris 1969).

A. B. E. HOOD, 'Sulpicius Severus and his Background' (unpublished Oxford B.Phil thesis, 1968).

D. HOSTER, *Die Form der frühesten lateinischen Heiligenviten von der Vita Cypriani bis zur Vita Ambrosii und ihr Heiligenideal* (Cologne diss. 1963).

J. M. HULL, *Hellenistic Magic and the Synoptic Tradition* (Studies in Biblical Theology, 2nd ser. 28; pb. edn. London 1974).

E. D. HUNT, 'St. Silvia of Aquitaine: the role of a Theodosian Pilgrim in the Society of East and West', *JTS* n.s. 23 (1972), pp. 351-73.

P. HYLTÉN, *Studien zu Sulpicius Severus* (Lund 1940).

A. H. M. JONES, *The Later Roman Empire, 284-602* (3 vols., Oxford 1964).

— with J. R. MARTINDALE & J. MORRIS, *The Prosopography of the Later Roman Empire* (Cambridge, in progress); esp. vol. I (1971).

C. JULLIAN, 'La Jeunesse de saint Martin' (= 'Notes gallo-romaines' §47), *REA* 12 (1910), pp. 260-80.

— 'Remarques critiques sur les sources de la vie de saint Martin' (= 'Notes gallo-romaines' §§93-5), *REA* 24 (1922), pp. 37-47, 123-8, 229-35.

— 'Remarques critiques sur la vie et l'œuvre de saint Martin' (= 'Notes gallo-romaines' §§96-9), *REA* 24 (1922), pp. 306-12; *REA* 25 (1923), pp. 49-55, 139-43, 234-50.

C. JULLIAN, *Histoire de la Gaule* (8 vols., Paris 1908-26), vols. VI-VIII.

H. C. KEE, 'Aretalogy and Gospel', *Journal of Biblical Literature* 92 (1973), pp. 402-22.

E. & M.-L. KELLER, *Miracles in Dispute* (ET London 1969).

J. N. D. KELLY, *Jerome: His Life, Writings, and Controversies* (pb. edn. London 1975).

F. KEMPER, *De vitarum Cypriani, Martini Turonensis, Ambrosii, Augustini rationibus* (Münster diss. 1904).

P. LAMBRECHTS, *Contributions à l'étude des divinités celtiques* (Bruges 1942).

G. W. H. LAMPE, 'Miracles in the Acts of the Apostles', in *Miracles*, ed. Moule (q.v.), pp. 165-78.

H. LECLERCQ, art. 'Paganisme', *DACL* XIII, 1, cols. 241-375.

— art. 'Primuliac', *DACL* XIV, 2, cols. 1781-98.

— art. 'Sarabaïtes', *DACL* XV, 1, cols. 756-60.

C. LELONG, 'Études sur l'abbaye de Marmoutier: (1) Histoire monumentale de l'abbaye', *Bulletin trimestriel de la Société Archéologique de Touraine* 39 (1980), pp. 279-319.

J. T. LIENHARD, *Paulinus of Nola and Early Western Monasticism* (Theophaneia 28; Cologne-Bonn 1977).

H. LIETZMANN, *A History of the Early Church* (4 vols.), vol. IV (ET pb. edn. London 1961).

A. LONGNON, *Géographie de la Gaule au VIᵉ siècle* (Paris 1878).

— *Atlas historique de la France depuis César jusqu'à nos jours* (Paris 1907), plate II.

R. LORENZ, 'Die Anfänge des abendländischen Mönchtums im 4. Jahrhundert', *Zeitschrift für Kirchengeschichte* 77 (1966), pp. 1-61.

L. T. A. LORIÉ, *Spiritual Terminology in the Latin Translations of the Vita Antonii* (Latinitas Christianorum Primaeva, 11; Nijmegen 1955).

F. LOTTER, *Severinus von Noricum, Legende und historische Wirklichkeit* (Monographien zur Geschichte des Mittelalters, 12; Stuttgart 1976).

R. MACMULLEN, *Soldier and Civilian in the Later Roman Empire* (Cambridge Mass. 1963).

E. MÂLE, *La Fin du paganisme en Gaule et les plus anciennes basiliques chrétiennes* (Paris 1950).

R. A. MARKUS, 'Paganism, Christianity and the Latin Classics in the Fourth Century', in *Latin Literature of the Fourth Century*, ed. Binns (q.v.), pp. 1-21.

H.-I. MARROU, *Saint Augustin et la fin de la culture antique* (Bibliothèque des écoles françaises d'Athènes et de Rome, 145; Paris 1938).

— *A History of Education in Antiquity* (ET pb. edn. London 1977).

F. MARTROYE, 'La Répression de la magie et le culte des gentils au IVᵉ siècle', *Revue historique de droit français et étranger* 9 (1930), pp. 669-701.

J. F. MATTHEWS, 'A Pious Supporter of Theodosius I: Maternus Cynegius and his Family', *JTS* n.s. 18 (1967), pp. 438-46.

— 'Gallic Supporters of Theodosius', *Latomus* 30 (1971), pp. 1073-99.

— *Western Aristocracies and Imperial Court, A.D. 364-425* (Oxford 1975).

M. MESLIN, *Les Ariens d'Occident, 335-430* (Patristica Sorbonensia 8; Paris 1967).

— 'Hilaire et la crise arienne', *Hilaire et son temps* (q.v.), pp. 19-42.

A. MOMIGLIANO, ed., *The Conflict between Paganism and Christianity in the Fourth Century* (Oxford 1963).

A. MOMIGLIANO, 'Ancient History and the Antiquarian', *Studies in Historiography* (a collection of M's essays; pb. edn. London 1969), pp. 1–39.

— 'L'età del trapasso fra storiografia antica e storiografia medievale (320–550 D.C.)', *Settimane di Studio del centro italiano di studi sull'alto medioevo*, 17: *La Storiografia altomedievale* (Spoleto 1970), I, pp. 89–118.

— *The Development of Greek Biography* (Cambridge Mass. 1971).

— *Essays in Ancient and Modern Historiography* (Oxford 1977), esp. 'Pagan and Christian Historiography in the Fourth Century A.D.' (pp. 107–26), and 'Popular Religious Beliefs and the Late Roman Historians' (pp. 141–59).

P. MONCEAUX, *Histoire littéraire de l'Afrique chretiénne* (7 vols., reprinted Brussels 1963), vol. III, pp. 126–31 (which reprints Monceaux's 'Étude critique sur la Passio Tipasii veterani' from *Revue archéologique* 1904, pp. 267–74).

C. F. D. MOULE, ed., *Miracles: Cambridge Studies in their Philosophy and History* (London 1965).

F. X. MURPHY, 'Rufinus of Aquileia and Paulinus of Nola', *Revue des Études Augustiniennes* 2 (1956), pp. 79–91.

F. MURRU, 'La concezione della storia nei *Chronica* di Sulpicio Severo: alcune linee di studio', *Latomus* 38 (1979), pp. 961–81.

P. NAUTIN, 'Études de chronologie hiéronymienne (393–397)', scattered through *Revue des Études Augustiniennes* 18 (1972), pp. 209–18; 19 (1973), pp. 69–86 and 213–39; 20 (1974), pp. 251–84.

A. D. NOCK, *Conversion* (Oxford 1933).

T. K. OESTERREICH, *Possession, Demonical and Other* (ET London 1930).

J.-R. PALANQUE, 'La *Vita Ambrosii* de Paulin', *Revue des sciences religieuses* 4 (1924), pp. 26–42, and 401–20.

— *Saint Ambroise et l'Empire romain* (Paris 1933).

— 'La Date du transfert de la préfecture des Gaules de Trèves à Arles', *REA* 36 (1934), pp. 359–65.

— 'Les Dissensions des églises des Gaules à la fin du IVᵉ siècle et la date du concile de Turin', *Revue d'histoire de l'église de France* 21 (1935), pp. 481–501.

— 'Du nouveau sur la date du transfert de la Préfecture des Gaules de Trèves à Arles?', *Provence Historique* 23 (1973), pp. 29–38.

J. PÉPIN, *Théologie cosmique et théologie chrétienne* (Paris 1964).

J. PERCIVAL, *The Roman Villa* (London 1976).

P. PETIT, 'Sur la date du "Pro Templis" de Libanius', *Byzantion* 21 (1951), pp. 285–310.

C. PFISTER, obituary notice on E.-C. Babut, *RH* 122 (1916), pp. 224–6.

T. G. E. POWELL, *The Celts* (pb. edn. London 1963).

S. PRETE, *I Chronica di Sulpicio Severo* (Collezione 'Amici delle catacombe', 24; Vatican 1955).

F. PRINZ, *Frühes Mönchtum im Frankenreich* (Munich & Vienna 1965).

R. REITZENSTEIN, *Hellenistische Wundererzählungen* (Leipzig 1906).

L. ROSE, *Faith Healing* (revised pb. edn. ed. B. Morgan; Harmondsworth 1971).

P. ROUSSEAU, 'The Spiritual Authority of the "Monk-Bishop"', *JTS* n.s. 22 (1971), pp. 380–419.

—— *Ascetics, Authority, and the Church in the Age of Jerome and Cassian* (Oxford Historical Monographs; Oxford 1978).

A. ROUSSELLE-ESTÈVE, 'Deux exemples d'évangélisation en Gaule à la fin du IVe siècle: Paulin de Nole et Sulpice Sévère', *Fédération historique du Languedoc méditerranéen et du Roussillon*, 43e Congrès (Montpellier 1971), pp. 91–8.

A. ROUSSELLE, 'Du sanctuaire au thaumaturge: la guérison en Gaule au IVe siècle', *Annales* 31 (1976), pp. 1085–107.

—— 'Aspects sociaux du recrutement ecclésiastique au IVe siècle', *Mélanges de l'École française de Rome: Antiquité* 89 (1977), pp. 333–70.

Saint Martin et son temps (*Studia Anselmiana* 46, Rome 1961).

W. SCHATZ, 'Studien zur Geschichte und Vorstellungswelt des frühen abendländischen Mönchtums' (unpublished diss. for Freiburg in Bressau, 1957; a microfilm is available in the Bodleian).

P. L. SCHMIDT, 'Zur Typologie und Literarisierung des frühchristlichen lateinischen Dialogs', in *Christianisme et formes littéraires de l'antiquité tardive en occident*, Fondation Hardt *entretiens*, vol. 23, arranged by M. Fuhrmann (Geneva 1977), pp. 101–80, and discussion pp. 181–90.

K. SCHREINER, '"Discrimen veri ac falsi": Ansätze und Formen der Kritik in der Heiligen- und Reliquienverehrung des Mittelalters', *Archiv für Kulturgeschichte* 48 (1966), pp. 1–53.

H. H. SCULLARD, *Martin of Tours, Apostle of Gaul* (London n.d. [1891]).

W. SESTON, 'Remarques sur le rôle de la pensée d'Origène dans les origines du monachisme', *Revue de l'histoire des religions* 108 (1933), pp. 197–213.

P. SINISCALCO, *Massimiliano: un obiettore di coscienza del tardo impero* (Historica, Politica, Philosophica, vol. 8; Turin 1974).

M. SMITH, 'Prolegomena to a discussion of aretalogies, divine men, the Gospels and Jesus', *Journal of Biblical Literature* 90 (1971), pp. 174–99.

C. E. STANCLIFFE, 'Sulpicius' Saint Martin' (unpublished Oxford D.Phil. thesis, 1978).

C. E. STANCLIFFE, 'From Town to Country: the Christianisation of the Touraine 370-600', *Studies in Church History* 16, ed. D. Baker (= *The Church in Town and Countryside*; Oxford 1979), pp. 43-59.

E. STEIN, *Histoire du bas-empire* (rev. edn. and Fr. tr. by J.-R. Palanque, 2 vols. in 3; Amsterdam 1968).

B. STUDER, 'Zu einer Teufelserscheinung in der Vita Martini des Sulpicius Severus', *Oikoumene: studi paleocristiani pubblicati in onore del Concilio Ecumenico Vaticano II* (Centro di Studi sull'Antico Cristianesimo, Università di Catania, 1964), pp. 351-404.

J. TAMBORNINO, *De antiquorum daemonismo* (Religionsgeschichtliche Versuche und Vorarbeiten, no. 7, part 3; Giessen 1909).

Théologie de la vie monastique: Études sur la Tradition patristique (Collection 'Théologie', 49; Paris 1961).

D. L. TIEDE, *The Charismatic Figure as Miracle Worker* (Society of Biblical Literature Dissertation Series, 1; Montana USA 1972).

G. K. VAN ANDEL, *The Christian Concept of History in the Chronicle of Sulpicius Severus* (Amsterdam 1976).

— 'Sulpicius Severus and Origenism', *Vigiliae Christianae* 34 (1980), pp. 278-87.

J. VAN DEN BOSCH, *Capa, Basilica, Monasterium, et le culte de saint Martin de Tours* (Latinitas Christianorum Primaeva, 13; Nijmegen 1959).

F. VAN DER MEER, *Augustine the Bishop* (ET London 1961).

R. VAN LOY, 'Le "Pro Templis" de Libanius', *Byzantion* 8 (1933), pp. 7-39, 389-404.

J. VANSINA, *Oral Tradition: A Study in Historical Methodology* (ET pb. edn. Harmondsworth 1973).

B. R. VOSS, 'Berührungen von Hagiographie und Historiographie in der Spätantike', *Frühmittelalterliche Studien* 4 (1970), pp. 53-69.

— *Der Dialog in der frühchristlichen Literatur* (Munich 1970).

E. M. WIGHTMAN, *Roman Trier and the Treveri* (London 1970).

A. WILMART, 'L'*Ad Constantium Liber Primus* de S. Hilaire de Poitiers et les *Fragments Historiques*', *Revue Bénédictine* 24 (1907), pp. 149-79, 291-317.

— 'Les *Fragments Historiques* et le synode de Béziers de 356', *Revue Bénédictine* 25 (1908), pp. 225-9.

Index

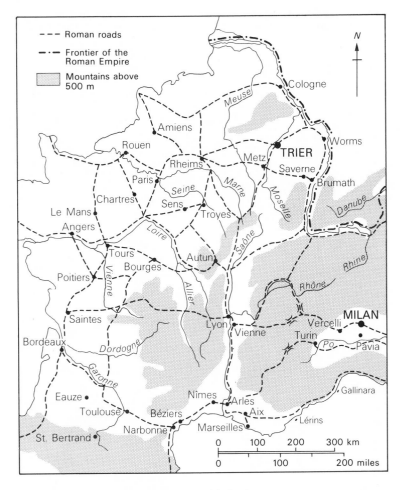

Map 1. Martin's Gaul

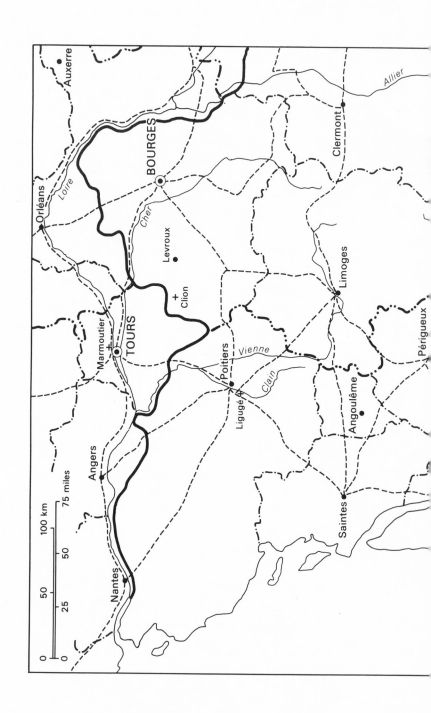

Auxerre

Allier

Clermont

BOURGES

Orléans

Loire

Cher

Levroux

Clion

Limoges

Marmoutier

TOURS

Poitiers

Vienne

Périgueux

Ligugé

Clain

Angoulême

Angers

100 km

75 miles

50

50

Saintes

50

25

Nantes

0

0

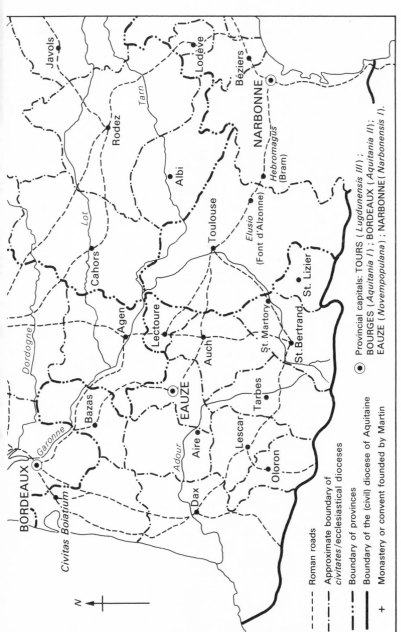

Map 2. South-West Gaul c.380–400

- - - - Roman roads
—··—··— Approximate boundary of *civitates*/ecclesiastical dioceses
—···—···— Boundary of provinces
———— Boundary of the (civil) diocese of Aquitaine
+ Monastery or convent founded by Martin

⊙ Provincial capitals: TOURS (*Lugdunensis III*);
BOURGES (*Aquitania I*); BORDEAUX (*Aquitania II*);
EAUZE (*Novempopulana*); NARBONNE (*Narbonensis I*).

Note on Map 2:

I give the *civitates* and provinces as they are found in the *Notitia Galliarum* of *c*.400 AD, taking the boundaries from A. Longnon, *Atlas historique de France* (Paris 1907), pl. II. The ecclesiastical organization at this date corresponded exactly with the civil administration: see Duchesne, *Fastes épiscopaux*, especially vol. II, pp. 17, 89.